THE END OF ANTIQUITY

Archaeology, Society and Religion AD 235-700

Jeremy K. Knight

TEMPUS

First published 1999

PUBLISHED IN THE UNITED KINGDOM BY:

Tempus Publishing Ltd
The Mill, Brimscombe Port
Stroud, Gloucestershire GL5 2QG

PUBLISHED IN THE UNITED STATES OF AMERICA BY:

Tempus Publishing Inc.
2A Cumberland Street
Charleston, SC 29401

Tempus books are available in France, Germany and Belgium
from the following addresses:

Tempus Publishing Group	Tempus Publishing Group	Tempus Publishing Group
21 Avenue de la République	Gustav-Adolf-Straße 3	Place de L'Alma 4/5
37300 Joué-lès-Tours	99084 Erfurt	1200 Brussels
FRANCE	GERMANY	BELGIUM

British Library Cataloguing in Publication Data.
A catalogue record for this book is available from the British Library.

ISBN 0 7524 1448 8

Typesetting and origination by Tempus Publishing.
PRINTED AND BOUND IN GREAT BRITAIN.

Contents

Introduction

This book tries to explore some of the routes by which people in the westernmost provinces of the Roman Empire developed into the Christian societies of medieval western Europe. Near the heart of this long process lay two basic shifts in authority. On a secular level, the western half of an Empire covering most of the known world outside Persia, India and China fragmented into successor states of very variable size, often quite small, and often ruled by peoples who had first come within the orbit of the Empire as invaders or intruders. On a religious level, the multifarious local cults of the Roman Empire, which made no real attempt to regulate or coerce the beliefs of individuals (the Christians were a special case, for special reasons), were replaced by a centrally organised religion with professional priests in an administrative hierarchy from the Metropolitan (equivalent to a later Archbishop), spiritual counterpart to a Roman provincial governor, down to parish priests little different to the peasant flock they served. Through this hierarchy, meeting in church councils and diocesan synods, rules could be passed down from the assembled bishops to the city churches, or to the village priest and his flock. These covered such topics as the responsibilities of landowners and magnates, the role of women in society, traditional calendar customs, sexual behaviour, clerical discipline, church property, the place of Jews in the community and the roles of the public and private sectors in providing rural churches. How far many of these admonitions were obeyed, even by the priest himself, is another matter.

My book begins with the third-century crisis, and with the murder of Severus Alexander in 235 which marked the end of the Severan dynasty. Our sources for the third century are notoriously bad. Classical historians like Tacitus had ceased to write, and late Roman authors like Ammianus Marcellinus or the Christian authors had not yet begun. Cassius Dio ended his History in 229, Herodian in 238. The surviving section of Ammianus begins in 353. In between, the Empire had undergone changes in some respects more radical than those of the early fifth century. I have used a biological metaphor for those changes, and to see the crisis merely as an unfocussed tale of woe is to ignore the efforts of able Emperors like Gallienus, Aurelian or Probus, whose attempts to cope with the hard times in which they lived provides our most informed comment on the nature of the crisis, and on the society which followed.

The first section (Chapters 1–3) deals with the later western Empire and the way in which those who governed it failed to cope with the fifth-century crisis as their counterparts had done successfully in the third. The second (Chapters 4–6) covers the ways in which the Christian Church set about replacing areas of this lost authority, initially in the cities, then in the countryside. The pre-Roman tribal areas had been re-organised by the Romans into administrative units imitating Graeco-Roman city states, with magistrates from the local land-owning élite, and the usual urban amenities — temples to the Roman gods, law courts, public bath buildings and local government offices. This monumental townscape provided a setting for consensual pageantry which emphasised the communal identity of the city, and the status of its élite families, who had often paid for elements of its building. Outside the city, its territory was divided into pagi or rural districts, with vici or small market towns. Vicus and pagus had their own petty magistrates, and industries such as iron smelting or pottery were normally based in vici rather than in cities. This may help to explain why the cities of Gaul proved so fragile in the third-century crisis. The city walls, built by central government after this crisis around small areas of what had once been large open cities, re-use in their foundations sculptures and inscriptions from the very temples and public buildings through which the local élite had once expressed their status. The classical ruins which have cast such a shadow over the architecture of Europe and America mostly belong to the first two centuries of the Christian era (some of course are much older). In areas like north Africa, some of the latest were built under Severus Alexander. Later buildings, like the Basilica of Maxentius in Rome, or the late Roman walls of Rome or of Gaul, belong to a different world. Their solidity and scale, like their confident use of vault and pier, show that they were not the mere result of decline and loss of powers. The world had changed, perhaps had turned upside down. The aristocrats who had followed careers as army generals and colonial governors, and the more modest local élite who had expressed their status in urban pageantry, had been eclipsed. There were new men, many of them salaried Imperial officials or military men of modest origins from the frontier provinces. In Gaul, many cities gave up their own name for that of their tribe, as if its own identity had been replaced by its role as local capital. *Avaricum*, capital of the tribe of the Biturgi, became the *Civitas Biturgum* (Bourges) and Lutetia, capital of the Parisi, became Paris.

The church modelled its organisation on that of Roman provinces and cities. The Archbishop of Bourges, metropolitan of Aquitania Prima, continued to rule the tribal territory of the Biturges until the French Revolution when his city became the head of the new Department of Cher, named after the local river, in a system designed to sweep away the feudal and ecclesiastical geography of the ancien regime. The bishop of Paris, despite the status of his city, remained a suffragan of the archbishop of Sens until the eighteenth century, for Sens, not Paris, had been capital of the Roman province of Lugdunensis IV. From such cities, Christianity spread outwards to the rural *pagenses*. Bishops built churches with the help of Christian landowners, and ensured that they were properly staffed with clergy. At the roots of rural pastoral care was an institution that went under many names — Minster, *Collegiale*, Baptismal church, Clas church, *Ecclesia Diocesana*. In it, a group of priests served a rural district much bigger than a later parish, equivalent indeed in Britain to the medieval Rural Deanery. Sometimes the *parochia* or sphere of influence of such a church corresponded to a unit of secular government — a *pagus*, hundred, *cantref*, *tuath* or *commote*, or whatever such a local subdivision was called. These were far from being the only kind of rural church however. In the same period, private landowners were founding churches on their estates for their clients and tenantry, and it was this process which contained the seeds of the later parochial system. Between the fourth and seventh centuries, and much later in some areas, country people were taught by their clergy to abandon their more overtly pagan rural beliefs and customs; to bring themselves and their children to the baptismal churches at the proper time; to abandon many customary ceremonies of the pre-Christian calendar and replace or supplement them with those of the Christian year; and finally to bring their dead for burial not to the long established family or community burial places, but to an enclosed Christian churchyard, where one existed. This was to affect not only the rural landscape and settlement pattern but also the archaeological record.

Though written sources for post-Roman Gaul are plentiful they present their own problems. This is particularly true of the Lives of saints. Often written centuries after the time when their subject lived, and with little or no earlier written material to draw on, many of their stories were borrowed from the lives of other saints, or from the Bible. To the medieval writer, and his reader, this did not matter. The parallel with an Old Testament Prophet or with Christ was intended as metaphor, and was meant to be recognised; Martin of Tours was the new Elijah; Germanus of Auxerre and his followers crossing the English Channel were like Christ and his disciples on the Sea of Galilee. One story of Germanus was even borrowed from a ghost story by Pliny. If the saint's miracles had been forgotten through the carelessness of later generations it was up to the author to put this right. Modern ideas of historical truth are anachronistic, and would have been regarded by contemporaries as naïve and unsophisticated. Hagiography has its own rules. Faced with these an historian or archaeologist may fall into various traps. He may analyse the Life as if it were a classical text by Tacitus. He may extract some nugget of apparent information without regarding the context, or the needs of the story line. He may simply dismiss the whole as historically valueless (it would be unfair to cite specific cases!). I have tried to look at a few of the more important Lives on their own terms, even when this means extended treatment.

Geographically, my treatment is partly delimited by the extent of my first hand knowledge of the landscape and archaeology of western Europe. I have said little directly of England, save where its development mirrors that of its neighbours. The story of the English Church and people has a distinguished historical tradition going back to Bede, and the archaeology of the Saxon settlements leads to areas of northern Europe outside my main themes. I hope, however, that this account of their neighbours may throw a little oblique light on the already well-illuminated kingdoms of the English. Similarly, I have not used the extremely rich Italian evidence for this period, save for comparative purposes, since its adequate treatment would need far more space than I have available. The 'changing horizons' of my last section are, however, as much geographic as cultural. By the sixth century at latest, a distinctive Christian culture was in place south of the Loire, with a pattern of shrines, churches and clergy, and strong links to the rest of the Mediterranean world. This influenced societies much further north, as the latin memorial stones and Mediterranean pottery of western Britain show. By the end of the same century however, there had been a profound cultural and political shift away from the shores of the Mediterranean, as barbarian successor states developed into territorial kingdoms of Franks, Anglo-Saxons and Visigoths. A Parisian abbot could regard the offer of a southern see by a Frankish king as a sentence of political exile, and Pirenne's analysis of the nature of this shift is still being debated.

The diversity of the French landscape, its geology and soils, fertility or austerity, water supply and irrigation, and the uses made of that diversity by man, are central to the French historical tradition and to its literary writers. This neatly complements the British tradition of archaeological fieldwork which looks back to the rural pursuits of its landowners and clergy. The greatest of English prehistoric sites was first seen by John Aubrey during a foxhunt.

Much of the travel on which this study is based was made possible by the hospitality of friends, both archaeological colleagues and others, in whose company I have got to know particular areas at first hand. Of particular value has been the chance to see some rural societies from the inside and compare them with more familiar British norms. This has helped my understanding even of such matters as church organisation and rural pastoral care. Thus the way in which in areas of the Mediterranean town dwellers (including my daughter's family) work land from a 'country house', returning home at night, would leave in some areas little need for rural churches. In a variant of this in the Vaucluse, a town-based landowner worked a *mas* with resident labourers (in this case north Africans), who cultivated an irrigated area around the farm and areas of arable in the surrounding fields. Latouche pointed out that Gregory of Tours cites a vernacular term for the irrigated area, suggesting that the system was already current in the sixth century and could be of Gallo-Roman origin. Elsewhere, it was possible to see something of the contrast between closed/open, arable/pastoral (chalk and cheese) communities, familiar in Britain since the time of John Aubrey, in a Spanish guise.

Leslie Alcock first suggested that I should write this book. Charles Thomas and Ken Dark found the time to read an earlier draft, saving me from errors and infelicities, and the former also introduced me to Peter Kemmis Betty in that hub of British archaeology, the tea-room of the Society of Antiquaries. Among my many Irish friends, Etienne Rynne added to his hospitality at Athenry and Galway the arrangements for a lecture tour of Irish universities in 1985. The Colt Fund of the Society for Medieval Archaeology made it possible for me to spend several weeks in Vienne, studying and re-drawing the Early Christian inscriptions there and elsewhere. French and Spanish colleagues have been generous in showing me their excavations and sites, giving me access to museum collections, giving me copies of their works, answering questions and providing photographs. Among them were Claude Seillier (Boulogne), M.J. Bazin (Dieppe), E. Louis (Douai), Dominique Cliquet (Evreux), R. Diehl (Jublains), Dominique Costa (Nantes), Marcel Baudoin and Christian Ganichaud (Noirmoutier), Professor P.R. Giot (Rennes), M.J. Ruf (Vienne), Jacques Sirat in the Vexin and R. Gavelle (St Bertrand de Comminges). Antonio Poveda Navarro (Elda) has introduced me to current work on late and post-Roman pottery in Spain. Mark Redknap made available to me a copy of his important forthcoming book on the Mayen pottery industry. Dan Bish has been a highly proficient adviser on computer problems. To my former colleagues in the Inspectorate of Ancient Monuments in Cadw (Welsh Historic Monuments), I owe an immense debt of gratitude for many personal kindnesses, and for a scholarly and stimulating working environment.

The first draft of this book was completed in the summer of 1992. Circumstances then made it necessary for me to lay it aside for some time, and I am grateful to kind friends who reminded me, in various ways, of a Biblical adage about setting hand to the plough. My partner and friend Annie Burns, by her support and help, has made it possible for me to finish the work. My greatest debt is to my late wife, Marion Knight, my travelling companion for over thirty years and partner in the fieldwork on which this book is based. Sadly, she is not here to see the work, to which she contributed so much, brought to fruition. This book is dedicated to her memory.

PART 1. THE ENDING OF AN EMPIRE

1. Mid-Life Crisis: Gaul and the west in the third century

The contemporaries of Severus, in the enjoyment of the peace and glory of his reign, forgave the cruelties by which it had been introduced. Posterity, who experienced the fatal effects of his maxims and example, justly considered him as the principal author of the decline of the Roman Empire.

Edward Gibbon *Decline and Fall of the Roman Empire* Book 1, Chapter 5

Great Rome is full of triumphal arches,
Over whom did the Caesars triumph ?
. . . So many reports,
So many questions.

Bertolt Brecht *A Worker's Questions While Reading*

When the young Roman Emperor Severus Alexander was murdered by his troops in the legionary fortress at Mainz on the Rhine in March 235 it brought to an end the dynasty which had come to power, through another military coup, with Septimius Severus in 193. The Empire was still recognisably that of Augustus or Trajan. The legions and auxiliaries held the frontiers against barbarian incursions. The legions, and most provinces, were governed by Roman senators. The coinage was basically that of Augustus, with the gold aureus, silver denarius and a range of copper alloy coins. The inflationary double denarius, or *antoninianus*, introduced by Caracalla, had been discontinued. In the cities there were still a few wealthy men willing to advertise their status, and that of their families, by conspicuous spending on buildings and public amenities, though the burdens on city magistrates were far heavier than they had been and the rewards of office less obvious. Severus Alexander had ruled for thirteen years. No one else was to be sole Emperor for as long until Constantine the Great, in very changed circumstances, at the end of the century.

For Gibbon, writing in the eighteenth century, the Roman Empire had already begun its long decline and fall, and Septimius Severus was one of the chief culprits. To Gibbon, the problem was that the Roman Empire was becoming less and less Roman. Rule by the senatorial aristocracy in Rome had long been a legal fiction, but the Emperor and his army commanders were at least members of the Senate. Septimius Severus, though a senator, was a North African, married into a Syrian family, and had been raised to the purple by the frontier army of the Danube. His great-nephew Elagabalus (218–22) introduced to Rome official worship of the Semitic sun-god Helios-Baal from Emesa in Syria. Though senatorial Emperors remained the norm, the murderers and successors of Caracalla and of Severus Alexander were Macrinus (217–8), the first non-senatorial Emperor, and Maximinus (235–8), a Thracian from the Danube frontier and the first soldier-Emperor to rise from the ranks. Threats or perceived threats to the frontiers from 'barbarians' had been useful since the time of Julius Caesar to justify the large army which underpinned the existing power structure. The malfunctioning of this system was one of the immediate causes of the third-century crisis, but Gibbon, thanks to a classical historiography which saw history as the acts of great men, blamed Severus.

Septimius Severus's alleged death bed advice to his sons, 'pay the troops, ignore everyone else,' had some logic. The army absorbed roughly half the Empire's gross tax revenue. In the absence of any major new sources of gold and silver since Trajan's conquest of the Dacian gold mines, and with many older mines in Spain and elsewhere running dry, the fall in the silver content of the denarius — which had begun in earnest with the heavy costs of the Danubian wars of Marcus Aurelius — continued under the Severi with increasing velocity. The aureus, too, had steadily shrunk in size and weight. This would have had a serious effect on fixed salaries including (despite pay rises) army pay, and the stability of the Empire depended on the army. The army itself was also changing. In the early Empire the legions were recruited from the Mediterranean provinces, the auxiliary units from less developed areas. There had been virtually no Italians in the ranks of the legions, however, since the time of Trajan, recruitment from Gaul and Spain soon dried up, and the very process of Romanization made military recruitment less attractive to the people of other provinces. Most troops were now from the frontier regions in which they served, and were often the children of army veterans. This has been seen since the days of Gibbon as a cause of the third-century crisis. In times of crisis (and there were plenty in the third century) the paramount loyalty of army units could be to their native province, where their families and lands were, and to the regional army which secured their safety, rather than to any grand strategy of the wider Empire. In the following century, the army mutineers in Paris in 360 underlined this dilemma with particular clarity. The Gallic army under Julian had freed Gaul from the invading Alemanni after hard fighting. Constantius II now demanded the pick of Julian's troops for his eastern campaign. Whatever his motives, the threat from Persia was real enough. 'We are being exiled to the furthest points of the earth like condemned criminals,' the troops complained, 'and our families will become slaves of the Alemanni after we have already freed them once from captivity by desperate battles.' They mutinied, and proclaimed Julian Emperor.[1]

It was not only local recruitment which bound the army to its permanent bases. The siting of the Empire's thirty legions owed more to political arithmetic, and to a balance of power designed to deter military coups, than it did to military grand strategy. From the latter viewpoint, it would have made little sense to station three legions on the borders of upland Britain, where they had ended up after the first century campaigns of conquest, or another in a remote area of northern Spain (though one with important gold mines). However, the four neatly balanced the four Rhineland legions, themselves divided two and two between Upper and Lower Germany. There were also problems of logistics. A division of over 5,000 heavy armed infantry required formidable amounts of leather, iron and other metals, (over 5,000 pairs of army boots to be kept in repair for a start), and above all grain, and the land on which to produce this. Medieval parallels suggest that some 4,700 acres of land would be needed for the corn supply of a legion, not counting the needs of families and other dependent civilians, though in practice much of this would be requisitioned from civilians or shipped in. Until the 160s it was still possible to move legions for specific campaigns, but in practice it was easier to post detachments, known as vexillations from their *vexillum* or banner, from the parent legion as required. These were often of about 1000 men (two legionary cohorts). A silvered bronze disc of third century date, now in the Cabinet des Medailles in Paris, shows vexillations of two British legions, II Augusta and XX Valeria Victrix, brigaded together. Ultimately, this led to the new Diocletianic legion with a strength of about 1000 men, equivalent to a vexillation. This is sometimes seen as an almost casual process as vexillations were drafted away and not returned. At Isca (Caerleon), however, though much had changed, the birthday of the legionary Eagle was celebrated on the proper date in 234 by the *primus pilus*, the senior centurion, who had charge of the Eagle, and presumably by the main body of the legion. It was similarly celebrated there in 244 under Gordian. Under Valerian and Gallienus (253–60), a cohort was posted back to Caerleon after a period on detached duty. Though improving the mobility and readiness of the army was central to army reform from Gallienus onwards, the new legions of the late Empire were both a characteristically pragmatic rationalisation of an existing trend and a recognition that the old style legions were too large and immobile for rapid response in a crisis.[2]

These were some of the parameters against which the military and political aspects of the third century crisis were to unfold. The Roman army was still formidable in battle but had put down roots and evolved from an army of conquest into an integral part of Roman provincial society in the frontier regions. Its priorities had changed. For the Emperor army pay and support costs, which already took up perhaps half of the Empire's tax revenue, were an increasing burden at a time of depreciating currency and of economic and probably fiscal decline. Gibbon saw this process through the eyes of a classically educated English gentleman, but his analysis of its problems — the increasing power of an army drawn from the 'barbarous' frontier regions — commands respect.

The cities of Gaul in the early third century

Though the frontiers of Britain and Gaul were still secure in the early third century, the condition of the towns is less clear. By the following century the Gallic cities had changed radically. Many of the temples, bath buildings, market halls and basilicas that marked them out as part of Graeco-Roman civilization had been demolished, and their masonry used in the foundations of massive fort-like town walls enclosing only small areas of the former open cities. Amiens (*Samobriva*) may have covered as much as 160 ha at its second-century

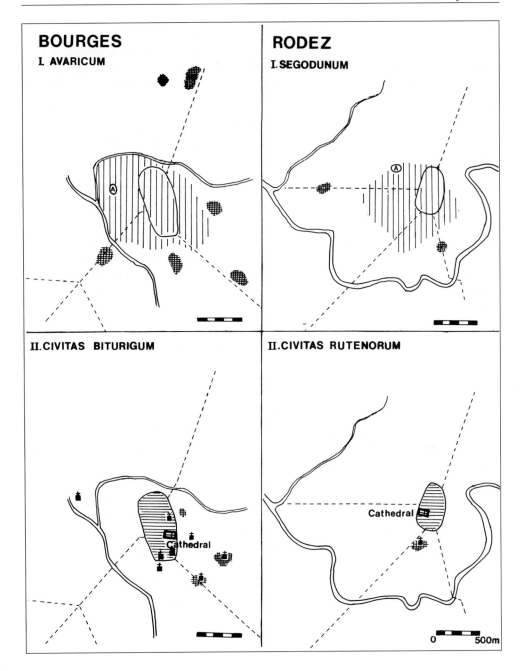

1   *Rodez (Aveyron) and Bourges (Cher). Early Roman towns and late Roman* civitates *. I. The early towns , with roads, cemeteries (cross hatched) and amphitheatres (A). II. The late walled towns, with their cemeteries and churches. The towns were by now known not by their own name, but by that of their tribal area. Based on T.C.C.G. VI (Aquitania Prima)*

peak, with a population of perhaps 15,000. Like most ancient cities, though, much of this may have been only lightly built up with large areas of parks and gardens. By about 270, it had shrunk to 30–40 ha, and the late Roman walls enclose 20, though this may not be an accurate reflection of the city's size. At Boulogne, not far from Amiens, Claude Seillier estimates that the late Roman fort and cross-channel port, with its suburbs and cemeteries, was only half the size of its second-century predecessor, despite its role in linking Britain and the Rhine frontier zone. At Langres in Burgundy, the Roman town occupied a long narrow north-south ridge, and extended some 2,000m along it. The late Roman walled town at the tip of the spur was about 500m square, a quarter the size of its predecessor. Similar figures could be quoted from many other Gallo-Roman cities, but it would be misleading to talk of the failure of the cities. They were to revive spectacularly in later centuries, and the list of Gallic Civitas capitals is also one of medieval French cathedral cities. The two questions that need to be asked are what caused this third-century eclipse, whether internal crisis and failure or external causes such as barbarian invasion; and how the open, undefended classical cities of early Roman times developed into medieval walled cathedral towns.[3]

Julius Caesar's conquest destroyed the existing power structure over much of Gaul, and the administrative towns loosely based on the Mediterranean city state and on existing tribal territories were intended to replace this. Of over 100 such towns, a few were old trading cities like Marseille, Lyon and Vienne, some were on the sites of pre-conquest oppida, as at Bourges, Chartres or Poitiers, but most were new Julio-Claudian foundations, their location determined by road lines and river crossings. Since the role of these new towns is central to their rise and decline, three aspects of this role deserve mention. In much of the Mediterranean towns are closely spaced on the more fertile and better irrigated land, as a glance at the map of Roman towns in Tunisia or southern Spain will show. The inhabitants work the land of its surrounding territory by day, returning to the city at nightfall. In contrast, the area of Gallic *civitates* is often very large, corresponding broadly to a modern French Department, or even, as with the huge territory of the Pictones of Poitiers, with several. This means that there is space for smaller towns or for rural cult centres as subsidiary centres within the *Civitas*, affecting both settlement patterns and local power structures. Members of the new tribal élite needed to buttress their novel and perhaps insecure social status, based on acquired land and the fruits of government service, by conspicuous spending on municipal buildings and public amenities, whose building inscriptions would advertise (in the fully modern sense) their wealth and standing in the community. The role of the city was not merely parasitic on the surrounding countryside, however. Medieval parallels suggest that a town of about 3,000 inhabitants would consume more than 1,000 tons of grain a year, needing around 8,000 acres on which to grow it. The town would thus create a market for the grain grown by local land-owners and for the produce of peasant farmers. The effect on bringing new land under cultivation and on such things as the growth of villas is obvious.[4]

Until the mid-third century the towns seem to have prospered, though the base of their prosperity may have been narrower than before. Until 1677, when it was demolished by order of Louis XIV, a classical ruin stood outside the Roman walls of Bordeaux, overlooking the Garonne. A podium of rusticated ashlar supported lines of Corinthian

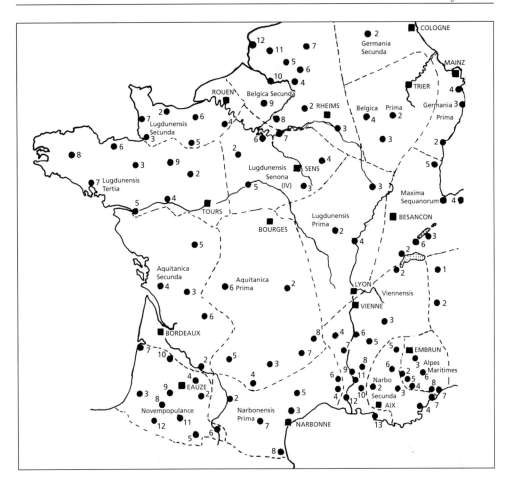

2   The Cities and Provinces of late Roman Gaul, from the Notitia Galliarum. *For key see Table 1, with the late Roman name, as it appears in the* Notitia *(eg* Civitas Aedorum*); the earlier Roman name (eg* Augustodunum*) and the modern name in brackets*

columns around an open rectangular space. Excavation has shown that the 'Pillars of Tutela' stood within a monumental precinct, and it may have housed an open air altar, perhaps for the Imperial cult. Architectural parallels suggest a Severan date. Dedications to the *Tutela Augusta* of AD 224, and to the *Tutela Bourdigalensis*, the guiding spirit of Bordeaux, have been found nearby. Marcus Aurelius Lunaris, who dedicated the latter in AD 237 under Maximinus, had business interests in Britain, and held civic office in York and Lincoln. Bordeaux acquired other monuments at this time, some with sculptured maritime and military themes. They are known, like the Tutela inscription, from blocks re-used in the foundations of the late Roman walls. Bordeaux may be a special case, a major Atlantic trading city, capital of Aquitania, and with a prosperous hinterland which in the next century contained many luxurious villas, but it did not stand alone. At Vieux in Normandy, Sennius Sollemnis, who had held most of the honours that his small town could provide, finished in 238 the public baths begun by his father, and set up a statue with an inscribed base of red marble — the 'Thorigny marble' — recording his career and links with the great and powerful. At Sens in northern Burgundy, C. Amatius Paterninus could list his local government posts in the time of Decius (249–51). Other less precisely dated examples are known from excavation, as at Beauvais, where private houses were swept away for a monumental Severan complex, including a colonnaded hemicycle, perhaps one of a pair flanking an open piazza in front of a public building.[5]

Most Gallic cities were still open and undefended at this date, save for a few whose venerable Augustan walls proclaimed their city's antiquity and long links with Rome. Things were already beginning to change, however. Behind the Danube frontier, cities like Serdica, Phillipopolis and Nicopolis ad Istrum were being walled in the 170s following barbarian invasion, and by the turn of the century Tongres and Trier on the Rhine frontier zone were acquiring defences. When Maximinus besieged Aquilea in north Italy in 238, its ancient walls were in ruin 'because after the extension of the Roman Empire, the citizens of Italy did not need walls…and in place of war enjoyed peace and Roman citizenship.' The sequel had its lesson for the future, for, in the face of desperate resistance by the Aquileans, Maximinus's army starved in front of the repaired walls and eventually murdered him.[6]

A change in the weather? Dating the onset of decline

Against this picture of an Indian summer in early third-century Gaul must be set other evidence for the beginnings of depopulation in town and country. In the Rhône Valley, and parts of Provence, there are signs of serious urban decline by mid century. The fine series of mosaics of Vienne become much rarer after AD 200 and seem to end about 225. During the second half of the century, the left bank suburbs of Sainte-Colombe and Saint-Romain-en-Gal were abandoned, as was the once densely occupied right bank area outside the Augustan walls. The population withdrew within the walled area, which continued as an important city in late Roman and early Medieval times. This retreat from the suburbs seems to have been a gradual process, not the result of some sudden crisis. When the right-bank suburb was re-colonised at the end of the fourth century, it was by the cemeteries and funerary churches of the now Christian city. At Lyon, the city centre area on the hill of Fourviere with its shops and monumental public buildings was also abandoned, though this may have been offset by continued dense occupation of the low lying commercial area between the Rhône and the Saône.[7]

Further north, Provost, in his survey of the Loire valley, sees its cities as in a state of stagnation and slow decline from the late second century onwards as a result of their failure to develop beyond administrative centres and their lack of industrial or commercial functions, an analysis strikingly similar to that of Whittaker. However, the scarcity of early third-century coins as archaeological site finds could mean that this dating is slightly too early. Evidence from Amiens suggests that decline set in somewhat later. About 170–80 it suffered one of the periodic fires which afflicted ancient cities. Recovery was swift. The forum was quickly rebuilt, and palatial public baths replaced the smaller earlier set. Decline set in about the time of Severus Alexander. A fire of about 250 was probably accidental, but marks the onset of serious eclipse. The town may already have been substantially smaller.

Various explanations have been put forward at different times to account for this long term urban decline. An older generation of French historians saw the way in which late Roman walls enclose only small areas of what had once been large open cities as evidence of violent sack by barbarian invaders and consequent demographic catastrophe. The cities perished by fire and sword, and the survivors salvaged stone from ruined buildings to build defences around a few streets that were now enough to house the much reduced population. There are reasons why a Frenchman of the generation after 1914 (or 1940) should think in terms of violent destruction by German invaders, but (leaving aside for the moment the nature and purpose of the town walls) archaeological evidence makes it clear that the decline was a gradual process, and had set in well before the third-century invasions. Natural or environmental causes have also been suggested as a contributory factor. There is some evidence of a climatic downturn after AD 200, and this could have led to a shorter growing season, a reduction in food output, and in the longer term to population decline, or the inability of the population to support itself on food from the surrounding countryside. As with the better-attested demographic crisis in fourteenth-century western Europe, this could have been accompanied by plague, to which populations weakened by poor diet are particularly susceptible, and which is known to have spread to western Europe with the returning armies of Marcus Aurelius. Soil exhaustion due to intensive agriculture and even lead poisoning from water pipes have also been suggested.[8]

One major factor may have been that the cities lacked a sufficient economic base to withstand change. Whittaker has noted the absence of any real industry above craft level at such excavated towns as Silchester or Amiens, and quotes Henry Cleere on the absence of major primary industries from the main urban centres of Roman Britain and their concentration in rural locations or in the vici. Similarly, Provost has noted how at Angers industries such as pottery and bronze-founding existed in Augustan times but were later driven out, leaving the city as solely an administrative and residential centre. Whittaker and Provost quite independently paint similar pictures of towns stagnating whilst rural vici and small towns are often flourishing centres of pottery production or iron smelting. In many ways this was a natural development. Leafy and select residential areas do not always welcome industrial smoke and pollution, and land for clay digging, an adequate water supply and wood for fuel might be expensive or unobtainable in the city suburbs, even if the landowners were to permit such activities near their town houses. This view may underestimate the role of the city as a market centre and as a focus for regional trade, but it does help to explain why cities were vulnerable to change once the local élite no longer saw advantage in participation in urban consensual activities, whether as building patrons or as office holders. A Gallic landowner whose ancestors had endowed a bath building or helped build a forum for 'his' town may have shunned urban life and saved his resources for his country villa.[9]

The cornlands of north Gaul and Germany lend themselves well to systematic field survey, whether on the ground or from the air. Roger Agache's air photographs of the Somme basin show several hundred Roman villas in their setting of roads, streams, and hills, together with several of the rural cult centres characteristic of Celtic Gaul, isolated rural temples, vici, and a few villages. He thought that this prosperous rural scene had largely disappeared by the end of the second century, with most villas deserted.

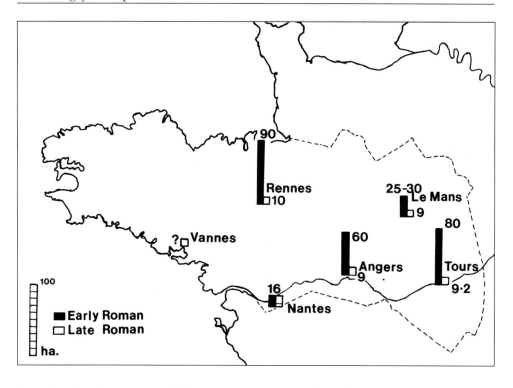

3   Province of Lugdunensis III (Britanny). Areas of the early and late Roman towns. Whilst the former vary considerably in size, the latter, save for Nantes, are a standard 9–10ha

Drinkwater contrasted this chronology with that of the funerary reliefs from Igel and Neumagen, which show the Belgic wool textile industry flourishing until at least 250. There is other evidence for a flourishing woollen industry in the fourth century, which made the territory of the Atrebates synonymous with fine cloaks. Agache's pioneer work has now been followed up by detailed field surveys of areas of northern France, Belgium and west Germany, brought together and analysed by Paul Van Ossel. These depend on surface finds of pottery and coins, supplemented by a few excavations. Chronological precision is therefore less than one would like, but they show that in sample areas the number of rural sites occupied in the late Empire is consistently smaller than in the early Empire, ranging from 65% in the Vexin near Paris to 9% in the Nijmegan area behind the Rhine. The late Edith Wightman suggested that late Roman rural sites were fewer but larger due to nucleation of peasant settlements and a return to pre-Roman settlement patterns, but Van Ossel could find no evidence of this. Similarly, though evidence of violent destruction was not uncommon, particularly on villas, there was little evidence that this had any real long-term effect compared with an overall continuous and progressive decline.[10]

In Germany west of the Rhine, rural settlement also shows decline well before the onset of the third-century troubles. Gechter and Kunow have charted a steady rise in the number of sites during the first century, and in the second century marginal areas like the wooded Hürtgen plateau were colonised. From about 200, however, there is, within the

16

margins of statistical error, a symmetrical decline in site numbers matching the earlier rise, and marginal sites are largely abandoned. Well after the onset of decline, the authors conclude, 'many rural settlements were destroyed during the Germanic raids of 275, after which (few) were rebuilt.' The latter statement, derived from historical rather than archaeological data, needs to be supported with more specific evidence, but decline was already well underway before the invasions. We also need data to show how the experience of Belgic Gaul compared with, for example, south Gaul or Aquitaine, which had (like Britain) many large and richly appointed fourth-century villas. In central Italy, the South Etruria Survey produced figures based on surface finds of African Red Slip ware and other fine wares which suggested that late Roman rural sites were about 30–45 % of the number occupied in the earlier Roman period, and much less in one area — a conclusion not unlike that of Van Ossel. However, these figures (for AD 80–320 and 350–450) give no indication of whether the decline was in progress before the third-century crisis, and their significance has been debated (we are, after all, dealing with surface finds of pottery rather than with actual population figures), but Timothy Potter has noted how the decline also affected the small towns of Etruria '. . . prosperous market centres in early Imperial times seem . . . to have fallen slowly into decay during the later centuries of the Empire.' The pattern of rural decline seen in Belgic Gaul seems to have been widespread in the late Empire, but we do not yet know if it was universal.[11]

Late Roman industry moved from the centre to the peripheral frontier regions because the frontier armies dominated the market. The red-gloss samian pottery industry of south-central Gaul and Spain came to an end in the third century, but Gaulish samian had itself grown from offshoots of north Italian Arretine production, and what, seen from one angle, looks like a decline of long distance trade, might be viewed from another as the establishment of healthy indigenous industries at the expense of products of more distant origin. The first African Red-slip wares copy late first-century Gaulish samian. By the later Empire, the latter had been replaced by flourishing red-gloss or red-slip industries in north Africa and the Mediterranean (African red slip); in south Gaul (terre sigillée claire B from the Rhône valley); in north Gaul (Argonne ware) and by local British industries such as Oxfordshire ware. The standards of Gallic samian had certainly fallen, and a more novel or attractive product may have made it seem dull and out of date. A fashion for imitations of expensive high-status silverware in pewter or in colour coated pottery (in the ancient world, silver was probably not kept highly polished) may also have provided competition. Pottery beakers with a metallic colour coat were made in Savoy ('Luisante'), the Rhineland and Britain. The distance of the main centres of Gallic samian production from their main markets and competition from rival products no doubt hastened their decay. In contrast, the glass industry of Cologne and north Gaul flourished under the late Empire; it had a solid base in the purchasing power of the soldiers and officials of its production area and export was secondary to local demand.

The early third century also saw the virtual end of the south Spanish olive oil industry which had previously supplied Rome and the northern frontiers with vast quantities of oil, carried in distinctive globular amphorae. Baetican oil may have been driven from some of its markets by north African oil, whose own distinctive amphorae now appear in large numbers on Mediterranean sites and filter in much smaller quantities to the Danube, the

Rhine and Britain. African red slip wares and amphorae first appear in quantity on Mediterranean sites at about the same time, perhaps the product of state purchase of African olive oil. This cannot have been the case further north where African amphorae are not common, but on the frontiers local army recruitment may have led to north European ways of cooking and lighting with animal fats replacing Mediterranean olive oil. Much wine was now shipped in wooden casks and barrels (a Celtic invention), often of impressive size. Unlike amphora sherds, these rarely survive, save in wet conditions. Boon has mapped their find spots in relation to the natural distribution of Larch and Silver Fir, the former in the Alpine area, the latter in the Alps and Pyrenees. The main trade probably came down the Rhine, with some on the Atlantic sea routes via Bordeaux and Nantes. Literary references suggest that such barrels were common, and the sixth-century import of fine slip wares (Insular D ware) from western France to Britain was perhaps an incidental by-product of a trade in wine carried in cask.[12]

The Roman Empire had been undergoing complex change in the first half of the third century. In the thirty years between the murder of Caracalla in 217 and that of Philip in 249 eleven successive Emperors died by violence, most of them at the hands of their own troops. This near-continuous crisis led to an outpouring of money on military pay and donatives which can only have weakened the economy. The *antoninianus*, or double denarius, taken out of circulation by Severus Alexander, was re-introduced by the senatorial Emperors Balbinus and Pupienus in the crisis of 238. It rapidly pushed aside the denarius, itself of increasingly debased metal. The priority of most Emperors was survival, not reform. In order to survive they increased the quantity of money in circulation for military pay by debasement, with little understanding of the long term consequences. Attempts to resist this trend by reforming Emperors could lead to military discontent with literally fatal results for the Emperor concerned. It may say something for the underlying strength of the western economy that it held up, as it seems to have done, until well past the mid century. It is possible to argue whether the symptoms of malaise represented a chronic but curable complaint or indicated a more deeply rooted disease. For the moment the patient was, on the surface, basically sound despite some worrying symptoms. The real crisis was not yet. When it came later in the century he survived, though he was never the same man again. Specialists are still arguing what was wrong with him.

The eye of the storm: Decius to Diocletian, AD 249–85

In Britain and the Rhineland, the Roman frontiers of the early third century had an air of permanence. The legions contributed vexillations from time to time for frontier campaigns elsewhere. Between, they were busy with the affairs of peace-time soldiering, improving the defences and amenities of their forts, and holding the usual yearly round of parades and religious ceremonies. The military centre of gravity had shifted to the Danube with the wars of Marcus Aurelius, and, as so often in European history, it was in the Balkans that the third-century crisis finally detonated. Pressure had been building up along the Danube for many years. From the 170s onwards towns behind the frontier were being fortified. This re-fortification spread to the Rhine frontier with the walls of Trier and Tongres. These, however, have more in common with the first-century town defences of north Italy or south Gaul than with late Roman urban fortifications. They enclosed large and evidently populous towns, their mural towers were relatively few (large circular mural towers had already appeared on the Rhine in the first-century walls of Cologne) and gates were often large, monumental structures like the Porta Nigra at Trier.[13]

The Emperor Philip (244–9) garrisoned Concordia and Aquilea in Venetia at the hinge of Italy and the Balkans. To the east, however, the army of Moesia, in present day Bulgaria and Serbia, faced the Goths, lately arrived from the Ukraine. These had invaded Dacia (Romania), a great salient of Roman territory which had projected northwards across the Danube since the conquests of Trajan. The army of the Danube was unhappy that Philip was not giving the threat the attention it required, and, hoping that an Emperor on the spot could cope better with the crisis, proclaimed their commander Marinus as Emperor. When he failed they tried again with their new general. Decius (249–51) was a reforming military Emperor and the first systematic persecutor of the Christians. When the Goths destroyed him in battle the first attempt at reform had failed. After a power struggle in which several pretenders perished, the elderly Valerian (253–60) emerged with his son Gallienus (253–68) as co-Emperor. Gallienus took command in the west, becoming in effect the first western Emperor, his father commanded in the east against the Persians. Gallienus's first campaigns were against the Goths on the Danube, but even before he moved his headquarters to Cologne in the spring of 257 vexillations from at least one British legion were fighting on the Rhine frontier. Coins announce victories against the Germans and hail Gallienus as saviour of Gaul. Gallienus has had a bad press which has obscured his very real achievements. His work on the defences of Germany and north Italy included town walls. A late source depicts him as sending teams of architects and engineers on inspection tours of cities to organise defences, and this is supported by inscriptions from Cologne and Verona. That from Cologne, on the central arch of the north gate, is something of a puzzle. The inscription, VALERIANA GALLIENA (ie of 253–60) was later erased, perhaps by Postumus, and replaced by C(olonia) C(laudia) A(ra) A(grippiensium) — the official name of the city The walls are usually dated to the first century, and little other evidence of later rebuilding has been found. The text does not read like a normal building inscription and may simply record some short-lived honorific title bestowed on the city. The inscription from Verona, commanding the strategic road south into Italy from the Brenner Pass, is more informative. The Augustan ramparts were encased in new walls dated to 265. Their lower part was faced with blocks of stone, robbed from buildings and cemeteries, around a rubble core. The upper part was of coursed tufa blocks. No mural towers are known on the surviving part of the walls, but at one corner they project out to include the amphitheatre in a salient. There are marked similarities to the later Gallic town walls, and these may owe more than has been realised to the military engineers of Gallienus and Valerian in north Italy and further afield.[14]

Gallienus's greatest problem lay in the mobility of the Emperor and his field army. The two thousand mile frontier from the Rhine mouth to the Black Sea was threatened by Franks (about to make their first recorded appearance in history) on the Rhine, the Alemanni in the centre, and the Goths on the Danube. The legions were still formidable in battle, but lacked the mobility to reach a threatened frontier in time to prevent military disaster or the army of the province taking matters into their own hands by making their own Emperor. Urban defences were one response. Gallienus's field army of cavalry based on Milan was another. This was backed up by another innovation to ensure the regular pay of the troops. The main mint at Rome was supplemented by a field mint. Initially in north Italy, probably at Milan, it moved with Gallienus to Cologne or Trier in 257. When this was lost to Postumus a fresh field mint was established at Milan, with others serving the Danube frontier and the eastern provinces. This energetic and innovative response to crisis hardly squares with Gibbon's damning portrait of an incompetent and indolent ruler whose personal deficiencies were largely responsible for the darkest days of the third century.

Gallienus's sole rule from 260 saw unparalleled disaster, with the senior Augustus a prisoner of the Persians, the western provinces defected to the Gallic Empire, much of the east in the hands of Zenobia, and with revolts and barbarian invasions in the remaining provinces. As if these were not enough, Gallienus has also been blamed for depriving the senatorial aristocracy of its monopoly of high military command which it had long enjoyed. This, which was probably in fact a more gradual process, agreed with Gallienus's other military reforms. It removed a source of frustration from those most likely to back a military coup by opening the higher command to professional soldiers, often men of modest birth, from the frontier regions, but the reform was bitterly resented by the aristocracy, always good haters. This is reflected in the bitterly hostile fourth-century 'biography' in the *Historia Augusta*, with its heavy senatorial bias. It meshed neatly with Gibbon's view that one of the main causes of the downfall of the Roman Empire was an army drawn from the 'barbarian' frontier regions. His account of Gallienus draws heavily and uncritically on the *Historia Augusta* whose strong element of forgery or hoax was not then known.[15]

The lack of reliable contemporary sources makes it difficult to follow the course of events in Gaul. Here, the crisis seems to have broken almost simultaneously with the capture of Valerian by the Persians. Gallienus moved to north Italy from Gaul in the autumn of 259. Shortly afterwards Postumus, governor of Lower Germany, mutinied over the booty taken from a German raiding party, exactly as Carausius was to do later in the century. Threats from Franks and Alemanni may have been building up, heightening tensions. Postumus seized Gaul, Britain and Spain, and set up a Gallic Empire that lasted for fourteen years. The loss of the western provinces, with their military manpower and economic resources, seriously weakened Gallienus. His coinage deteriorated sharply as a result of the loss of British and Spanish silver mines. In Gaul, Postumus was faced with heavy fighting. Aurelius Victor, over a century later, wrote how about 262 'The Frankish people plundered Gaul and seized Spain. After laying waste and almost destroying . . . Tarragona, some eventually seized boats and got as far as Africa.' He is clearly drawing on a Spanish source, and is less well informed on what happened in Gaul. His mention of Franks has sometimes been seized upon as the first reference to the perceived ancestors of the French, but Eutropius and Orosius call the invaders simply 'Germans' and the reference could be anachronistic.[16]

Postumus restored the situation, but after his death in 269 it deteriorated again. The *Historia Augusta* may for once be dependable when it describes how Probus set out for Gaul 'which since the death of Postumus had been in turmoil, and after the death of Aurelian (275) had been seized by the Germans.' This puts the Gallic invasions in a wider context, for about 267 the Goths had forced the Dardanelles with a fleet they had acquired on the Black Sea and sacked Greece. For whatever reason, the rising barbarian tide was becoming a flood. Though Claudius II 'Gothicus' (268–70) defeated the Goths at Nish in Serbia before his death in a plague epidemic, and his chosen successor Aurelian repulsed the Alemannic invasions of north Italy at the beginning of his reign, these brought only a limited respite. Nevertheless, Aurelian's achievements during his short reign (270–5) were remarkable. His 18km (12 mile) circuit of walls around Rome, completed by Probus, is still one of the most imposing monuments of the city. Its architectural inspiration lies in the Hellenistic east, and presumably there was as yet little in the way of an up to date western tradition of fortification that he could draw on. Aurelian's conquest of Zenobia's eastern Empire and Tetricus's surrender to him of the Gallic Empire in 274 ended the danger that the Empire would split into a series of separate regional states, as it did in the fifth century. His abandonment of the trans-Danubian province of Dacia showed, like the walls of Rome, his recognition of the need for a defensible and fortified frontier. His reform of the coinage looks forward (like much else) to Diocletian and Constantine. His new reformed *antoninianus*, at 2,500 to the pound of gold, was better looking than the old, at 5000 to the pound, but it was still base metal. In Gaul, it made little headway against the mass of debased billon and its even more debased imitations now circulating in bulk north of the Loire. Aurelian's reform of the Rome mint led to a mutiny among its workers, presumably because he was trying to stamp out lucrative abuses, which needed a pitched battle to suppress it. He claimed the title of *Restitutor Galliarum*, but there was not time between its recovery in 274 and his murder the following year to ensure peace. A fresh wave of invasions followed his death.[17]

Probus and the recovery of Gaul

This fresh wave seems to have marked the final breakdown of the defences of Gaul. Its effects on rural settlements in *Gallia Belgica* are clear from excavations, though since the latest coin from a site can only give a *terminus post quem* (a date *after* which something happened), it is difficult (and probably unwise) to try to correlate the destruction of an individual site with a particular historically attested event.

At Haccourt, north of Liege, the huge villa was destroyed by fire some time after 263 and not rebuilt. At Vodelée in south-west Belgium, a villa destroyed in a fire whose debris sealed a coin of Tetricus (270–4) was rebuilt in Constantinian times, only to be burnt down again about 350, probably in the disturbances in the time of Magnentius. At Echternach in Luxembourg, a large villa was destroyed by fire about 275. A circular stone fort with internal towers was then built on a hill above, using masonry salvaged from a cemetery. The villa was later partially rebuilt, and, though archaeological evidence does not go beyond the fifth century, the estate of *Epaternacus* may have survived to the seventh when it was granted by a daughter of Dagobert II in 698 to the Anglo-Saxon missionary Willibrord and became the site of a celebrated monastery. All three were probably destroyed in the invasions on the death of Aurelian, but their subsequent fates are equally instructive. However, Van Ossel argues that the longer term effects of the invasions, however destructive they may have been, has probably been overestimated. Where destruction or abandonment can be identified in the areas studied by him, the dates do not belong to a single horizon and many sites survived the crisis. Gechter and Kunow have demonstrated a similar pattern of long term decline behind the Rhine frontier from early in the third century onwards. They conclude that, well after this process had begun, many sites were destroyed in 'the Germanic raids of 275' and never rebuilt. This may be a sound conclusion though the date 275, derived from literary sources, cuts across a series of histograms otherwise calibrated at half centuries, so skewing the chronological pattern. Elsewhere, this reliance on historically derived dates can be seen in the tendency to assign the many large coin hoards of the period and any archaeological evidence for abandonment or destruction to 'The Great Invasions', often hopefully dated to 275, or, hedging bets, to 'circa 275'. Without evidence from well excavated and well published sites it can be difficult to be sure of such identifications. Sometimes in the past hoards have been mapped to show the routes of particular groups of invaders, with arrows like the lines of advance of army divisions on a modern battle map. The coin hoards, however, need to be put into context.[18]

By the third century, the silver denarius of the early Empire, over 90% fine silver, was a distant memory. Its silver content had dropped to 50% under Severus and continued to slide under his successors. By the accession of Valerian and Gallienus in 253 it was 35% and this halved by the time Gallienus became sole ruler in 260. Even this almost token silver content fell within a decade to a mere 2.5%, whilst the gold aureus was now a quarter of its weight at the beginning of the joint reign. The Roman mint doubled its *officinae* or workshops to keep pace with demand, and the equally debased coinage of the Gallic Empire, and the products of the other regional mints, added their share. Even this flood of coinage was not enough, for north of the Loire a mass of smaller and cruder copies of the debased official coinage ('barbarous radiates') poured out of clandestine mints. The almost worthless individual coins were accepted by weight rather than by number.

Similar debasement of the currency is not unparalleled, though it has seldom been allowed to go so far. It is wrong though to think in terms of the catastrophic effects of hyper-inflation in pre- Hitler Germany, for that was a highly monetarized society with most of the population living on salaries or fixed incomes. Interestingly, when the silver value of the French coinage was reduced by two thirds between 1295 and 1306 the Crown was forced to abandon its income from *monnayage* (the profits of debasement) by the protests of the church and nobility who relied on fixed incomes and moneys of account. The third-century debasement would have hit some social groups hard, and may have had an unsettling effect on the army. More widely its effects may have been no more than those complained of by a traveller in Spain in 1724: 'the major part of payments is made . . . in alloy (copper, with a little silver added); its transport is very cumbersome and expensive; moreover it is customary to accept it by weight.' Though the many vast hoards containing coins of Tetricus and their crude copies have often been associated with the invasions, they also sometimes contain copies of issues of Probus and in those cases must post-date the invasions. The bulk were probably simply abandoned when the government repudiated them. Possibly some residual hope of redemption may have saved them from melting down as scrap metal. The presence of a large radiate hoard on a site has sometimes been used to suggest that it was destroyed during the invasions and never re-occupied. A cautionary tale (if one is needed) is provided, however, by the rural cult centre of

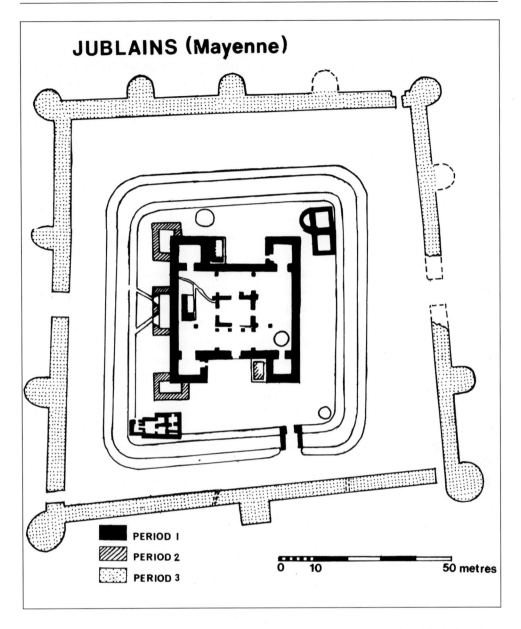

JUBLAINS (Mayenne)

PERIOD 1
PERIOD 2
PERIOD 3

0   10   50 metres

4   *Jublains (Mayenne). Late third-century burgus, with defensive tower and double ditches, the latter backfilled when the later fort was built under Diocletian or Constantine*

Montbuoy (Loiret) in the Aveyron valley south of Montargis. Here a hoard of 45kg of coin, including many barbarous copies of Tetricus, was found in 1938, and taken as evidence that the site was destroyed in the Great Invasion. In 1951–3, however, four more hoards were found. Three (or rather one hoard in three pots) ended under Gordian and one about 310. There is no reason to associate any one hoard with an assumed sack, and the latest post-dates the invasions by thirty-five years. The site evidently generated much coin use, and attracted large amounts of small value coin, much of which stayed there. It may not have been easy to exchange this for gold, and the hoards may have been cached pending an opportunity to do so.[19]

Despite the disasters of the third quarter of the century, one trend marked a significant move towards stability. Thanks to Gallienus's much decried opening of high command to non-senators, there now existed an officer corps of men of modest origins, often from Illyria (the Balkans). They had usually risen from junior commands under earlier Emperors, so ensuring a measure of badly needed continuity. A professional army career structure had been created. On the death of Aurelian, M. Aurelius Probus, son of a military tribune from Sirmium in Pannonia, became Emperor (276). He marched west, crossed into Gaul, and attacked the Alemanni, whilst his generals fought the Franks to the north. The author of the *Historia Augusta* tells how Probus '. . . fought so great and victorious battles that he recovered from the Germans sixty very famous cities of Gaul', killing many raiders who were wandering 'through all the country of Gaul' and settled prisoners as *numeri* and *limitanei*. Julian, himself victor of a similar campaign, spoke with admiration of 'Probus, who set seventy cities on their feet in less than seven years.'[20]

One site perhaps associated with Probus's recovery of Gaul is Jublains (Mayenne). South-west of the Roman small town is a bastioned rectangular fort which Rebuffet thinks was built under Diocletian by the workforce responsible for the walls of Le Mans. Inside is an earlier tower surrounded by a double ditch which was backfilled when the later fort was built, sealing copies of Tetrican coins including a small hoard. Inside it were two small bath buildings of a kind found on sites housing small military detachments. The site may be associated with the collection and storage of the *annona*, a tax in foodstuffs and in kind, but its first phase is linked by coin evidence to the aftermath of the Gallic Empire. It recalls the ditches added around the Great Monument at Richborough at just this time and the way these were backfilled to make way for the Carausian fort. Such *burgi* may once have been more widespread.[21]

Despite Probus's victories the west was still unsettled. There were brief coups by a governor of Britain, by Bonosus the commander at Cologne, a Spaniard with a British father and Gallic mother, and at Lyon by Proculus from Albenga in Savoy, an area proverbial for bandits. Probus's successor Carus took command in the east, leaving his son Carinus in the west. Gaul was now quiet, save for peasant resistance to the re-imposition of Roman 'order' (and taxation). There was still trouble in Britain, and by the end of 284 Carinus could claim the title of *Britannicus Maximus*. Judging by the Carausian revolt five years later, Saxons and other sea raiders may have been involved. Despite these last gusts the storm was blowing itself out, but by this time Carinus's father was dead and Diocletian was marching west against him.[22]

2. Soldiers and Civilians in the Gallic Late Empire

Our Lords the Emperor Caesar Gaius Aurelius Valerius Diocletian, Father of his People, Invincible Augustus, and the Emperor Marcus Aurelius Valerius Maximianus, Pius, Felix, Invincible Augustus, by their Providence ordered the walls of Cularo (Grenoble), with their interior buildings, to be built and completed, together with the Vienne Gate, otherwise the Gate of Hercules.

One of a pair of inscriptions once built into the face of the late Roman walls of Grenoble

By 285, Diocletian was sole master of Rome. Just over a century later, in 395, Theodosius I was briefly the last ruler of an undivided Empire. Diocletian's division of the Empire between the eastern and western Augusti and their Caesars, or junior Emperors, had good earlier parallels for good military reasons, from Valerian and Gallienus to Carus and Carinus. The eastern Emperor was normally the senior colleague. Diocletian was Jupiter, ruler of the world. His western partner Maximian was Hercules, a slightly lesser god, freeing the world of monsters and rebels by his exertions. The same Herculean symbolism was retained by later western Emperors (and much later by Charles the Bald when he was trying to cope with the Vikings). The distinction encapsulates the differences between the two halves of the Empire, and goes some way towards explaining the breakdown of the Tetrachy after the retirement of the two Augusti in 305. The east had long been familiar with the semi-divine king, and here the system was fairly stable until it was overthrown by Licinius and Constantine from the west. In the west, however, the Emperor was above all an *Imperator* or army commander.[1]

Maximian was sent to Gaul to consolidate the fragile peace established by Probus and Carinus. Frankish invaders were still in control of areas behind the Rhine frontier, and Maximian agreed to their settlement in the territories of the Nervii and Treveri, in the Ardennes, Luxembourg and Rhineland-Pfalz. A panegyric delivered before the Caesar Constantius about 293 tells of Frankish *laeti* tilling the waste cornlands of north Gaul, and other sources speak of Frankish settlers serving the Empire under Constantine by their agriculture and military service and of barbarian oxen tilling the fields of Belgic Gaul. This response to rural depopulation and the shortage of army recruits was far from unique. Severus Alexander, for example, is said to have settled prisoners of war on deserted farmlands in Phrygia. We shall need to consider changes in rural settlement patterns in north Gaul later, but behind this frontier zone the towns of Gaul were also in need of attention.[2]

Gallia Renascati: the late Roman town walls

Julius Caesar began his account of the Gallic Wars with his famous statement that all Gaul was divided into three parts (*Gallia est omnis divisa in partres tres*), inhabited by the Aquitanians, the Gauls and the Belgae. This did not include Gallia Transalpina ('Gaul across the Alps'), the Mediterranean coastal strip, already a Roman province (hence the modern Provence). Not only did this tag become familiar to schoolboys for centuries, but it was used by Augustus to divide Gaul into four provinces — Gallia Aquitanica; Gallia Lugdunensis (from its capital, Lyon); Gallia Belgica; and Gallia Narbonensis (Transalpina). These were not ethnic or racial divisions but convenient-sized administrative units, rather as a modern police authority might take the name of an Anglo-Saxon kingdom. By the late fourth century, through a series of local government reorganisations, these four provinces had increased to seventeen, including the two Rhineland military frontier provinces of Upper and Lower Germany. These make a useful framework within which to study late Roman Gaul for two reasons. Many correspond to familiar modern regions of France, and whilst even an historian might pause for a moment before identifying Lugdunensis II or III, most people will be familiar with their modern counterparts of Normandy and Brittany, though the latter extended as far south-east as Tours. The second reason is the survival of a late Roman document known as the *Notitia Galliarum* which lists 115 cities and 7 lesser places under their respective provinces. It must date from after 367 for Grenoble appears as *Gratianopolis*, after the Emperor Gratian, rather than under its older name of *Cularo*.[3] ·

Following the recovery of the cities of Gaul by Probus and Maximian, many were equipped with formidable defences surrounding part of the earlier urban area. Some, like Bourges, Le Mans, Tours or Évreux, still have impressive remains of these walls in the city centre. Elsewhere, they have been demolished or replaced by medieval walls or modern boulevards and are only known from archaeological excavations, records of old discoveries, and from old plans and drawings. In one notorious case, at Dax in the Pyrenees, a finely preserved circuit of late Roman walls was demolished by the local municipality in 1856, despite protests from leading French and British scholars. The walls are of distinctive construction. Their foundations and lower parts are of large blocks of stone, often re-used from earlier buildings. These include sculptured friezes, tombstones, inscriptions, fragments of columns, and even statues. Sometimes, parts of a standing building were incorporated in the masonry, as at Bourges where an elegant apsed fountain house was encased in the wall structure. Above this broad and solid base, the walls were faced with small squarish blocks of coursed ashlar (*petit appareil*), neatly coursed, around a rubble core which was often dry-laid with wet mortar poured around it like concrete. Spaced at intervals in the wall face were bands of tiles, levelling courses several tiles thick which would have speeded up construction by enabling the mortar to dry more quickly. Often these bands of tile are associated with the square putlog holes which held the timber scaffolding during the building process. The wall faces are sometimes patterned with coloured stone-dark ironstone, orange sandstone or white limestone, a technique already used in the first-century walls of Cologne. Spaced along the wall at intervals were projecting towers, most commonly round fronted, from the tops of which the faces of the

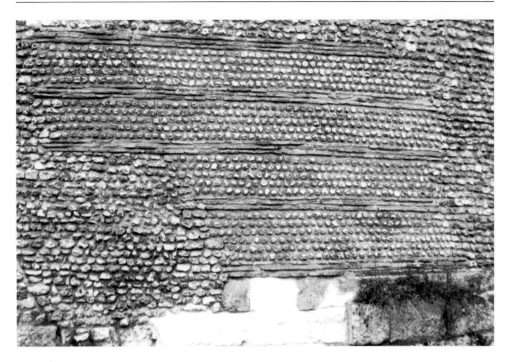

*5   Evreux (Eure). South-west angle of the Roman town walls, with small coursed blockwork facing (*petit appareil)*, tile bonding courses and large re-used masonry blocks below. The rougher masonry above and to the sides is medieval. Photograph J.K.K.*

walls could be protected by covering fire. Where they survive to sufficient height, as at Le Mans, Senlis or Bourges, the towers stand some height above the curtain wall with three arched windows looking outwards. In contrast to medieval castles arrow loops are extremely rare. At Le Mans, the upper chamber of one tower was big enough to be turned by a seventh-century bishop into a chapel of St Michael the Archangel. The Tour Saint-Michel survived until the eighteenth century.[4]

Far from being emergency defences run up in haste, the Gallic town walls are impressive works of military architecture, functional and strong. They compare favourably with major medieval castles. Many, like Le Mans, Évreux or Pevensey, stood siege in medieval times when they were regarded as formidable defences. Philip Augustus had the amphitheatre at Amiens, which formed part of the Roman defences, demolished lest it be utilised by his enemies. The origins of the developed medieval castle, its curtain wall protected by projecting circular mural towers and with twin-towered gatehouses like those of late Roman town defences, is still not wholly understood. But innovative castle builders like Philip Augustus or Richard I of England did not need to go on Crusade to see fortifications of impressive scale and sophistication, and the late Roman town walls may have played a much greater part in the evolution of the castle in western Europe than is usually thought.

The building of this defence system was a labour worthy of Hercules himself, but any attempt to understand it and the reasons why it was built raises a number of problems. These include:

(1) The origins of this distinctive and innovative style of military architecture.

(2) The chronology of individual walls, and of the system as a whole.

(3) The significance of the re-used material, much of it from public buildings.

(4) The purpose of these defences, and whether the initiative for their building came from central government, the provincial governor, or from local communities. Were they for the protection of the townspeople against barbarian attack; fortified bases for the Imperial field army; protected regional seats of government; or for another purpose?

Origins

These citadels, enclosing only a fraction of the earlier city, are very different from early town walls in Gaul. The latter enclosed large areas, had relatively few towers (most commonly large circular towers spanning the defences) and were equipped with impressive monumental gateways. They are as much symbols of the city's status as defensive circuits. Town walls with closely set rectangular projecting towers were an ancient tradition in the Hellenistic east and were still in use in the third century, whether by Septimius Severus at Kifrin on the Euphrates or by Aurelian in the walls of Rome. A possible link with later western developments is the Severan fort of Ain Sinu II in northern Iraq, a hybrid of the traditional and the new, with close-spaced rectangular towers on one face, semi-circular central towers on two others and solid circular angle towers. Sites like Ain Sinu II suggest that these new model fortifications developed on the eastern frontiers where their counter-siege defences would have been of greater use against the Persians, skilled in siege warfare, than they were against Germanic invaders in the west. In the west, however, they were combined with more local traditions. There is more variation within the late Roman Gallic city walls than their generalised description above might suggest, and Stephen Johnson has shown the existence of distinctive groups within individual provinces, the work of specific groups of engineers or masons. The style of masonry, *opus mixtum*, with its bands of brickwork, calls for no special comment. It was a normal style of the late Empire in Gaul and elsewhere, seen in the forum of Bavai and in the late second-century *Barbarathermen* and the Constantinian Imperial Baths at Trier. The influence of earlier western styles of fortification is also apparent. Large circular towers of Cologne-Tongres type recur in Belgica Secunda and at Brest. The wall patterning at Le Mans and elsewhere in Aquitania Secunda matches the first-century north-west corner tower at Cologne. Similarly, the city walls in Lugdunensis II, with the 'playing card' shape of earlier Roman forts, as at Bayeux, Lisieux and Évreux, may be inspired by the second-century *classis Britannica* fort at Boulogne or by the earlier forts of the 'Saxon shore' series. Medieval parallels show that innovation in military architecture is often, as here, the result of the conjunction of an existing local building tradition with an outside model. We know little of the fortifications built by Gallienus and Philip in northern Italy, but the walls of Verona, of 265, with re-used masonry blocks below and coursed tufa above suggest that some elements of the system were already in place. Though isolated towns in Gaul may have been fortified earlier, perhaps by Probus, the type must have been introduced to the west under the Tetrarchy, though many individual walls may be much later.[5]

6   *Evreux (Eure). The interior face of the same wall, with re-used masonry and columns, in the archaeology gallery of the Musée Municipal. Three putlog holes (scaffolding holes) visible at top. Photograph Musée Municipal, Evreux*

Chronology and context

The only Gallic town walls dateable in historical terms are those of Grenoble. Until they were destroyed early in the nineteenth century, two long narrow inscriptions in the wall face recorded the building of the walls, and of their Jovian and Herculean gates (otherwise the 'Rome gate' and the 'Vienne gate') under Diocletian and Maximian (286–305). Grenoble however may be a special case. It was not at that time a Civitas capital, but commanded (as the names of its gates show) the strategic highway between north Italy and Gaul at a key river crossing. It may have served a different initial function to other Gallic walls. Away from Grenoble we are reliant on archaeological dating, which in practice usually means coins sealed in the construction levels of the wall or in its masonry. Pottery evidence and radio-carbon dating are at present too inexact to be of much help. In some cases, where walls pass through marshy ground, they are built on timber piles, and here dendrochronology offers the possibility of precise dating. At Xanten in Upper Germany, for example, we know from tree ring dating that work on the Trajanic Colonia walls began in the spring of AD 106. Sealed coins give a less exact date for they can only provide a *terminus post quem* — the date *after* which the coin could have been lost. Beauvais, north-west of Paris, had walls belonging to a group in Belgica Secunda whose common features suggest a similar date. Coins of Postumus (259–67) and Diocletian (286–305) found in the wall core suggested a date soon after Diocletian's capture of Gaul. Later, two more coins, of 307–10 and 311–13, were found in debris cut by the foundation trench of the wall, making the walls some 25 years later. Similar evidence is now available from many French cities, and is useful both for dating individual wall circuits and for dating the Gallic town walls as a whole. A medieval parallel may, however, serve to put the dating problem into perspective. In thirty years, between 1277 and 1307, King Edward I built seven castles in north Wales which represent the peak of medieval castle building and drew heavily on the material and financial resources of his kingdom — a major medieval realm covering much of Britain and France, and near the height of its power. Maximian's Gaul was ruined by barbarian invasion, and control had only recently been re-established. Even if he and his successors achieved the truly Herculean task of building sixty Gallic town walls in the same time span as Edward's seven castles, this would take us, allowing a couple of years in which to organise the building programme after his arrival in Gaul in 286, down to 318, almost mid way through the reign of Constantine I. In fact, work at Beaumaris, the latest of Edward's castles, continued as late as 1331, the equivalent on our Gallic timescale of 340, two years after the death of Constantine. We might therefore expect a programme of work of this magnitude begun under Maximian to be on-going until at least 320 or 340. Only when coins show that a particular circuit of walls is considerably later than this can we conclude that they belong to a separate campaign of work. It is now becoming clear, however, that many Gallic town walls are much later. At Tours, a sequence of stratified fourth-century coins pre-dated the walls, and one of Valentinian I (364–75) came from its foundation trench. A link has been suggested with the creation of Tours as capital of the new province of Lugdunensis III in 374, and the walls of the neighbouring city of Orleans are now thought to be of similar date (350–75). Similarly, the walls of St Bertrand de Comminges in the Pyrenees now seem to be little, if at all, earlier than 400, and carry most of the distinctive town walls of the province of Novempopulana with them.[6]

Sometimes, excavation within cities has made it possible to relate their walls to wider patterns of development. At Bourges (Rue Eduoard Branly) a bath building inside the north rampart was demolished, its rubble sealing 5 coins of Diocletian and Maximian ending in 292–3. If this was connected with the building of the walls, it suggests an early date, as at Grenoble. At Rouen (Rue des Fosses Louis V) an Antonine market hall, perhaps a fish market, was levelled soon after a coin hoard of Carausius and Allectus had been hidden in it, again suggesting a Diocletianic date. However, it appears that the site lay open for some time, and was used to dump waste, and the adjacent town walls may not be earlier than the mid-fourth century. Similarly at Poitiers, where an important sequence has been uncovered on the site of the medieval bishop's palace, it seems that the city walls post-date an east-west inhumation cemetery in use until the mid-fourth century. Possibly lack of resources, or the inability of central government to impose its will at local level, meant that official building programmes, starved of funds, dragged on for many years.[7]

Second-hand stonework

Many visitors to the British Museum will be familiar with the memorial stone of Julius Classicianus, Imperial procurator of Britain in the aftermath of the Bouddican revolt. His tombstone survived because in the fourth century it was re-used in the foundations of one of the bastions of the walls of Roman London. Many of the great collections of Roman sculpture and inscriptions in French provincial museums have a similar origin, sealed in the foundations of city walls and so saved from destruction in a medieval lime kiln or breaking up for rubble. It shows how much the ancient city had changed that these one-time sources of civic pride could be used in this way. Sometimes the reasons why monumental stonework was available for re-use are clear enough. Cemeteries on the fringes of the town would need to be cleared for the wide defensive ditches of late wall circuits. If some circuits are as late as they now appear to be, material from pagan temples demolished by Christian Emperors could have been available for re-use.

Such cases do not, however, account for the wholesale demolition of public amenities like the bath building and public fountain at Bourges, and the fish market at Rouen. At Beauvais, the Severan colonnaded hemicycle and the monumental complex of which it was a part were demolished and their stones incorporated in the defences. In Sens the public baths received similar treatment. Constantine's confiscation of municipal revenues may have had much to do with this, though Gallienus was already using *spolia* from demolished buildings in the walls of Verona a generation earlier. Municipal magistrates could no longer afford to pay for the upkeep of public baths or the maintenance of aqueducts, or preferred to spend what money they had on their villas. Equally, the value of the large blocks of masonry to military engineers is obvious from Ammianus Marcellinus's accounts of the use of battering rams and other siege engines by Persians and Romans alike on the eastern frontiers.[8]

The reason why — the use of urban space

Such demolitions are only the start of the story. The use of the vacant spaces afterwards may help us towards the reasons why the walls were built and what they were protecting. At Rouen the area of the fish market lay empty for many years, like a modern city-centre

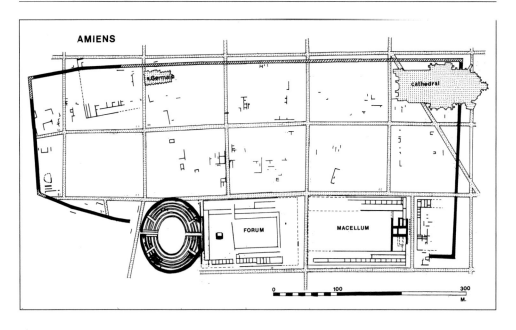

7   *Amiens (Somme). Late Roman town wall, overlying the streets and buildings of the earlier town. The Amphitheatre, Forum and Macellum (market) have been requisitioned by the state, and turned into a military stores depot and arsenal. After Bayard and Massy (1983)*

car park in an area awaiting re-development. At Poitiers two town houses remained in use until 320 or 340. By mid century, however, they had been replaced by two low status timber buildings (*Masures*) with chalk and mortar floors and an east-west inhumation cemetery.[9]

Open spaces created by demolition would make a clean sweep for the line of the walls and may have influenced their planned circuits. Some areas within the walls may have remained as open space. At Évreux, a large area of paving within the walls may have belonged to the forum. Elsewhere buildings were left standing, perhaps officially requisitioned. At Amiens, a monumental forum and market-building complex occupying two city-centre blocks along with the amphitheatre were turned into a fortified complex which occupied a quarter of the area of the new walled town. A coin of Probus of 277–8 is known from its masonry. Excavation of the market building (*macellum*) has revealed a large granary and extensive traces of metalworking, perhaps associated with the state armaments factory recorded in the *Notitia Dignitatum*. Along the Amiens-Cologne highway at Bavai, a similar double forum complex was encased in defensive walls turning it into a fortification. Nearby at Famars (*Fanum Martis*), the baths were included in the walled area and re-used, possibly as a corn mill. As at Bavai, the walls are of two periods though the overall chronology is not yet clear.[10]

Evidence for the fourth-century use of intra-mural space comes from Tours. Sulpicius Severus mentions the *Praetorium*, or provincial governor's residence, and the prison, both within the walls. The cathedral of Tours also moved within the city walls shortly before Martin's ordination as bishop in 372. In the ninth century a Basilica, perhaps that of the

Praetorium, was pressed into service as a church when Martin's body was brought within the walls during the Viking raids. The church of *S. Martini de Basilica* (de la Basoche) was in the south-east corner of the Roman town, near the present Rue de la Bazoche. A charter of 903 describes it:

> An open area with the hall adjoining, once called the accursed (*Maledicta*), but now, because it has received Martin, the House of God (*Domus Dei*), situate within the walls of Tours, with its wall and postern, being in circuit from the Orleans Gate (*Porta Aurelienensi*) round to the amphitheatre, 96 perches.[11]

Such examples suggest that late Roman city walls were built to serve the needs of central government, not primarily for local defence or to protect the townsfolk. The size of the wall circuit need not therefore reflect the size of the urban population. Those of *Lugdunensis* III in Brittany and the Loire valley enclose an area of 9–10 ha, irrespective of the earlier size of the town. The exception is Nantes, a naval and military base of the *Dux Tractus Armoricani et Nervicani*, whose different function may be reflected in its greater wall circuit. Unlike medieval town walls, the late Gallic ones did not necessarily seek to enclose the whole community, or reflect its size. Indeed, they recall the acropolis towns of Mediterranean Europe, with a fortified citadel above and the town below. The 'Wall of Valerian' built on the Athenian acropolis after the Gothic invasions offers an even closer parallel. It may, however, be possible to go beyond this role as *castra* or proto-castles and to suggest a more specific function.[12]

Town walls and the Annona Militaris

The fourth-century poet Ausonius in his poem on the Moselle describes the fortifications of northern Gaul as *non castra, sed horrea Belgis* – 'not the castles, but the granaries of Belgica.' Granaries not for the civilian population but for the armies of the Rhine frontier. One victim of third-century inflation and unrest had been taxation. As the value of fixed cash payments plummeted, Emperors replaced taxation mostly in money with requisitions of foodstuffs and other goods. This *annona militaris* was well suited to a period when the most pressing need was to feed and equip the army. Cash payments made a comeback when the monetary system and a closely ordered society had been re-established, but the need remained to store and safeguard large quantities of army provisions. Corn had to be collected in central depots for re-distribution to military units, obvious targets for Bacaudae or barbarian raiders. Ammianus describes how the Isaurian rebels of 354, driven by hunger, attacked the walled fortress of Palaea on the coast where 'supplies are regularly stored even today, for distribution to the troops that defend the frontier.' Elsewhere he notes, with the eye of an experienced staff officer, Julian's care in bringing corn supplies for the Army of the Rhine from Aquitania and Britain, and how he built forts and granaries to protect the British supply route and store its products. In the fortified forum complex at Amiens, part of the *macellum* was turned into a vast hall with a floor of hypocausted channels, perhaps a storehouse or granary for Julian's Rhineland campaign. It may also be reflected in the official corn mills at Famars and at Ickham in Kent.[13]

The towns would also have been involved, for the collection of taxes, in cash or kind, was a prime function of the *civitates* and their magistrates. One duty of third-century magistrates was to escort corn supplies. Rebuffet suggested that the defences of Jublains were built, to store locally collected annona, by the same masons who built the walls of Le Mans. In England, Alchester has a late third-century granary, perhaps connected with the annona. This was not contemporary with the town walls, however, for it was demolished in the mid-fourth century to provide stone for their building. Similarly, an inscription of 387 from the town of Oretum in central Spain records the building of a granary by the *praeses* or governor. It is characteristic of the late Empire that the person who now appears on an inscription as the donor of a basilica colonnade, the restorer of a bath building, or the builder of a granary, is no longer a local magistrate but the *praeses*. Landowners no longer exercised the trappings of power through the *civitates*. To that extent the attempt to transplant the Graeco-Roman city state to northern climes had failed, but the cities still performed a necessary function. Field Marshal Lord Wavell once said that 'supply is the essence of victory,' and corn supply must have occupied a place in the late Empire like that of petrol in modern mechanised warfare. The building of city walls was imposed from above, like so much at that time, but it marked one of the decisive steps between the towns of antiquity and those of the middle ages. The city was not longer merely a centre for administration and trade but a defended place which gave domination of the area around it to whoever controlled its walls. The citizens had some measure of control over their destinies by deciding to whom they should open their gates, or against whom they should close them. The Civil War began when Sir John Hotham refused to open the gates of Hull to Charles I. Nor was their role wholly military. In post-Roman Gaul, the cathedral and city churches were within the walls, the cemeteries and extra-mural basilicas outside. When the cemeteries invaded the space within the walls the medieval city was complete. In Medieval Spain, the definition of a city was simple, 'a city (*Ciudad, Civitas*), must have a bishop, and walls.'[14]

The city as strongpoint: some military aspects of the late Roman towns

In military terms 'Defensible hard points' or 'boxes' for defence in depth serve as fortified supply depots, enable an army to move without the encumbrance of a supply train, deny the enemy food supplies, and delay them by inhibiting the use of passes and river crossings. The Romans were well aware of the dangers with such systems — that field units might be pinned down as garrison troops. The division of the army into the *comitatenses* of the field army and the frontier *limitanae* was partly designed to prevent this, but since the latter could not be withdrawn from the frontiers the fortified towns were separately garrisoned with units of *laeti* drawn from the soldier-settlers of Gallia Belgica — Batavians, Franks and Teutons — and with *gentiles* recruited from prisoners of war — Suevians, Sarmatians or Taifali. The military units based on the late Roman towns of Gaul are listed in the *Notitia Dignitatum*, though the list is incomplete due to a missing page in the manuscript, and any such list for Britain is also missing. Leaving aside units of *milites*, which were part of the frontier army and came under separate command, the military units based on the towns can be listed under their provinces.[15]

Lugdunensis Prima		**Not Dig. (Occ)XLII**
Sarmatian gentiles	Langres	69
Lugdunensis Secunda		
Batavian laeti and Suevian gentiles	Bayeux and Coutances	34
Lugdunensis Tertia		
laeti and Suevian gentiles	Le Mans	35
Frankish laeti	Rennes	36
Lugdunensis IV (Senonia)		
Teutonic laeti	Chartres	33
Sarmatian gentiles	Paris	66
Belgica Prima		
Lingonian laeti	dispersed	37
Aeduan laeti	Epuso	38
Belgica Secunda		
Nervian laeti	Famars	39
Batavian laeti	Arras	40
Batavian laeti	Noviomagus (Yvois-Carignan)	41
Laeti and gentiles	Reims and Senlis	42
Sarmatian gentiles	Between Reims and Amiens	67
Germania Prima		
Lagensian laeti	Tongres	43
Aquitania Prima		
Laeti and Suevian gentiles	Clermont	44
Sarmatian gentiles	Rodez and ?	68
Aquitania Secunda		
Sarmatian and Taifal gentiles	Poitiers	65
Sarmatian gentiles	Au . . . ? Agen	70
(Folio missing in Ms. After XLII, 70)		

Strictly speaking, the *Notitia* does not list the location of units but of their commanding officer, and detachments may have been stationed in other walled towns of the province. Though there is some variation and the list is incomplete, the units were often brigaded in pairs, following normal late Roman practice, with *laeti* and *gentiles* sometimes serving together. Since the Sarmatians were cavalry (and sometimes stationed outside the towns), this implies a mix of infantry and cavalry, able to fulfil the variety of roles that Luttwak has suggested. The two Aquitanian provinces further from the frontiers managed with a pair

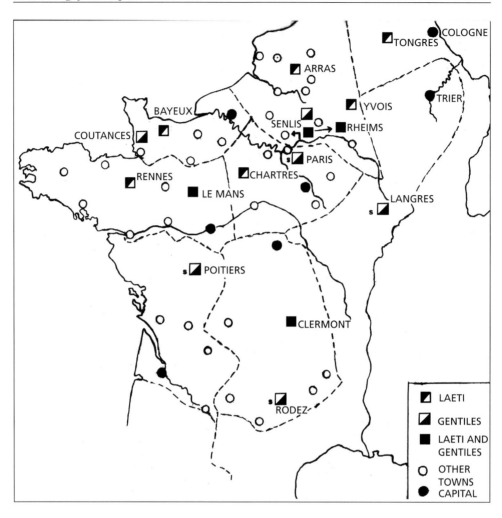

8   *Barbarian* laeti *and* gentiles *in late Roman Gaul (*Notitia Dignitatum *Occ.XLII).
     Locations may be those of the commander and company headquarters and elements could have
     been stationed in other nearby towns. Sarmatian cavalry (S) were often rurally based*

of Gentile units apiece, mostly Sarmatians, plus some *laeti* in the key central town of
Clermont. Here a rapid reaction force to deal with any barbarian penetration may have
been more use than city garrisons. The possibility of identifying these units in the
archaeological record is another matter. There would be many soldiers present in late
Roman towns from time to time, for many reasons, and it is not usually possible to
associate items of military equipment with the permanent garrison. The soldier of the field
army unit of *Mattiaci Seniores* buried at Bordeaux was presumably in the provincial capital
for other reasons. However, two Theodosian barracks parallel to the town walls in the
castrum at Arras, apparently housing a cavalry unit, could have belonged to the unit of
Batavian *laeti* recorded there in the *Notitia Dignitatum*. Finds of military equipment from

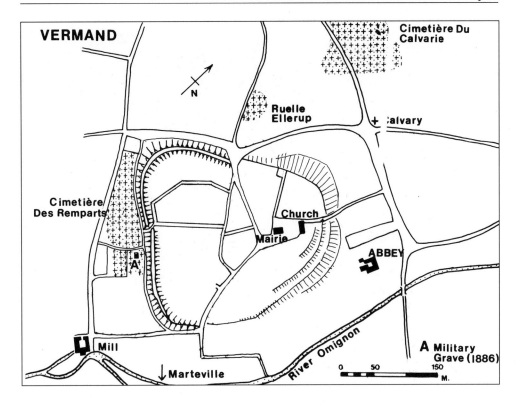

9   *Vermand (Aisne). The hillfort and the cemeteries (after Eck 1891)*

within the walls of Tours may also indicate a military garrison, though the evidence has not yet been published in detail. These could have been a detachment from the laetic units at Le Mans or Rennes. A fine late Roman military buckle from Poitiers could have belonged to an officer of the Gentiles stationed there, but other explanations are again possible.[16]

A late Roman officer from Vermand

From Amiens, with its fortified forum complex, a major Roman and modern road runs due east along the Somme valley. The many First World War cemeteries on each side are reminders of the importance of this road for the military control of northern France. 50km from Amiens the road crosses the river Omignon at Vermand, site of the pre-Roman oppidum of the Viromandui. In early Roman times their capital moved to *Augusta* (St Quentin), but by the late Empire it had returned to the defended river crossing at Vermand which was to give its name to the medieval County of the Vermandois.

Outside the ramparts of the hillfort were three late Roman cemeteries with some 700 north-south inhumations of the kind normal in pre-Roman times over much of western Europe, and which revived in the late Empire when cremation was no longer used. The community was wealthy and probably pagan, though a separate Christian cemetery may have existed elsewhere. Its dead were buried in their everyday clothes, men often in stout nailed boots, and women with their costume jewellery. Their graves were equipped with pottery, glass and metal vessels, and with food and drink for the last journey — a cold chicken, a hare, a young pig or a plate of veal chops. Many of the vessels were flasks or flagons suitable for wine or beer. The dead were equipped for their journey not only with boots, but also with Charon's penny in their hand or mouth, a purse of coins, silver siliquae or even a gold solidus. Though a few items from graves have Christian motifs it is doubtful if these reflected the beliefs of their owners.[17]

In 1886 a large rectangular grave pit was found in a cemetery outside the south-west defences of the hillfort. Set under a circular barrow, of which the ditch remained, the grave pit — 2.7m wide and 3.5m long — was cut into the chalk to a depth of 2.5m. In the centre of its floor a man lay in a cist of mortared limestone blocks, re-used from some demolished structure. Around him was an array of weapons. At his feet on the wall of the chamber hung a circular shield 80cm across, with traces of a purple internal lining and elaborate gold-leaf decoration around its silver-gilt boss. Near his right hand were an axe, spear and ten light javelins. Richly decorated silver-gilt fittings may have belonged to a military baton or standard. Eck noted that their diameter did not match that of the spear shaft, and they would have been out of place in an otherwise functional weapon set. The tomb had been rifled by grave robbers — perhaps at the time of excavation — and only a few silver buckles and strap ends remained of his personal accoutrements, but a gold solidus of Arcadius (of 383–8) may have come from it.[18]

Whilst there is no evidence of the ethnicity of the Vermand warrior, a number of features suggest that he was both a Roman military commander and a barbarian chieftain of noble blood. The purple lining of the shield (a colour reserved for Imperial use) and the ceremonial baton may denote an officer commanding troops in personal attendance on the Emperor. The lining can be matched on a shield on the fourth-century Beast Hunt mosaic at the probably Imperial villa at Piazza Armerina in Sicily, and Elton has suggested that circular shields were confined to those in close attendance on the Emperor. On the other hand, the timber grave chamber under a barrow can be matched across the Rhine from Halstatt times onwards, and in post Roman contexts in rich weapon graves throughout the barbarian west. His grave is one of some seventy in the northern frontier zone with weapons and military belt fittings. Though equivalent women's graves have brooches and jewellery of Germanic affinity, these were the graves of Roman soldiers and their families. The military element at Vermand may not have been high. Among 700 graves are 13 'Germanic' or 'Military' burials — four women and nine men — and Böhme's estimate that 20% of the population could have been Germanic is on the high side. Army fashions like belts may have spread among the civilian population, for at St Quentin, in an otherwise normal late Roman cemetery, nine of the ten men and a young child wore belts with buckles. The way in which the Vermand cemeteries cluster around the ramparts of the hillfort might suggest a military garrison, but a civilian settlement (and another cemetery) is known across the river at Vermand Marteville.[19]

Buckles and brooches: aspects of military dress in the frontier region

Though the sword and belt of the Vermand warrior had fallen victim to grave robbers,

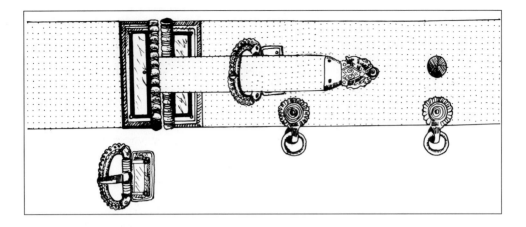

10   *Late Roman military belt set and buckle, late fourth century (Vermand Grave 190)*

many military graves in north Gaul contain metal fittings from the heavy military belt or *cingulum*. The *cingulum* had considerable symbolic significance. A Christian soldier might throw down his belt before the standards in an act of formal disobedience during a pagan sacrifice, another might hang up his belt in a church as a votive act before retiring from the world as a hermit. Late Roman ivories and silverware show how such metalwork formed part of the uniform of late Roman soldiers and officials, though representations of the military belt are rare, partly because soldiers are usually shown holding a large oval shield in front of them. The military cloak, bulky enough to be used as a bed cover or to be cut in half to be divided with a beggar, was fastened at the right shoulder with a crossbow brooch worn foot upwards. An ivory diptych shows the Roman general Stilicho so dressed, with military cloak, sword and sword belt. His son is in similar military dress, and his wife Serena has a necklace, jewelled belt and elaborate earrings. Though these to some extent match the costume jewellery from the north Gallic graves, she wears the normal accessories of a late Roman lady of rank, and a catacomb painting shows that these could be equally appropriate for the Virgin Mary. On the Missorium of Theodosius, a late Roman silver dish now in Madrid, the Emperor Arcadius is shown in a decorated belt with rectangular mounts and an elaborate terminal.[20]

A variety of late Roman military belt types and belt fittings are known. In the later fourth century wide belts between 50mm (2in) to about 25mm (5in) across made possible elaborate fittings, often with *kerbschnitt* (chip-carved) decoration. The belt sets vary in style. The simplest buckles have oval loops of cast bronze with sheet bronze plates, folded double, and riveted on to the end of the belt. More elaborate types are of cast bronze throughout. A finished belt may have up to eight separately cast components, all with matching decoration, plus half a dozen studs and suspension rings. The belts themselves may have had matching decoration, for leather baldrics among military equipment from Danish bog deposits at Vimose and Thorsbjerg have punched triangular motifs and peltae very like the chip carved metal fittings. Silver and niello or silver-gilt belt sets are known, and there is a sold gold buckle from Saint-Croix-au-Mines (Haut-Rhin). Such a hierarchy

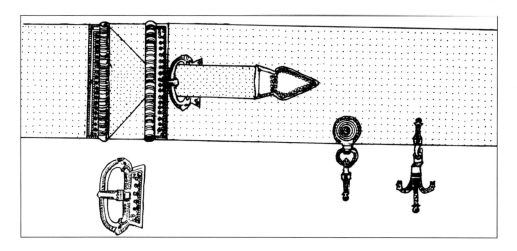

11   *Late Roman military belt set and buckle, early fifth century with cast-in-one buckle (Belleray, Meuse). The alternative strap arrangement is conjectural*

emphasises both the status implicit in such belt sets and the well organised system of large scale production. This was largely in the state arms factories recorded in the *Notitia Dignitatum*, though mould fragments and an unfinished casting from sites on the Rhine frontier — including the legionary fortress at Bonn — show that these did not enjoy a monopoly. Böhme has divided the buckles into seven types, each probably the product of a separate workshop.[21]

In 1952, part of a belt set of nielloed silver was dredged from the Loire at Chécy (Loiret) with a hoard of gold solidi of AD 402–6. The belt, its purse, and probably its owner were lost in the Loire at the time of the invasions of 406–7 and the usurpation of Constantine III. The find throws useful light on workshop practice, for the buckle is from the same workshop as others from Richborough (Kent) and Rouvroy near St Quentin. The buckles from Chécy and Rouvroy match so precisely in form and dimensions as to suggest the use of the same model for casting, despite different decoration. One technique for the series production of small bronzes at this time was a version of the *cire perdu* (lost wax) process using a lead die. A clay mould was formed around a wax model of the object to be cast, and the wax melted out. The mould was then used to cast a lead die, which could be used to make further moulds, from which the finished objects were cast. Without a lead master die it would have been necessary to repeat the whole process from wax model on for each object. The decoration would then be sharpened up in the mould before casting, or a plain lead die used and decoration added in the mould at the final stage. Sometimes chip-carved decoration might even be added to the finished object. This process explains the near-identical decoration on objects like pairs of Anglo-Saxon saucer brooches, which nevertheless show variation in detail.[22]

State arms factories may sometimes have been housed in disused public buildings. One for shields and spears is recorded at Amiens in the *Notitia Dignitatum* and may now have been found by excavation in the fortified forum complex there. The *macellum*, previously a storehouse or granary for military supplies, was converted under Valentinian I into a metallurgical workshop of factory scale. Its floor was covered with a thick layer of metallurgical debris, and a series of circular furnaces 2–3m across survived as burnt areas on the underlying floor. Burnt fragments of late Argonne ware, some with Christian symbols, suggest that production continued to the mid-fifth century. Such *fabricae* were organised like the Imperial mints with specialised *officinae* or workshops for each unit of production. They were based in walled cities not only for security, but because it was here that tax revenues, whether food and raw materials or bullion, were collected and stored. One product of the Amiens shield factory may be the shield boss with an official stamp from a weapon grave at Miséry (Somme).[23]

Soldiers and civilians in Gallia Belgica

Burials like the Vermand warrior, with belt furniture and weapons, are those of Roman soldiers, uniformed and armed from the state factories of the late Empire. Many were no doubt ethnic Germans, as the jewellery of their womenfolk suggests, though often the jewellery, though in Germanic style, was of types made within the boundaries of the Empire. There is no need to associate them with the *laeti* settled in Gallia Belgica by Maximian and Constantius, though letes serving in the army may have worn similar equipment. *Laetus* is a late Latin term of Germanic origin meaning a peasant or settler of low status. It reappears in the early seventh-century laws of Aethelberht of Kent, where by an ethnic inversion it seems to refer to peasant farmers of Gallo-Roman origin. When Julian refused to send his crack troops like the *Petulantes* to Constantius in 360, he offered instead recruits from the laeti, 'a tribe of barbarians from this side of the Rhine, or rather who come over voluntarily to us', though he expressed concern that if such recruits, who had volunteered only for service in Gaul, were forced to serve in the east 'Barbarian volunteers who often come over to our side (of the Rhine) under such conditions' might stop doing so. In fact, it was Julian's Gallic regulars who objected and mutinied. His wording shows that this immigration was not the result of one act of settlement by Constantine or anyone else, but was a continuing process through much of the fourth century.[24]

These soldier settlers and their families must have been familiar figures in fourth-century Gaul. The legal prohibition on their marriage with Gallo-Romans implies that there was no other barrier to their integration. It was probably designed to prevent a fusion making it more difficult to enforce obligations to military service. Their settlement does not imply that Rome was surrendering control of these areas. In the sixth century, Procopius has an interesting comment on how the (Gallo) Romans and the 'Germans' united and became one people, and in practice Roman control must have become less direct as barbarian settlement took root. In the territory of the Nervii (broadly the modern Department of Nord) where Maximian had settled *laeti*, the forum of their capital, Bavai, was turned into a bastioned fort with the civil power falling back on Cambrai to the west. Famars, a vicus within the civitas, became a similar fort, headquarters of the *Praefectus laetorum Nerviorum*. Unlike other *laeti*, these were stationed in their own tribal territory, and it has been suggested that the Prefect may have been responsible for recruiting and training rather than being commander of an army unit. Such arrangements were not

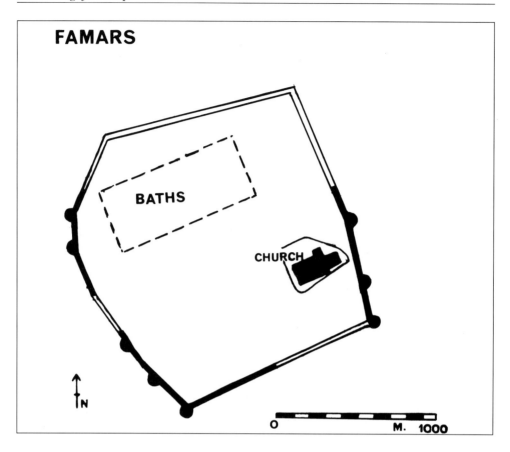

12   *Famars (Nord). Late Roman defences of the* vicus *or market town (after Bersu and Unverzagt). The bath building was probably re-used in the same way as the forum complex at Amiens. Famars was garrisoned until the time of Aetius*

unknown in British India. A gold solidus of Valentinian III and early fifth-century pottery suggest a Roman military presence at Famars until the time of Aetius. The capital of the neighbouring Menapii was pulled back from Cassel above the Flanders plain to Tournai. At the end of the century, when Paulinus of Nola spoke of the missionary work of Victricius, bishop of Rouen, in the territory of the Morini east of Boulogne 'at the end of the civilised globe' (*terra Morinorum situ orbis extrema*), one is inclined to dismiss this as rhetoric and faulty geography, for the Morini were not even in the same province as Rouen. If, however, the land beyond was now being settled by the Franks, and Roman control was only indirect, the phrase would be more exact.[25]

Something of this process of settlement can be seen at Vron (Somme), south of Boulogne. The cemetery was totally excavated by Claude Seillier between 1969 and 1984. About AD 370–5, a group of about fifty people, probably three family groups, settled near a Roman shrine on a limestone ridge overlooking the coastal flats and the Channel beyond. They had access to Roman pottery, glass and coinage, including silver siliquae, some

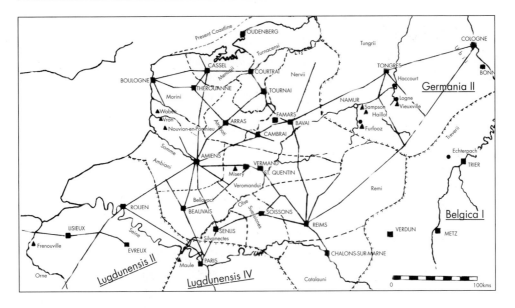

13   Belgica Secunda and parts of adjacent provinces in the late Empire. Solid triangles — cemeteries mentioned in the text

clipped like their British counterparts. Each family buried in its own sector of the cemetery. One (Group 2) seems to have been of superior status, with large and deep grave pits, three with timber chambers, and rich grave goods. One man was in a wooden coffin, with a spear, glass and pewter, a Theodosian coin and a belt with a small plain buckle. In the belt was a knife with a decorated silver-gilt and niello handle. Early Merovingian examples are seen as high status table knives. Another man of this group had pottery, glass, and a coin of Valens. His belt and knife set included a worn and repaired bronze belt buckle whose repoussée plate had a facing (? Imperial) bust within an ovulo border. The belt, though not normal army issue, would be appropriate to someone who had been granted some official status. Another family (Group 1) had a stronger Germanic element, with most of the Germanic style tutulus and bow brooches from the cemetery. Seillier estimates that both family groups contained about 20 people, the third group being smaller with about 10. The combination of Gallo-Roman and Germanic elements is striking. One man buried on the periphery of the early cemetery had a chip-carved belt set and an axe (one of the rare weapons from the cemetery), suggesting service in the Roman army.[26]

We shall need to return to Vron later to see how the community developed after the barbarian invasions, but in the Seine Valley and Normandy small groups of soldiers or ex-soldiers are found settled in indigenous rural communities. These could be ethnic Germans or simply time-expired veterans. At Cortrat, east of Orleans, of 38 graves only five are other than the poorly furnished graves of late Roman peasantry. Of the five, two men had belt-buckles and crossbow brooches, implying a military background, whilst the three women (two buried alongside each other) had triangular bone combs and Germanic brooches. These suggest a Germanic family group with a military background settled

43

peacefully among a Gallo-Roman population. At Frenouville in Calvados, in one corner of a large cemetery of late Roman north-south burials are four graves with military belts but no weapons and little else. If they were soldiers billeted on the estate the buckles are of surprisingly diverse types. They are probably no more than an indigenous family with a tradition of army service and some standing in the village as *anciens combattants.*[27]

Montana Castella: late Roman hillforts

One testimony to a changed society is the return to small hillforts and promontory forts — some re-used Iron Age sites — through much of Gaul from Gallia Belgica to Provence and the Alps. In Gallia Belgica they begin at the time of the Gallic Empire. At Nismes-Vironival in Belgium, a promontory defended by a double ditch and a stone rampart, the coins do not go beyond the Gallic Empire. The stone ringwall with square internal turrets near the villa at Echternach in Luxembourg followed its burning about 275. In the Massif Central, Iron-Age promontory forts like Clapas-Castel and St-Bonnet-de-Chirac (Lozère) were re-occupied, and the former has produced Constantinian coins. Sidonius refers to hillforts, *montana castella*, as a familiar feature of the landscape in those parts, and his tale of the woman carried off by 'our local bandits' and sold into slavery suggests the sort of conditions that led to their building. Such defences may be the work of local leaders at a time when state security had broken down. A similar background has been suggested for the third-century Bacaudae. However, one group of fortifications in Gallia Belgica may have a different and military origin.[28]

In the absence of excavation we know nothing of any refortification of the Iron Age oppidum at Vermand, but the cemeteries around its ramparts make such reoccupation likely. In the Ardennes and southern Belgium a group of late Roman cliff fortifications cover river crossings south of the strategic Amiens-Cologne highway. Furfooz is on a cliff-girt promontory (the Heights of Hauterecenne) above a crossing of the Meuse south of Namur. The neck was cut off by two successive defensive walls. The earlier, of Roman style masonry, was associated with a small bath building outside the defences, suggesting the presence of an army detachment. The coins begin under the Gallic Empire, and this first period may end at the time of Magnentius around 350 whose withdrawal of troops led to widespread devastation on the frontier. The second wall, to the rear of the first, was of rougher masonry and included re-used material from the baths. Burials with military belt furniture, weapons, pottery and glass lay in and around the bath building, sometimes cut through its ruins. These begin about the time of Valentinian, and coins run to Magnus Maximus, though it is uncertain which were from the cemetery and which from the fortification.[29]

At Éprave a similar river cliff overlooks a crossing of a tributary of the Meuse. Semi-circular defences with a ditch, a mortared stone wall of coursed ashlar blocks and an earth rampart back on to the cliff. The coins begin with late third-century radiate copies and issues of Constantine I and the ironwork includes a spearhead and axe. Nearby, La Roche a Lomme at Dourbes has a propeller shaped stiffener from a military belt of Constantinian date. This, like the Roman masonry at Furfooz I and Éprave, may indicate the presence of regular soldiers. The second phase at Furfooz may indicate *laeti* like those defined by Julian, or like the first settlers at Vron.[30]

3. How the West was lost: Valentinian I – Valentinian III

After the Romans had given over the possession of the Realme, it seemeth probable that their coyne was still current here a long time: for there never as yet, as farre as I understand, beene any coines found of *Vortiger*, *Vortimer*, *Aurelius*, *Ambrosius*, *Arthur* and any other which lived in those times.

William Camden *Remains Concerning Britain* (1605), ed R.D. Dunn (Toronto 1984), 168

The Emperor Valentinian I (364–75) was a formidable man. He and his brother, the eastern Emperor Valens (364–78), were sons of a Pannonian officer of peasant origin who had risen from the ranks through service in the *Protectores* and a military tribunate to be military commander in Britain. Valentinian's two pet bears had, perhaps unjustly, a reputation to match his own, and he died, characteristically, of apoplexy when confronted with a deputation of barbarian ambassadors. Ammianus Marcellinus tells how he fortified the Rhine with *castra*, *castella*, and towers, personally supervising the diversion of the River Neckar to lay a foundation of piles and oak beams on its bed. He returned to the cities one third of their confiscated annual revenues for the repair of public buildings, and the walls of Tours, and perhaps of other cities, may date from his reign. In Britain, his Spanish born general Count Theodosius is said to have restored cities and forts (*urbes et praesidiaria*). Though there are problems in matching the historical and archaeological evidence so far as Britain is concerned, Valentinian's restoration of the western frontiers was the last stage in their history before the final calamity.[1]

Valentinian was surrounded by a circle of pious Christian officers, often men of similar backgrounds to himself, from the same Danubian frontier regions. Many of these were attracted to the cult of the martyrs and ascetics whom they saw as the soldiers of Christ, gaining victory in a struggle against the devil and the powers of the world. His *magister militum* Flavius Jovinus was buried in a church at Reims containing relics of the north Italian martyrs Agricola and Vitalis. The career of Martin of Tours, son of another Pannonian tribune who had risen from the ranks and who became bishop of Tours in the time of Valentinian, can best be understood against this background of strenuous soldierly Christianity. The last generations of the western Empire were to see much rivalry between various groups of Gallic magnates and with Italian or other outsiders. One strand in this was the dissonance between the well born landowner, country gentleman, magistrate, and often bishop, whose faith far from excluded an educated interest in the pagan gods and their mythology, and the ascetic — often with a military background and an origin outside Gaul — who saw the world as a battlefield between Christ and his martyrs and the demons who inhabited the pagan temples. There was also potential hostility between the majority of the Gallic aristocrats, whose paramount loyalty was to Gaul where their estates and power base lay, and those who held office as provincial governors or courtiers in what was being increasingly seen as an 'Italian' administration which neglected the security of Gaul in the face of threats elsewhere.[2]

Valentinian's son Gratian (378–83) was overthrown by Theodosius's client and fellow Spaniard Magnus Maximus, military commander in Britain, and murdered in Lyon in August 383. Magnus Maximus involved the bishops of Gaul in bitter controversy by Imperial intervention in a theological quarrel between the Spanish ascetic Priscillian of Avila and his accusers. The bishops of Agen and Bordeaux became embroiled in what was initially a Spanish matter because Priscillian had made converts among the Aquitanian aristocracy. The trial and execution of Priscillian and some of his followers (the first time a Christian ruler had executed any of his subjects for heresy) divided the Gallic bishops. Mathisen sees the 'Felicians' (so named from Felix, bishop of Trier, the Imperial capital where the trial had taken place, who favoured Imperial intervention) as isolationists who preferred to deal with Gallic problems within Gaul, whilst the 'anti-Felicians', who included Martin of Tours and Ambrose of Milan, were prepared to look outside Gaul for support. The Felicians may have found support among the aristocrats from whom so many bishops came, whilst the anti-Felicians were connected with the ascetics and the soldierly Christianity of the court of Valentinian, many of whose leaders came from outside Gaul.[3]

Magnus Maximus once boasted to St Ambrose of the 'many thousands of barbarians who fight for me, and take their pay (*annona*) from me' and Ambrose accused him of threatening Italy with his *turmae translimitanae* — troops of soldiers from across the frontier of the Empire. The names of his *magister peditum* Merobaudes and *magister equitum* Andragathius tell their own story. When Theodosius I (379–95), son of Count Theodosius, defeated and slew his rival at Aquilea in 388, the Frankish general Arbogast, who had family links in the Trier area, was sent to hunt down his remaining adherents. He invaded across the Rhine. Sulpicius Alexander attributes his success there to his familiarity with his native terrain, and claims that Arbogast was motivated by personal involvement in Frankish tribal feud. No doubt it was all part of the Great Game of frontier politics. It is a pity that Gregory of Tours was only interested in the early rulers of the Franks mentioned by Sulpicius whose *Historia*, a continuation of Jerome's Chronicle from 379 onwards, is only known from fragments quoted by Gregory. It was well informed on the Rhine frontier, mentioning not only cities like Neuss and Mainz but individual areas of forest, Frankish tribes, and military commanders. Sulpicius, probably a military man, is scornfully hostile towards Arbogast and the Franks in Roman service. He may represent the viewpoint of the Gallo-Roman element of the army. A Roman army could normally defeat Franks and Alemanni in the field, but over-confident invasion across the Rhine could lead to disaster — as it did for Magnus Maximus's general Quintinus in 387–8, perhaps because he lacked Arbogast's knowledge of the country.[4]

If Magnus Maximus received a surprisingly favourable press in later literary sources, it was in part because he was looked back to as almost the last Emperor who accorded the defence of Gaul the priority it required. Valentinian's younger son Valentinian II was installed in the west after the fall of Maximus, but when he was found hanging in his palace at Vienne in May 392 suspicion fell on Arbogast who proclaimed a puppet Emperor, the scholarly pagan Eugenius. They were destroyed by the avenging army of Theodosius at the River Frigidus. Soon after the battle, in January 395, Theodosius died in Milan, last sole ruler of the Roman Empire. The two halves of the Empire were drawing apart. Their coins had been distinct since the time of Valentinian, and the Empire was now divided between Theodosius's two sons — the elder, Arcadius, in the east, and the younger, the ten year old Honorius, in the west. The east, as usual, took precedence. Power lay in the hands of their mutually hostile chief ministers.

Arbogast's successor as *magister militum*, the half-Vandal former *Protector* Stilicho, led an army to the Rhine in the following year, as much to levy recruits as to strengthen the frontier. In the face of almost continuous crisis in the next few years the west became a rapidly emptying reservoir of manpower from which some last reserves might be siphoned off. In 401 the Visigoths under Alaric invaded Italy. Stilicho, desperate for troops, withdrew what he could, including legions from Britain and the Rhineland. Alaric's retreat in 403 gave a short respite before a fresh barbarian invasion of Italy in 406. The situation was already critical before the collapse of the Rhine frontier on the last day of 406 when an army of Vandals, Sueves and Alans crossed the frozen river near Mainz. Frankish federates withstood them and routed the Vandals before Alan reinforcements turned the day. The towns of Belgica Secunda were sacked before the invaders reached the sea near Boulogne.[5]

Constantine III and the loss of Britain

This was the background to the British *pronunciamento* of 406 when one Marcus, presumably an army commander, was proclaimed Emperor. Zosimus thought that this was due to a fear that the barbarians would seize the Channel ports and cross to Britain, but the coup preceded the invasion of Gaul. We do not know its cause, but the barbarian build up across the Rhine may not have passed unnoticed and there may have been some attempt to withdraw troops from Britain. Whatever the cause, the rapid succession of three pretenders, Marcus, Gratian and Constantine, shows that its authors were divided among themselves. Gratian, described by Orosius as *Municeps eiusdem insulae* — a city magistrate — may have represented the views of the urban magistrates and rural landowners against that of the army. The former may have wished to retain the army of Britain, or what was left of it, to defend Britain, whereas the emphasis on the 'auspicious' name of Constantine implies a policy of taking the army to Gaul in a bid for supreme power and to protect Gaul from the invaders. Gratian lasted four months before falling to Constantine. It is probably no more than coincidence that it was the Emperor Gratian who brought the land-owning classes of Gaul to political prominence at court, but again we see conflict between the army and the land-owning classes and between the defensive needs of individual provinces and those of the broader western Empire.[6]

Constantine crossed to Boulogne in the spring of 407. His advance guard under Justinianus and the Frank Nebiogastes was defeated (late Roman armies normally operated as a brigade of two units), but the main army — under their replacements Edobichus and Gerontius, a Frank and a Briton — forced the loyalist general, the Goth Sarus, back over the Alps where he had to buy safe passage from the notorious Alpine bandits. Constantine set his court at Arles, stabilised the military situation, and established control over the long strip of Gaul not in the hands of the invaders. Most of the Gallic aristocracy supported him, for the old reason that an Emperor on the spot was better placed to deal with the crisis and because his arrival marked the end, for the time being, of the haemorrhage of the western armies to meet the needs of Italy. For the most part only Imperial officials and former officials remained loyal to Honorius. Among them were Claudius Postumus Dardanus, praetorian prefect of Gaul and former governor of Viennensis, and his brother Claudius Lepidus, ex-governor of Germania Prima, both former Imperial courtiers. Of the rest, most would have echoed Ammianus Marcellinus when he had written of the situation fifty years earlier that 'from long neglect, the Gallic provinces, having no help on which to rely' [after the fall of Magnentius] 'had borne cruel massacres plunder and burnings from barbarians, who raged through the land with impunity.' One writer made the significant claim that Constantine III was the most effective defender of the Gallic frontiers since Magnus Maximus. Historians have made little of Orosius's statement that Constantine's son Constans was a monk, but Constantine, as Emperor, secured the election of Heros *vir sanctus et beati Martini discipulis* as bishop of Arles, and of Lazarus, a protégé of bishop Proculus of Marseille, to the see of Aix. Heros tried to save the life of Constantine after the fall of Arles in 411 by ordaining him. Both bishops were attacked by Pope Zosimus as creatures of the fallen tyrant forced upon an unwilling Church and people. It is possible that the Caesar Constans had indeed been a Martinian monk.[7]

Constans was sent into Spain to suppress a loyalist rising by kinsmen of Theodosius. He took Gerontius as his *magister militum*, and Apollinaris, grandfather of Sidonius Apollinaris, as praetorian prefect. The Theodosians raised an army from their estates around Coca and Palentia, south of the Upper Duero valley, but were defeated. So far Spain had escaped the invaders, but whilst Constans was visiting his father at Arles, Gerontius conspired with the barbarians and raised one Maximus to the purple. The name is not uncommon, but as with Constantine it may have been 'auspicious' and Magnus Maximus had been Spanish. Constans replaced the Spanish defenders of the Pyrenean passes with his own barbarian troops, and in September 409 the barbarian hordes from Gaul invaded Spain. Constantine III was besieged in Arles around which four armies now fought — those of Constantine, his besieger Gerontius, a relief force of Franks and Alemanni from the Rhineland under Edobichnus, and Honorius's general Constantius, the final victor. Constantius became virtual ruler of Gaul and eventually Emperor as Constantius III before his death in 421.[8]

Apollinaris's successor as Constantine III's praetorian prefect, Decimus Rusticus, was involved in the brief attempt at power by the Gallo-Roman Jovinus after the defeat and death of Edobichnus. When this had been suppressed, the loyalist prefect, Claudius Dardanus, carried out a bloody purge of his fellow Gallic aristocrats, including Decimus Rusticus and probably Apollinaris. The latter's grave at Lyon bore no memorial until the time of his grandson, Sidonius Apollinaris. Despite this their sons followed the normal career structure for young Gallic notables, serving as Tribunes and Notaries at the court of Honorius. One became praetorian prefect under Valentinian III. Claudius Dardanus was a devout Christian, a correspondent of Jerome and Augustine. He retired to live in religious seclusion on his fortified estate in a valley above Sisteron (Basses-Alpes) which he re-named *Theopolis* — City of God — as we know from an inscription cut on a rock face nearby. Sidonius knew other landowners who had retired to their estates in this way after a career in the public service.[9]

One lasting effect of the regime of Constantine III was to transfer the post of praetorian prefect of Gaul into the hands of the Gallic aristocracy. Aristocrats from central and south-east Gaul now had a virtual monopoly of the official career structure to the exclusion of lesser folk. The stream of patronage now ran in a much narrower bed, and competition for posts was intense. This spilled over into ecclesiastical affairs where episcopal elections were often keenly contested between rival groups of local magnates. Here the only real rivals to the Gallic *potentissimi* were ascetic monk-bishops like Martin of Tours, usually men with a military or official background. When Constantius of Lyon wrote the life of Germanus of Auxerre about 480–90 he presented him as an ideal bishop; a local landed magnate, whose parents lay in a church on a nearby estate; a distinguished public servant; and, like Martin, an ex-soldier and ascetic.[10]

By 418 conditions were stable enough for Honorius to revive the annual Council of the Gauls at Arles. The Burgundians had been settled at Worms in 413 in the first federate kingdom, and Constantius, after using the Visigoths to clear much of Spain of barbarian settlement, placed them in Aquitania Secunda to protect Gaul against its enemies, internal or external. His death in 421 was followed by that of Honorius two years later. Constantius's infant son Valentinian III became Emperor, with his mother Galla Placidia, sister of Honorius, as Regent.[11]

After the deluge: early fifth-century communities in northern Gaul

The newly restored Gaul of Constantius and Valentinian III was not that of the opening of the century. Effective, direct Roman rule extended only over the centre and south, in Provence, Languedoc, the Rhône Valley and the Auvergne. To the west, Aquitania and Novempopulana were in the hands of the Visigoths. North of the Goths, Armorica was in obscure periodic revolt, and the Bacaudae, a peasant self-help militia, were out. Though the Rhine was still held, behind it in Belgic Gaul, the Seine Valley and Normandy, barbarian settlement was continuing among the indigenous population. Beyond were the lost provinces of Britain.

In Britain, the end of Roman administration was followed by the rapid demise of the material culture of the fourth century. No fresh bronze coin reached Britain after the issues of 395–404 and silver later than c400 is rare, though gold coinage continued to arrive under Constantine III. In contrast to earlier periods when coin supply failed there were no attempts to produce local copies and the search for sub-Roman imitations has proved a quest for a chimera. The Romano-British pottery industries came to an end, and what Roman pottery there is in early Anglo-Saxon graves seems to be the result of salvage, not survival. The continuance of Romano-British metalworking skills — in the form of hanging bowls derived from the late Roman 'Irchester' bowls and of penannular brooches and belt buckles — is credible but hard to prove. A few early fifth-century brooches and belt fittings and a little glass arrived in Britain from north Gaul, but these relate to incoming Germanic invaders rather than to any surviving British entity. The situation across the Channel is in sharp contrast for here coins, pottery, glass and metalwork continued to be made and used. The political situation in early fifth-century Britain is unknown, though there is just enough evidence to suggest that Romano-British organisation continued well into the first half of the century. Constantius of Lyon assumed that Germanus of Auxerre found in Britain in 429 a functioning late Roman society, and an early fifth-century Gallic tract on church organisation confidently includes Britain and assumes a normal late Roman Church there.[12]

Across the Channel many of the Frankish settlers who had established themselves in fortified *castella* in the frontier areas of north Gaul were still there in the fifth century. The invasions of 406–7 caused some disruption. A number of cemeteries begin or end at this time, and may have been re-sited when the initial shock was over. Furfooz, though the excavated cemetery ends with the invasions, has produced gold solidi of Constantine III (407–11), John (423–5) and Valentinian III (425–55) — noted as having been 'found apart' from the cemetery — as well as a triangular cast-in-one buckle of early fifth-century type. The heights of Hauterecenne, where the *castellum* was sited, was later used for a medieval castle. A similar fortified site under the medieval castle of Logne, on a crag above the river Ourthe south of Liege, has produced Roman coins down to Arcadius, and late fourth or early fifth-century Argonne ware. In 882 the monks of Stavelot-Malmedy sought refuge from the Vikings in the 'castle above the Ourthe called Lonniam' (*Castrum supra Urtae Lonniam nomine*). A mile away at Vieuxville, a rich cemetery of 190 graves begins in the early fifth century.[13]

In contrast to Britain, the late Roman material culture of north Gaul not only survived but continued to develop. One change is the replacement of the earlier military zoomorphic belt buckles by 'cast-in-one' or ' fixed plate' buckles (Böhme's *Schnallen mit festen Beschlag*). Unlike the earlier buckles, these have loop and plate cast together as one solid piece of metal instead of being two separate hinged pieces. Bohme identifies four sub-types which spread out from Belgic Gaul along the Rhine, west to Normandy, north to the Bremen-Hamburg area, and to eastern England.[14]

Two of the earliest graves at Vieuxville contained a gold solidus of Arcadius of 402–6 and two silver siliquae of Constantine III (407–11) and Jovinus (411–3) with a chip-carved belt set. If Logne began as a late Roman fortification like Furfooz there may be an earlier cemetery nearer the castle. The earliest graves, including the two coin-dated ones, lie at the northern tip of the cemetery. They include weapon graves with swords, belt sets, and glassware. Thereafter burials move progressively southwards, and Vieuxville is a classic example of horizontal stratigraphy. Alenus-Lecerf has published a chronological sequence, beginning with a seventh-century burial from the southern end and proceeding northwards with successively earlier grave groups. The average size of the community may have been about 20–30 people. The early fifth-century graves, between the rich founders graves on the north and the later fifth-century burials to the south, include a cremation with eight light javelins and a cast-in-one gilt bronze buckle of Trier-Sampson type. Others contain Argonne ware, Mayen type pottery, a carinated bronze cauldron with triangular lugs, and much glass, including two bowls with indented decoration, a type also found in Anglo-Saxon cemeteries in Kent and Sussex, and two others of a type with moulded decoration which sometimes includes Christian chi-rho symbols and inscriptions. One, from an Anglo-Saxon grave at Darenth in Kent, names two Gallo-Roman martyrs from the Soissons area.[15]

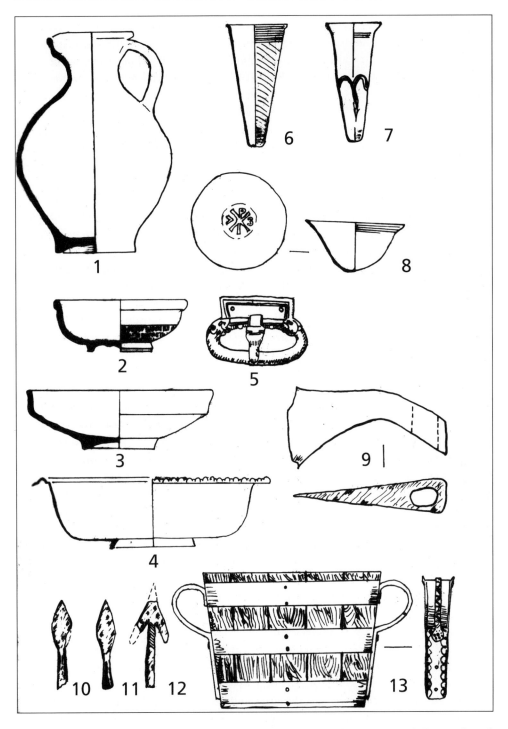

14   *Haillot (Belgium) - selected gravegoods. 1. Pottery jug, 2–3. Argonne ware, 4. Bronze 'bossed rim' bowl, 5. Cast in one bronze buckle 6–8 Glass, 9–12 Ironwork. 13 Bronze bound wooden tub (after Breuer and Roosens)*

At Vireux-Molhain in the Ardennes, the late Roman castellum on the promontory of Mont-Vireux is again under a medieval castle. The nearby cemetery again shows a sequence from north to south, but is earlier than Vieuxville and ends where the latter begins. The oldest graves are Gallo-Roman. The latest, at the south end, have military belt sets, Argonne ware, glass, a gold solidus of Honorius, and two silver siliquae — one a Trier coin of Theodosius II, of c440–50, the other a barbarian copy. One of the two belt sets is of normal late fourth-century chip-carved type, the other a cast-in-one buckle of Haillot type. Such burials are not confined north of the Seine. At Fel in southern Normandy a cemetery began with two women with Germanic jewellery and two men, one with a cast-in-one Haillot type belt set, the other with an indented glass bowl like those at Vieuxville and a coin of Valentinian III of about 445.[16]

Cemeteries like these show a still economically functioning late Roman society in north Gaul in the first half of the fifth century, with access to mass-produced pottery from the Argonne, Mayen, and other centres; to a flourishing glassware industry with new and distinctive products; and to metalworkers with the skills to produce cauldrons like that from Vieuxville, and belt sets, even if the latter had to be simplified because the skilled craftsmen who worked in the state armaments factories were no longer available or were working for new masters. Gold and silver coinage from the Imperial mints not only continued to circulate but was supplemented by copies in both metals. Possibly access to such manufactured goods was no longer broad based, but was the prerogative of an élite already established, like later feudal lords, in their castles.[17]

How far this sub-Roman economy reflected Roman military control of the Rhine frontier is another issue. It has sometimes been assumed that the Rhine defences did not survive the invasions of 407. It is now possible to test this against evidence from the fifth-century pottery industry. Argonne ware is a red-slip pottery derived from samian ware, with complex rouletted decoration made with a wheel. Detailed study of individual rollers or roulettes gives a chronological sequence which can be correlated from dated grave groups. Chenet believed that the industry ended in 407, but Hübener's original study of its survival into the fifth century has now been extended by Didier Bayard who has identified four phases of the industry covering the period 350–530. Finds from British sites are all of Phase 1 (c.350–400), agreeing with the traditional date for the end of Roman Britain, but pottery of Phase 2 (c.400–40) is found on Roman military sites in north Gaul, though it is rare on villas or civilian sites. The presence of pottery or military metalwork on a site at this date does not prove that it held a Roman military unit, or what the role of that unit might have been. Nevertheless, it does give us some guide to the shape of the Rhine frontier in the time of Aetius.[18]

The age of Aetius

Since the murder of Gratian in 383, Britain, Gaul and Spain had, as actual or *de facto* rulers, a series of military men, often of local origin, and with close links to barbarian soldiers and commanders. Earlier in the century Magnentius, a soldier born in Amiens of a British father and a possibly laetic Frankish mother, had become a Christian Emperor. The Spanish born Magnus Maximus (383–8) with his *turmae translimitanae* was followed by the

Frankish Arbogast (388–94), by the half-Vandal Stilicho (396–408), and by Constantine III (407–11), whose generals included the Franks Nebogastes and Edobichus and the Briton Gerontius. On the death of Honorius in 423 Galla Placidia, widow of Constantius III and regent for their infant son Valentinian III, was faced with Flavius Aetius, a native of Durostorum on the Danube in modern Bulgaria. Aetius was the son of a Vandal nobleman and of a mother from an Italian senatorial family. As a young man he was a hostage among the Visigoths, and later among the Huns. His alliance with the latter was the essential underpinning of his later power base but gave his career a curious ambiguity. Aetius was both 'last of the Romans' and a semi-barbarian warlord allied with the most savage and feared of barbarian nomads. He could be seen as the essential support of the young Valentinian and his mother or as a dangerous and over mighty subject who might have designs on the Imperial purple for his son Gaudentius.[19]

Aetius's first recorded exploit sounds a characteristically ambiguous note. On the death of Honorius, a civil servant, John, was declared Emperor in Ravenna by the *magister militum* Castinus. The eastern Emperor Theodosius II sent an army against him accompanied by Galla Placidia and her child. Boniface, count of Africa, placed its corn supply at her disposal, but Aetius was sent by John to Pannonia to raise an army. John was captured and executed in the summer of 425. Immediately afterwards Aetius appeared at Ravenna backed by a large army of Huns. Placidia had little alternative but to accept him as a supporter of the new Emperor, her son Valentinian III. The Visigoths, settled in Aquitaine by the treaty of 418, were now trying under Theoderic II to seize the former Imperial capital of Arles, equipped — unlike Bordeaux or Toulouse — with the trappings of an Imperial city. This would also have given them access to a port for African grain supplies. Shortly before, under Athaulf, they had tried to seize Marseille but had been repulsed by Boniface. The threat to Arles was a mortal danger to what remained of the western Empire, for its loss would sever land communications with Spain, usurp the Gallic capital, and threaten the routes northwards into Gaul. Arles was the key to the survival of the Gallic Prefecture. Under the *magister militum* Flavius Constantius Felix, Aetius relieved Arles from a Gothic siege in 427 and destroyed a Gothic force at *Mons Colubrarius*. Felix had been responsible for several political murders, including that of Patroclus, bishop of Arles. When Aetius had Felix and his wife Padusia murdered by a group of soldiers in 430 he could make a plausible claim that they had been plotting his death and that he acted in self-defence. In the same year a treaty with the Goths ended the war.[20]

If Felix, Aetius and Boniface had acted together under the regency of Galla Placidia there might have been some chance of salvaging the remaining core of the western Empire. As it was their rivalry, and the opportunist tactics of Galla Placidia, led to disaster. Whilst the Goths were besieging Arles in 427, Galla Placidia recalled Boniface from Africa in disgrace and declared him a public enemy. He refused to leave Carthage and defeated an expeditionary force. This led directly to the Vandals leaving Spain in 429 and crossing into Africa, perhaps at the invitation of Boniface. They advanced rapidly eastward. Galla Placidia, isolated by the murder of Felix and alarmed by events in Africa which threatened Italy's corn supply, reinstated Boniface, who was now besieged in Hippo (with the dying St Augustine). In 432 Boniface abandoned Africa and returned to Italy to deal with his rival Aetius, whom he defeated near Rimini, though he died of wounds shortly after. In 435 a treaty surrendered all Africa, save an enclave around Carthage, to Gaiseric and the Vandals. In 439 they occupied Carthage, gaining control of the corn supplies on which the cities of the west depended, of the direct sea route between the east and west Mediterranean, and of a powerful fleet. Trade and commerce continued, as abundant African pottery exports show, but the western Empire was rapidly losing control of its own destiny.

In the meantime Aetius had been active in Noricum in modern Austria, where Roman authority had collapsed and the provincials were in obscure revolt. His campaigns of 430–1 may have briefly restored Roman rule, but by the 450s it had vanished save for the odd garrison, cut off and with its pay badly in arrears. In 488 the ruler of Italy, Odoacer, abandoned Noricum north of the Alps and evacuated its population to Italy with their possessions and even the body of their patron saint, Severinus. After the death of Boniface, Aetius withdrew to exile among the Huns (there are hints that he feared assassination by Galla Placidia), but by 433 was back as *magister militum*. By 434 he was a Patrician, and the following year was able to turn his attention back to Gaul.[21]

The Arles-Marseille road from the supply port to Imperial headquarters was put in repair, and the Spanish soldier-poet Merobaudes put down unrest in the Alps, whose notorious bandits threatened the lines of communication with Italy. Aetius, with his Huns and the Roman troops under his command, faced the Burgundians on the Upper Rhine, the Franks to the north, Goar's army of Alans, the Bacaudae of Armorica under Tibatto, and the powerful Visigoths. He moved against the Burgundians around Worms. Massacred by the Huns, what was left of them were resettled in Sapaudia (Savoy) in 443. The Goths under Theoderic in 436 laid siege to Narbonne, still seeking access to the Mediterranean and its food supplies. Aetius's general Litorius raised the siege and in the following year put down the Bacaudae and captured Tibatto. By 439 he had carried the war as far as the Gothic capital at Toulouse, but was wounded and taken prisoner. Aetius made peace with the help of his *magister militum per Gallias*, the Gallo-Roman aristocrat and future Emperor Eparchius Avitus who was on good terms with the Goths. Some sort of stability had been restored, and for some years after the peace of 439 the bishops of Gaul were able to hold regular church councils.[22]

This bald narrative serves to document a number of problems. The identity of the Bacaudae has been much debated. They have been seen in terms of separatist revolt, or of Marxist class struggle. Banditry was endemic in the ancient world at all periods. Sidonius tells of a woman kidnapped by the *Vargi* 'as our local bandits are called' and sold as a slave. The Bacaudae have a different dimension. They first appear in the late third century with the requisition in kind of the *annona militaris*, disappear from our sources in the fourth century when monetary taxation and an effective western regime had been restored, only to reappear in the early fifth century. Van Dam sees them not as rebels or separatists but in terms of a reversion to traditional patterns of local leadership in troubled times, when central authority had failed, and men were 'rallying around local leaders out of a need for security.' Drinkwater, on the other hand, sees the fifth-century Bacaudae as the result of more tax burdens falling on fewer tax payers, so forcing land owners to increase pressures on their tied tenants, perhaps at a time when pressure for land had been increased by landowners moving in from areas taken over by barbarians. He notes that western France has a long tradition of resistance to central authority. Salvian wrote of the Bacaudae as people who live like barbarians because they are forced to do so, but they cannot be seen simply as a peasant revolt.[23]

Our sources associate them with forests and woodlands. Thanks to Aetius, says Merobaudes, Armorica, accustomed to hide in its forests plunder gained by savage crimes, has lost its old ways and learns to entrust grain to its untried fields. Another source seems to depict them setting up forest courts beneath the boughs of an oak tree. Earlier, a panegyric spoke scornfully of 'these peasants, strangers to arms . . . the peasant an infantryman, the shepherd a cavalryman, the countryman imitating the barbarian.' The last word (which echoes Salvian a century later) is revealing, for it all but equates 'soldier' and 'barbarian'. It was illegal for provincials to take up arms in their own defence, but for the Gallo-Roman peasant there must have been little apparent difference between a band of barbarian looters hostile to the Roman order and another band of barbarians in Roman service, requisitioning grain and livestock for the army of Aetius.[24]

The governing class no doubt bracketed all unrest together under one title, but the Bacaudae fall into place with later phases of peasant unrest in the woodland and forest-edge areas of the western fringes of Europe. They recall the English west country Clubmen of the Civil War, or the Chouans of the Vendée in western France, itself part of the Armorican forest area. These are 'self-defence' or 'self-help' movements, directed against the agents of central government and its army, whose requisitions of grain, livestock and recruits are seen as 'illegal' exactions, contrary to customary law. In the ninth century, similar self help groups against the Vikings among the peasantry of western France were bloodily suppressed by the Carolingian nobility who saw them as a worse social threat than the pagan Norse. This was to become an all too familiar scenario in Armorican history, down to the 'Bandes Infernelles' of French Revolutionary soldiers sent against the Royalist and Catholic Vendée, a mirror image of the events of 1798 in Ireland, and leaving equally long lasting scars.[25]

Historians of the Civil War in England have noted how the Clubmen were not from those arable areas whose villagers had suffered most from Royalist exactions, but from the forest-edge areas which, until late in the war, had largely escaped them. In many regions of western Europe there is a contrast between areas with nucleated villages working largely arable land and those with more scattered communities and a greater reliance on pasture, common land, and customary rights to forest or forest edge resources. The former are usually under tighter and more direct seigneurial control, and the working of the arable demands the structured co-operative effort of the village community. Apart from external pressures, there can be marked pressure from within for conformity and cohesion. In open 'forest edge' communities, seigneurial control is less direct, and any interference with access to resources such as common grazing, timber, game, or woodland forage, or any attempt by outside forces to requisition supplies can arouse militant reaction. The distinction between 'chalk' (arable) and 'cheese' (pastoral) has been familiar in areas like Wiltshire since John Aubrey, and has even been used to explain how that county divided in the Civil War between the radical 'cheese' and the royalist 'chalk'. In times of trouble the population of forest areas swells with refugees and outlaws, increasing the tendency to resist any interference on the part of central government whose reaction is often much the same. Rupert put down the Herefordshire Clubmen with his cavalry, just as Aetius sent

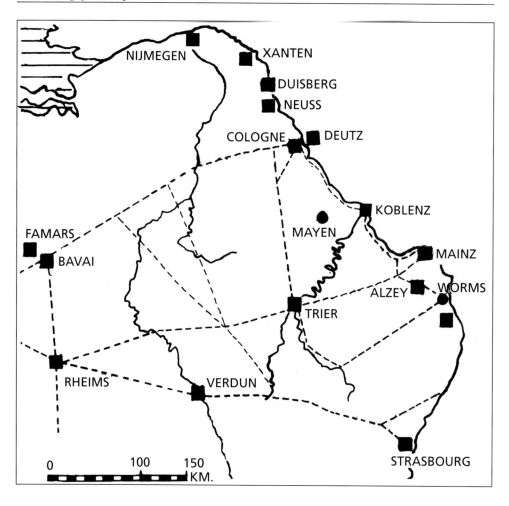

15   Map of the Rhine frontier in the early fifth century

Goar and his Alan cavalry against the Bacaudae.[26]

Aetius's relations with the other major power of north Gaul, the Franks, poses other questions. We know of the battle of *Vicus Helenae* of about 428 from Sidonius's panegyric of Majorian who took part. Its most probable location is Vis-en-Artois, where the Roman road from Arras to Cambrai crosses the river Sensée. The Franks had invaded Atrebatic territory in modern Somme or Nord. Aetius's attack was directed at a Frankish gathering for a wedding feast in a vicus at a road junction where a wooden bridge crossed a river. It was enough to make the Frankish ruler come to terms and abandon Roman territory. In the following century, Procopius had a story of the Roman army in Gaul which emphasises the relationship of Gallo-Romans and Germans in that frontier society. The Rhine, he explains, enters the ocean in an area full of lakes where the Germans (Franks) once dwelt. Next to them were the Arborychi (Armoricans), the Gallo-Romans of north Gaul. At the time the Visigoths seized Spain and Aquitaine the Arborychi were soldiers of the Romans. The Germans attacked them, but the Armoricans, 'proved their valour, and their loyalty to the Romans' (so much for the Bacaudae), intermarried with the Germans 'and were united into one people, who came to have great power.' He goes on to tell how Roman troops in Gaul, unable to return to Rome, joined the Arborychi and the Germans, with their military standards and the land they were guarding. The fate of the last Roman units in Noricum about this time shows that this is wholly credible. More surprising is Procopius's claim that in his own day these men were still recognisable as Roman legionaries, down to their shoes. However, his point about the role of Gallo-Romans and Franks in the making of Merovingian society is a valuable one.[27]

The new evidence from fifth-century Argonne ware puts this last phase of the Roman frontier into some degree of focus. The main military artery was the Amiens-Cologne highway, a *Limes* in the sense of a fortified road. The area north of the road may have been no longer under Roman control. The Constantinian fort at Xanten had been abandoned about 350 under Magnentius. Though Phase 2 Argonne ware of about 400–40 is known from Rhineland forts from Cologne-Deutz north to Nijmegen, there is nothing in the huge empty space behind them and Roman control of the lower Rhine may have been confined to keeping open the river supply route. The Amiens-Cologne road, however, was firmly held, and to the south groups of Frankish settlers in their fortified *castella* still guarded the river crossings. The state arms factory at Amiens seems to have been still in production in the time of Aetius, and the fort in the old forum at Bavai was still occupied. At Famars, the evidence for military occupation under Aetius from a gold coin of Valentinian III has now been reinforced by fifth-century pottery. Similarly Tongres, on the eastern half of the military road, has Argonne ware and military belt fittings of the early fifth century. Further north, an important early fifth-century sequence at Duisberg shows the beginnings of early Germanic settlement on the Rhine, with both Argonne ware and Germanic style pottery, whilst the associated animal bones show significant differences from the late Roman assemblage. Roman military occupation continued, however, and excavation at the fort built by Valentinian I at Alzey between Mainz and Worms has made it something of a type site for the fifth-century frontier with three well-defined phases, the final one running from about 425–50 or beyond.[28]

The soldier-poet Flavius Merobaudes summarised the achievements of his patron Aetius at the time of his third consulship in 446. The peace of 439 was holding. Aetius had brought peace, and the Rhine had made a treaty with Rome. The Armoricans were quiet, and corn could now grow peacefully in their fields. Aetius had used the Alans against the Bacaudae and settled the former around Orleans and Valence, guarding crossings of the Loire and the Rhône. However idealised Merobaudes's picture, Aetius had restored stability. He may have received other congratulations on his consulship. Whatever civil power now ruled southern Britain thought that, with Gaul at peace, Aetius might now aid them. It is unfortunate that their appeal to Aetius is usually discussed in the context of the chronology of Gildas and of the so called *Adventus Saxonum* rather than as evidence for fifth-century Britain. There is no doubt that Flavius Aetius is intended, since he is the only person who could be described as *ter consulis* – 'thrice consul'. The style of the appeal is different to Gildas's normal prose, and it is generally accepted that he is quoting an authentic document. There were persons of similar name active in Gaul at this period, but it is hard to believe that the British would have thought that Aegidius, a Roman warlord active around the Loire and at Soissons, would have been able to intervene effectively in Britain. It needs special pleading not to regard the document as what it is — an appeal from whoever now controlled southern or south-west England to the *de facto* ruler of what was left of the Prefecture of the Gauls. They may have sent a delegation to congratulate the Roman patrician on his third consulship and implore his aid. Fifteen years earlier, the people of northern Spain had made a similar appeal to Aetius through bishop Hydatius, asking for help against the Sueves. It was equally unavailing.[29]

Aetius's treaties with the Franks and Alans probably involved subsidies in gold, as it did with the Huns. Military pay was also in gold, and these factors may account for the amount of late Roman gold coinage in north Gaul, and for the various groups of irregular gold solidi struck in Gaul in the names of fifth-century emperors. The practice of including coins in rich burials is a separate matter, but does not account for the 100–120 solidi from Valentinian I to Honorius recovered from cliff falls at Hautot-sur-Mer near Dieppe between 1844 and 1861, or the early fifth-century solidi from Furfooz or Famars. Such gold was not confined to Frankish areas, as solidi of Julius Nepos and Zeno of the 470s from Saint-Nicodeme in western Brittany show. The gold must have been reaching the frontier as pay or subsidies. Normally it would have found its way back to the Imperial treasury as tax, or in exchange for goods and services. There was still a functioning exchange economy in early fifth-century Gaul, but with broader patterns of trade and taxation breaking down the gold was less likely to find its way back. This would pose a problem for those responsible for Imperial defence.[30]

The Gallic coinage is of two types. One, of gold and silver in the names of Honorius, Theodosius II and Valentinian III, was probably struck by the Visigoth Theoderic II about 425–30 when he was trying to capture Arles. It is less clear who struck the later Gallic solidi in the names of emperors from Valentinian III to Julius Nepos (473–80) and Anastasius I (491–518). These began about the same time as the Visigothic solidi and outlast the western Empire. Though they bear mint signatures of Rome or Ravenna there is no question of fraudulent imitation. All five groups have distinctive features serving as privy marks to identify the issue. Lafaurie suggested that the commonest group of gold and silver could have been struck by Aetius at Trier. Some could have been struck for the subsidies to allies, and many travelled beyond the former Imperial frontiers to Sweden, Germany and eastern Europe They were far from being the only late Imperial gold to reach those parts, but this would accord with subsidy payments. The logic behind local mintage if it were the work of Roman commanders such as Aetius or Aegidius may have lain in the rivalry between the Gallic Prefecture and the 'Italian' government for available resources, particularly for military pay. If bullion from Gallic taxes had been sent to mints at Rome or Ravenna it could have been diverted to other urgent uses rather than returned as struck coin. Though a breach of Imperial prerogative, the Gallic solidi may have been a money of necessity, for the payment of Imperial allies.[31]

When Attila invaded Gaul in 451 the Franks, Burgundians and Visigoths fought with Aetius in a war of nations against Attila's conglomerate of tribes. Aetius's victory near Troyes that summer was the prelude to his fall, for the guarantee of his power was his alliance with the Huns. For Valentinian, the uncomfortable fact was that Aetius effectively was the Imperial power west of Italy. Aetius was murdered in the Imperial palace in Rome in September 454 by Valentinian III in the middle of a meeting to discuss tax revenues and military spending. Six months later two of his retainers struck down Valentinian. Aetius's right to the title 'last of the Romans' may be questionable (Majorian would be a better candidate), but the alternative view of an unscrupulous plotter whose ambition was a danger to the Empire is not always supported by evidence that would stand up in court. With subsidies to barbarian 'allies' to find from a greatly depleted tax base it is hardly surprising to find that money to pay the army was scarce, but there is little need to see a plot to keep Valentinian starved of funds with an eye to Aetius's hopes for the Purple for his son. Similarly, Sidonius's claim that the future Emperor Majorian was rusticated to his estates through the jealousy of Aetius's wife need not involve intrigue over the hand of an Imperial heiress. The story bears a suspicious resemblance to that of Joseph and Potiphar's wife and Sidonius may be glossing over the embarrassing fact (for a panegyrist) that Majorian had been passed over for promotion. Aetius's strategy may have been flawed by his reliance on the Huns, his concentration on Gaul, and his failure to ally with the Goths, the most effective military power in south Gaul, but his options were very limited. As regional commander he was fairly successful, and with his limited resources his non-intervention on other fronts was prudent. Marcellinus's judgement found much support: 'With Aetius fell the Western Empire', he wrote, 'and up to the present has not been able to raise its head.' Bede echoed him much later: 'So fell Valentinian, and with him fell the Empire of the west.'[32]

Events after the death of Valentinian bear this out. The efforts of the Gallic senator Avitus and of Aetius's former *magister militum* in Gaul, Majorian, to maintain the western Empire failed, since an effective western Emperor suited neither the Vandals or Ricimer, puppet master in Italy. On the murder of Majorian in 461, his *magister militum* Afranius Syagrius Aegidius refused to recognise the 'Italian' Emperor Libius Severus, and was only stopped from marching on Rome by the Goths, probably bribed by Ricimer with the surrender of Narbonne. Aegidius was both a rebel against Libius Severus and a loyalist supporter of the eastern Emperor Leo I, to whom Severus was a usurper. His defeat of the Goths at Orléans in 463 bought a breathing space, and on his death two years later his son Syagrius succeeded him in a shadowy sub-Roman realm in western and northern Gaul, centred on Soissons, until he was defeated and killed by Clovis in 486, having outlived the western Empire by a decade. The 'End of the Western Empire' in 476 was of the same order of significance as Napoleon's abolition of the Venetian Republic.[33]

St Germanus in Britain: fact and allegory in the *Vita Germani*

Sometime between 418 and 448, bishop Germanus of Auxerre was making a journey through Aetius's Gaul with a group of his clergy. Overtaken by darkness, they sought shelter in a deserted and ruinous villa with a fearsome local reputation for hauntings. During the night a ghost appeared and politely explained that he and a friend, evidently executed criminals, lay unburied in the ruins, chained together and unable to rest. With a torch carried before them, the ghost led Germanus through the ruins. Next day, with a locally recruited excavation team, Germanus recovered the bodies. When they had received Christian burial the house ceased to be troubled and was rebuilt.[34]

The story, from Constantius of Lyon's *Vita Germani*, perhaps the only contemporary account of a ruined fifth-century Gallo-Roman villa, contains elements familiar from Roman Britain — skeletons buried in the ruins of a villa, a few habitable rooms among many, casual visitors scattering the remains of their supper. It may also explain why, at the Brislington villa, the skeletons of four or more people were thrown into a well and 6 ft of building rubble tipped in over them. Its value in this respect is not diminished by its suspicious resemblance to a well-known ghost story told by Pliny the Younger, where the philosopher Athenodrus played the same role as Germanus of Auxerre, and where a skeleton in chains was found, and the house rebuilt. If Constantius knew his Pliny so did many of his readers, and they would have taken his point that the wisdom of the Christian bishop matched that of the pagan philosopher.[35]

The *Vita Germani* is dedicated to Patiens, bishop of Lyon from 449, and Censurius, bishop of Auxerre from 470. Levison dated it around 480, thirty years after the death of its subject. It contains an account of Germanus's two visits to Britain in 429 and around 435–45. These have been the subject of so much discussion that it might be thought that no more could be said of them. For sub-Roman Britain the *Vita Germani* is a unique source, but when a bright light is thrown into a dark place it is often difficult to separate shadow from substance. The ghost story shows how the narrative operates on several levels. A straightforward Biblical *topos* can be obvious enough. When Germanus, crossing to Britain with his clergy, stills a storm in the Channel, the comparison with Christ and his disciples on the Sea of Galilee is clear, but there are other less obvious forms of metaphor. An understanding of the life's literary and rhetorical conventions is necessary if we are to avoid taking as fact what was meant as metaphor or allegory. Germanus was born in Auxerre about 378 and after reading law in Rome became a barrister and later a military commander, perhaps *Dux Tractus Armoricani et Nervicani*, which could explain his later links with Armorica and Britain. In 418 he was elected bishop of Auxerre. The account of his election makes much use of military metaphor. A war is declared against Germanus by the people to force his (unwilling) election. He is a conscript forcibly enrolled in the heavenly militia, and when bishop he used his old military cloak as a bed cover. The ascetic, as usual, is seen as the counterpart of the soldier.[36]

Constantius's choice of subject matter is governed not only by the literary tradition within which he was writing but by his intended audience. The Life has some splendid stories for public reading, whether to the people of Auxerre and the surrounding countryside gathered in their cathedral on the feast of Germanus, or to the monks of his monastery across the river from the city. Its horizons are local, despite the wide geographic spread of the stories. Its focus is Germanus's tomb in the suburban basilica once dedicated to the soldier martyrs Maurice and the Theban Legion, but now to a local bishop, here Germanus. Apart from Auxerre, the place which receives most attention is Alesia (Alise-Sainte-Reine, Côte d'Or), an important vicus 75km away, where the aristocrat Senator was priest. Constantius records several miracles here, and there may have been a cult around the tomb of Senator and his wife, whose family may still have been prominent locally. An early church has been excavated at the site though its significance is not clear. Germanus also healed a girl at Autun, but, apart from such centres of Imperial rule as Arles and

Ravenna, the interest in places declines in direct relationship to their distance from Auxerre. Thompson has remarked on the short, colourless account of Germanus's visit to Constantius's own city of Lyon, and the interest of his audience diminished as the distance increased.[37]

The one exception is Britain. This may be explained by a link with Auxerre and the person of Germanus in the form of relics brought back from Verulamium. The earliest version of the *Passio Albani*, recording the martyrdom of St Alban of Verulamium, was written in Auxerre between 515 and 540. Embedded in it are borrowings from earlier lives, including those of Burgundian martyrs from Lyon, Autun and Dijon, written in the time of Bishop Gregory of Langres (506–40). This (Levison's 'T' text) ends with an account of how Germanus visited St Albans, spoke with the martyr in a vision, and carried away 'dust' from his tomb, presumably to Auxerre, where a church of St Alban was said to have been founded by Germanus. Soon after it was written, 'T' was abridged to produce a second version ('E') and then expanded again to a third version ('P'), probably used by Gildas and certainly by Bede. One function of the Burgundian Lives was to authenticate relics by suitable documentation, and Hugh Williams long ago suggested that the *Passio Albani* was linked to Germanus's visit to the tomb. The first visit to Britain, which follows shortly after the ghost story, is dated by Prosper of Aquitaine to 429. He tells how Pope Celestine sent Germanus to Britain on the advice of Palladius the Deacon. Germanus routed the Pelagian heretics, steering Britain back to Catholic orthodoxy. There is no conflict with Constantius's statement that the mission was in response to an embassy from Britain. Deputations to men who had the ear of the powerful were the normal way of getting things done, and a similar embassy from Britain must have waited on Aetius some years later. The earlier deputation would have had no difficulty in conveying the concern of factions of the British Church to Pope Celestine via Germanus or Palladius.[38]

Germanus crossed to Britain with bishop Lupus of Troyes, a former monk of Lerins, who may have acted as theological adviser. He stilled a storm in the Channel with holy oil, and was met on arrival by a large crowd, including Pelagian magnates in formal dress and a man holding the rank of Tribune (*tribuniciae potestatis*) whose blind daughter Germanus healed. The stilling of the storm is a straightforward Biblical *topos* and the daughter is obviously Britannia whom Germanus freed from the blindness of heresy. This is what should have happened, and in hagiographic terms therefore what no doubt did. Germanus's silence on British bishops or secular rulers is frustrating for historians, and is sometimes taken to imply that society in Britain had broken down or was in some way abnormal. Had this been so Germanus would have stressed that his hero was venturing outside the boundaries of the civilised world. His silence says the exact opposite, for it implies a normal functioning late Roman society which was too familiar to need explanation. In this context the Tribune, whether a military officer or a young man pursuing a secular career (Tribune and Notary), makes sense. He had presumably been sent to welcome these distinguished official visitors on behalf of the civil power. We are in some danger of circular argument here, however, for Constantius knew perfectly well what official protocol in such matters was, and may be assuming that it was followed.

After the Pelagians had been condemned in debate, presumably by a church council, Germanus and Lupus went on a post conference excursion to the tomb of the martyr

Alban. Much of Constantius's vagueness about conditions in Britain might be explained if his primary concern lay in documenting the relics of Alban then at Auxerre. When Germanus, laid up with an injured ankle, is saved by relics of Alban from a fire, this common stock miracle emphasises this again. Another leading theme of the Life is Germanus as the ideal bishop. Ian Wood has called it 'a handbook for bishops' and the account of his preaching 'at cross-roads, in rural areas, and in out of the way places' reflects what a good bishop should do, and which Germanus therefore no doubt did. The emphasis on pastoral care in rural areas is interesting. The Life may not be our only source for the importance of this to the fifth-century British church. *On the Seven Offices of the Church*, perhaps addressed to Rusticus of Narbonne (427–61), discusses the right of priests in Gaul to preach, as well as bishops. It claims that they already enjoyed this right in other parts, including Britain. The issue can be connected with debate about rural clergy and the provision of rural pastoral care. Perhaps the latter was a concern in Britain at this time.[39]

The same theme of rural pastoral care is implicit in the account of mass baptisms before the battle against the Picts and Saxons. The Alleluia victory has been variously located in Flintshire (where an obelisk of 1732 and early editions of the Ordnance Survey map record its exact site at Rhual near Mold) and in the Chilterns. Ian Wood, on the other hand, suggests that its inspiration may have been Joshua's victory at Jericho (*Joshua* VI, 2–20). One feature of the battle calls for comment. The alliance between, as Hodgkin put it, 'Pictish speaking Highlanders and German speaking Saxons' was, as Thompson notes, 'the only instance of such co-operation to have been recorded from the age of the migrations.' Both give Constantius the benefit of the doubt, but 'Picts and Saxons' is no more than a rhetorical stock phrase appropriate to barbarian invaders of Britain. Any reader of Sidonius, or of Claudian before him, will be familiar with the tedious catalogues of barbarian tribes that sometimes take over the narrative. Each tribe has its own attribute or descriptive phrase like characters in a pageant, or the representations of Roman provinces and cities from which this rhetorician's trick was borrowed. Cameron has remarked on the German tribes whom Stilicho, according to Claudian, subdued on the Rhine in 396, with 'the Cimbri, specially resurrected for the purpose, together with the Cherusci, fresh from the pages of Tacitus.' Jerome uses the same trick in describing, from the safe distance of Jerusalem, an improbable mix of invaders in Gaul in 406–7. 'Julius Caesar,' says Sidonius, 'took his victorious legions over to the Caledonian Britons, and . . . routed the Scot, the Pict and the Saxon', and the same trio appear in Claudian's description of Theodosius the Elder's campaigns in Britain: 'the Orkneys ran red with Saxon blood, Thule was wet with the blood of Picts, ice-bound Ireland wept for the heaps of slain Scots.' Fortunately we can ignore Sidonius as a source for Caesar's invasions of Britain, or Claudian as evidence for Saxon settlement in Orkney, but one may also doubt whether the almost identical phrase has any more substance when used by Sidonius's contemporary and friend Constantius. His Life of Germanus is a valuable source for early fifth-century Britain, but to decode it we need to understand its conventions of metaphor and rhetoric.[40]

PART 2: BUILDING THE CHRISTIAN CITY

4. The Christian City

And church-yards are our cities, unto which
The most repair, that are in goodnesse rich.
There is the best concourse, and confluence.
There are the holy suburbs, and from thence,
Begins God's City, New Jerusalem.

John Donne, *Obsequies to the Lord Harrington*

'A city must have a bishop, and walls.' This medieval Spanish prescription defines two essential elements of those late antique cities which, in Peter Brown's phrase, 'collapsed inwards around their bishop.' The bishop was the elected overseer and protector of the Christian family within the city and its territory. The walls offered physical protection to the inhabitants and defined the city's space. For as long as the Roman rule of burial outside city limits was maintained, they separated the city of the living from that of the dead. Inside the walls were the cathedral and the city churches. Outside were the cemeteries and the funerary basilicas, though in practice reality was often more complex than this neat formula.

The survival of the Roman civitates as bishoprics, with the civitas capital as the seat of the bishop, is a central fact of French history. To take one example from many, the Breton tribe of the Namnetes were governed in Roman times from Condivincum, an ancient trading port on the estuary of the Loire. By the late Empire, throughout Gaul the names of towns had reverted to that of their tribe, as if their own independent role as a city was now less important than their function as local capital. Condivincum became the *Civitas Namnetum* — the city of the Namnetes. Their bishop, from his fifteenth-century cathedral in Nantes, is still spiritual head of what was once the tribal territory, even though the old feudal and ecclesiastical geography of pre-Revolutionary France was swept away by the Revolutionary government and the old names replaced by river names, so that Nantes is now capital of the Department of Loire-Atlantique. In Britain, by contrast, bishoprics, even in Roman cities, were founded or re-founded after the conversion of the English. In much of Spain they were re-founded after the re-conquest from the Moors, and some are converted mosques.[1]

The best vantage point from which to see how the Christian bishop attained this role is through the eyes of a fourth-century Gallo-Roman magnate. If his was an old family (and few were), they may once have held office as local 'senators' and 'pagan' priests (the latter an honorific, not a salaried post). Their names might have appeared on inscriptions in the forum or baths, or there might have been a statue somewhere. They might even have aspired to a civil or military post outside their own province. Most of that was now gone. The city revenues had been confiscated by Constantine. The forum and baths had been demolished, and their inscriptions and statues were now part of the foundations of the city walls. In a Christian Empire there was no longer a place for pagan priests. Though aristocrats might still lay claim to local senatorial status and still had the wealth to maintain and embellish their country villas, there was no longer any power or glory to be had in urban office holding — only ruinous expense and *munera* (compulsory public duties). Yet public office holding was still important, not least in cities where there might be more than one family contending for power and status. Even in the fifth century, Sidonius chided a friend that if he stayed on his estate and did not show his status through public office he would lose it.[2]

What qualified a sixth-century Gallic aristocrat for the title of senator has been much debated. In the late Empire, it could denote either a member of the Roman senate or of a municipal city council. Its use in the sixth century has been seen as a term for large landed proprietors (Kurth), as a formal title for descendants of Imperial Roman senators (Stroheker), or as denoting people of varied social origins united mainly by their economic wealth (Gilliard). This last is, interestingly, the view of an American scholar. Brennan suggests that whilst the essential qualification was a senatorial family background, the use of the title might imply that the Gallo-Roman aristocracy felt a rivalry for power and status from the parallel Frankish aristocracy and from those Gallo-Romans who had risen through service with the Frankish kings. The somewhat self-conscious assertion of status could signal a certain siege mentality. There seems to have been some attribute by which Gregory of Tours could identify some of his friends as 'senators', though the term could have been as elastic as the English usage 'public school'. I have used the term 'senator' (in quotation marks) or 'local senator' to indicate that these were not members of the Roman senate.[3]

The landed aristocrat with ambitions outside his own city passed his life in alternate spells of public office in some other province than his own (it had been illegal for someone to govern his native province since an unfortunate episode in the time of Marcus Aurelius), and in retirement on his estate when out of office. There was a polite convention that office was a tiresome duty, but in reality it was highly profitable and much sought after. A provincial governor would have a staff of 'friends' whose appointments were in his gift, and this formed part of a wide network of clientage. The process can be seen in action on an inscription from Normandy, the 'Thorigny Marble'. Titus Sennius Sollemnis was a magistrate of the small tribe of the Viducassi in modern Calvados, and the friend and client of Tiberius Claudius Paulinus, sometime commander of the Second Augustan Legion in Britain and governor of several Gallic and British provinces. When allegations were made against his patron before the Council of the Three Gauls at Lyon, Sennius Sollemnis used his influence to get the charges dropped. The grateful Paulinus sent him presents and promised him a job as Tribune on his staff at York, where Paulinus was now governor, with a salary paid in gold. Earlier, when Paulinus had been legionary commander, he became patron of the tribe of the Silures. He obtained for them some substantial official favour, probably a tax concession, and the tribal senate in gratitude voted him a statue. Its inscribed base, like the Thorigny marble, still survives. Similar patronage was expected of the Christian bishop. St Germanus's return from his British visit in 429 had been prayed for by the people of Auxerre 'since he was regarded as their protector both in the Courts of Heaven and in the storms of this world', and a heavy new tax assessment had just been made.[4]

In the altered circumstances of the late Empire, the range of middle ranking civil and military posts had disappeared. It was no longer possible for the like of Sennius Sollemnis to obtain through patronage a well paid job at York. What few posts remained were the preserve of the *potentissimi* and were keenly contested. Most available jobs were now within Gaul, though the career of a young aristocrat with the right connections might include the post of tribune and notary (private secretary) at Rome or Ravenna, or that of governor of one of the now much smaller provinces of the late Empire. One of the biggest plums of all, the Praetorian Prefecture of Gaul, was now held by Gallic aristocrats, but the stream of patronage now flowed in much narrower channels, and office was not easy to come by. It is hardly surprising that competition for episcopal posts was so keen.

The civil power within the city was represented by the *comes civitatis* or count of the city, a post of Gallo-Roman origin but whose functioning we know most of (as usual) from Gregory of Tours. Although appointed by the Merovingian kings, the counts were almost all drawn from the same Gallo Roman 'senatorial' families as the bishops. Gregory's grandfather Georgius had been count of Clermont Ferrand. Nicetius, count of Dax in Novempopulanae, was the brother of Rusticus, the bishop of Aire, and himself later became bishop of Dax. When count Maracharius of Angoulême became bishop, he was succeeded as count by his nephew Nantius. Similarly at Javols, count Palladius inherited the post from his father Britanus. We quite often hear of counts like Nicetius or Maracharius becoming bishops, and this was seen as a distinct promotion. For several reasons it was not possible for ordained churchmen or bishops to become counts, but it is doubtful if such a demotion would have occurred in any case, though in the unsettled conditions of the seventh century bishops may have taken over some of the functions of the *comes civitatis*.

It was unusual for an outsider to be made count of a city though they were royal appointees, and when, for example, the Merovingian king Chilperic took over a number of cities from his brother Guntram, he appointed new counts with orders that they were to forward all taxes to him. The count was both civil governor and, when necessary, led the men of the city in war, sometimes even against a neighbouring city on the orders of the king. Thus count Sicharius of Bourges led an armed force against Poitiers for king Guntram, and Firminus of Clermont attacked Arles for king Sigibert at the head of the city's forces. Sometimes several cities were brigaded together for military or other purposes, and the leader of such a group would sometimes assume the late Roman military rank of *Dux* (Duke). Counts could also act as an internal security police, arresting those who spoke ill of the king or denouncing those who opposed him. The titles of Duke and Count were, of course, to have a long later history, for with the fragmentation of the Carolingian state they were often assumed by regional military commanders who had attained a *de facto* independence. The Duke of Aquitaine and the Counts of Anjou and Flanders became major medieval rulers.[5]

Gallic bishops of the fifth century had a variety of roles. They interceded with rulers for their city. They might, in a crisis, take charge of its defence. A bishop, 'like a second Joseph', might organise famine relief, ransom prisoners, or persuade the Emperor to call off the agents of his wrath. Germanus of Auxerre intervened when Aetius sent Goar and his Alans against the Armorican rebels. Martin slept on the doorstep of Count Avitiacus until he released the columns of chained prisoners with whom he had arrived in Tours. He also prevented tribunes being sent into Spain by Magnus Maximus to hunt down suspected Priscillianists. The *topos* or rhetorical cliché of the ruler being forced to recognise the authority of the bishop or holy man passed into the hagiographer's stock in trade, and became a standard episode in saints lives. Much of the posthumous fame of Magnus Maximus and his wife as Macsen Wledig and Helen of the Hosts stems from the account in the *Vita Martini* of the Emperor at dinner with Martin whilst his wife waited silently on Martin like a servant. Earlier in Martin's career, Valentinian I had refused to rise to greet him until forced to do so by the application of divine fire to that part of the royal person with which he sat upon his throne.[6]

Hagiography apart, such roles were not solely the product of crisis. Ransoming of captives had the best biblical and patristic authority, and the involvement of the Church in famine relief is not confined to the ancient world. Freeing captives and slaves fulfilled various functions, apart from demonstrating Christian charity and serving as a practical allegory of the doctrine of redemption. It called for such episcopal skills as fund raising and negotiation. It extended the all-important circle of the bishops clientage, for a freed captive (like a freed slave) owed a legally enforceable debt, which could be redeemed by service. Where those freed were pagans it was an effective means of missionary activity. St Patrick could refer to the role of the Gallic Church in ransoming captives as if it were common knowledge, even in Ireland. A praetorian prefect might give Martin 100lb of silver to be used in redeeming captives, and St Severinus of Noricum was a natural go-between in freeing hostages and kidnap victims on the Danube frontier. Such good works were not confined to bishops. The memorial of Eugenia 'of illustrious blood' in the Abbey of St Victor at Marseille told how 'Her wealth freed unhappy captives from their bonds, and returned exiles to their homes.'[7]

Famine relief performed similar functions. When Euric laid waste the Rhône Valley and Provence, bishop Patiens of Lyon organised convoys of grain carts at his own expense. 'When the crops had been consumed by fire and the Goths', wrote Sidonius, 'you sent free supplies of corn . . . At your own private expense to relieve public destitution.' At the same time Sidonius's kinsman, the 'senator' Ecdicius, sent his servants through the devastated areas with carts and horses to bring in the starving. He brought large numbers of people (Gregory of Tours said 4000) to a central relief point, fed them until the crisis was over, and then returned them home. Ecdicius was not a bishop, but even in more normal times the help of a powerful man could be all-important. The letter files of the fifth-century bishop Sidonius are full of requests to other magnates, or to fellow bishops, on behalf of what one can only describe in modern terms as a constituent. These are people of modest status — a deacon or a widow involved in family quarrels over a will; another deacon, a refugee from the Goths, who was squatting on a piece of church glebe and wanted to regularise his position; a letter of introduction for a young man setting off to seek his fortune as a merchant at Marseille; help for the family of a woman kidnapped on the road by bandits. Merchants or traders would particularly need the support of their bishop, for in a strange town they might be suspect as outsiders, and a letter of introduction from their bishop to his fellow diocesan would vouch for them. Such folk also performed a useful function for bishops, for at a time when communications were difficult they could serve as messengers and letter carriers.[8]

Seat of power: the intra-mural Cathedral complex

The earliest Christian focus in many Gallic cities may have been in the cemeteries and funerary chapels. City centre space was a scarce and valuable asset, and until the Church had the wealth and the patronage to acquire land in the city centre it had to make do with less central locations. At Bordeaux, the demolished church of St Etienne in the cemetery area of St Seurin was of late Roman style *opus mixtum*, with small square blocks of ashlar and tile bonding courses, and was aligned on the Roman street grid. The Marquise de Maillé thought that it might have been a late Roman extra-mural cathedral, but it was strikingly similar to the recently excavated cemeterial basilica at Colchester and may have performed a similar function.[9]

We are well informed on Christian origins in Tours thanks to its two most celebrated bishops, Martin and Gregory. According to Gregory, the first church in Tours was built by a local aristocrat Litorius, the second bishop (337–70), who converted the house of a fellow 'senator'. Similar 'house churches ' are known at Dura Europos on the Euphrates, and possibly at Merida in Spain. The town walls of Tours had not then been built, so that Litorius's church was neither intra or extra mural. It lay in the suburban cemetery area, 1000m along the road to Angers from the later walled town. Litorius was buried there in what became the *Basilica Litorii*. His successor Martin lay nearby, and the first small church over his grave, built by his successor Bricius, developed into one of the greatest abbeys of medieval France. In the middle ages, Tours was divided between the rival *Bourgs* of St Martin on the west, around his Abbey and tomb, and the walled cathedral area to the east. Litorius also built the first intra mural cathedral where Martin was ordained as bishop in 371–2, though the walls were not built, on the evidence of a sealed coin, until after 364, and they and the new cathedral must have been nearly contemporary.[10]

By the early fifth century, bishops from wealthy local families of 'senatorial' status were building new cathedral complexes in city centre locations, often with the financial help of fellow aristocrats or Imperial officials. When bishop Rusticus of Narbonne rebuilt his cathedral around 441–3, after being burnt down in the troubles at the beginning of the century, the subscription list was headed by the praetorian prefect Marcellus who seems to have had family connections in the city. He gave a donation of 600 solidi from the profits of two years of his office, together with an additional 600 or 1500 solidi (the reading is uncertain) from his own resources. Rusticus also built a church of the Spanish martyr Felix of Gerona at Narbonne, with subscriptions from local 'senators' including Consentius, a friend of Sidonius, who stayed with him on a visit to Narbonne about 465. In 441 the bishops of Viennensis gathered in the cathedral at Orange for a church council. The *Ecclesia Justinianensis* had probably been built by a kinsman of the then bishop Justus. Eighty years later their successors combined a further council with the dedication of a new cathedral, paid for by Petrus Marcellinus Felix Liberius, *vir clarissimus*, praetorian prefect of Gaul and Patrician. He signed the minutes immediately after the bishops, followed by seven other grandees, all *viri inlustres* of senatorial rank, including one of the Syagrii of Lyon.[11]

Since intra-mural space was so limited, it is scarcely surprising that many early cathedrals re-used the sites of major Roman buildings. Indeed, they could scarcely have avoided doing so. In some cases this was the house of a local 'senator', as at Tours. At Aix-en-Provence it was the forum and basilica, at Cimiez the North Baths, at Alba and Beauvais the sites of monumental Severan public buildings. In most cases these would have been out of use, as at Cimiez and Aix, or long demolished, as at Beauvais. Such cases often gave rise in older literature to claims that a cathedral had been built on the site of a Roman 'temple', but they must date from the time when the bishop did not have to beg a house from a local magnate. Rather he could be given a public building or its site (perhaps no more than a vacant building plot) by the municipality or by the Count of the City.

The cathedral complex included the cathedral itself, the baptistery, and the bishop's palace. In the apse of the cathedral was the bishop's throne or *cathedra* where he sat, flanked by his clergy, facing the congregation gathered in the nave like a civil magistrate seated in an urban basilica. The buildings of the cathedral complex were often grouped around a large square or atrium in which crowds from all over the civitas territory would gather on the great feasts of the Church. All Christians were expected to come to the city at Easter, Christmas and Pentecost. Landowners were forbidden to keep those feasts on their estates or villas, as were their estate clergy. They should celebrate the festivals with the bishop in the city 'and so must all adult citizens'. This gave a wholly new emphasis to the role of the city. Sidonius describes a hot autumn night in Lyon in 469 when great crowds had gathered to celebrate the feast of the monk-bishop Justus in the great extra mural basilica where he lay buried. Similar scenes must have been familiar in the cathedral cities at times such as Easter, when crowds of catechumens and their families came in from the surrounding countryside for baptism, or for the other great feasts of the Christian year.[12]

A number of cathedral complexes are known from excavation. At Aix-en-Provence, capital of Narbonensis Secunda, the fifth-century baptistery south of the cathedral survives. Excavation has shown that the cathedral itself overlies a monumental first-century public building with a columned facade on its south, opening out onto a porticoed public square paved with stone slabs and measuring 50m by 25m. These have been identified as the main forum and basilica of the city. A large seventeenth-century crypt has removed the evidence for the Early Christian cathedral, but it would be hard to imagine a more telling illustration of the changing pattern of authority within Aix; the cathedral had replaced the judicial and administrative seat of its magistrates, and the forum had become a great atrium beside the cathedral, dominated by its baptistery and filled with crowds of townsfolk and country people at the great Christian feasts. The bishop and his clergy had replaced the urban magistrates and 'senators'. The transformation may have come about at the end of the fifth century, in the time of bishop Basilius whose metrical epitaph survives.[13]

At Valence (Drôme), bishop Apollinaris, the contemporary of Basilius and kinsman of Sidonius Apollinaris, built two churches within the Augustan walls some time between 490 and 518 and invited his brother, bishop Avitus of Vienne, to the consecration of one of them. An alignment of three early churches is known running east-west along the axis of the south wall of the present Gothic cathedral. From west to east these comprise a square cruciform baptistery with mosaics, excavated in 1866 outside the south-west angle of the cathedral nave; a church with rectangular nave and eastern apse found in 1960 under the present south transept; and the now demolished polygonal rotunda of Notre Dame de la Ronde to the east. The central building may be bishop Apollinaris's cathedral of St John the Evangelist. The baptistery, once dedicated to St John the Baptist, could have stood in a rectangular atrium west of the church, as at Aix-en-Provence and elsewhere. Notre Dame de la Ronde recalls the celebrated and vanished church of Notre Dame de la Daurade at Toulouse. If the latter was, as has been suggested, a converted Roman temple, the Valence church could either have been a copy or a similar Christianised pagan temple. The early cathedral was later re-dedicated (like so many early Gallic cathedrals) to St Stephen and finally demolished in 1094 when the body of St Apollinaris was translated into the newly built predecessor of the present cathedral of St Apollinaire. As was so often the case the name of an early bishop has replaced the primitive dedication.[14]

At Geneva a large building within the late Roman walls, possibly the residence of an official, was given over to the Church in the later fourth century for a twin cathedral like that at Trier with a baptistery in an atrium between the two churches. Differing liturgical arrangements suggest that the north church, much enlarged in the fifth century, was the cathedral proper where the divine offices were celebrated, the south church serving for catechumens who were excluded from the main part of the Mass (as they are in the Orthodox Church). The baptistery was also rebuilt in the fifth century with marble (no doubt re-used), mosaics, and a hydraulic system with wooden water pipes. Excavated parts of the bishop's palace include a private chapel, a large heated room with a decorated mosaic floor, perhaps a reception hall for the bishop, and possible store and service rooms. This complex, which survived until about AD 1000, now forms an archaeological display under the standing twelfth-century cathedral of St Pierre. We shall need to consider these double cathedrals later in an architectural context, but they are essentially a late Roman feature of the period of the conversions.[15]

Originally a cathedral would not have needed a dedication. It was simply the *ecclesia* or cathedral church of Paris or the like, sometimes bearing the name of its founder, like the *Ecclesia Justinianensis* at Orange or the *Basilica Litorii* at Tours. A Basilica was a church with important relics, as opposed to an *ecclesia* or cathedral or to a mere *oratorium*. The need to distinguish between churches by means of a distinctive dedication arose in the late fourth and fifth centuries, partly because of the multiplication of urban churches and partly because of the growing cult of relics. Many French cathedrals are dedicated to St Stephen whose relics were discovered in Palestine in 415 and reached Gaul soon after. Gregory of Tours gives an impressive catalogue of relics that he and his predecessors had placed in various churches and chapels in Tours. He begins his *In Gloria Martyrorum* with accounts of miracles wrought by relics of the protomartyr St Stephen, and of St Mary (who was not, of course, a martyr), to whom many churches were now being dedicated. The paramount saint of Tours, however, was its third bishop Martin whose successor and spiritual heir Gregory was.[16]

Possible remains of the bishop's residence, the *domus ecclesiae*, are known from several sites, including Aix-en-Provence and Geneva. Here, documentary evidence gives a clearer picture than do the fragmentary excavated remains. The domus may not have been very different from its medieval successor, the bishop's palace, save in scale. The composite picture would fit a smaller and simpler version, perhaps not unlike a medieval abbot's lodging. It had a large hall, sometimes on an upper floor, which served at times to entertain the leading townsfolk. The bishop's reception hall at Geneva no doubt saw similar gatherings. Private chapels are known at Geneva and at Tours, where Gregory formed one out of a fine room which his predecessor had used as a store. There was a camera, or private chamber, for the bishop, but one feature not found in later clerical residences was the camera for the *episcopa* or former wife of the bishop. It was to be kept well apart from the bishop's camera lest her maidservants proved a temptation for the younger priests in the bishop's household. The *domus ecclesiae* must have been a busy place with many callers and petitioners, and the bishop was forbidden to keep hounds or hunting dogs on the premises lest they frightened poor and nervous visitors. Sometimes the bishop's palace was tucked away in a corner of the city in an angle of the town walls. At Angers, bishop Audouveus built a solar or gazebo on the ramparts where he could sit and drink with his friends, but there was an unhappy accident when a deacon fell from the wall after an evening's drinking, nearly taking the bishop with him. A more sober bishop, Bertram (Bertechramnus) of Le Mans, built a chapel of St Michael the Archangel, the guardian of high places, in the top room of one of the towers of the Roman wall after a vision of an angel. In his will in 616, Bertram refers to the cathedral bakery (*pistrinis aecclesiae*) which he had added to the bishop's house, a reminder that much food preparation would be necessary, for the bishop's household and for the poor who would be fed there. In the area of the bishop's palace at Poitiers, excavation has revealed a complex for smoking fish or meat of the sixth to eighth century with a large oven and five rectangular hearths of brick herringbone masonry.[17]

Outside the city walls: martyrs, graves and bishops

In the cemeteries outside the walls of many Gallic cities were the graves of Christian martyrs. Events after such a death followed a common pattern throughout the Empire. The body would be buried in a suburban cemetery in the normal way. Pagans and Christians alike marked the anniversary of the death of a family member at the graveside with meals and libations, and grave altars with lead pipes for libations, going down from the surface to the burial chest, are known from Britain, Gaul and Germany. To Christians this was the 'Heavenly birthday', and whilst most Gallic Christian tombstones record the day of death only a few record the year. The 'Heavenly birthday' of a martyr would be a matter for the whole Christian family in the city. This does not mean that a martyr cult need have developed immediately or spontaneously. Our knowledge of the beginnings of Gallic martyr cults is limited, but the first clear evidence comes from the world of soldierly Christianity of the time of Valentinian I, much of it relating to the north Italian martyrs whose cults were sponsored by St Ambrosius of Milan. When Flavius Jovinus founded a church at Reims, it contained not the relics of local martyrs but of the north Italian saints Agricola and Vitalis. Martin of Tours brought relics of the Milanese martyrs Gervasius and Protasius, whose bones had been discovered by St Ambrose in 386, to Gaul, and a widespread cult developed. Martin's biographer Sulpicius Severus was soon equating him with the military martyrs of the persecutions and claiming this monk-bishop as the equal of the martyrs.[18]

It is thus uncertain how much the genesis of individual martyr cults owed to popular pressure from below, and how much to the sponsorship of bishops and other grandees from above. In north Africa Augustine, beleaguered by the Donatists, distrusted popular martyr cults though he also preached some notable sermons on the feasts of individual martyrs. 'We should not be like the pagans', he told his congregation on the feast of the martyr bishop Fructuosus of Tarragona, 'for they venerate dead mortals.' The martyrs, he told them on another occasion, 'hate the clatter of your pots and pans, the martyrs hate to be worshipped.' In Gaul conditions were different. The main problem was not the divisions caused by the final persecutions but the conversion of the pagan masses. Even here, however, Martin of Tours ended one popular cult by calling up the ghost of the 'martyr' who confessed that he was an executed criminal. One common theme in Gaul is the role of the bishop as critic and censor of newly emerging cults and the need for episcopal sanction. At Dijon, the bishop thought the tomb of St Benigne to be a pagan sarcophagus until a miracle, an apparition, and a passio brought from Italy proved otherwise. At Troyes, the bishop at first accused the priest at St Patroclus's oratory of forging his passio – 'it is a mere invention on your part' — until confronted with a second copy, again brought from Italy.[19]

Until the early fifth century most Gallic martyrs still lay in unimportant tomb chapels in the city cemeteries. At Autun, St Symphorian lay in a little *cellula* until a basilica was built over his grave by bishop Euphronius shortly before 452, and St Reverendius in a small tomb chapel in the cemetery of St Pierre l'Estrier (*de Strata Via* – 'On the Roman road') until the priest Aboleno built an oratory. At Troyes, St Patroclus had only a small oratory with a single priest and the inhabitants paid him scant regard until his passio was discovered. At Toulouse, St Saturninus was buried in a wooden coffin in a timber roadside chapel a few hundred yards from the site of his martyrdom. About 360 St Hilary covered it with a brick vault, but it was left to bishop Silvius at the very end of the century to build a basilica over the grave. These stories, like those of initial episcopal scepticism, have a rhetorical element, designed to enhance the glory of the bishop responsible for the new basilica or the merits of the martyr for overcoming apathy and neglect, and to emphasise that his cult had episcopal sanction. They do, however, reflect a phase when the martyrs lay in tomb chapels no different to those of wealthy lay folk with no especial claim to sanctity.[20]

The descriptions of early tomb chapels and martyria in the Gallic passios can now be matched from excavated evidence. The cemetery of St Pierre l'Estrier at Autun grew up in the second and third centuries outside the Augustan walls, alongside the road to Langres. Its church, secularised at the French Revolution and now a barn, developed from a square third-century mausoleum like those at Lyon, Poundbury or Stone by Faversham. Though the site is structurally complex and difficult to interpret, and direct dating evidence scarce, the general pattern of development can be followed. The surrounding area was packed with earth cut graves and sarcophagi including a third-century Greek Christian inscription, an epitaph of 378 on a sarcophagus lid, and an early fifth-century *Hic Iacet* inscription. A second structure to the west was demolished in the fourth century and replaced by a two-

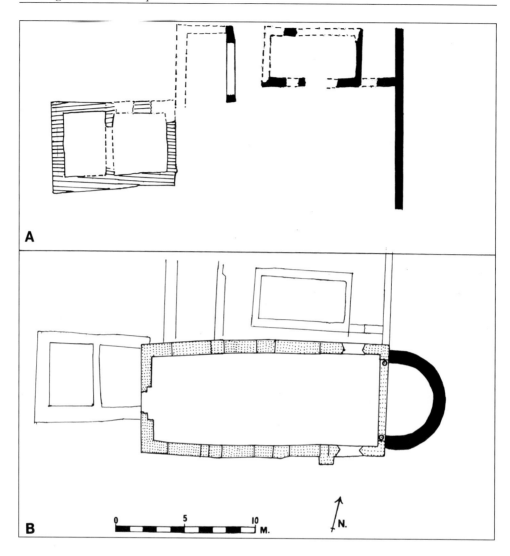

16   *Church of St Pierre l'Estrier, Autun. A: Third-century (black) and fourth-century (shaded) mausolea. B: Standing church (stippled) with demolished fifth-century apse (after Sapin 1986)*

chambered building with a vaulted roof, cut into the hillside like St Hilary's brick vaulted tomb for St Saturninus. Later the two structures at Autun were joined up, and in the fifth century an eastern apse added. Later still an arched arcosolitum tomb was added against the north wall, perhaps for the remains of the fourth-century theologian-bishop Rusticus. Its Romanesque successor, with a much later inscription, was recorded by an eighteenth-century scholar, and the sarcophagus over which it stood is still in place.[21]

The tomb chapel of a martyr would often be one of several similar mausolea standing amid the graves of a cemetery as can be seen at Poundbury, Grenoble or Lyon. At the latter, the tomb of the praetorian prefect Syagrius was in a chapel with its own park, complete with concierge. At Dijon, apart from St Benignus there was the mausoleum where the 'senator' Helarius was buried with his wife in a sarcophagus of 'Parian' marble. They were joined there by a holy woman named Florida. In the eleventh century the three were re-housed in the monastery of St Benigne and their chapel demolished. Another *religiosa*, Pascasia, had her own grave chapel nearby and was translated at the same time. Several early bishops were buried near the church of St Pierre at Autun, Reticius with his wife, and were later translated inside the church. St Symphorien's little *cellula* nearby developed into a major monastery where St Germanus of Paris was later abbot. Thus in the fifth century the graves of martyrs were being supplemented by those of a growing number of bishops, ascetics, and other holy men and women. Sometimes the oratories over their graves developed into major medieval churches.[22]

The same process can be seen at the basilica of the Holy Apostles or St Pierre at Vienne. A rectangular *memoria* with a shallow square apse was built in the late fourth century and burials took place around it. Later, a large aisled basilica was built to the west by bishop Mamertius who died about 475. The earlier structure was kept as an eastern annexe in an ambulatory with a second memoria to the east. In the sixth century the *memoria* and ambulatory were replaced by the church of St George, probably an episcopal funerary chapel. The sequence below the Abbey of St Viktor at Xanten in the Rhineland is similar and can be put into clearer focus by Bridger's re-assessment of its chronology. The late Roman cemetery 'at the place of the saints' (*Ad Sanctos* — hence Xanten), outside the legionary fortress and town of Vetera, was the burial place of the martyr St Viktor, though in the time of Gregory of Tours the site of his grave was unknown. After AD 348 (from a sealed coin) two men were buried in a double wooden coffin. The date would seem to rule out martyrs unless the curious double coffin means that we are dealing with a translation. Successive wooden structures over their grave recall St Saturninus's wooden martyrium at Toulouse. Later these were replaced by a square stone *memoria*, perhaps the oratory of St Mallosus known to Gregory of Tours. There were rich late Roman and Merovingian graves around the chapel, but it was not until the late seventh century that the *memoria* was replaced by a stone oratory which became the nave of two successive Carolingian churches, predecessors of the present Abbey.[23]

The graves of martyrs and other holy men and women not only provided heavenly guardians for a city but a focus for the common identity and loyalty of its townspeople. However, the distribution of martyr graves was uneven. There were few in western Gaul south of the Seine or west of the Massif Central. A town lacking such a patron had two options — to adopt the cult of an early bishop, or to obtain relics from elsewhere. Two of the most important early bishop cults grew up on the fringes of western Gaul in cities which lacked martyrs, at Tours in the Loire Valley and Auxerre between the Seine and Loire. The alternative was for the city or its bishop to obtain relics from elsewhere. The arrival of relics in a city was greeted with the Adventus ceremony which had previously marked the arrival of a Roman Emperor. The townsfolk were led by the bishop, the various grades of clergy, and the leading men of the town. The citizens were all ranked in order according to age, sex and status. They would meet the messengers bearing the relics some miles outside the city gates and escort them to their new home in the cathedral where the bishop would preach a sermon of welcome. That preached by bishop Victricius of Rouen on such a happy occasion has come down to us. A sixth-century ivory now in Trier shows the arrival of relics at Constantinople, carried by two metropolitan bishops on a triumphal chariot, preceded by the Emperor and his court carrying torches, and with crowds of spectators watching from balconies and rooftops.[24]

Sometimes the translation of relics from a distant source led in time to the mistaken belief that these were local martyrs. It is improbable that the small number of Gallic victims of the Imperial persecutions included three separate men called Genesius, and Genesius of Tarbes in the Pyrenees and Genesius of Thiers in the Auvergne must be doublets of the better attested martyr Genesius of Arles. Some time in the fifth century, relics were perhaps sent from Arles to Tarbes and Thiers as a piece of ecclesiastical diplomacy in the period when Arles was seeking to assert its metropolitan primacy over the churches of Gaul. By the late sixth century, Genesius of Tarbes was seen as a local martyr-priest and a homily had been written with an account of his death for reading to the citizens on his feast day. In Thiers, bishop Avitus of Clermont (571–94) built a church over what was claimed as the recently discovered tomb of the martyr, though the church also contained relics of Genesius of Arles. Such localisations of cult could have been due to simple amnesia or intended to counter attempts to extend the influence of Arles. Interestingly, neither place was a civitas capital where the relics might have challenged the diocesan bishop too directly. Neither cult took root, and nothing further is heard of these 'martyrs'.[25]

Five French towns: the geography of the Heavenly City

The best way to see how the themes explored in this chapter worked out in practice is to look at some towns in various regions of France and from different late Roman provinces. Vienne, capital of Viennensis, was in origin a trading town on the Rhône, in pre-Roman times an interface between the Greek colonies of the Mediterranean coast and the Celtic hinterland. Later it became an Augustan colony. Arles and Marseille lay within its province, but an adequate study of either of these in late antiquity would take up more space than is available here and an excellent study of Marseille has recently been published. At Bourges in central France, in Lugdunensis Secunda, the late Roman walls followed the line of the defences of the oppidum of Avaricum taken by Julius Caesar in 52 BC. Bordeaux, metropolis of Aquitania Secunda, was (and is) a major Atlantic seaport. It had imposing late Roman walls, and excavation has revealed sixth-century occupation inside them. Langres, in Lugdunensis Prima, was a modest sized inland town on the northern margin of Burgundy.[26]

Vienne (Isère)

The walls of the *Colonia Julia Augusta Florentia Viennensius* enclosed 30 ha within their 7km. In late Roman times the city contracted to an inner core, and suburbs across the Rhône and south of the walled area were abandoned. Claims of a smaller late circuit within the Augustan walls are unproven. Vienne contained an Imperial palace occupied by Emperors such as Julian and Valentinian II, though the only later reference to it relates to the supernatural fire fighting abilities of a fifth-century bishop. Two important remains of the Augustan Colonia also survived in a Christian context. Two blocks from a monumental

17   *Memorial stone of Foedula, from church of St Gervaise and St Protasius, Vienne, recording her baptism by St Martin and her burial 'at the seat of the martyrs'. I.C.G. 412. C.I.L. XII, 2115*

inscription recording the building of the MUROS (et) PORTAS — the wall and gates — were re-used as coffins, and the temple of Livia and Augustus survived as the church of Notre Dame la Vieille. Suppressed at the Revolution it was later a museum. An engraving prior to its restoration by the Monuments Historiques shows the classical temple with Gothic arches in the blocked-up walls, and the word 'Musée' over the door.[27]

A deacon from Vienne was among the Lyon martyrs of 177, and the city had its own martyr shrine of St Ferreolus south of the city where the apse of a basilica built by the fifth-century bishop Mamertius is known. A ninth-century bishop list would carry their succession back to the later third century, matching the evidence for third-century Christianity from Autun, Marseille, Arles, and elsewhere in the province. The presence of Christian Emperors would have demanded a cathedral of suitable size near the Imperial palace, and Julian, then still a Christian, attended service in such a basilica in 361. By Carolingian times the cathedral complex included a north church of Notre Dame, a south church of the Maccabees, and a baptistery with a central lantern tower re-built by bishop Avitus (490–518). This may have been a late Roman double cathedral like those at Geneva or Trier.[28]

The wide compass of the Augustan walls makes it difficult to talk of intra and extra mural space at Vienne. However, the early Christian centres of cult fall into three clusters. One lies north of the Gére, across the little river (d'Outre Gére); one in the central late Roman urban core around the cathedral; and the third in the cemetery area south of this. The latter had been a flourishing extra mural suburb until the third century. Apart possibly for the cathedral, it was the earliest centre of Christian cult in Vienne. Outside the

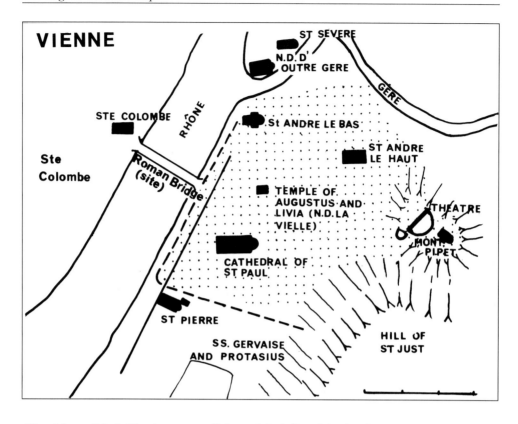

18   *Vienne (Isère). The Augustan walled area (stippled) and the churches*

Augustan south gate lay a major necropolis. Its two fourth-century foci were the church of Gervasius and Protasius and the *memoria* on the site of the later church of St George. Relics of the Milanese martyrs Gervasius and Protasius were brought to Gaul by Martin of Tours, who was in Vienne with Paulinus of Nola and Victricius of Rouen between 386 and 389. The tombstone of Foedula, a woman baptised by Martin, was found in the cemetery around the church. It uses the early fifth-century *Hic Iacet* formula. The church was destroyed in the sixteenth-century wars of religion. In 1853 a railway line was cut through its forgotten site. A mass of tile tombs, sarcophagi and long cist graves was found. Le Blant published a contemporary sketch showing the tombs, but the site was destroyed almost without record, many inscriptions being broken up for building material. Some were salvaged by Auguste Allmer, an archaeologist responsible for a number of important excavations in Vienne, and are now in the lapidary museum in the church of St Andre le Bas. They are all fifth century, using the formulae *Hic Iacet* or *Hic Requiescit In Pace*. The relics of Gervasius and Protasius were housed not in an intra mural church but in a suburban funerary basilica, so that those buried there were *ad sanctos* (or, as Foedula put it, 'at the seat of the martyrs'), close to the saints who would intercede for them on the Last Day. The site is now marked by the railway station whilst Allmer is commemorated in the Rue Allmer, a rare if fitting honour for an urban archaeologist.[29]

The churches of St George and of St Pierre (once the Basilica of the Holy Apostles) were 700m from St Gervaise. They may even pre-date the latter and have produced the oldest Christian inscription from Vienne, of late fourth century type. The complex began with a late fourth-century *memoria*, next to which Bishop Mamertius built his basilica of the Holy Apostles about 475 as a funerary basilica for the bishops of Vienne. His *Arcosolitum* tomb is set into one side of the apse. It rapidly became a favoured place for burial, including the graves of many bishops. The interior was crammed with tombs, mostly sarcophagi, many with inscriptions with consular dates. The earliest, of a *vir spectabilis*, was of 483, according well with the foundation date. The standing remains will be considered in a later chapter, but the most important citizens of Vienne now rested not with the relics of the saints but with their bishops.[30]

North of the Gére were the late fifth-century churches of St Severus, St Martin, and Notre Dame de l'Outre Gére. The priest St Severus founded a basilica of St Stephen which later took his own name. It has produced a dated tombstone of 511. There is another, of 495, from St Martin's and one of 502 from Notre Dame. Inside the urban nucleus the most important early church, save for the cathedral, was St Andre le Bas, a nunnery founded by Ansemond and his wife Anslebana for their daughter Remila or Eugenia. The original foundation of about 543 seems not to have taken effect until about 570, perhaps on the death of Remila's parents. As was often the case with urban nunneries, the nuns were replaced by secular canons in the ninth century, and later by Benedictine monks. Excavation and study of the standing fabric has shown a remarkable sequence. On the vaulted substructure of a major Roman building was a late or sub-Roman building with crushed tile mortar, possibly that given by Ansemond for his daughter's nunnery. The third phase comprises the lower part of the north wall, of small irregular masonry, with a round headed window with voussoirs of brick and stone. Phase IV is an eleventh-century church, perhaps built after the installation of Benedictine monks.[31]

Bourges (Cher)

Avaricum, capital of the Biturges Cubi, captured by Julius Caesar in 52 BC after a hard siege, was said to be the fairest city of all Gaul, the defence and pride of their nation. After the Roman conquest the town spread down the slopes outside the ramparts on their limestone promontory, but these must have been still visible for under the late Empire they provided a convenient line for formidable city walls. There were no known martyrs at Bourges and the first recorded bishop, Leo, attended the Council of Angers in 453. A lost eleventh-century ivory diptych places him twelfth in a bishop list, but this would not carry the bishops back before Constantine. At some date a local aristocrat Leocadius, who claimed descent from one of the Lyon martyrs of 177, gave his house inside the walls for a church.[32]

References to the baptistery and the *domus ecclesiae* or bishop's palace show that the normal cathedral complex grew up around the cathedral of St Stephen inside the east rampart. Nearby a Roman gateway gave access to the cemeteries. These lay 400m from the walls, separated from them by the extra-mural area of the Roman town. Whether this was still occupied by suburbs or merely encumbered by ruins is unknown. A fifth-century ascetic Agustus built an oratory in the cemetery zone with relics of Martin of Tours, which, by the following century, developed into a monastery. As at Vienne, the relics were not at this date housed inside the walls but in the suburban cemetery. Bishop Probianus founded another monastery dedicated to the martyr Symphorien of Autun nearer the town, in the former suburbs, and installed Agustus as abbot. St Germanus of Paris was abbot of St Symphorien at Autun, and had probably given relics of the martyr to Probianus. Unlike the oratory of St Martin the monastery did not attract burials, perhaps because it lay in the former built up area. Bourges, however, lacked a native saint until Agustus and Germanus found the tomb of the alleged first bishop, Ursinus, in a vineyard outside the town and translated his sarcophagus to a basilica. By the seventh century there were three monasteries of men in the suburban areas — those of St Martin, of St Symphorien, and the funerary church of St Austrigisilus. In contrast the three nunneries were all within the walls. This reflects not only any perceived greater need of security (apart from anything else, the abduction of heiresses from nunneries was not unknown), but the existence of monastic lands and vineyards outside the city worked by the monks. If the Church had retreated inside the city walls during the troubles of the late Empire it was now re-occupying the ground outside them. The founder of one nunnery, Eustadiola, lay in the church of St Paul the Apostle outside the walls. The lamp over her tomb was still working miracles when the church was destroyed by the Protestants in 1562, but here, as elsewhere, by the eleventh century all three nunneries had become houses of canons. For the building of churches the Roman town left a useful legacy. Bishop Austrigisilus installed an ascetic, Amandus, in one of the towers of the city wall (we shall find parallels at Le Mans), and another bishop, Sulpicius, built his nunnery with stone taken from ancient buildings.[33]

Bordeaux (Gironde)

Martyr graves were scarce in western France. There were none in Novempopulanae save for Genesius of Bigorre, a duplicate of Genesius of Arles, and in Aquitania Secunda only Fides of Agen. A bishop seeking to establish a cult as focus for the identity of his city and people would need to look elsewhere — either to local holy men, or to relics brought from outside. Bishop Palladius of Saintes (573–600), built a church of St Peter and St Paul in his cathedral city, and obtained relics of the Roman apostles and martyrs for it from Pope Gregory the Great. He also acquired relics of St Martin from Gregory of Tours. Saintes still lacked its own saint, however. There was a neglected church said to contain the grave of an early bishop in one of the cemeteries. Palladius dug up the body, identifying it by an axe mark on the skull as the martyr Eutropius. For once even Gregory of Tours was cautious. This early exercise in palaeo-pathology is an example of the way in which a Merovingian bishop could build up, from relics or from the discovery of holy bodies, a religious identity for his city. Something of the sort can perhaps be seen in the neighbouring city of Bordeaux.[34]

The plateau north-west of Bordeaux where the basilica of St Seurin now stands had been used for burial since the second century. There are sculptured sarcophagi, amphora burials, and the tombstone of Flavinus, a soldier of the *Numerus Mattiacorum Seniorum*. The church of St Etienne, demolished in 1787, may have been a late Roman cemeterial basilica, or even an early cathedral. The focus of cult, however, was the tomb of a certain Severinus (St Seurin), claimed as an early bishop. Fortunatus, Gregory of Tours, and a local life confused him with St Severinus of Noricum, or his namesake at Cologne, and

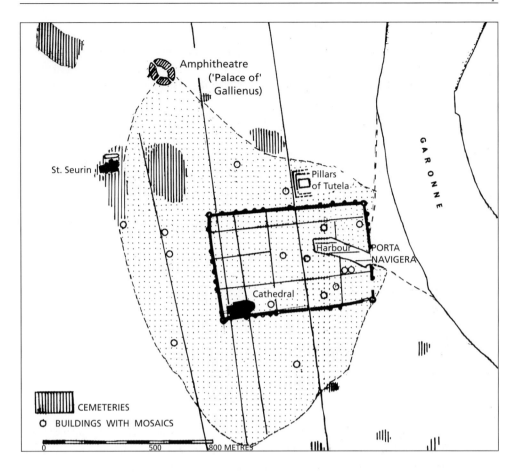

19   Bordeaux (Gironde). The early Roman town (stippled) and cemeteries, and the late Roman defences (after Etienne)

brought him from 'The East' or the Rhine to replace bishop Amandus at Bordeaux. Amandus, a friend of Paulinus of Nola, became bishop in 405. Gregory claimed that he gave up his see to Severinus but reclaimed it on his death. This sounds like a drastic attempt to reconcile conflicting traditions. The Marquise de Maillé thought that the cult may have been the creation of bishop Bertechramnus (d.585), a contemporary of Gregory of Tours and Eutropius of Saintes, but the description suggests an established cult rather than a newly created shrine. Like Eutropius, Bertram was an avid collector of relics. Gregory tells stories, set in Bordeaux, of Bertram and a relic of the Syrian martyr Sergius of Resafa and of a vision of St Stephen which led to Bertram acquiring a handkerchief soaked in water from his robe which was cut up and distributed as relics.[35]

Bertram had reasons for wanting to acquire sources of supernatural authority. Until the late 560s the metropolitan see of Bordeaux was dominated by the local senatorial family of the Leontii. The last of these, Leontius II, clashed with the Frankish king Charibert over the appointment of a bishop of Saintes, challenging the king's right to appoint bishops. Bertram, his successor, was a kinsman of Charibert's brother, king Guntram. This cannot have made his position with the local aristocracy or his fellow bishops easy. Gregory of Tours, a personal and political enemy, was scornful of his pretensions, and may not have been alone in this. Relics could reinforce Bertram's authority and prestige, as could the grave of a saintly bishop whose spiritual heir Bertram was. Evidently a cult had grown up around the *memoria* of a holy man named Severinus, who could be placed, perhaps by a dated tomb inscription, as a contemporary of bishop Amandus. Whether he was already identified as a bishop before the time of Bertram is less clear. There were cases in the disorders of the early fifth century where a bishop was deposed but regained his see after the fall or death of his rival. Martin's successor at Tours, Bricius, was one example. Constantine III 's replacement of the bishops of Aix and Arles by Martinian ascetics is another. Amandus might also have been driven from his see by the Arian Visigoths in 418. However, such cases usually made a stir, and if Amandus had been deposed in this way we might expect to have heard of it. Perhaps there were difficulties in fitting Severinus's known date into the bishop list, making it necessary to split the episcopate of Amandus to fit him in.[36]

Langres (Haute-Marne)

Langres provides a variation on the theme of intra and extra mural space. The capital of the Lingones had always been here, though the bishops spent much of their time at nearby Dijon, a strongly walled town where Bishop Gregory of Langres, great-grandfather of Gregory of Tours, had left them large estates. Gregory of Tours praised the amenities and natural resources of the city, and its wine. 'Why Dijon has not been elevated into a bishopric', he said, 'I cannot imagine'. Competition from Dijon may have affected the development of Langres. The Roman town stretched along a north-south ridge for 2000m. Post-Roman Langres was a quarter of this size, and, like mercury falling in a thermometer in hard weather, occupied only the northern end of the ridge. One Roman gate survived until 1840, and the piecemeal demolition of the walls provided a rich harvest of re-used sculptures and inscriptions. The cemeteries remained where they were, separated, as at Bourges, by the area of the early Roman town. In the fifth century Langres acquired the relics of some Cappadocian martyrs. Those of St Mammetis were installed in the cathedral within the walls, those of the brothers Speusippos, Elisippos and Melasippos in a basilica in the Roman cemetery south of the city. It was at the basilica of the Holy Brothers that Ceolfrith, abbot of Jarrow and Monkwearmouth, died on his way to Rome in 716. In the early seventh century these cults were supplemented by that of bishop Desideratius (St Didier), who was translated from his tomb outside the city to a new intra-mural church and provided with a *passio* which claimed that he had been martyred in the third-century invasions. These events determined the religious geography of Langres. Today the cathedral of St Mammetis stands within the medieval ramparts with the disused Romanesque church of St Didier, now the Musee Lapidaire, nearby. 3km south is the thirteenth-century church of the Holy Brothers, with the area of the Roman town lying between.[37]

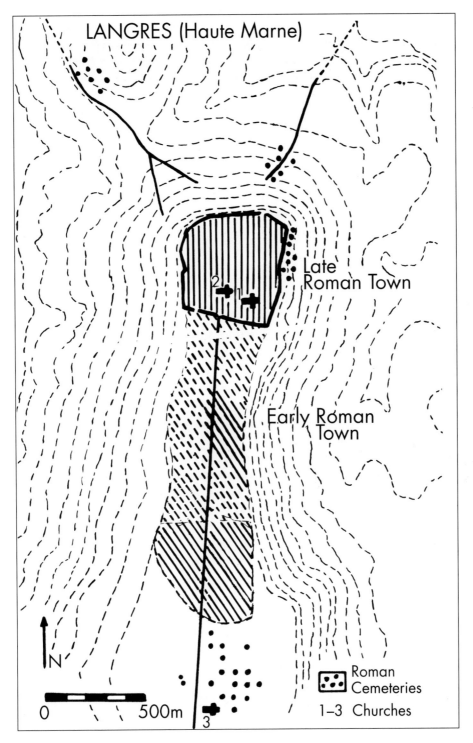

20 Langres (Haute-Marne). The early Roman town extended for 2000m along a north-south spur. The late Roman town occupied only the northern quarter of this. After T.C.C.G.

Le Mans (Sarthe)

The city of the Cenomanni, on its ridge above an important crossing of the Sarthe, may have carried, like Bourges, a pre-Roman oppidum. Under the late Empire the ridge was enclosed by particularly massive walls enclosing nine of the city's 25–30 ha, and garrisoned by a unit of Suevian irregulars. There is little evidence of fourth-century Christianity, the first recorded bishop being at the Council of Angers in 453. Early traditions centred on St Julian, said to be the first bishop, and on relics of the Milanese martyrs Gervasius and Protasius which he brought to the city. Julian may have been a contemporary of Martin of Tours. According to a ninth-century source he received a house from Defensor, 'first man of that place,' and built a church of St Mary with relics of the two saints. This could be borrowed from accounts of similar gifts at Tours and Bourges, but is otherwise perfectly credible. The cathedral, within the north-east angle of the city walls, was rebuilt by bishop Innocent (524–59) who installed the relics of the two martyrs in the main altar of the cathedral, with Julian's altar of St Mary on the north, and an altar to St Peter on the south. In 835 the relics of St Julian were translated from their cross-river grave to the newly rebuilt cathedral which then took his name. The changes of dedication, from a universal saint like Mary to the two martyrs and then to an early bishop, reflect patterns that we have already seen elsewhere.[38]

The cemeteries of Le Mans lay across the Sarthe. Julian lay in the monastery of Notre Dame du Pré where an early crypt marks his tomb. Nearby, another episcopal funerary basilica, the Church of the Holy Apostles, matched the dedication of Mamertius's basilica at Vienne. It was built for the burial of bishop Liborius by his successor Victurius (450–90), a contemporary of Mamertius. Victurius was later buried there and the church then took its name from him. Another abbey was built by bishop Domnolus in 572 to house relics of the Spanish martyr Vincent of Saragossa. Domnolus, a Parisian abbot, was appointed bishop of Le Mans by Lothar I whose brother Childebert had brought relics of Vincent back to Paris from Saragossa as war loot. Domnolus was originally offered Avignon but pleaded that he, a simple man, could not be expected to sit at table bored by the conversations of old senatorial families. Like that other Merovingian royal appointee Bertram of Bordeaux, he may have felt the need for a spiritual power base to set against the established power of their Le Mans equivalents, and this the relics of St Vincent provided. His foundation developed into a major monastery with the suburb of St Vincent a flourishing *bourg* with many craftsmen and their families. By this time, there was little room inside the cities for large bodies of monks with their manual workers, agricultural labourers and craftsmen, and the monks needed ready access to their fields and vineyards. The cities which had retracted within their walls were now moving outside again and the suburban monasteries were leading the way. In Norman times St Vincent's Abbey had important possessions in Britain, including Abergavenny Priory.[39]

The walls of Le Mans also enclosed, by Carolingian times, some half dozen small chapels and oratories, two in towers of the city wall. One of the latter was the chapel of St Michael the Archangel, built by bishop Bertram following a vision. The other, dedicated to St Albinus, was associated with a small nunnery.[40]

Some time in the fifth century, Nantes was under siege from unidentified barbarians. The citizens retreated behind their Roman walls, but food was scarce and the situation

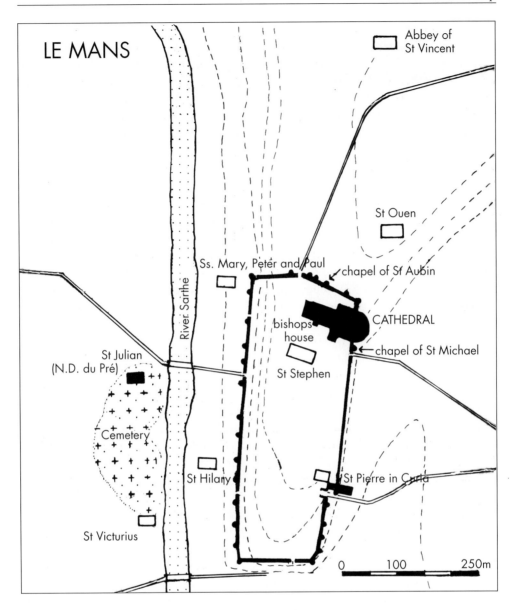

LE MANS

Abbey of
St Vincent

River Sarthe

St Ouen

Ss. Mary, Peter and Paul

chapel of St Aubin

CATHEDRAL

bishops
house

chapel of St Michael

St Julian
(N.D. du Pré)

St Stephen

Cemetery

St Hilary

St Pierre in Curia

St Victurius

0   100   250m

21   *Le Mans (Sarthe). The walled town, churches and Christian cemetery, demolished churches in outline (after Butler and Biarne)*

22   *Lost tenth-century onyx cameo, showing the saints Gervasius and Protasius (GERBA and PROTA) guarding the late Roman walls of Le Mans, from J. Gruter* Inscriptionum Romanorum Corpus *(Heidelberg 1615), courtesy of the Society of Antiquaries of London*

became critical. After two months of siege, two processions of men in white robes bearing candles were seen coming out of the basilica of the martyrs Rogatianus and Donatus, and from the church where the confessor Similinus lay buried. When the solemn white robed figures processed around the city walls the barbarians fled. Similar events were reported in other cities in times of stress, in Gaul, in Spain and in Byzantium. A now lost tenth-century onyx intaglio shows the Roman walls and gates of Le Mans and their supernatural protectors Gervasius (GERBA) and Protasius (PROTA). An earthly city needed a bishop and walls, but it also needed the supernatural protectors who ringed those walls with their graves and their *memoriae*.[41]

5. The Buildings of Jerusalem: churches and inscriptions in Post Roman Gaul

The great church gleams with light, and . . . its towering front faces the summer sunrise. Inside, the shafts of light play, and the sun is drawn to the gilded ceiling, travelling over its tawny metal, matching its colours. Marble of many shining colours fills the vaulting, the floor, the windows. With multicoloured patterns, a grass green encrustation brings winding lines of sapphire stone over the green glass. Outside the church, three lines of columns of Aquitanian marble rise proudly, and a second colonnade of the same kind shuts off the fourth side of the cloister. A stone forest fills the nave, with columns standing well apart. On one side is the noisy road, on the other the river . . . Towards this place all should make their way, for through it runs the road to salvation.

Sidonius Apollinaris (*Letters* II, X), describing the church built by bishop Patiens at Lyon

Basilica and Rotunda

The Christian Church inherited two basic architectural forms from the pagan and classical past — the rotunda and the basilica. Variations on these two themes were to dominate church architecture to the end of the Middle Ages and beyond, when Renaissance architects went back to surviving Roman buildings and drew afresh on those basic types. When Michaelangelo was coping with the engineering problems of the dome of St Peters in Rome in 1546–64, he spent much time studying two of the major surviving buildings of ancient Rome — the rotunda of Hadrian's Pantheon and basilica of Maxentius in the Roman Forum.

The basilica was a rectangular hall like the nave of a church. It might be roofed in a single span, or, more usually, its normally timber roof might be supported on rows of columns or piers with flanking side aisles to the central space. Both arrangements have remained normal for the naves of churches down to the present day. Its origins go back to Republican Rome where it was used for law courts and other places of public assembly, often with an apse or recess at one end for the presiding magistrate. Under the late Empire the apse could sometimes serve as a setting for the presence of the Emperor or his representative. In the basilica of Maxentius, as completed by Constantine, the western apse housed a colossal statue of the Emperor with a secondary apse in the centre of the side wall for the magistrate's platform. At Trier a basilica forming part of the Imperial palace, with an apse at one end, still survives. Unusually, it was built not of the usual brick-faced concrete but of solid brick throughout, an eastern technique at this date. It is now a church. The similar basilica at Metz, later St Pierre aux Nonnains, used similar stamped bricks. It may have been a judicial basilica for the provincial governor, like that recorded at Tours by Sulpicius Severus. The basilican assembly hall, with the apse as a symbol of the presence of authority and housing the representatives of authority presiding at its ceremonies, made a natural model for the first great urban churches.[1]

The rotunda is a centrally planned structure, circular or polygonal, normally with a domed roof. Like the basilica, it was used in the lay out of monumental bath buildings and royal palaces, but its form also made it suitable for temples like Hadrian's Pantheon in Rome, or for important tombs. A number of large circular rotundas were built as burial places for late Roman Emperors or their families, like Diocletian's mausoleum at Split (Croatia), S. Costanza in Rome, or the rotunda for the Honorian dynasty attached to the south transept of Old St Peters there. A surviving example, possibly in origin an Imperial mausoleum, is the Chapel of St Aquilino in the church of San Lorenzo in Milan. Built about 370, it is of two storeys, octagonal inside and out. Its clerestory has tall windows lighting an internal gallery below the domed roof. The otherwise plain interior is enriched with mosaics, and has alternate rectangular and semi-circular niches in its eight sides, the latter set in the angles. It may have served as a model for the slightly later cathedral baptistery at Milan, known from excavation, and attributed to St Ambrose (bishop 374–97). From here, similar centrally planned baptisteries spread to southern Gaul and elsewhere. A mausoleum very like S. Aquilino appears as Christ's tomb on an ivory diptych of the Resurrection, also now in Milan. Contemporary with S. Aquilino, it shows a two storey circular building with tall windows at the upper level, and a conical tiled roof.[2]

Some late Roman churches in Gaul

In the centre of the German city of Trier are two large medieval churches, the eleventh-century cathedral and the Gothic church of Our Lady. This area of the city once contained the Imperial palace of Constantine the Great, and the fabric of the cathedral still includes parts of a monumental fourth-century building. In the years after the war, excavation showed that the area around these churches contained two huge parallel aisled halls over 70m in length. These formed a late Roman double cathedral, the ancestor of the two medieval churches, dating back to the time of Constantine. One church was probably for the catechumens, under instruction and awaiting baptism, who were excluded from the main part of the Mass. Double cathedrals were not confined to Trier. There are others in Italy and the Balkans, and at Geneva a double cathedral with a baptistery between the two churches, as at Trier, is preserved in an archaeological display under the present cathedral. Others may have existed at Rouen and Vienne. They belong to the fourth century, when large numbers of new Christians were entering the church and separate provision had to be made for them. That at Trier was re-modelled by Gratian about 380 (the surviving fragment in the present cathedral belongs to its elaborate east end); Geneva is of similar date, Vienne was an Imperial city where the Emperor Julian, then still a Christian, attended Mass. They belong to the world of late Imperial architecture, rather than to that of post Roman church building.[3]

Several other late Roman churches are known in north Gaul and the Rhineland. St Gereon at Cologne is an elaborate oval version of the mausoleum-martyrium theme, possibly built over the tomb of a martyr in the late fourth century. To its west was a colonnaded atrium and forebuilding. The *Basilica Joviana* stood in the southern cemetery area at Reims. Its founder, Flavius Jovinus, was *magister militum* in 362–9 and consul in 367. The nave had a polychrome wall mosaic above its arcades with figures set in a field of gold and an inscription in letters of gold. The late Roman church of St Maurice and the Theban Legion at Cologne, with similar mosaics, was known as the 'Church of the Golden Saints'. West of the Reims basilica was an atrium where Jovinus lay in a marble tomb, perhaps the fine lion hunt sarcophagus from the church now in Reims museum. There is a minor puzzle concerning the date of the church. The dedicatory inscription, recorded by the ninth-century historian Flodoard, makes no reference to Jovinus's consulship, suggesting a date before 367, but the martyr Agricola of Bologna, whose relics lay in the church, was only discovered by St Ambrose in 393. The obvious explanation is that the relics were added to an existing church, but the late Edith Wightman neatly snipped the Gordian knot by suggesting that Jovinus built his church late in life, having retired to Reims after a long and distinguished career.[4]

Unlike the *Basilica Joviana*, known only from literary texts, the fourth-century church at St Bertrand de Comminges (Haute-Garonne) is known only from its excavated ground plan. Discovered earlier this century, it has now been re-excavated and re-planned. St Bertrand, *Lugdunum Convenarum*, lay on a flat plain below the foothills of the Pyrenees, near the marble quarries at St Béat from which much of its prosperity derived. From Augustan times onwards it acquired impressive public buildings, but in medieval times the city retreated to a hill overlooking the plain where the medieval cathedral and modern town now are. The church was in the lower town. It had a rectangular, unaisled nave, 26m by 14m overall, and a rectangular chancel flanked by annexes which may have served as vestries. Apart from these, its plan recalls the late fourth-century *memoria* which formed the first phase of the basilica of the Holy Apostles at Vienne. The latest excavations show that the St Bertrand church stood on the edge of the ornamental garden of a large town house, and its site could have been given by a local 'senator' as in other Gallic towns. It is dated by sealed late Roman coins (giving a *terminus post quem*, a date after which the church could have been built) and by a funerary inscription of AD 347. In a later phase it acquired a polygonal apse, a type with a long history in central and western Gaul.[5]

Poets, priests and archaeologists: some problems of sources

Standing churches of the fourth to seventh centuries are rare in western Europe outside Italy, and their dates have often been the subject of controversy. St Bertrand and the *Basilica Joviana*, one known from its excavated ground plan the other only from literary sources, illustrate the sorts of fragmentary data we have to use. Both types of source present problems, and we shall need to consider what these are.

Literary descriptions of churches can be by contemporaries like Prudentius, Sidonius or Fortunatus, or by later antiquarian writers, describing buildings since demolished. The church of St Martin at Autun, built by Queen Brunehaut about 600, was destroyed at the

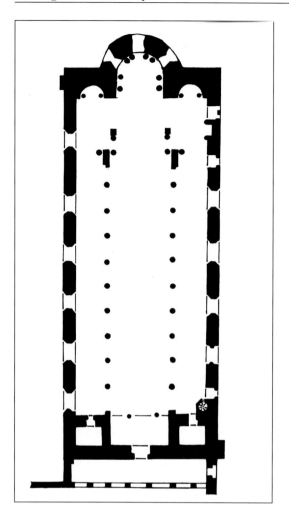

23 *Church of St Martin, Autun (Saône et Loire). From a plan of 1658 (after Sapin 1986, fig 88). The church was demolished during the French Revolution*

French Revolution, but two early plans and three descriptions written between 1647 and 1740 enabled Jean Hubert and Christian Sapin to describe it in some detail. The usual reason for a literary account of a church by a contemporary is praise of the bishop or abbot who built it. Sidonius began his description of the new cathedral of St Jean at Lyon by saying that all could here admire the work of Bishop Patiens (c.449–91). Its Eastern apse has been found in excavation, and Sidonius's poem adds details such as the use of polychrome marbles, the window glass, the Aquitanian marble pillars of the external atrium, and the ceiling of gilded timber. The description is clear, particularly to anyone who has seen the luminous interiors of surviving churches of this date in Rome or Ravenna. There are, however, limits to the information we can draw from it. We are dealing with a literary tradition which valued erudite reference to approved literary models above mere originality, and phrases and images may be borrowed from earlier poems on the same theme — though common sense suggests that what the writer describes corresponds to what was actually there. Moreover, the vocabulary is determined not by the needs of architectural historians but by those of metre and assonance, so that when we come across an unusual word it may be little use looking up its precise meaning in a dictionary of late Latin.[6]

One interesting feature of Sidonius's description is that he is not so much concerned with exact architectural description as with the play of light over its surfaces — the dawn Mediterranean light on its west front, the pale sunlight of the interior playing on the tawny gold of the ceiling (probably of coffered wood), the light from the green glass on the marble floor, all reflecting the light of Christ, which was the light of the world. We may be seeing a new aesthetic here, one which preferred pillars of variously coloured marbles, red, green, dark grey, blue or white, to the solid uniform columns of classical antiquity. The choice of columns was often limited by what was available for salvage from older buildings, but the polychromatic interiors of the Poitiers baptistery, St Martin d'Autun or the crypt at Jouarre, could reflect deliberate choice.

Our other main source of information, that of excavated churches, has expanded radically in recent years, particularly in France and Germany. The problems of archaeological evidence are much more mundane than those of literary sources. One is that of dating excavated structures. Churches by their nature usually lack the occupation deposits found in secular buildings, and what levels do exist have usually been badly cut up by burials. In addition, the impoverished material culture of post-Roman times means that sealed coins and pottery are rare, save for residual Roman material which can only provide a *terminus post quem*. A fourth-century coin only shows that the floor which seals it is of later date than the coin; it does not prove that the building is late Roman. With modern excavation and recording techniques this problem can sometimes be overcome. At Lyon, a late phase of the cathedral baptistery was dated by a coin of the Burgundian king Gundobad (473–56) in the fill of a water pipe trench and the second church of St Just by a sequence of coins, the latest an issue of Gundobad of 506–10.[7]

Sometimes a church or its cemetery will contain dated tombstones, and these can show when a church was in use. At Vienne, those from the church of Saints Gervasius and Protasius are all of fifth-century type, the earliest from the church of St Pierre of AD 483 and from St Sévéré of 511, whilst the earliest dated tombstone from the funerary basilica of St Lawrence at Choulans in Lyon is of AD 599. A tombstone can, of course, also be centuries later than the church itself. Also, fashions change, even in tombstones, and the dated inscriptions may belong only to one phase of the church's history. Another problem is the use of historical evidence of variable reliability or relevance to date excavated structures. Older literature often identified Roman structures under a church as those of a pagan temple 'no doubt' destroyed by early Christians and replaced by a predecessor of the existing church. This model, which gives the church an impressive degree of antiquity and seniority, derives from a comment by Sulpicius Severus, taken out of context, about St Martin replacing demolished pagan temples with Christian churches. At other times an antiquary, often in France or Spain a cleric, filled with commendable local *pietas*, may seek to identify the scanty remains of an excavated church with that recorded as having been built by an early saint or bishop rather than with some later rebuild. The common factor is the difficulty of marrying together the historical and archaeological evidence for a site and a temptation to interpret the latter subjectively in terms of the former.[8]

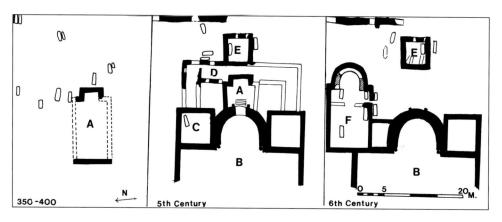

24   *Vienne (Isère). Development of church of St Pierre, originally the basilica of the Holy Apostles, fourth to sixth centuries (after Jannet-Vallat 1986)*

The great church in the city: urban basilicas in the fifth and sixth centuries

In recent years our understanding of early Christian architecture in France has been transformed by the excavation of major urban churches in Paris, Lyon, Vienne, Rouen, Geneva, Grenoble and elsewhere, notably by J.F. Reynaud and his colleagues in the Rhône Valley. Our knowledge of major fifth-century basilicas is still limited. Only the apse of bishop Patiens basilica at Lyon has been excavated, though it is displayed, with other parts of the cathedral complex, in an 'archaeological park'. At Vienne, bishop Mamertius's funerary basilica of the Holy Apostles (later St Pierre) of c.475 partly survives, now used as a museum of Roman sculptures and inscriptions. The apse was flanked by two square eastward projecting chapels or vestries, a plan-type which can be paralleled in fifth-century churches across the Mediterranean as far as the coastlands of Asia Minor. The dedication echoes both Constantine's funerary basilica in Constantinople and St Ambrose's church of the Holy Apostles in Milan. East of the Vienne basilica, an earlier mausoleum had been incorporated in a colonnaded precinct recalling the similar treatment 'of the martyrium shrine of St Just in Lyon and the Anastasius martyrium precinct of c.426 at Salona (Croatia). The other excavated fifth-century church at Vienne was the martyrial basilica of St Ferreol. It was an aisled basilica with an eastern apse. The masonry of the apse is impressive, with a solid foundation of coursed rubble 1.3m deep, an offset of massive re-used masonry blocks above this, and walling of *opus mixtum*, with tile bonding courses. Not only were architects and masons in the Rhône valley still able to draw on plan-types of pan- Mediterranean range, but they were still able to build in a distinctive and solid late Roman style.[9]

About 382–3 bishop Justus of Lyon resigned his see and retired to Palestine where he became a monk. At his death his body was brought back to Lyon and buried in the cemetery near the tomb of his predecessor, St Irenaeus. Here, one of his successors built a church dedicated to the Maccabees which later took the name of St Just. The sequence

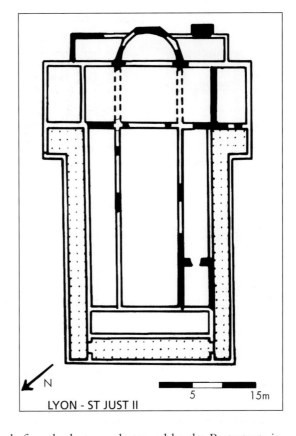

25   *Lyon (Rhône). The sixth-century
      basilica of St Just (after Reynaud
      1986). The porticos surrounding
      the nave are stippled*

LYON - ST JUST II

N

5   15m

of five churches built over his grave, before the last was destroyed by the Protestants in 1562, has been excavated by J.F. Reynaud. The first, St Just I, is not known in detail, save that it had a large rectangular nave and an eastern apse. North-east of it was the first mausoleum or martyrium of St Justus. This was square, with a broad eastern apse and an ambulatory on the other three sides, and can be paralleled at St Pierre, Vienne, and at Salona, whilst the burial apse recalls those in the transepts of the church of the Holy Apostles at Milan. In the early sixth century (the latest sealed coin prior to the rebuilding was of Gundobad of AD 506–10), the martyrium was demolished and the body of St Justus translated to a new basilica. The nave remained the same size, but the east end of St Just II was more elaborate, with a long cross-transept and eastern apse. The central liturgical area, in the apse and square crossing bay, was flanked by six vestries or sacristies, two in each transept arm and two eastern transeptal vestries flanking the apse. This can be paralleled among the great churches of Rome and north Italy, as in Milan at St Ambrose's cathedral of St Tecla, and in Rome at S. Maria Maggiore (432–40) and Old St Peters. These were seminal buildings whose influence was long lasting, and the difference in date in no way implies that St Just II was old fashioned or out of date.[10]

One pair of transeptal vestries may have served as *prothesis* and *diaconicon*, the former for the storage of the elements of the Mass, the *diaconicon* for the reception of offerings from the faithful, and as a vestry and robing room for the clergy. A story of Sulpicius Severus depicts St Martin before a service in one of a pair of transeptal vestries, with his clergy in

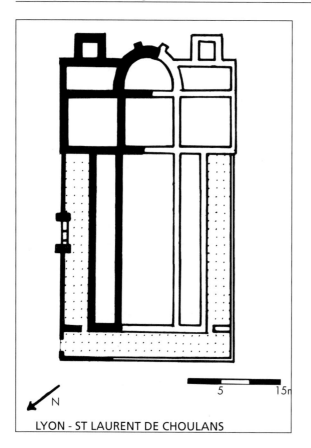

26 *Lyon (Rhône). Church of St Laurent de Choulans, built c.590 (after Reynaud 1986). The porticos surrounding the nave are stippled*

LYON - ST LAURENT DE CHOULANS

the other. The inner chambers flanking the apse, reached from the transept areas, may have served for the safekeeping of valuables and relics (Gregory of Tours had a cupboard containing many relics, locked with a key which he kept on his person). They may also have housed the book cupboards and archives (one of the original functions of the *diaconicon*). These clergy rooms may reflect more complex functions and the growing numbers of clergy, but is a quite distinct line of development from later architectural elaborations of chancel areas with ambulatories and radiating chapels, designed for liturgical processions or the circulation of pilgrims.[11]

St Laurent de Choulans, whose remains can be seen under a motorway flyover at Lyon, was a funerary church crowded with rectangular and trapezoid sarcophagi (the latter a type absent from St Just). The earliest dated tombstone is of 599, and St Laurent shows how the architectural tradition of St Just continued until the end of the sixth century. Its plan is similar, with a rectangular nave flanked on three sides by colonnaded porticos which would have increased the area available for burials. It has a tripartite cross-transept, like St Tecla or St Just, with the crossing probably roofed at a higher level than the flanking arms. A seventeenth-century drawing shows that the eastern apse was polygonal above its foundations. It was flanked by a pair of eastern transeptal vestries like St Just, but with two additional projecting square sacristies.[12]

Baptisteries and bishops

Ever since its foundation by Greek settlers from Phocea in Asia Minor about 600 BC Marseille had occupied a distinctive and often anomalous position among the cities of Gaul. Founded because of its superb natural harbour, not because of its rocky and not very fertile hinterland, its territory in ancient times was small, despite its economic and social importance. In the fifth and sixth centuries, Marseille and Gallic trade were almost synonymous and the city played a large role (perhaps too large) in Henri Pirenne's survey of the Merovingian economy. At this time Marseille was a major trading city, with a busy waterfront, striking coins in all three metals, and a major entrepot for eastern goods such as papyrus, luxury cloth, spices and fine wines. In political and religious terms, its pre-eminence was less marked. Its rival and neighbour, the former Imperial capital of Arles, claimed the religious Primacy of Gaul, backed up by the Imperial government at Ravenna. This claim was vigorously opposed by Proculus, bishop of Marseille (c.382–428). These circumstances may explain the size and splendour of the cathedral baptistery at Marseille, probably built by Proculus.[13]

Like most Gallic baptisteries it was octagonal, like S. Aquilino in Milan, or St Ambrose's baptistery there. For Ambrose, eight was the numerical symbol for re-birth and resurrection. The world had begun on the eighth day, after seven days of creation, and Christ had risen from the dead on the eighth day of his passion. The form was fitting for a baptistery or a Christian mausoleum, but there were also sound structural reasons, and Ambrose's exergesis reflected extant octagonal buildings rather than the baptisteries reflecting Ambrosian number symbolism. The fourth-century villa at Carignan in the Ardennes had a large octagonal *laconicum* or sweating room with corner apses, just like the Gallic baptisteries, and the architectural origins of the latter lay as much in such secular buildings as in religious architecture.[14]

Unlike the Milan structures, octagonal inside and out, Gallic baptisteries are usually an octagon inscribed in a square. A mausoleum is usually free standing, but a baptistery, like a rotunda in a bath house complex, has to be integrated with disrobing rooms, vestries for the clergy, housing for altars, and other spaces. Such rooms, known from excavation at Aix-en-Provence and Marseille, can be more readily integrated with an externally square form. Indeed, early baptisteries like the fourth-century one at Trier were square or rectangular, and this remained the norm in areas like Africa. The octagon or octagon-in-square form was a regional type.

The baptistery at Marseille, the largest in France, was still intact in the sixteenth century, identified by antiquaries as a Temple of Diana. Pillaged for its marbles, only one of its four tall corner niches still stood when the building was re-discovered (and finally demolished) in the 1850s, during the rebuilding of the cathedral. A fraction under 23m square, its interior was not an open dome but its roof was carried on an octagon of re-used Corinthian columns. Its interior, and rooms to the south, were carpeted with spreads of patterned mosaic like those of north Italy or Istria. The internal octagon of columns recalls the mausoleum of S. Costanza in Rome, and they recur in other Gallic baptisteries, as at Riez and Aix-en-Provence. Riez (Alpes-de-Haute Provence) is a much smaller cube like building (8.25m by 9.25m) with a low pyramidal roof, octagonal within, with an apse recessed into

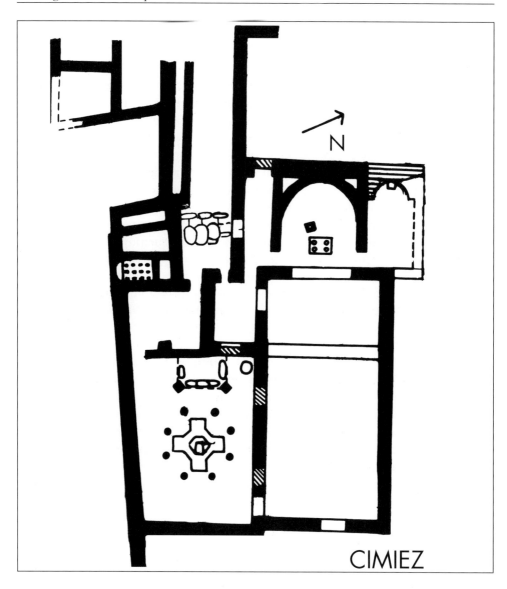

27   Cimiez (Alpes-Maritimes), the cathedral and baptistery (after Andre Blanc)

each corner. Eight columns of re-used grey-blue granite form an octagonal central space.[15]

At Aix-en-Provence (Bouches du Rhône) the baptistery, probably of the end of the fifth century, is similar to Riez, though larger (c.15m square). It shows a further move away from the octagonal plan type. Whereas Riez was an octagon in a square, Aix was planned in terms of a square. The eight central columns are set around a square space, and the four angle niches which convert the interior into an octagon may even be an afterthought. It stood originally at one end of a large piazza in front of the cathedral, once the main forum of the Roman city. At Valence (Drôme), Frejus (Var) and at Porec (Parezo) in Istria, baptisteries similarly stood west of the cathedral, separated from it by a space which probably held a similar atrium or piazza. These would be filled on the great feasts of the Church with crowds of townsfolk and country people, particularly at Easter, the usual date for baptism. Church councils forbade local magnates and their estate clergy from celebrating Easter and the other great feasts at their villa churches. They must celebrate them in the city with the bishop. How effective this was in maintaining Easter as a paramount urban baptismal festival is uncertain. Baptism was often postponed until late in life, and life itself could be short and uncertain. Baptism of the sick was often necessary as a matter of urgency, and by the late fourth century rural baptisteries were becoming more common. The withdrawal of magnates from urban life to their rural estates may have been threatening to erode the status and authority of the bishop as leader of the civitas and its people, much as it had earlier helped to undermine the role of the Gallo-Roman city. In parts of Spain the separation of the city and its territory as a result of this internal emigration may have had a severe effect on the life of the towns. The baptistery and atrium, by providing a stage for the celebration of the great Christian festivals within the city, may have helped to maintain the role of the city and that of its bishop, though in the longer term the solution to maintaining that role was the provision of an effective network of rural pastoral care.[16]

At Valence, the alignment of early churches known under the south facade of the present cathedral comprise, from west to east, the cruciform baptistery of St Stephen, an aisled basilica with an eastern apse, and the polygonal rotunda of Notre Dame de la Ronde. Bishop St Apollinaris of Valence built *intra muros* — within the Augustan walls — two churches, and invited his brother, bishop St Avitus of Vienne (490–518) to the consecration of one of these. The baptistery is in a different architectural tradition to those of Provence. It was an equal armed cross with eastward facing apses in three of its arms and a tiny narthex and porch in the west arm. Its floor was of decorated mosaic. The short, stumpy plan is like that of a series of fifth-century martyr churches in north Italy. That at Vicenza is an exact contemporary of Valence. A similar cruciform but centrally planned baptistery is now known from Grenoble.[17]

The baptisteries, like the urban basilicas, show that the cities of southern Gaul were in touch with the architectural traditions of Italy and the Mediterranean throughout the fifth and sixth centuries, with access to stonemasons, architects, mosaic workers and mural painters. This raises the questions of to what extent similar baptisteries existed in other parts of Gaul, and what provision there was for baptism at this time outside the cities.

The baptistery of St Jean at Poitiers still stands, though in an altered state. There has been controversy about its date, but in its first, probably fourth century, form, as recovered by the archaeologist-priest Camille de la Croix in 1890–7, it comprised a series of successive rooms and halls, like a Roman bath building. It may date from before the fifth-century north Italian / south Gaulish tradition of rotunda baptisteries had spread north. A simple rectangular block, as reconstructed in plan it had three symmetrical doorways facing on to a street to the west. The centre door led to a vestibule, the side doors to a pair of square flanking rooms, perhaps disrobing rooms for men and women baptismal candidates. The centre of the building was a large rectangular hall, and beyond was a second similar hall housing the octagonal baptismal piscina. A stone and tile conduit

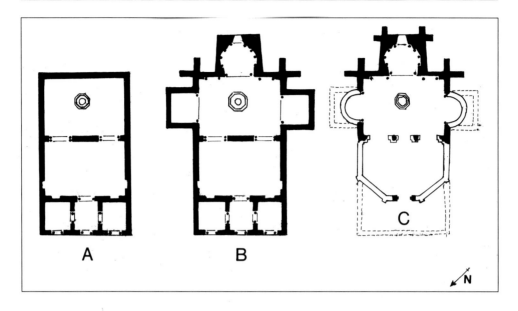

28   *Poitiers (Vienne). Development of the baptistery of St Jean (a) fourth century, (b) sixth century (c) tenth century*

supplied the baptistery from a Roman aqueduct to the west, and a tile drain took waste water away to a deep sump. These hydraulics again argue for a late Roman date. By the sixth century, Gregory of Tours could regard similar hydraulics in a baptistery as miraculous. The first phase masonry, where it survives, is of small, rather irregular coursed blocks.[18]

Later, the baptistery was re-modelled to a cruciform plan with square projections each side of the baptismal hall, and an eastern apse-like feature holding an altar, perhaps with relics of John the Baptist, as in other cathedral baptisteries. The masonry is of larger, neatly squared ashlar blocks, like those in early Roman buildings in Poitou, and is probably re-used. In its second phase, St Jean falls into place with other late fifth–sixth century cruciform baptisteries, as at Valence or Grenoble. At some stage it suffered a fire which made some rebuilding necessary. The remarkable internal and external decoration may not therefore be all of the same phase.[19]

The church of St John the Baptist at Nantes was demolished in the fifteenth century when the adjacent cathedral was built. Excavation around the bishop's palace before the First World War revealed a large late Roman building, overlying one demolished when the fourth-century town walls were built. The late Roman building contained two octagonal baptismal pools at different levels. Durville thought these to be of the fourth and the sixth centuries. The nature of the building and its relationship to the medieval church of St Jean remain uncertain, though its plan has similarities to the first phase of the Poitiers baptistery. Fresh excavation would be needed to put the site into context.[20]

By the end of the fourth century baptism was not confined to the urban cathedrals. Archaeologically baptisteries can sometimes be difficult to distinguish, even in a Christian

29   Poitiers, baptistery of St Jean from the east. Photograph J.K.K.

context, from other forms of ritual ablution, or even from fountains and water tanks, but rural baptisteries are known; from the fort at Richborough in Kent, which probably ranked as a vicus; from the rural vicus of Civaux (Vienne); from the monastery of Lerins; from a rural site at Port-Bail in Normandy; and possibly from villas at Chedworth in Gloucestershire and Primuliacum in Gascony, the latter from literary sources. These are smaller and simpler than the urban baptisteries. Richborough, Civaux and Port-Bail all have six-sided baptismal basins for reasons of scale. The evidence from Chedworth centres on re-use of an octagonal basin fed by a natural spring.[21]

Miro opere fabricatum: Merovingian church building in western Gaul

Some time before its replacement by a Romanesque cathedral, a chronicler at Nantes described that built centuries before by bishop Eumerius (533–48) and completed by his son and successor bishop Felix (549–82):

> Bishop Felix put in the cathedral of Nantes marble altars, the like of which are not to be found even in Rome. He had made very many columns, with sculptured capitals of divers marbles, for supporting the arches, and on each of

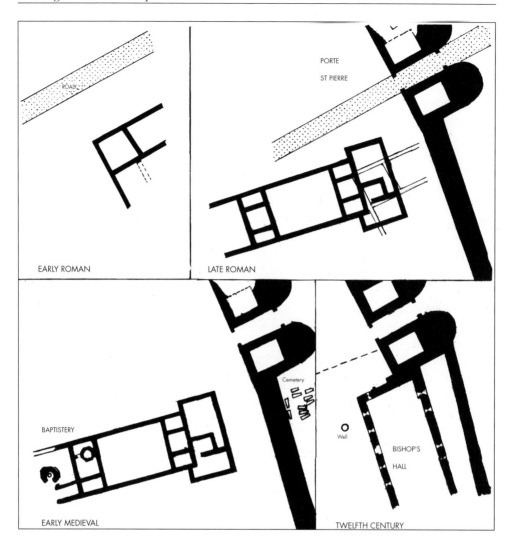

30   Nantes (Loire-Maritime). Roman and early medieval development of the area inside the Porte St Pierre, immediately north of the cathedral (after Durville)

the two walls were mosaics of marvellous workmanship and, on the arcades, flowers in stucco distinguished by a variety of colours, and before the altars were crowns of gold and silver vases . . . and the pavement was marvellously made of divers marbles.[22]

A poem by Fortunatus describing the same cathedral contains the usual mixture of important detail and frustrating poetic diction. The church had an aisled nave of great height with a central tower, square at the base but circular and internally arcaded above, and with mosaics or paintings which shimmered in the light below a lead dome. The east end was cruciform with a high altar dedicated to St Peter and St Paul and transept chapels. That on the south had altars to St Hilary and St Martin, the north chapel one of the martyr St Ferreolus. In the crossing a marble column supported a silver cross. It is uncertain whether the east end was cruciform or simply ended in three apses, like St Martin d' Autun, but Madame de Viellard-Troiekouroff has made the sensible point that the transepts would be structurally necessary to support the thrust of the tower. The central arcaded space and the silver cross on its marble column recall St Ambrose's *Basilica Apostolorum* in Milan. This was cruciform, with transeptal side wings opening to the crossing through triple arches. In the centre of the crossing were relics of the Apostles in a silver shrine brought from Constantinople. Ambrose's basilica was based on Constantine's *Aposteleoin* in Constantinople, and was itself the model for other north Italian churches like the fifth-century cathedral of Pavia, the *ecclesia maior*. Nantes, apart from its links along the western seaways, was in touch with developments in north Italy and Milan and, through them, with the wider Mediterranean world.[23]

However rich the interiors of early Christian churches, their exteriors were usually austerely plain, perhaps in deliberate contrast to the luminous interiors. However, when the baptistery at Poitiers was remodelled in the sixth or early seventh century, both interior and exterior were given elaborate decoration. The arcaded interior of the eastern apse and the triple arcade fronting it have columns of a variety of marbles, with freshly carved capitals of St Béat marble from the Pyrenees of a series found across western Gaul from Gascony to Paris and the Seine valley. The use of polychrome columns in arcading around a triple apse recalls the east end of the now demolished church of Saint Martin at Autun, built by Queen Brunehaut and bishop Syagrius in 589–601, as known from early plans and descriptions. The external decoration is more unusual. Flat pilasters with crude foliage capitals rest on a string course, whilst above are a series of semi-circular or triangular decorative panels in stone or brick with radiating flower-like patterns. The whole effect is somewhat reminiscent of children's building bricks. In a later (probably tenth-century) phase, the western parts of the original structure were demolished and replaced by a five-sided western narthex opening to the baptismal chamber through a trio of tall Romanesque arches.[24]

Eygun noted parallels for the external decoration at Mazerolles near Poitiers, a church re-founded in the seventh century by bishop Ansoald for an Irish *peregrinus*, Romanus. Other evidence of date comes from around Nantes. Fragments of the cathedral described by the *Chronicle of Nantes* and by Fortunatus, recovered in excavation, include sculptured capitals and impost blocks of St Béat marble and column fragments of variously coloured marble, some spirally fluted. It contains, however, nothing matching the exterior of the Poitiers baptistery, suggesting that this must be later than the mid-sixth century. Fragments in this latter style are, however, known from the abbey of Vertou outside Nantes, founded by St Martin of Vertou before his death in 601, agreeing with the evidence from Mazerolles.[25]

About 847–50, with the Vikings encamped around Nantes, the monks of St-Martin-de-Vertou fled with the bones of St Martin to St Jouin des Marnes (Deux-Sevres), where the early church was excavated by Dom. Coquet. Vertou became a cell of St Jouin, and when the twelfth-century church there was demolished in 1876 fragments from an earlier one were found. These included a series of the moulded decorative bricks known from other churches in the Nantes area with classical and biblical motifs, including Adam and Eve, chi-rho monograms and vine scroll. There are also plain stepped forms and lozenges in brick, matching some of those used externally on the Poitiers baptistery, and square tiles with acanthus decoration, like the capitals of the pilasters there. The stone sculpture, all of local white limestone, includes copies of the marble St Béat series and triangular panels with marigold and 'sunburst' motifs, again like those at Poitiers, and a pair of doves flanking a chalice. They may not be from external decoration (Costa thought they might be from an ambo), but form and decoration link them to Poitiers. A fragment of a Roman sculptured sarcophagus, unique in the region, may be from the original shrine of St Martin.[26]

There is another large collection of terra cotta plaques from the church of the fourth-century bishop St Similien at Nantes. Gregory relates a miracle involving his church set in the time of Clovis (481–511). When its fifteenth-century successor was demolished in 1894, an earlier church with rectangular nave and western apse, perhaps of the ninth or tenth century, was found. There were sculptured fragments and over fifty decorated bricks with sea monsters, flying victories, hunting scenes with parallels in provincial Roman art, vine and plant scrolls. Many examples of each kind occur, but since they are so little abraded they cannot have been floor tiles. Possibly they formed decorative friezes. Some, in the form of long, narrow voussoirs, have tall monogram-crosses and figures of a bishop, presumably St Similien. These must be from some arcaded structure, possibly a shrine. They presumably pre-date the church found in excavation.[27]

The stones of heaven and earth: building materials in Post Roman Gaul

The decorative use of ornamental brick at Nantes and Poitiers shows how a building material still used in Rome for structural load bearing walls had in Gaul become merely an artistic craft. Normal masonry construction, however, was still in late Roman tradition, either of *petit appareil* — 'little coursed blocks' — or in *opus mixtum*, with bands of tile at intervals in the wall face. The *petit appareil* tends to be untidier than work of the Roman period, with the blocks neither as neatly squared nor as regularly laid. Where large, well-dressed ashlar occurs, as in parts of the Poitiers baptistery, or massive squared blocks, as at St Ferreol in Vienne or in St Martin d'Autun, it was probably re-used from some earlier Roman building. *Opus mixtum* was widely used throughout the later Roman Empire, both east and west. We have already met it in the Gallic town walls, and its continued use in post Roman Gaul calls for no particular comment. In Carolingian times (and perhaps earlier) arches were often turned in *opus mixtum* with alternate bands of brick and stone voussoirs. Whether builders realised that this hastened the setting of the mortar by allowing its water content to escape more rapidly or whether it was simply used for decorative effect is not clear.[28]

Literary sources often stress the floors of shining marble, and there was plenty of Roman marble available for re-use. At times the floor must have been largely of stone tomb-slabs with inset marble panels carrying the funerary inscriptions. Mortar floors, known from excavation, were probably bedding for mosaics or stone flagging rather than finished surfaces. Gregory of Tours tells of a floor of *opus signinum*, a durable and waterproof aggregate of crushed brick and mortar, in a church near Aire-sur-l'Adour (Landes). Three priests were buried in the church under a floor 'of lime and crushed bricks, hard as the hardest stone', but this had worn through or subsided, exposing the tombs. Gregory implies that this was miraculous, but the building was evidently old and in need of repair. Perhaps by that time such floors were uncommon enough to merit special comment. *Opus signinum* floors are also known from excavation in seventh-century monasteries at Monkwearmouth and Jarrow in Northumbria where Benedict Biscop, once a monk of Lerins, had acquired stonemasons and glassmakers from Gaul, and at Nivelles in Belgium. In both cases, however, most of the floors are of white concrete, with a surface layer of pink brick- aggregate.[29]

Window glass was common, though its availability depended on that of skilled glassmakers. Sidonius describes the light shining through the green and sapphire glass of bishop Patiens' basilica at Lyon, and Gregory of Tours explains that the rural church built by bishop Eustocius at Yzeures in Touraine in 443–60 had the 'usual' glass windows — though a thief managed to steal them from their wooden frames, melt them down, and sell the cullet to a merchant. Other thieves broke into St Martin's basilica at Tours by breaking the glass of an apse window. Even the little seventh-century village church at Hordain near Douai had glass windows. However, when bishop Ruricus of Limoges was building a church in his cathedral city soon after 485, he had to write to a fellow bishop asking him to send a *vitrarius* for its windows, just as Benedict Biscop had to do in Northumbria. Patronage of such craftsmen may have been confined to bishops and other churchmen, and glass workers were perhaps more readily available in major episcopal centres.[30]

This is not the place for a discussion of Merovingian sculpture and decorative arts. We have noted the use of relief panels of terra cotta and of cut and shaped brick for wall decoration, and both wall mosaics (largely an invention of the late Empire) and mural paintings are well attested. The wife of bishop Namatius of Clermont-Ferrand sat in the church of St Stephen with a book on her lap, reading to the painters stories 'of events long ago' which she wanted illustrated on the walls. A visitor seeing an elderly lady in black mistook her for a beggar, and gave her some bread. Stucco flowers, painted in bright colours, are known from the ninth-century description of the cathedral at Nantes, though like the surviving stucco work in St Laurent at Grenoble they could have been of Carolingian date. For Gregory of Tours, however, the most noteworthy feature of the churches were their burial crypts and the miraculous tombs they contained. Sometimes these had sarcophagi of 'Parian' marble, though it is not always clear whether they were late Roman sarcophagi, like those at Arles, or post Roman sculptured sarcophagi of the 'Visigothic' or 'south-west Gallic' school.[31]

Of graves and epitaphs

The 'south-west Gallic' sarcophagi are among the most remarkable products of post Roman Gaul. At a time when the economic life of Gaul is sometimes thought to have largely reverted to a subsistence economy, or to trade in luxury goods for an élite, well over two hundred sarcophagi, freshly sculptured of marble from St Béat and from other Pyrenean quarries, were traded over a wide area of southern Gaul, between the Loire and

31 *Christian inscription of AD 405, found in a grave in the cemetery of the church of St Ausone, Angoulême, (Charente), placed vertically behind the head of the corpse. 'Basilius was buried on Sunday, January 22, in the year after the sixth consulship of Honorius'. Presumably news of the consul for the new year had not yet reached the city (after Le Blant). N.R. 277. C.I.L. XIII, 1118*

the Rhône. Some have figure sculpture derived from late Roman sarcophagi like those from Arles and Marseille, but most are in a fresh and distinctive style with panels of vine scroll, ivy branches or acanthus, canthari (decorative urns), chi-rho monograms (sometimes in a wreath), circular rosettes, strigil decoration, and with miniature pillars or pilasters dividing the zones of decoration. Discussion of this series has centred on two problems — their date and historical context, and the sources of their distinctive style of decoration. They have been seen as associated with the fifth-century Visigothic kingdom of Toulouse; as the memorials of the sixth-century contemporaries of Gregory of Tours; or as products of a 'seventh-century Renaissance' associated with the court of Dagobert I. The latter view was influenced by a few sarcophagi associated with seventh or early eighth-century bishops, but these were a result of the well attested practice of re-using earlier sarcophagi for the translation of the bodies of saints. What follows is not intended as a full discussion of these problems but only as a summary of our present state of knowledge.[32]

The late Roman sculptured sarcophagi of Marseille are less well known than those of Arles because the former were mostly broken up during the French Revolution and only remnants survive. Parallel with them were a series of marble altar tables with decorative sculpture around their raised borders. Ward Perkins emphasised the links between the Massiliot sarcophagi and altars and the beginnings of the south-west Gallic school, and this link has now been strengthened by the discovery of a Massiliot type altar with vinescroll decoration and an inscription at St Bertrand-de-Comminges, near the source of the St Béat marble. Other sources of inspiration can also be suggested. The distinctive shape of the south-west Gallic sarcophagi, with sloping slides and roof shaped lid with inward sloping gables, can be paralleled in late Roman silver caskets like the Casket of Projecta in the British Museum (some of the rosettes on the sarcophagi can also best be

32   Christian inscription of fourth-century type, from the church of Valcabrère, St Bertrand de Comminges (Haute-Garonne). '(The memorial) of Severinus, In Peace, who was buried on the 15th of February (? In the consulship of Valerius)'. The inscription is heavily trimmed and incomplete (drawing - the author). N.R. 296. C.I.L. XIII, 300

paralleled on late Roman silver). There are also striking links between the art of the sarcophagi and that of the fifth-century mosaics of the luxury villas of Aquitaine.[33]

The possible link with aristocratic villa owners is an important one, for much late Roman industry was organized through the great landowners and their estates. The initiative in opening the quarries, and the first market for their products, may have come from the villa owners. For ease of transport and to prevent accidental damage in transit, sarcophagi in the ancient world were roughed out at the quarry and shipped to the marble workshop for decoration and finishing. The initial workshop, in Toulouse, also produced sarcophagi of late classical type, with Christ and the Apostles in a columned arcade, but the master mason soon devised an original and distinctive type. This was inspired by late-Roman silverware (so pre-figuring the American usage 'casket'), by the mosaics of its luxury villas, and perhaps by the vernacular art of the region. The low relief style may be due to workshop technique. Motifs like the plant scrolls and rosettes are often repetitive, with near-identical patterns recurring on a series of sarcophagi or even as a 'repeating pattern' in a series of panels on the same sarcophagus. This suggests the use of stencils, like those identified on Anglo-Saxon sculpture. The technique would involve painting or scribing the pattern on the surface of the marble, and then cutting away the low relief areas. Too mechanical an appearance could be avoided by minor variation in the panels before final cutting. From the mason's yard, the finished products could be shipped to the new Christian cemeteries that were rising outside the city walls of southern Gaul. The popularity of these new memorials was so great that in time other workshops opened to serve areas such as Narbonne, Bordeaux or the towns of the Pyrenees (a fragment of an unfinished sculptured sarcophagus is now known from St Bertrand). Some of these drew on new marble quarries near Pau in the western Pyrenees, as scientific analysis of the marbles used has shown.[34]

Parallel with the sarcophagi were the equally remarkable series of sculptured capitals of

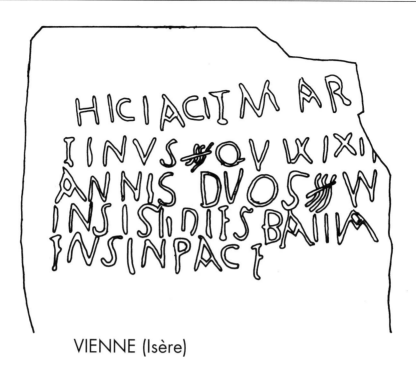

VIENNE (Isère)

33   *Early fifth-century inscription, cemetery of Gervaise and Protasius, Vienne (Isère) 'Here lies*
      Martinus, who lived two years, two months, ? three days (inscription garbled by illiterate
      stonecutter). In peace.' Iacet *is spelt* Iacit, *as on the insular inscriptions (drawing - the author).*
      I.C.G. 422a. C.I.L. XII, 2126

Pyrenean marble, found throughout western Gaul from the Marne to the Pyrenees. The
commerce in marble sarcophagi and capitals was, however, merely the top end of the
market. Sarcophagi were meant to be displayed against the wall of a church (the back is
usually undecorated) or in a crypt. There was also, however, a wide regional trade in
undecorated stone coffins (also referred to as sarcophagi). Sarcophagus quarries are
known both archaeologically and from place names such as Serqueux (Haute-Marne and
Seine-Maritime) or La Roche Taillee ('The rock of dressed stone') at Arcy-sur-Cure
(Yonne). Though little work has been done to relate the stone coffins to their geological
sources, the distribution of, for example, coffins in shelly limestone or red sandstone in
Maine (Mayenne and Sarthe), the similar use of Saintenay oolite from quarries west of
Carentan in western Normandy, or stone from Vergelé (Seine-Maritime) further east
suggest the existence of active local trade.[35]

In southern Gaul, many graves were marked by a horizontal stone slab carrying an
inscription, or with an inset inscribed marble panel. Many of these inscriptions carry a
consular date, the names of the two Roman consuls (or later the single western consul)
who gave their names to the year. These epitaphs are not only a major source of

CAMIAC (Gironde)

34   Early fifth-century inscription, Camiac (Gironde), 'Here lies Peculia in peace', from Gallia *25 (1967), 341*

information on post Roman Gaul, but since some of the memorial formulae used, particularly *Hic Iacet* — 'Here he (or she) lies' — also occur on the British Insular memorial stones, they have the potential of throwing light on the obscure relations between Celtic speaking Britain and continental Europe.

At first, the memorial inscriptions of Christians in the west did not differ greatly from those of their pagan counterparts, but by the early third century phrases like *Receptus ad Deum* or words like *Decessit* and *Dormit* began to appear. Third-century Christian inscriptions are rare in Gaul, and usually of non-local people. There is one from Autun in Greek and from Bordeaux is the memorial of a lady from Trier, of the time of the Gallic Empire, in the form of a Roman altar with a double Christian-pagan epitaph. The alleged memorial of two third-century martyrs from Marseille probably commemorates the victims of a shipwreck.[36]

By about the time of Constantine, a form of Christian epitaph had emerged giving in varying order the name of the deceased, the date of death (the 'heavenly birthday', important for his or her annual commemoration), sometimes the consuls of the year, and a verb such as *decessit* or *depositus*. A few other phrases sometimes occur — *In Pace, Hic Iacet* or *Puer Nomine* ('A Boy by the name of'). The earliest dated Gallic Christian inscription is of this type. Found in the St Irenée-St Just cemetery at Lyon in digging a water pipe trench

35   *Later fifth-century inscription, cemetery of Gervaise and Protasius, Vienne. 'Here lies in peace Leonia, who lived four years and six months.' (drawing - the author). I.C.G. 416 C.I.L. XII, 2120*

in the seventeenth century, it is now lost but carried a date equivalent to AD 334: *Optato et Paulino Consulibus, Kal(endas) Febr(u)aris Depos(itus) Selenioses* – 'In the consulship of Optatus and Paulinus, on the First of February, Selentiosus was buried'. There are similar dated inscriptions from Valcabrere below St-Bertrand-de-Comminges (Haute-Garonne) of 347 and 405; from St Pierre l'Estrier at Autun (378); and from the cemetery of Saint-Ausone at Angoulême (Charente) of AD 405. Undated inscriptions of similar fourth-century type occur at Lyon, Vienne and Valcabrere. A separate group from Angoulême (Charente), Civaux (Vienne) and Rom (Deux-Sèvres) in Aquitania use the formula *Vivas In Deo* ('May he live in God'). All save Civaux are urban, but two others, from St-Croix-du-Mont (Gironde) and St-Cyr-en-Talmondois (Vendée) are probably from villas, matching the literary evidence for Christian chapels on villa estates.[37]

The latest of this fourth-century series dates from AD 405, two years before the

VIENNE　　　　　LLANERFYL

36　　Late fifth-century memorial stones from Vienne (Isère) and Llanerfyl (Powys) (a) 'Here rests
in peace in peace Iniuriosus, who lived four years, nine months and one day. He shall be raised again in
Christ. His mother Euladia had this made'. I.C.G. 414, C.I.L. XII, 2118 (b) 'Here in the
tomb lies Rosteece, the daughter of Paterninus. She lived thirteen years. In Peace'. E.C.M.W. 294

barbarian invasions. It was strongest in Aquitaine. The subsequent early fifth-century
stones, now using the initial memorial formulae like *Hic Iacet*, are mostly from Provence
and the Rhône Valley. If the stone of the Treveran lady buried at Bordeaux in the time of
Postumus (259–67) is genuine (Le Blant thought it a fake), the prolific Rhineland series
of *Hic Iacet* inscriptions may have begun as early as the late third century; her double
epitaph uses both the pagan *Dis Manibus et Memoriae* and the Christian *Hic Iacet*. The close
links between the Imperial cities of Trier and Milan may be enough to explain the spread
of this north Italian formula to the Rhineland and thence, in this isolated case, to
Bordeaux. The *Hic Iacet* formula was certainly current in Italy in the late third and fourth
century. However, within a few years of the sack of Rome in 410, it began to appear at the
head of the text — along with related phrases like *Hic Positus Est, Hic In Pace Quiescit* or *Hic
Requiescit* — as part of a more structured form of epitaph, replacing the more variable order
of the fourth century. It is this use of the phrase as an initial formula, rather than its mere
employment, that marks out the new series.

In southern Gaul the earliest dated example is of AD 422, one of a sequence of six
inscriptions from the St Irenee-St Just cemetery at Lyon.

AD 422　*Hic Requiescit Pascasia Dulcissima Infans* (I.C.G. 53, C. I. L. XIII, 2353)
AD 431　*In Huc Locu Requievit Leucadia* . . . (I.C.G. 44, C. I. L. XIII, 2354)
AD 438　*Hic Iacet Aspasius Aduliscens* . . . (JJ Martin 'Inscriptions Chretiennes Decouverts a
　　　　Lyons' *Bulletin Archaeologique de Comite* 1904, XLI–II; C.I.L. XIII, 11, 207)

37   *Christian symbolism from the tombstone of Peleger, church of Notre Dame d'Outre Gere, Vienne, AD 502. Birds representing the souls of the faithful feed on a vine scroll springing from a* cantharos *or chalice (drawing — the author)*

AD 447 *Hic Iacet Decora Mercurina . . .* (I.C.G.35, C.I.L. XIII, 2355)
AD 448 *Hic Requiescit Innox Infans Vrsus . . .* (I.C.G. 68, C.I.L. XIII, 2356)
AD 449 *Hic Iacet Sanctulus Famulus Dei . . .* (I.C.G. 532, C.I.L.. XIII, 2357)
  (Only the beginning of each text is given)

The next dated inscription, of AD 454, introduces the later fashion for 'four figure' formulae such as *Hic Requiescit Bon(a)e Memoriae* or *Hic Requiescit In Pace*, which are thereafter standard until about 480 when new and longer forms appear.

These fifth-century formulae recur in the Insular memorial stones of western Britain, though there are now enough *Hic Iacet* inscriptions from western Gaul to suggest that the immediate source of the Insular series may have been western Gaul rather than the Rhône Valley. Some Gallic fifth-century memorials have the late vulgar Latin *Hic Iacit* for *Hic Iacet*, as on the Insular stones. The text is usually headed by decoration, often symbolic, of the Eucharist — a cross, chi-rho monogram, or a chalice, from which spring vine scrolls, on whose grapes a pair of doves are feeding — the souls of the faithful feeding upon the True Vine. Sometimes a pair of peacocks, whose flesh was thought to be incorruptible, replace the doves. The increasing elaboration of the texts themselves is best explained by a few dated examples, beginning with one of the *Hic Iacet* inscriptions already cited from Lyon:

> *Hic Iacet Decora Mercurina Qui Vixit Annos XV Obiit XIII Kal Maias Vigelia Pasce*
>   *Calipio V.C. Cons*
> Here lies Decora Mercurina, who lived for 15 years, and died on Easter Eve, the

19th of April, in the consulship of Calipius, *vir clarissimus* (a senatorial title, rather like our 'Right Honourable') and consul (AD 447)

By the following decade the longer 'four figure' formulae had come into fashion:

> *Hic Requiiscit In Pace Constantiola Qui Vixit Annos XX Menses III. Recessit III Kl. Martias P.C. III Leonis*
>
> Here rests in peace Constantiola, who lived for 20 years and 3 months. She died on the 28th of April in the third year after the consulship of Leonius, AD 467
> From an early church and cemetery site at Saint-Romain d'Albon (Drôme)
> N.R. 34, C.I.L. XII, 79

By the 480s a longer initial formula appeared, with was to remain standard (with minor variations) throughout the sixth century and into the seventh:

> *In Hunc Tomulo Requiescit In Pace Bertefrida Innox Honesta Decora Blandautfles Cauta Qui Vixit Annus Polpus Minus VIII Obiet Kal Septebrs Anno LXVI P.C. Basili V.C.C. Ind VIIII*
>
> In this tomb rests in peace Bertefrida, innocent, fair, decorous, charming and modest, who lived for more or less 8 years, and died on the 1st of September in the 66th year after the consulship of that most illustrious man Basil, in the ninth indiction
> AD 606 Luzinay (Isère). I.C.G. 397, C.I.L. XII, 2096

Whilst virtually all stones carry the date of death, only a minority name the year. After the division of the Empire, one of the pair of consuls who gave their name to the year was appointed by the eastern Emperor and one by his western colleague. It is the latter whose name appears on the inscriptions. Even so the system was cumbrous and clumsy. Barbarian invasions, usurpers (who often appointed their own consuls), diplomatic ruptures between east and west, and the simple shortage of Roman senators able to bear the expense of the consulship, meant that there were frequent gaps in the *fastes* (list of consuls), and it was often necessary to date an inscription to the year *after* the consulship of someone. The tombstone of Constantiola is an early example of this. The western Emperor Libius Severus had died in August 465, and his successor Anthemius was not appointed until April 2nd 467. In the absence of an emperor no consul could be appointed. Her family could only record her death as in 'the third year after the consulship of Leonius'. At this date this was still exceptional and tombstones continued to carry the consul's name until Justinian effectively abolished the consulship in 541. Thereafter, some areas chose to use the increasingly archaic and irrelevant post-consular dating system for another seventy years ('sixty-six years after the consulship of Basil'), whilst to add to the confusion Lyon and Vienne, always rivals, chose different 'final' consuls as their baseline. Eventually, this redundant system gave way to more relevant and resounding dating systems: 'In the twelfth year of the reign of our most Glorious King, our lord Chlodovech'.[38]

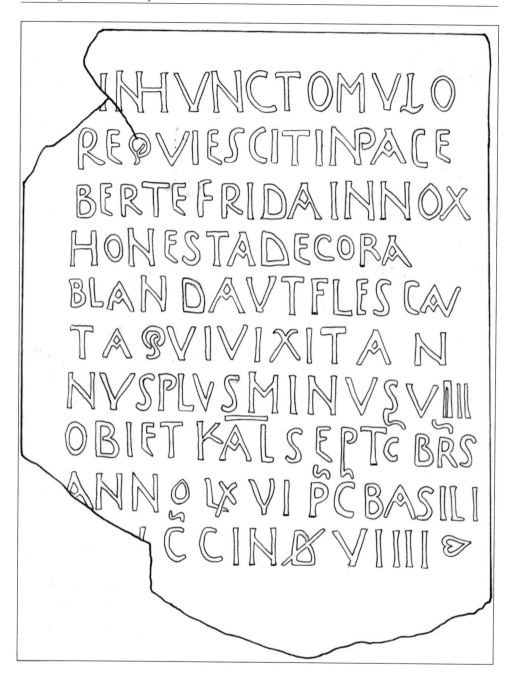

38   *Memorial of Bertefrida from church of St Germanus, Luzinay (Isère), AD 606. For text and translation see p.109. I.C.G. 397, C.I.L. XII, 2096 (drawing — the author)*

39   Some Spanish sixth-century memorial stones. They use the formula Famulus Dei (Slave of God) and are dated by the Spanish era. (1) Octavius, Seville AD 532 (2) Bulgaricus, Arcos de la Frontera (Prov. Cadiz), AD 562 (3) Simplicius, Mertola (Portugal) AD 537 (4) Britto, a priest, Mertola AD 546 (after Vives)

6. The world turned upside down: the Christianisation of the Gallic countryside

Someone, whether Gentile or Christian, whether man or woman, whether boy or girl, whether slave or free, has stolen from me, Annianus son of Matutina, six silver coins from my purse. You, lady Goddess, are to exact them from him.

B.Cunliffe (ed) *The Temple of Sulis Minerva at Bath, Vol 2. The Finds from the Sacred Spring* (1988), no 98, p.232

Sanctuary and stage: rural shrines and magnate display

We do not know exactly where or when in the late Roman Empire the word *paganus*, a rustic who lived in a *pagus* or country district rather than in town, came to mean a non-Christian, but it would fit well with the time of Valentinian and Theodosius, when Martin of Tours and bishops like him set out from their urban bases to evangelise the *pagenses* of the surrounding countryside.

Even today, the Gallo-Roman pagan sanctuaries are among the most striking field monuments of the French countryside. Their ruins, in finely dressed Roman masonry, usually include, when fully excavated, a temple in a spacious *temenos* or precinct; a forum or market square; sometimes a circular tholos-like building; large public baths; a theatre; and a varying number of shops and houses. The monumentality of these complexes, at times the size of a small town, is emphasised by their symmetrical layout and architecturally imposing buildings, carefully aligned in their landscape for maximum visual effect. They are often prolific in finds, with large numbers of coins and small objects; bronze statues and statuettes of gods and animals; masks in repoussé bronze and fragments of votive inscriptions. Some have produced temple treasures like that from Berthouville (Eure), with over ninety silver and silver-gilt vessels, many with dedications to Mercury Canetonensis, Berthouville being the Roman *Cenetorum*. Sanxay (Vienne) has produced metalworking debris and enamel crucibles, suggesting the production of enamelled trinkets for sale to pilgrims or to local people visiting the market. The role of such sites in rural society must have extended beyond the purely religious, combining the roles of pilgrimage centre, fair and market venues and probably centres of local administration. An inscription from Vendoeuvre-en-Brenne (Indre) lists its buildings — the temple, the basilica with its decoration, the *dribitoria* or offices, the forum, the portico and the baths. These *concilabulae* were perhaps the political and religious centres of smaller rural tribes which had not attained full civitas status.[1]

Nearly fifty such sites are now known, spread over the Somme and Paris basins, Normandy, the Loire Valley, Maine and Poitou, Charente, Limousin and Berry, in the territories of some twenty Roman cities. Many are sited on the boundaries of their tribal territories, perhaps to attract pilgrims from more than one area, though since many have pre-Roman origins they may once have had a role in inter-tribal trade. Berthouville, for example, is close to the boundaries of the Lexovii of Lisieux, the Eburovices of Evreux and the Veliocasses of Rouen. A few are close to their civitas capitals, like Allonnes (Sarthe) or Vieil-Evreux, but here the Roman administrative town may have replaced the pre-conquest tribal meeting place. Provost has shown how the rural cult centres of the Loire basin were spaced at regular intervals of around 70km, so that no peasant was more than 35km (23 miles or 15 Gaulish leagues) from a cult centre — a day's trip there and back, ignoring other centres such as civitas capitals. This emphasises their role in local life. Though their architectural inspiration lies in the fora, temples and baths of nearby towns, and more distantly in the rural healing shrines of classical Greece, like Epidaurus or Delphi, many perpetuate important pre-conquest religious or market centres. Drevant (Cher), the ancient *Derventum*, lies on the Roman road from Bourges to Neris, across the river from the Iron Age oppidum of the Camp de César. Its name is from *dervos*, 'an oak', and *venta*, a market or meeting place — 'The meeting place by the Oak Tree'. It has a temple off centre in a large temenos, suggesting some now vanished central feature, public baths, and a theatre. Alleans (Cher), Aubigny (Sarthe) and Amboise (Indre-et-Loire) are also associated with major oppida, and Genainville (Val d'Oise), Ribemont-sur-Ancre (Somme) and Aubigny overlie Iron Age cemeteries and cult centres. Others have produced large numbers of pre-Roman 'Celtic' coins — over five hundred at Bois l'Abbe (Seine-Maritime) alone.[2]

The sanctuaries flourished in the first century and a half of the Christian era. The names of some combine *magus* — a plain or market — with a Latin personal name, sometimes that of a member of the Imperial family, suggesting that they were organised or re-organised under official patronage in Julio-Claudian times. Bouchards and Chassenon in Charente were *Germanicomagus* and *Cassinomagus* and Clion (Indre-et-Loire) was *Claudiomagus*. For their subsequent history, Ribemont-sur-Ancre near Amiens is fairly typical. The first temple was built under Augustus or Tiberius, and a theatre to hold 3000 spectators added early in the reign of Nero. Under Trajan public baths were built, and under Pius or Marcus Aurelius the temple was rebuilt with rich sculptural decoration in fine limestone brought from a distance. Shortly after 160, the theatre was remodelled as one of the theatre-amphitheatres characteristic of Celtic Gaul. At its peak, the sanctuary and its associated settlement covered some 25 ha. At Genainville, the temple and theatre were also rebuilt in Antonine times with lavish sculptural decoration. The rural theatre at Canouville (Seine-Maritime) also dates from this time, and at Lillebonne, where the theatre was again remodelled as a theatre-amphitheatre, baths were added no earlier than the time of Commodus. Such site histories, however, merely follow the trajectory of building chronology, particularly of urban buildings, throughout Gaul and the west. What is more important from our point of view is the role of such sites in the rural power structure, and how far they continued that role in the late Empire.[3]

The urban architectural style of these rural sanctuaries and the lavish expenditure on

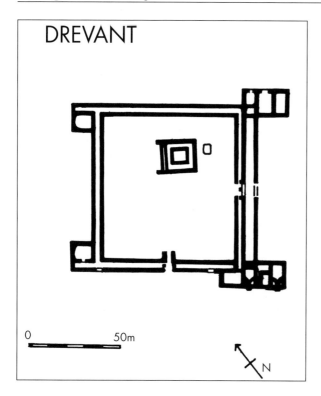

DREVANT

0   50m

N

40   Drevant (Cher) Romano Celtic temple and precinct. The name means 'the meeting place by the oak tree' and the temple is set off centre in its temenos. The focal point may have been a sacred tree rather than the temple itself

their buildings, sculpture and temple treasures suggests that they were part of the hierarchy of urbanism and office holding within the land-owning class. At Bois l'Abbé near Dieppe, a second-century temple and theatre complex was excavated in the nineteenth century by Cochet. In 1965, during fresh excavations, a large inscription was found lying in fragments in the theatre, where it had fallen from the stage building or *frons scenae*. It records the gift of the proscenium, with its decoration, to the pagus of the Catuslugi by Lucius Cerialius Rectus. He had held various offices, including Priest of Rome and Augustus and Prefect for the suppression of bandits. The Catuslugi were one of the lesser tribes of Belgic Gaul, recorded by Pliny but included officially within the tribal territory of the Ambiani. The latest coins pre-dating the *frons scenae* were unworn issues of 164–8. Bethouville, another Norman site, lies on a wide fertile plain which also contains a large Roman villa. The treasure was found in 1830 by a farmer digging stone from the ruins of the shrine. When it was confiscated for the Cabinet des Médailles in Paris, the finder pulled much of the site apart in a frantic search for more treasure (this was, after all, de Maupassant country). Babelon, who published the find, suggested that Q. Domitius Tutus, donor of some nine pieces, may have been the owner of the villa estate, rather as English landowners often gave items of silver to 'their' parish church to mark family events. This raises questions about the relationship between the sanctuaries, the land-owning classes, and the crowds who gathered there for fairs and festivals. Local magnates could list their offices in vicus or pagus just as they could grander posts. Thus C. Amatius Paterninus could record in the reign of Decius that he had been *aedile* of the vicus of *Agiedincensus*, aedile of the *Civitas Senonum* at Sens and actor publici of the *pagus Toutiacus*.[4]

Vici, shrines and rural society

A local Gallic magnate thus had more than one stage below the level of the civitas capital on which he could demonstrate his status and importance. The very large size of many of the Gallic civitates in comparison with the much more compact territories of the Mediterranean cities made secondary centres of administration and trade very necessary. The vicus was a small rural market town, similar to the 'small towns' of Roman Britain, and sometimes with an important local role in manufacture and industry. Some were pottery making or iron smelting centres. These needed waste land where clay could be dug, and timber cut for firing, and these might not be readily available in urban areas. Medieval urban pottery kilns were strictly controlled as a fire risk and a nuisance, even where they were permitted. The landowner or the estate owner would take a render, whether in the form of a cash rent or as a percentage of the output, though there is no need to see such industries as being directly controlled by magnates in such matters as production and marketing. Nevertheless, these economic aspects emphasise the involvement of local potentates and estate owners in vici and other rural centres. Similarly inscriptions record the activities of magnates as benefactors and patrons of pagi and vici. At Gargarius, now St-Jean-de-Gar (Bouches-du-Rhône), the *pagani* of the small town put up an inscription to their patron, Q. Cornelius Zosimus, in the time of Antoninus Pius. He had obtained a tax relief for them, possibly connected with the building of public baths. Similarly, at Yzeures-sur-Creuse (Indre-et-Loire) a local magnate M. Petronius . . . milius (the last name is incomplete) built an altar and column dedicated to Mercury and the divinities of two second-century emperors. Both vici were later the sites of important early churches.[5]

Until late in the second century, the rural sanctuaries went on adding to their buildings, often in grand style, with monumental sculpture and expensive non-local freestone. By the late Empire, however, their great days were over. The coins from Sanxay have been poorly published, but on present evidence do not go beyond the Gallic Empire. Ribemont-sur-Ancre near Amiens reached its final grandeur under Marcus Aurelius or Commodus, and has produced abundant coins of the Gallic Empire. Burnt down in the later third century it was restored under Constantine, but its revival was short lived with drystone huts invading the monumental precincts and perhaps only the amphitheatre remaining in use. By c.380–90 even this ghost town existence had come to an end. At Bouchards the 197 coins end with a Tetrican copy and four Constantinian issues, whilst Drevant fell into disuse about 300 and by the mid-fourth century was abandoned and in total ruin. Elsewhere in the Roman Empire, the spread of Christianity has been linked to a collapse of pagan religion and the disuse of its shrines seen as an indirect result of the third-century crisis. In Gaul it has been claimed that many rural cult centres were destroyed in the third-century invasions, or fell into disuse as a result of them. If this were so, Christianity would have spread into a countryside where pagan religion had already received a mortal wound.[6]

One problem here is that many older excavations were poorly published and were subjectively interpreted in terms of assumed violent destruction by barbarian invaders in the third century or by Christian monks in the fourth. We shall need to look later at the evidence for Martin of Tours' undoubted activity (probably with military aid) in this field, but some early excavators were all too aware of this literary evidence which formed a model for their site interpretations. These depended upon two observed phenomena, that the site showed signs of destruction and that the coins ended under a particular Emperor — Tetricus, Magnentius or Magnus Maximus. In some cases the site was no doubt violently destroyed at the date indicated, but destruction could be the work of barbarian invaders, Christian monks, or recent stone robbers. Smashed cult statues of marble or limestone could be the work of iconoclasts or of lime burners. Burnt masonry could be the result of barbarian pillage or of a lime kiln. The broken statues piled in a heap at Mont-Martre, Avallon (Yonne) sound like the work of lime burners, and some sites, like Vieux-Poitiers, have unfinished early medieval sarcophagi still on site. Sanxay (Vienne) produced many small fragments of inscriptions, rarely with more than a few letters, from many different inscriptions. Christians might well have smashed stones bearing the names of such 'devils' as Apollo or Mercury, who both plagued the sleep of the demon haunted Martin of Tours. They would have been singularly unlikely, however, to have carried the pieces away as souvenirs. Sanxay was pillaged by stone robbers down to the time of Camille de la Croix's excavation and beyond. One of the larger inscribed fragments, a convenient cube of stone a metre square, was carried away from the excavations to help build a house. Berthouville was the only local source of building stone in that part of Normandy, and the adjacent hamlet was built from its ruins. It was whilst robbing it for building stone that the peasant proprietor found the treasure. It would be unreasonable to interpret all reported cases of destruction thus, but with many older excavations it is an option that needs to be borne in mind. In cases like Ribemont, Bouchards and Sanxay, we can at least say that destruction by militant Christian monks is not an option, for by that time the sites had long been in ruin.[7]

One element in the declining importance of the rural cult centres may have been changes within the local élite for whom they provided what David Cannadine has called, in a modern context, 'consensual pageantry'. They were not the only stage on which local potentates could act out their local leadership role, but their temples, colonnaded courts and processional routes offered much greater opportunities for religious processions and displays of rank and leadership than did a small French town or vicus on market day. Cannadine has shown how sensitive such ceremonies and the buildings associated with them can be to changes in society and in local leadership structures. A building can be adorned with elaborate statuary, designed to stimulate local pride but which can become meaningless within the same century. Significantly the vici, which had a more durable economic and social basis, did not show the same decline, and retained, as we shall see, a central role in local society in the late Empire and beyond.[8]

Similarly there is little evidence that other types of rural shrine were in terminal decline. Despite the end of rural coin hoards over most of rural Gaul by mid century, suggesting changing patterns of coin use in the countryside, rural temples continued to receive coin offerings until Valentinianic or Theodosian times. This again suggests that the end of the monumental rural sanctuaries was related, not to a decline of pagan religion, but to changes in local magnate power structures in the Gallic countryside. The rural cult centres end around the time that Constantine I confiscated the city revenues, but participation in their activities may already have been less attractive to rural magnates. Other kinds of rural shrine remained until the anti-pagan legislation of Valentinian and Theodosius. The life of Martin of Tours by the Aquitanian landowner Sulpicius Severus is a literary work following certain well understood hagiographic conventions, more interested in allegorical coded meaning than in biographical fact, and not above creating (for moderns) chronological problems for its own reasons. However, its accounts of Martin's assaults on pagan shrines, and their physical destruction by him, can be accepted as an authentic first hand account with good parallels elsewhere in the late Empire.[9]

The Vita Martini: a Christian manifesto

Compiled soon after Martin's death in 397, Sulpicius Severus's dossier on Martin consists of the *Vita Martini* itself, three short letters, and two conversation pieces or Dialogues — *Postumianus* (itself divided into two at an early date) and *Gallus*. Apart from being a celebration of Martin, and intended as homilies for reading aloud to monks and clergy (one section is clearly intended for nuns and other pious ladies), it is a Christian manifesto of a very specific sort. It reflects the militant evangelical Christianity of the soldierly men and devout women most clearly seen to us in the courts of the soldier Emperors of the late fourth century. It belongs to the church of the martyrs and of their spiritual heirs, the monks and hermits. Martin is contrasted with the aristocratic Gallo-Roman bishops rather in the way that Pugin in his *Contrasts* sets the Church of an idealised Gothic Middle Ages against that of the industrial nineteenth century. Martin is the new Elijah, the equal of the martyrs, who, though born too late for martyrdom, would have made a splendid martyr. He went everywhere on foot, unlike his successor Bricius, who was said to keep a stable of fine horses, and a train of male and female servants. The well-born Gallo-Roman bishop prided himself on his recondite classical education. To Martin the pagan Gods were demons, whose shrines had to be physically destroyed.[10]

Martin was born at Savaria (Szombathely, or in German Steinamanger) in modern Hungary, on the Danube frontier, son of a military tribune who had risen from the ranks. Brought up in the military base of Ticinum near Milan, he was forcibly enrolled in the army as a member of one of the hereditary professions of the late Empire. According to Sulpicius Severus, however, after five years service in the Horseguards, the *Alae Scolares*, he was discharged following a deliberate act of military disobedience during a parade at the time of Julian's Rhineland campaign (before his elevation to the throne) of 356. This introduces two basic themes of the Life — the bishop as the soldier of Christ, and the bishop-ascetic as the equal of the martyrs. As Jacques Fontaine has shown, this section is modelled on the passios of certain military martyrs and cannot be understood apart from these. Marcellus of Tangier was a legionary centurion who threw down his military belt as an act of disobedience during a parade to celebrate the Emperor's birthday in 298. Maximilian was a soldier's son from Tebessa in Numidia who refused to be enrolled in the army, and was executed at Carthage in 295. St Maurice and the Theban legion, who enjoyed a wide cult in Gaul, were said (rather less historically) to have been executed for refusing to take part in a pagan sacrifice. The theme of the Christian soldier would have appealed to the large military and official population of north Gaul, but if the military martyr was not to appear simply as a pacifist condemnation of the Emperor and his army it needed a pagan Emperor. Within a realistic time scale the only available candidate was Julian. This may have distorted the chronology of the Life.[11]

Whilst the dates of Martin's episcopate (371/2–97) are secure, the chronology of his early life thus has problems. Gregory of Tours, using the records of his own (and Martin's) see gives a birth date of 316, suggesting recruitment into the army at the normal age about 334, and discharge after a full term of service about 359. Sulpicius on the other hand suggests a birth date of 336, recruitment at the surprisingly early age of 15, and discharge after five years service. Both Babut and Fontaine argued that Sulpicius has telescoped Martin's early life, either because military service was seen as unfitting for a bishop or to create the dramatic confrontation essential to the military martyr theme. Happily, these problems do not affect Martin's later career or his assaults on Gallo-Roman paganism.[12]

Details of pagan cult in the *Vita Martini* can sometimes be matched archaeologically. Once, Martin met a pagan funeral procession, which was legal, but mistook it for a pagan sacrifice, which was not, 'for the peasants . . . were wont . . . to carry around their fields images of demons, covered with white veils'. The splendid cast-bronze horse with a dedicatory inscription from the temple treasure found in a sand pit at Neuvy-en-Sullias (Loiret), now in the Musee d'Orleanais at Orleans has a bronze ring at each corner of its base, for carrying the figure in procession on poles, like some later Christian shrines. The story is followed by that of Martin felling a sacred pine tree which stood next to a very ancient temple. The priest and a crowd of peasants accepted the destruction of the temple with resignation, only becoming agitated when Martin began to fell the tree. Some Romano-Celtic shrines like Drevant — *Derventum*, 'the meeting place by the oak tree' — are off centre in their temenos, which may have focussed on some now vanished central feature. Elsewhere, Martin destroyed a Jupiter column and one of the great circular temple cellae characteristic of western Gaul.[13]

Martin's activities can be put into a wider context by the career of his contemporary Maternus Cynegius, who held high office under Theodosius I before dying whilst consul and praetorian prefect of the east in 388. Like Theodosius he was Spanish and a devout Christian. Several of Theodosius's edicts against pagans and heretics were addressed to him, and whilst praetorian prefect he organised official tours of Syria, Mesopotamia and Egypt in which important pagan temples were destroyed by soldiers and squads of black-clad monks. Martin's activities may have been inspired by his example and must have had similar official support. Under normal circumstances a provincial governor, one of whose main responsibilities was the maintenance of public order, would have viewed with alarm a body of men who travelled around his province provoking public unrest and upsetting the local *status quo*. Even Sulpicius, who would hardly emphasise the role of such an official at the expense of Martin's position centre stage, admits that he had such help. At Amboise, the Christian priest in charge had been unable to demolish a temple built of large ashlar blocks, domed and of great height, even with the aid of his clergy, some local monks, the town garrison, and local workmen. At Levroux (Indre), 'a temple much enriched by the pagans', Martin was driven off by a hostile crowd. He returned with two angels armed with spears and shields, who sound suspiciously like Roman soldiers. Another bishop, Marcellus of Apamea in Syria, called in the army to help him demolish pagan shrines in the countryside around his city but was lynched by a mob whilst pulling down a shrine of Zeus.[14]

The laws of 385 and 391 against pagan sacrifices provide another context for Martin's activities. The lands and treasures of the pagan temples, particularly in the form of precious metals, attracted the Christian Emperors just as the riches of the British monasteries attracted Henry VIII. There was also the advantage of returning to the Treasury the large amounts of public money spent on pagan religion. Gratian confiscated all temple lands and gold, a law which has sometimes been linked to the ample good quality gold coinage of the late Empire. Under Theodosius and Honorius pagan priests were stripped of their tax revenues and privileges. As Theodosius told the Roman senate, the pagan cults were a burden on the state and the cash was needed for military necessities.[15]

According to Sulpicius Severus, wherever Martin destroyed a pagan temple he replaced it with a church or a monastery. As we have seen, some older antiquarians were all too aware of this, but Sulpicius does not say that the two were necessarily on the same site. At Richborough, the pagan temples had Theodosian rubbish pits cut through them and are unlikely to have co-existed for long with the Christian church and baptistery, but they stood on separate sites and we have no way of knowing whether the building of the church was related in any way to the destruction of the temples. At Amboise, the temple whose destruction by Martin is described in the *Vita Martini* has now been located and its site acquired by the state. We know, however, that there was already a church and priest at Amboise before the destruction of the temple. In a few cases Roman temples were taken over by the Church and converted into churches, and paradoxically this often ensured their survival. The two well preserved Augustan temples at Nimes and Vienne are examples of this. Usually, however, there was a lengthy gap, often of several centuries, before the redundant building was converted to Christian use. The Pantheon at Rome was closed by the fourth-century Christian Emperors, but it was not until 609 that it became the church of Santa Maria ad Martyres when the emperor Phocas gave it to the Pope.[16]

It was one thing to destroy a pagan shrine. It was even possible to effect some form of conversion on the crowd of gaping rustics who had witnessed the overthrow of their god. Martin, after felling the sacred pine tree, received the spectators into the Church as catechumens by the laying on of hands. It was quite another thing to provide enough pastoral care to prevent the peasantry from lapsing back into paganism once the immediate sensation was over. Sulpicius's double church and baptistery on his estate at Primuliacum in Gascony is significant here, for these late Roman double churches may have been for baptised Christians and for catechumens under instruction and not yet baptised. Martin's new converts should have come to the civitas capital the following Easter for baptism at the hands of the bishop after proper instruction. There was, however, no adequate framework of rural churches as yet, or enough rural clergy to provide proper instruction, or even to announce the date of Easter to their flock.

The real point of Sulpicius Severus's comment on Martin replacing pagan temples with Christian churches was that a start was being made on creating such a framework. Civaux (Vienne) in Poitou was a rural vicus or a cult centre with a temple, theatre and other buildings, though excavation is difficult because of the modern village and the huge Merovingian sarcophagus cemetery, still in use, which overlie much of the site. The cemetery began in Gallo-Roman times and must have served a wider area than the present settlement. The earliest post Roman phase, as at Chinon, a church founded by Martin's successor Bricius, is of simple earth-cut graves. The sarcophagus cemetery is later. A short distance from the cemetery, with its extraordinary boundary hedge of vertically set sarcophagus lids, is the parish church. Its oldest part is a polygonal apse of re-used Roman stonework, possibly Merovingian in date. The church is dedicated to Gervais and Protasius, the Milanese martyrs discovered by Ambrose in 386, whose relics were brought back to Gaul by Martin of Tours and distributed among churches founded by himself and his followers. In 1862 a late fourth-century epitaph reading *Aeternalis et Servilia Vivatis in Deo* with a chi-rho monogram above, was found built into its walls. In 1960 two concentric walls of Gallo-Roman masonry were found north of the church and identified as a Romano-Celtic temple. In its ambulatory was a baptismal font. The assumed temple may be some form of baptistery, but the church seems to go back to Martin's time and is in an adjacent diocese. It shows that a start was being made in providing pastoral care in the Gallo-Roman countryside.[17]

The retreat into magic

It was relatively simple for fourth-century Emperors to erase what had been the official state religion by legislation, by the confiscation of temple lands and revenues, and by permitting militant Christians like Martin to demolish pagan shrines with official help and connivance. What in the longer term proved impossible was the eradication of the dense undergrowth of popular magical belief that underlay the pagan forest. Marcel Mauss defined magic as 'any ritual that does not form part of an organised cult'. Though the names of the old gods were sometimes invoked, much as those of the old saints were in post Reformation spells and charms, most of what is sometimes described as 'pagan survival' in post Roman Gaul consisted of a range of popular customs, many of which have lasted to the present day as 'folk customs', 'magic', 'popular superstitions' or what you will. Such expressions belong to that interest in peasant culture which formed part of the intellectual baggage of the Romantic movement. 'Magic', as defined by Mauss or by Valerie Flint, is better provided that it does not restrict the range and variety of activities to those which consciously call on some supernatural power. Here, I have retained the traditional terms in order to emphasise the ubiquity of these customs in west European society at all periods. The church thus faced two closely linked tasks in Christianising the countryside — the replacement of these magical customs by the rites of the Christian Church and the establishment of its own network of rural pastoral care. Sulpicius Severus begins that part of the *Vita Martini* dealing with Martin's miracles whilst bishop with two stories. One deals with Martin's suppression of the popular cult of a false martyr, the other with his intervention in a (permissible) pagan funeral which he mistook for a forbidden pagan sacrifice. Martin's diocese held a mixed population of pagans and Christians, and Sulpicius makes it clear at the outset that Martin was concerned with imposing norms of Christian orthodoxy on both.[18]

Ritual animal disguise, cross-dressing on certain calendar dates, divination by means of dice, a sacred text (the 'Sortes') or by the stars, or the deposition of small objects at places thought 'special' or 'holy', are extraordinarily widespread in space and time. Some had their recognised place in pre-Christian religion, but were quite separate from its core beliefs and practices. Valerie Flint has shown how the Church came to distinguish 'Forbidden magic', dependent on demons and other unauthorised sources of spiritual power, from 'rescued' or permitted magic, which often set up parallel Christian procedures mimicking the old. There was, of course, also 'encouraged' Christian magic. Between were huge grey areas, and at times the category in which a Christian observer placed some magical event depended upon the practitioner rather than upon the magic. A miracle which proved the sanctity of an aristocratic Gaulish bishop might, if carried out by unauthorised hands, be seen as the work of a charlatan, or of the devil.[19]

The range of human needs which worshippers brought to pagan shrines in Britain and Gaul can be illustrated from a wide range of sources: the lead 'curse tablets' or *defixiones*, ill wishing some person and devoting them to the vengeance of a deity; a late Roman manuscript from a pagan shrine in south Gaul, forming a handbook for pagan priests dealing with questions from worshippers; and from medical instruments and *ex-votos* which show that some shrines, like their older Greek counterparts, had healing functions. New standards of excavation and finds processing have greatly increased the number of curse tablets available for study in recent years. Their range of concerns may at times remind one of a supernatural lost property office, but is overall very similar to those which a medieval French preacher at Béthune in northern France attributed to 'witches who want (to know) hidden things, such as who stole this or that, who did so and so, or who want to know what will happen in the future . . . so that (the devil) will reveal whether or not I have stolen something, . . . (or) the location of lost objects'.[20]

Similar concerns, with others, appear in the *Sortes Sangallenses*, the primary text of the palimpsested manuscript *St Gall 908*. We seem to be in a south Gallic context of the late fourth century, but in a higher social class than among the *defixiones*, perhaps among the citizens of a provincial town after the reforms of Constantine and Diocletian. They are much concerned with runaway slaves, lost property, career prospects, promotion (or the avoidance of municipal obligations), legacies, tax problems, mortgages, ill health and similar middle class worries. The questions were brought to the priest of an oracular shrine, and the answer (with twelve possible alternatives) decided by dicing. The manuscript may have remained in secular hands until it was acquired by the monks of St Gall as waste vellum in the eighth or ninth century, suitable for the eraser's knife. But in view of the evidence from Gregory of Tours that related forms of *sortes* were used in the Gallic church, with the help of its priests, and other survivals of pagan oracle books into medieval times, it could be significant that it passed into a monastic library.[21]

At some Gaulish shrines, medical help may have been available through a resident physician or through itinerant doctors who visited fairs and markets like the quacks of Victorian Britain. Some shrines have produced oculist's stamps, eye-shaped plaques of bronze or gold, medical spatulae, or other surgical instruments. Votive models of limbs or parts of the body imply healing cults, but these need not have involved medical care. Aline Rouselle suggested that the miraculous cures effected by Martin of Tours show once again how he sought to replace traditional pagan sources of help. Martin may have acquired some basic medical training in the Roman army (which certainly had professional doctors) and Rouselle shows that however miraculous his cures, they were based on sound current medical knowledge.[22]

By the end of the sixth century, with the structure of rural pastoral care largely in place south of the Loire, paganism had declined into 'magic' and 'superstition' using unauthorised spiritual powers. Sometime between 560 and 605 a diocesan synod was held at Auxerre. This is the only surviving record of a Merovingian diocesan synod attended by a bishop and his clergy rather than by the bishops of one or more provinces in a church council. Its horizons are more local, and, though isolated canons are sometimes quoted out of context as evidence for 'pagan' survival, its real concern is with the role of traditional customs and practices in a society already basically Christian. The church was seeking to implant the festivals of the Christian year into the annual round of the rural seasons and their traditional calendar customs, bringing peasant society within its social control. Thus the first clause, the oft quoted prohibition on dressing up as cattle, stags or old women at the winter solstice, and on the 'new years gifts to devils', distinguished from the permissible new years gifts of classical antiquity, comes first because of its place at the beginning of the year. It is followed by the ruling that priests are to find out the date for the beginning of Lent from their bishop and announce it to their flocks at Epiphany. The war between Carnival and Lent was to continue for centuries, and no one familiar with the Welsh Mari Llwyd or with the Padstow and Kentish 'Hosses' and their 'Judies' will have any difficulty in recognising the world wide calendar customs of ritual animal disguise and cross-dressing ('the world turned upside down'), together with the gifts of food or money to their companions, in a familiar west European guise.[23]

The third canon deals with a mixture of Christian and non-Christian customs. The agenda item no doubt read 'popular abuses'. It falls into four clauses, separated by *nec* — 'neither':

> Ceremonies in private houses are not allowed. Neither is the holding of night vigils before the feasts of the saints. Neither is the keeping of a vow at a thorn bush, or a holy tree, or a spring. If anyone has to fulfil a vow, he should hold a vigil in church, and make an offering to the church funds (*matriculate*) or to the poor. Neither shall anyone make carvings of a foot, or of a man, out of wood.

Convivial and rowdy gatherings before the feasts of the martyrs had much exercised St Augustine ('The martyrs hate the clatter of your pots and pans') and the fifth canon adds that even vigils in honour of St Martin are forbidden. Popular piety needed official sanction and control. The 'ceremonies in private houses' are too late to refer to the Agape, or early Church supper, though this was held in the house of a private believer. The wooden images, however, may be linked to the wooden *ex votos* of human figures or limbs from Chamaliéres near Clermont Ferrand or from the source of the Seine, but there is no need to link them with the quite separate reference to *fontes* in the previous clause nor with offerings to sacred springs. Similar wooden models of injured human parts were still displayed in a shrine near Cologne in the time of Theuderic I (511–33). It is also of interest to note, in view of the large numbers of Iron Age and Roman coins from sanctuary sites, that the fulfilling of a vow could be accompanied by an offering which could profitably be diverted to church funds.[24]

The next canon deals with fortune tellers and the *sortres quas sanctorum vocant*, 'the so-called sortes of the saints'. No one was to consult fortune tellers or to look at what soothsayers made out of wood or bread. Images of parts of the body in the form of wheat-flour cakes were being used by Christians around Arles at just this time, and the practice persisted until at least the eighth century. They recall the much later English 'cockle bread', one of many methods used by girls to divine the names of their future husbands. At a different level, there are many fortune tellers of dubious repute in Gregory of Tours, along with Merovingian princes and others consulting the *Sortes Biblicae* or the *Sortes Sanctorum* with the help of the church.[25]

The Church in the country: the beginnings of rural pastoral care

If we were to follow a Merovingian bishop through the gates of his city, past the extra-mural cemeteries into the countryside beyond, we would be entering a rural world where the Church was beginning to establish churches for a population which, though nominally Christian, in many areas still lacked the essential infrastructure of churches and clergy. The Church needed to bring individual communities within the orbit of an organization which was still mostly urban.

The essential elements of the rural settlement pattern were the villa and the vicus. Vici were small market towns, secondary centres within the area of the civitas. Some had industries such as iron smelting or pottery making and, as we have seen, a landowner could hold office in a vicus or pagus as well as in the city. The boundary between civitas city and vicus was not immutable. Late Roman cities like Boulogne or Grenoble had been mere vici under the early Empire. The area of the civitas territory was divided into pagi or rural districts. Civitas and Pagus could even be used as a kind of postal address. A late Roman 'desk instruction' for tax officials tells how land should be registered in the tax census under the name of the farm or villa, with the Civitas and Pagus within which it lay. A writing tablet of AD 118 from the Walbrook in London deals with land in the *Civitas Cantiacorum* (Kent), located by its pagus, and by neighbouring roads and properties. We know relatively little of the pagi, but five inscriptions found in the foundations of the late Roman town walls at Rennes in Britanny are dedications in honour of the Imperial family and their local gods by the constituent pagi of the *Riedones*, whose civitas capital Rennes was. They include the *pagus Matans*, the *pagus Sextanmandus* and the *pagus Carnutenus*.[26]

Just as the Christian church based its pattern of bishoprics on that of the secular civitates, so it based its pattern of rural churches on the vici and on the villas of private landowners. The *ecclesiae diocesanae* or churches in the vici were the basis which extended the organization of the urban church into the surrounding countryside. Each had its 'diocese' or sphere of influence, and was a 'diocesan church' in the sense of 'church with a diocese', rather than a 'church of the diocese', though it was that as well. Church councils speak of bishops touring their dioceses, the constituent units that made up their see. He was to visit them yearly and see that they were in good repair and that the roof did not leak. When bishop Maroveus needed a diplomatic excuse for his absence from Poitiers during the funeral of St Radegond (the two had quarrelled), he was 'unavoidably delayed' on a tour of his dioceses.[27]

At the same time, the word *parochia*, 'parish', Greek in origin, was coming into use. The original meaning was the community of Christians within a town under the charge of its bishop, but it soon came to mean the sphere of influence of a particular priest or church. The modern colloquial use of 'parish' for someone's patch or territory is very similar. It was 'that circuit of ground which is committed to the charge of one priest, having the cure of souls therein' and from the revenues of which the church and its priest were supported. Thus, confusingly for moderns, a bishop could have a parish (his see), whereas a diocese was only one of the constituent areas which together made up that see. The first use of 'parish' in Gaul in something like the modern sense was in 417. The bishops of Marseille and Aix both laid claim to two *parochiae*, churches with their territories, at *Citharista*, now Ceyreste south-east of Marseille near la Ciotat, and *Gargarius*, St-Jean-de-Gar, some 10km to the north near Aubagne. *Gargarius* had been a flourishing Roman small town, with mosaics, sculptures and inscriptions. In the time of Antoninus Pius, the *pagani* of the *pagus Lucretius* had set up an honorific inscription there to their patron, the freedman Q. Cornelius Zosimus. By coincidence, it was his namesake Pope Zosimus who was now asked to adjudicate on the dispute. The two adjacent parishes must have covered a substantial area between Marseille and the present eastern boundary of the Bouches-du-Rhone.[28]

Gregory of Tours lists the *ecclesiae diocesanae* built by the bishops of his see, from Martin (371–97) to Volusianus (491–8). Most were in Roman small towns like Clion (*Claudiomagus*) or Amboise (*Ambaticus*). Martin's foundations follow the pattern of the river valleys and of settlement. They were at Amboise and Langeais on the Loire; Candes (where Martin died) at the junction of the Loire and the Vienne; Sonnay and Tournon-St-Martin on the Vienne, and at Ciran-La-Latte west of the Indre. At Clion, where a 'double' monastery of monks and nuns existed under Martin, his successor Bricius added a church. Martin's successors filled out the pattern with sixteen more churches by the end of the century. Some of these churches are also known as the sites of important early post Roman cemeteries.[29]

Like urban churches, these rural episcopal foundations depended upon gifts of land and property from landowners. Magnates could display their piety and patronage in church building just as their predecessors had done with conspicuous votive gifts to pagan shrines. Bishop Eustocius of Tours, a man of 'senatorial rank', built a church at *Iciodorum vicus* (Yzeures-sur-Creuse, Indre et Loire) in the *pagus Iciodorum*, presumably with the help of local landowners. An earlier local magnate had built an altar and column here dedicated to Mercury and the divinities of (probably) Marcus Aurelius and Lucius Verus. Its sculptured blocks were found re-used in the foundations of Eustocius's church or a successor, and Merovingian burials are known from the site. Other early episcopal churches in the Touraine are also known from excavation. At Eustocius's other foundation at Loches (*vicus Loccae*) the foundations of an early church are known under the parish church of St Ours. At Chinon, where Bricius built a church, substantial Roman walls, sculptures, and inscriptions were found under the medieval castle in the nineteenth century, and the dominating rock ridge on which it stands probably carried a late Roman fortification of some kind. Aegidius besieged it shortly before 464, and by the tenth century it was the *Castrum Kaionense*. At its foot is the former Romanesque minster of St Mexme, founded by the fifth-century monk Maximus, a disciple of St Martin. Its

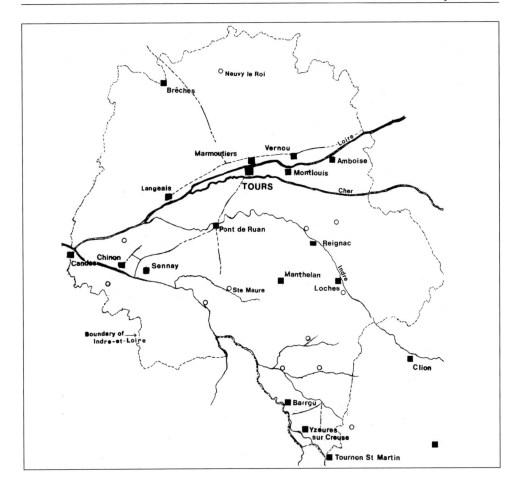

41   *Churches founded by the bishops of Tours in the vici of Touraine, AD 371–498 and other early churches mentioned in the text, with Roman roads and the present boundary of Indre et Loire (which does not correspond exactly with the ancient diocese)*

cemetery has east-west orientated earth graves of apparent fifth-century date followed by a sarcophagus cemetery.[30]

Sites such as these put into context both Sulpicius Severus's statement about Martin replacing demolished pagan shrines with churches and Gregory's account of Martin and subsequent bishops founding churches in the rural vici of Touraine. Such churches were served by a group of priests under an archpriest or archpresbyter. They were quite distinct from monasteries where groups of celibate monks lived a communal life under an abbot and a written rule or *regula* (hence 'regular clergy', who live according to a monastic rule). In England the word *monasterium* served for both until Bede, himself of course a monk, used it in its modern sense. This may have influenced common English usage which distinguishes between a monastery of regular clergy or monks (who may not even be priests), and a minster of canons or secular clergy who lived in the world, might well be married, and, unlike monks, had the cure of souls within their diocese or minster parish. The secular minsters, equivalent to the French Collegiales or Baptismal churches, or to the pioneer churches in the vici of Touraine, were the original units of pastoral care in England. In Wales, where an indirect reference to married clergy by Gildas shows that most sixth-century British priests were secular clergy, their churches later became known as *clas* churches from the *clas* or community of canons.

Such churches, though they formed the original units of rural church organization over most of western Europe, were not the immediate source of the developed parochial pattern of medieval and later times. A sixth-century church council held at Clermont in central France lists three kinds of clergy — those who belong to the canon (list of clergy) of the city, or of the rural parishes, and those who live in a villa and celebrate divine service there. The practice of building churches serving villas and their estates had begun with Roman villa owners, and the references to *oratoria villara* in church councils probably follow the semantic shift from Roman *villa* or farm to medieval *vill* or estate. The fourth Council of Orleans in 541 ruled that anyone wishing to establish a diocese (rural church) on their estate must provide enough land, property and clergy for its proper endowment. Other Councils ruled that relics were not to be placed in villa oratories unless there were clerics of a nearby *paruchia* to sing psalms over them, and proper provision made for a priest. Great men were not to celebrate the great Christian feasts on their estates but with the bishop in the city.[31]

There are a number of incidental references to villa churches by writers such as Ausonius in the fourth century and Sidonius Apollinaris in the fifth. One of the most striking is that of *Primuliacum* in south-west Gaul, where Sulpicius Severus, biographer of Martin of Tours, retired to live in religious seclusion on his estate around AD 400. Primuliac already had a church, but Sulpicius added a second side by side with it, linked to the old by a baptistery in the shape of a rotunda or tower. This recalls such urban cathedrals as Trier or Geneva, but the exact nature of *Primuliacum* is uncertain. The -acum termination suggests a villa, as does Paulinus of Nola's reference to *Primuliacus nostra*, 'our Primuliac', as being 'in the midst of your possessions.' Griffé, however, thought that the double church and baptistery suggested a vicus, or the centre of a pagus where Sulpicius was the main landowner. We hear of a priest, deacon and sub-deacon there, which would suit a rural minster, but Paulinus three times calls it *domestica tua ecclesia* – 'your private domestic church'. Primuliac was clearly an estate church of some kind, and the centre of that estate was probably (in modern archaeological terminology) a villa. Though the location of *Primuliacum* is unknown, the settlement pattern of the most probable area may help in explaining its context. Since the seventeenth century, one favoured location for it has been near the Roman town of Eauze (Gers) in the northern foothills of the Pyrenees. The pattern of closely spaced fairly, small civitas towns in the valley network of this wooded and hilly area would have left little room for subsidiary vici, and a pattern of large villa estates interspersed with civitas towns in the larger valleys seems probable.[32]

At Beaucaire east of Eauze, a large fourth-century Roman villa with fine polychrome mosaics was succeeded by a cemetery with over a hundred sarcophagi and many earth graves, in use until at least the ninth century. Other similar sites are known in the area, and whilst there is, of course, no reason to associate any of them with Primuliac, they do at least suggest the sort of context into which it might fit. The earlier church was presumably a simple villa chapel for Sulpicius and his household. His remodelling, with a baptistery and a second church for tenants or for catechumens on the model of the urban cathedrals, demonstrates that the evangelisation of the Gallo-Roman countryside was not just a matter for the bishop and the *ecclesiae diocesanae* but also for Christian landowners. Soon, though, the bishops would find it necessary to assert that these estate or villa churches were not private property, but as much part of the diocesan structure as the 'public' churches in the vici.[33]

The problem of churches and cemeteries on villa sites is a huge and contentious topic. Lullingstone, with its wall paintings, is a unique case, but mosaics with Christian themes, as at Hinton St Mary in Dorset or the Villa of Fortunatus near Fraga in the Ebro Valley in north Spain, at least provide circumstantial evidence. At the latter, a villa with a mosaic bearing the name of its owner flanking a chi-rho monogram, was succeeded by a Visigothic church and cemetery. Two Christian tombstones from France, from St-Croix-du-Mont (Gironde) and St-Cyr-en-Talmondois (Vendée), are probably from villas. Despite their archaeological elusiveness, villa chapels were probably not uncommon.[34]

In the fifth and sixth centuries rural estate churches continued to multiply. As usual we are well informed about those in Touraine. At Ste Maure, the graves of two virgins, Maura and Britta, were found in a Roman cemetery. A stone church was built over them by a local man, and dedicated by bishop Eufronius (556–73). Gregory makes clear the need for episcopal sanction in such cases. The landowner begs the bishop to come and consecrate the church, and the relics, as in similar cases, are taken first to the episcopal city and then out to the new church. Ste Maure developed into an important medieval abbey. A landowner at Neuvy-le-Roi north of Tours already had an estate church, though it lacked relics. During Chlodomer's invasion of Burgundy in 524, he 'rescued' a reliquary containing relics of St Andrew and of St Saturninus of Toulouse from a burning church set on fire by the Franks. This was placed in his estate church. Later his son built a separate church for the relics, so that there were now two churches at Neuvy. When men passed through the village carrying relics of St Vincent of Saragossa, the priest begged a fragment for the old church. The number of estate churches were growing steadily. Addleshaw noted that in the diocese of Auxerre in the sixth century, only thirteen churches out of thirty-seven were diocesan churches. The remaining twenty-four were all private estate churches which had acquired parochial status.[35]

Church councils were insistent that estate churches were not private property, outside the diocesan structure, but as much a part of it as the 'public' minsters in the vici. Provision was made for a landowner who wished to see his estate chapel attain parochial status, and in Italy anyone who wished to see an estate church consecrated had to renounce all rights to it save those of a normal Christian layman. Some sought to exclude their churches from episcopal control by declaring them to be monasteries, which were also exempt from many forms of royal taxation. These privatised pseudo-monasteries were to greatly worry Bede, but their seeds can be seen at Primuliac. By 524 the Council of Lerida in Catalonia was having to rule that laymen who built a church could not withdraw it from episcopal control as a monastery unless there were monks there and a rule drawn up by a bishop.

PART 3: TOWARDS NEW HORIZONS

7. The Prehistory of the Parish

> And if the persons that are to be married dwell in divers Parishes, the Banns must be asked in both Parishes; and the Curate of the one Parish shall not solemnize Matrimony betwixt them without a Certificate of the Banns being thrice asked, from the Curate of the other Parish.
>
> Book of Common Prayer. The Form of the Solemnization of Matrimony

From the Loire to the Rhine

If the career of Martin of Tours bridged the frontier in time between pagan and Christian Gaul, then his episcopal see lay on another such frontier. Tours stands on the south bank of the Loire. South of this river much of the structure of Roman urban society survived, and the church had been able to superimpose its own structures on it. The last chapter, 'The Christianization of the Countryside', should really have had 'South of the Loire' in its title. North of the Loire urbanism and late Roman Christianity were never as strong, though parts of the Rhineland and Gallia Belgica were an exception due to the presence of the Roman army. These pockets apart, there was a great swathe of territory covering five Roman provinces between the Loire and the Rhine where the invasions of the late Empire, subsequent barbarian settlement, and a less urbanised society, meant that the Church faced a more prolonged task in establishing its pattern of rural churches. In particular the dynamic by which Gallo-Roman magnates provided resources for building churches in the rural vici was much weaker, and the strategy of the Church had to change.

In recent years, new archaeological techniques of large scale open area excavation of rural cemeteries have produced a radically new source of evidence for the transition from a pre-Christian society in northern Gaul. Though many hundreds of late-Roman and early medieval cemeteries are recorded in north Gaul, most are known only from brief references in nineteenth-century antiquarian literature, or at best from the excavation of a few graves from part of a cemetery of unknown extent. Save for a very few earlier excavations, it was only with the advent of techniques of controlled mechanical topsoil stripping and the technical and financial backup necessary for large scale excavation that it became possible to reveal the full pattern of cemetery evidence.

Frenouville was one of the first to reveal the full potential of this new evidence. It lay in rich Norman farmland in the Orne valley south-east of Caen. There is a Roman villa nearby, and the cemetery begins after the third-century invasions which may have resulted in changes in the villa estate. To the east, Edith Wightman commented on the way in which the invasions resulted in changes in cemetery patterns in Belgic Gaul. There, late Roman cemeteries sometimes shift back to pre-Roman burial places, as if the intervening pattern of early Roman settlement and burial had been a mere interlude. There is no pre-Roman phase at Frenouville, but several recently excavated Normandy cemeteries run through from the pre-Roman Iron Age to Merovingian times. Usually the earlier phases are of north-south inhumations, a mode of burial normal in the pre-Roman Iron Age over most of north Gaul and Britain. St Martin de Fontenay (Calvados) begins in this way in pre-Roman times, changes to cremation in early Roman times, only to revert back to north-south inhumation under the late Empire. In some ways this reflects a pattern common to the whole western Empire, but the reversion to the old orientation might again suggest a return to older ways. However, these problems do not directly concern us at Frenouville.[1]

Frenouville is a twin cemetery of 650 graves, one half of late Roman north-south burials, the other, separated from it by a short space, of post Roman east-west inhumations. Without total excavation over a period of eighteen months, it might have passed into the literature as wholly late Roman or wholly post Roman. The late Romans were buried in their normal clothes, often with a flagon or drinking cup beside their head, and in a wooden coffin. Pilet has argued convincingly that Frenouville shows the unbroken history of a Norman rural community from the third century to the end of the seventh. A small group of burials with 'military' belt buckles in one corner of the first phase cemetery need represent no more than an indigenous family with some tradition of army service. The post Roman cemetery has a small group of early sixth-century weapon graves, including two with swords, a sign of status. Pilet sees these as leading members of the existing community who had achieved the status and authority of their Frankish masters. The question remains as to what factor could, some time in the fifth century, persuade this stable and conservative rural society to abandon their long-established cemetery and its tradition of north-south inhumation — which had been sufficiently strong to re-assert itself in the region after the end of cremation burial — and then to move a short distance away and begin again with a new cemetery. We can rule out the influence of Frankish or other new settlers. Neither was it due to purely local factors, for similar twin cemeteries with north-south inhumations followed by east-west burials are now known from a growing number of cemeteries, from Normandy, through Picardy and the Paris basin to the Rhine.

That the cemetery shift at Frenouville was not due to immigration is shown by cemeteries like Vron (Somme) or Bulles (Oise), which are those of new settlers and show the same shift. Vron, as we have seen, was founded by three family groups in the time of Valentinian I. They buried their dead north-south, but in the mid-fifth century the cemetery underwent a basic change. After a brief period of fluidity a new east-west cemetery began, tangential to the old, and probably, like it, polyfocal. This continued to the seventh century. Some of the earliest graves of the second phase cemetery contained silver coins of Valentinian and Theodosius II struck about 446–50. Roman pottery and glass continue as grave goods, though there is an interesting phase in the early fifth century when grave goods are reduced to one or two updateable minor objects per grave — an iron buckle, a knife or a pot. This may account for the apparent hiatus sometimes seen in the cemetery record at this time. Grave goods revive in the later fifth century. As with other cemeteries in the area, a small

42   *The cemeteries of Rhenen (Holland, Guelders) and Vron (Somme). The earlier phase of each cemetery consists of north-south burials (black) in the pre-Christian tradition common to much of north-west Europe. The later phase is of east-west burials (outline) in the Christian tradition*

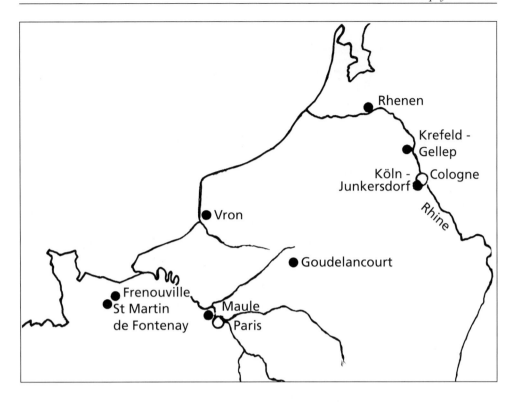

43   *Distribution map of twin cemeteries of the Vron-Rhenen type (1: 7,500,000)*

group of Anglo-Saxons appear at Vron about 485–540, buried in their own area of the cemetery, part of a wider spread of Anglo-Saxon material in Normandy and Picardy.[2]

A similar pattern can be seen at Maule in the French Vexin between Normandy and Paris. Here, a third-century cremation cemetery was followed by late Roman north-south inhumations in wooden coffins, with pottery and glass vessels. Sometime in the fifth century these are succeeded by rows of east-west graves which continue until the eighth century. Maule was a Gallo-Roman and Merovingian *vicus* in a favoured position for settlement. It is not typical of cemetery or settlement patterns elsewhere in the Vexin which are far more discontinuous. This shift from north-south burials to east-west graves a short distance away is repeated in a growing number of other cemeteries. Whilst the data from these other sites might seem repetitious, it is the variations between them that enable us to assess the likely cause. We have already seen that it cannot be attributed to immigration or new settlement. Similarly the date at which the change took place varies. The very large cemetery around the Roman *limes* fort of Krefeld-Gellep, on the Rhine near Dusseldorf, changes about AD 350 from north-south inhumations to east-west graves with few objects, though these include a military belt set and Germanic brooches. Rhenen, on the 'barbarian' bank of the Rhine near its mouth in modern Holland, has a group of thirty late fourth to early fifth-century north-south graves with military belt furniture and Germanic disc brooches, separated by a gap of some 15m from an east-west

44   Nouvion-en-Ponthieu (Somme). Plaque with Christian symbolism from a grave in the second, east west, phase of a twin cemetery. After Gallia *39, (1981), 287*

cemetery which continues until the eighth century. The cemetery shift at Vron was broadly contemporary. Bulles (Oise) has a central core of late fifth to early sixth-century cremations and north-south inhumations, one with a Frankish copy of a gold triens of Anastasius (515–20), and a one-piece buckle. Some time after this east-west burials replace the earlier mode. Finally, Goudelancourt-les-Pierrepont (Aisne) was founded about 525–75. It has the familiar pattern of twin cemeteries separated by a blank zone 10m across, and with the usual change in orientation This recurrent pattern can thus occur anywhere between the mid-fourth century and the mid or later sixth.[3]

It is necessary to look for a common factor which could persuade the inhabitants of a late Roman military vicus on the Rhine, a Normandy farming community, a group of fifth-century Gallo-Frankish settlers on the edge of the English Channel, the people of a Gallo-Roman vicus in the Paris basin, and of a couple of sixth-century Merovingian settlements to make, at very various dates, this fundamental change in one of the most conservative areas of human behaviour, and abandon their old cemetery for a new one only a few metres away. Whilst there is an understandable reluctance among archaeologists to associate grave orientation with religious belief, there is both historical and some archaeological evidence that this cemetery shift coincided with Christian conversion. At Frenouville, Christian Pilet explained the end of the east-west cemetery by a move to churchyard burial following conversion. Frenouville would thus have remained basically pagan until the late seventh century, suggesting a degree of Merovingian rural paganism quite unexpected from such sources as Gregory of Tours or the Church Councils, which, though they sometimes confuse historians by referring to traditional customs as 'pagan', in fact make it clear that these were merely survivals in a basically Christian environment.[4]

There is a distinction between the Christian conversion of an area and the establishment of a framework of rural pastoral care based within individual communities. Martin of Tours received converts at a rural pagan shrine into the church as catechumens

45   *Model of seventh-century church and cemetery at Hordain (Nord). Photo Musèe des Sciences naturelles et d'Archéologie, Douai*

by the laying on of hands. Sulpicius Severus's account, taken in context, implies not an instant replacement of one religious structure by another but a lengthy process of instruction, church building, and the provision and funding of clergy, designed to bring the rural *pagenses* within the orbit of the Church as baptised and instructed Christians. We have seen the establishment of rural churches and villa chapels from the level of the bishop and the local magnate. In our archaeological evidence, we are seeing the same process at the level of the villager and of the village priest. It would fit the observed evidence if the initial Christian evangelisation of these areas took place from rural churches or mission stations in the vici like the *ecclesiae diocesanae* in the vici of Touraine. South of the Loire, the surviving urban patterns of town and vicus, and of magnate patronage, together with the less dispersed settlement pattern, made possible a 'one stage' pattern of conversion with churches in the vici and pagi directly replacing pre-Christian cult centres. North of the Loire, however, there was a long interval, often of several centuries, before there were enough rural churches and clergy to provide adequate pastoral care. Conversion was thus a two stage process.[5]

Initial conversion might be marked by a shift to a new cemetery on an adjacent site, though grave goods and clothed burial continued. Some at least of those buried in the new east-west cemeteries were Christians. Objects like the glass bowl and bronze casket with Christian and Biblical scenes in graves at Vermand need not betoken the religious beliefs of their owners, any more than would a brass image of an Indian god in the home of a retired English Colonel. However, belt buckles with Christian crosses on the plates in graves of the second (east-west) phase at Goudelancourt-les-Pierrepont are more personal. Another grave in the same phase of the cemetery carried a headstone engraved with a large cross — a specific statement about the deceased, rather than an incidental possession. From Nouvion-en-Ponthieu (Somme), a large cemetery near Vron with a similar history, comes a square stone plaque with a Christian chi-rho monogram with alpha and omega from a sixth-century grave, again a positive statement about its occupant.[6]

The simplest kind of Merovingian field-church with cemetery is seen at Hordain near Douai (Nord). Here, a rectangular stone church of the early seventh century stood in the centre of a rectangular churchyard bounded by a ditch and hedge. Whereas the graves south of the church lay in neat rows east-west, those to its north were orientated to the north-west in irregular rows or long curving arcs. Among them were a ditched barrow covering a cremation and two small *grubenhauser*. The grave types were similar in both groups, with stone settings or grave markers, but possibly the church and churchyard took over the site of an earlier cemetery, perhaps not of pagans but outside the direct ambit of the organised church.[7]

The second, east-west phases of these cemeteries all end in the seventh or eighth centuries. Pilet associated this with a shift to burial in a newly established parish church on the site of the present village. At Hordain the cemetery and the first church were on the same site. Perhaps it was the *oratoria villara* or estate church of a landowner. Elsewhere, long established cemeteries attached to individual settlements shifted to fresh sites, presumably manorial centres, to which the settlement itself also moved. From Carolingian times onwards, there was a conscious aim that there should be a resident priest to minister to every settlement, and that laymen should pay tithe to make this ideal possible. The aim was achievable because a growing number of landowners were building churches on their estates with a plot of land as endowment for its priest. This process had been underway since the villa oratories of the fourth century, and by the ninth century most estates and villages in the more settled areas of western Europe probably had a church. Once this was supported, not only by seigneurial endowment but by the tithes and mortuary fees of its *parochia*, the definition of parish boundaries became essential. Tithes existed, if only as a moral obligation, by the sixth century in Gaul, as sources like Caesarius of Arles show, but were voluntary until Pippin III, 'The Short', made them compulsory in 765, an edict renewed by Charlemagne in 786. In England, they became obligatory under Edmund (939–46) and Edgar (959–75). These payments to the new seigneurial parish churches clashed with the ancient financial rights of the *ecclesiae diocesanae*, the older original units of rural pastoral care. In England, tithes were often divided between the 'Old Minster' and the new parish church. In France in 845, the Council of Meaux forbade priests to administer baptism save in vici (ie in 'minster ' churches) and baptisteries 'since the vici must be allowed to keep their ancient privileges'. At this time the number of landholdings was rapidly increasing, from population growth, from the growing number of land grants by lords to their followers, and from the fragmentation of ecclesiastical estates when the church was unable to recover lands which it had leased to secular lords. In this way the large early estates, secular and ecclesiastical, were fragmenting into smaller communities, though the breaking up of the old minster parishes took some centuries.[8]

The British Church

In Britain, similar post-Roman developments are obscured by the disappearance of Romano-British material culture in the fifth century, the pagan Anglo-Saxon settlements, and the problems presented by what literary sources we possess. It would need a different book to this to discuss such problems as when and where Gildas was writing, or how far Bede's account of the circumstances of the English conversions is dictated, and perhaps distorted, by his own agenda. Gildas knew little of late Roman Britain, and most of what he does say is derived from literary sources we still have. His emphasis on Magnus Maximus may derive from the latter's role in the *Vita Martini*, whose wording Gildas may echo. His notorious mis-dating of the two northern walls to after Magnus Maximus may be due to a muddled reading of Orosius, or of a source derived from him. Orosius attributes Hadrian's wall to Severus, who did repair it, and this became accepted historical wisdom known, for example, to Bede. Gildas may have read in Orosius, directly or indirectly, of Severus's Pictish wars, and confused these with the barbarian invasions of Picts and Scots (the standard rhetorical expression, as we have seen, for invaders of Britain) which marked the end of Roman Britain. On the other hand, he says nothing of Constantine III who is also in Orosius. The one original document he quotes is the appeal to Aetius 'thrice consul'. It would explain a lot about Gildas if he was working not from a library but from a collection of notes and extracts.[9]

Gildas is a first hand witness for the sixth-century British church, but we are usually reliant on oblique references made whilst Gildas was talking about other things. He refers to the grades of the clergy — bishops, priests and deacons, and to monks and abbots. He was probably a member of the secular clergy, perhaps a deacon. His words for these match those on contemporary Latin memorial stones. 'Bishops and priests' are *episcopi vel presbyteri*, like Veracius the priest (*Presbyter*) and Senacus the priest on two stones from Capel Anelog on the Llyn peninsular in Gwynedd. Another Caernarvonshire stone, from Bodafon, commemorates a *Sanctinus Sacerdos*, sometimes interpreted as 'Bishop Sanctinus'. The same word occurs at Capel Bronwen in Anglesey and Kirkmadrine in Galloway. If these were bishops it would be vital evidence for sixth-century British organisation, but Gildas uses *sacerdos* to refer, not to bishops, but to the priestly office as such – 'the priestly seat of bishop or priest', for example — *sacerdotalem episcopatus vel presbyterii sedem*. Overall, his usage is consistent. *Episcopus* and *Presbyter* refer to grades of the clergy — bishop and priest, *Sacerdos* to the priestly function, appropriate to the clergy as a whole.[10]

The Capel Bronwen stone was set up in memory of his wife by Bivatigirnus, Servant of God (*Famulus Dei*), *Sacerdos* and disciple (*Vasso*) of Paulinus, epithets appropriate to a senior and well born churchman. *Famulus Dei*, a phrase of literary rather than epigraphic origin, often used of a monk, suggests an educated man, even if we ignore the highly uncertain reading *Andoco Natione* which would make him a Gaul from Angers. If he were a bishop or senior churchman his wife would be equivalent to a Gallic *episcopa*, the wife of an important layman who separated from her husband on his becoming bishop, but retained her position and status.[11]

None of this tells us much about the overall structure of the British church at this time — the extent of individual sees; where these were located; how they were organized internally; the pattern of churches within them; and the relationship of these to the geographical structure of contemporary secular society. Gildas, however, alleges that the British clergy of his day would drive away a religious mother or sister from their house, but make light of keeping other ('strange') women. This neatly inverts the frequently repeated rulings of Gallic synods that priests should not keep 'extraneous women', *extranearum mulierum*, but be looked after by an aunt, sister, mother or daughter. Evidently most secular British clergy of Gildas's day were married, like their Gallic counterparts in the rural diocesan minsters. Presumably Gildas was citing the now lost rulings of equivalent British church councils with which his readers would have been familiar. These scraps of evidence suggest that the sixth-century British church was sufficiently like that of Merovingian Gaul to make comparisons meaningful. When Augustine met the British bishops at Augustine's Oak on the borders of the Hwicce and the West Saxons, he raised the issue of certain customs of the British church which were at variance with his own, but did not suggest that the position of the bishops was irregular in any other respect. The British church attracted educated men like Bivatigirnus into its ranks, and its bishops held church councils which concerned themselves with problems including that of married clergy. There were communities of monks, but most priests were probably based in rural *ecclesiae diocesanae*, and often married (in the sense of an open and socially accepted relationship) like their Gallic counterparts. These churches presumably had their parochiae (minster parishes, to use a deliberate anachronism), which may have corresponded to secular land divisions.[12]

The Latin memorial stones

In western Britain, from southern Scotland to Cornwall, the fifth century saw a surprising late flowering of Latin literacy in the form of some two hundred inscribed memorial stones (ie tombstones). These overlap with a parallel series of Irish language memorials in a home made Ogam alphabet, a system of notches on the same principle as the morse code. Latin and Ogams sometimes appear on the same stone in bilingual Latin and Irish inscriptions. The Latin series has little connection with Romano-British pagan tombstones, which are mostly early Roman, with a heavy bias towards the military and resident foreigners. Late Roman tombstones, reading *Dis Manibus et Memoriae*, common in Gaul, are rare in Britain and confined to south-east England. Other types of Roman inscription would have been more familiar to an untravelled British ruler. Milestones could have shown him how Roman emperors could advertise their name and titles. Carlo Tedeschi has also pointed out to me that the ligatures on early memorial stones, by which two or even three letters are joined together, are probably derived from Romano-British inscriptions rather than from continental practice. Nevertheless, the fifth-century inscriptions are basically a fresh departure, commonest in unromanized areas like Cornwall or west Wales, and less well represented in more romanized areas like south-east Wales.

Ogam inscriptions were presumably first to appear, since they must precede the ready accessibility of Latin literacy. There are other examples of native learned classes in societies on the fringes of early modern European literacy in west Africa or north America devising alphabets in this way through a process which the American anthropologist AL Kroeber called 'stimulus diffusion'. In this, a society mimics some invention or process which a neighbouring society has but which they cannot absorb directly because of technical difficulties. They may not know the sound values of a written script, or they may lack the kiln technology to make a certain kind of pottery. They therefore use something within their own cultural tool kit to attain the desired end, often producing something which appears fresh and novel rather than merely derivative. Thus the Dutch in the late sixteenth century did not have the high temperature kilns necessary to make Chinese porcelain but used their own technology of tin glazed Maiolica to mimic it, so producing Delftware. Similarly, the Goth Ulfila invented a script to translate Christian scriptures into Gothic. The immediate inspiration for Ogams may have been message sticks or tallies like the yew wands and wooden amulets with Runic inscriptions from Frisia.[13]

Similarly milestones standing beside Roman roads in Wales or Scotland could have shown fifth-century British notables how a Roman emperor could display his name and lineage. A sixth-century inscription beside a Roman road at Port Talbot (Glamorgan) was cut on the reverse of a milestone of the Emperor Maximinus Daia, but such indigenous sources cannot wholly explain the Latin memorial series. The *Hic Iacet* formula they use (in the late Roman vulgar Latin form *Hic Iacit*) derives from fifth-century Gaul. The memorial of a thirteen-year old girl from the church of Llanerfyl (Powys) must be close to the beginning of the series. It is cut horizontally, in the manner of conventional Latin inscriptions, and retains features like punctuation, the age at death, and a final *In Pace* common on the Gallic series, but dropped on the later Insular stones. The latter either use *Hic Iacit* ('Here he lies') like the Gaulish stones, or the form 'A son of B' (eg *Severini fili Severi* '(the stone) of Severinus son of Severus'), like the Ogam inscriptions. Some, mostly late in the series, combine the two in a 'compound' formula, eg *Catacus Hic Iacit Filius Tegernacus*. The great majority of such inscriptions are cut not horizontally but vertically. This is a distinctive Insular feature which may owe its origin to the tall, thin slabs available in much of west Britain, or to a parallel tradition of now vanished wooden grave markers like those indicated at Arfryn in Anglesey by the post-holes at the heads of several graves.[14]

This Latin literacy can only have been introduced to Britain through the medium of the Christian church and its cemeteries. Llanerfyl lies within the territory of the Cornovii, 50km west of its capital of *Viroconium* (Wroxeter), at a point where a Roman road running north from the fort of Caersws crosses the river Banwy. Erfyl, its patron, is an obscure female saint. An elaborate wooden shrine and reliquary in her church show that her cult still flourished in the fifteenth century. The memorial of Rosteece might be regarded as the earliest post Roman Latin memorial stone of Wales, or as a near unique epigraphic witness to the fifth-century Romano-British church. Llanerfyl could have been one of the rural churches, *ecclesiae diocesanae*, of a late Roman episcopal see of the Cornovii, based on Wroxeter, where there is a fifth-century Latin memorial stone, and possibly a late Roman Christian church.[15]

Only one Latin memorial stone from Wales has ever been found in an archaeological excavation. For many, the recorded context is no more than ' built into a barn' or 're-used as the lintel of a beast house'. Overall, though, we can distinguish three broad categories of context within which such stones occur. Some stand in churchyards, are built into the fabric of existing churches, or are displayed inside the churches where they were found. Others are from the sites of vanished chapels, recorded in early documentary sources, or in antiquarian literature. Those in this first category are, as Christian tombstones in

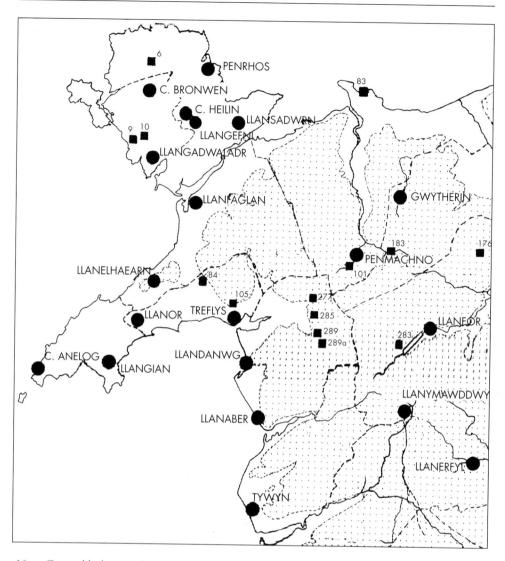

46   *Gwynedd, showing churches associated with early memorial stones (circles) and memorial stones not associated with churches (squares). Numbers for the latter from Nash-Williams E.C.M.W*

Christian churchyards, relatively straightforward, though there remain the problems of what kind of church they were associated with and whether they might have belonged to a cemetery which preceded the building of any church, as with the first phase at Hordain (in Charles Thomas's terminology to an 'undeveloped cemetery'). The second category includes the few stones that are known to be from just such undeveloped cemeteries in open country, with long cists and other types of burial but no sign of an associated church. Others again, in our third category, stand isolated on high moorland where there has clearly never been a church, alongside a Roman road or an early trackway, or even associated with a prehistoric barrow.[16]

These categories may help us to say something about the original archaeological contexts of our memorial stones, the kinds of churches with which some were associated, and perhaps why the people who put up these stones thought it important that their families should be remembered. Sometimes a Welsh *cantref* (equivalent to an English hundred), or a *commote* (the subdivision of a *cantref*) will have a church within it with an early memorial stone (often the only one within the area), and evidence from medieval sources that it was the mother church of that *cantref* or *commote* before the establishment of its later parochial pattern. Often the church will be dedicated to a locally important 'Celtic' saint, and there may be evidence that it once possessed relics in the form of his or her grave, or of metalwork or other objects associated with the saint. At times there may be a separate chapel, free standing or attached to the west end of the church, known as an *Eglwys Y Bedd* ('church of the grave'), where his body once lay. Such churches are equivalent to the English 'Hundredal Minsters'.

The 'seven *cantrefs* of Glamorgan' were said to have been an early kingdom whose seven sub-divisions were named after the sons of its ruler, Glywys, just as the *cantrefi* of Gwynedd were named after the sons of Cunedda. This could be simply a twelfth-century learned construct, but the 'seven *cantrefs*' are strikingly similar to the groups of English hundreds making up small early provinces or proto-kingdoms which have been seen by some Anglo-Saxon scholars as an early stage in Anglo-Saxon state formation. They may therefore have been of similar early origin. The three westernmost each have a church of the type discussed above with an early memorial stone, at Llansaint in Cydweli; Llanmadoc (Gwyr) and Merthyr Mawr (Margam). The eastern parts lie largely outside the distribution range of early memorial stones, though similar churches can be identified at Bassaleg (Gwynlliog), Llandough (Penychen) and Llanilltyd Fawr (Llantwit Major in Gorfynydd). It is possible that the 'seven bishop houses of Dyfed' listed in a late pre-Norman source, each a church associated with a corresponding *cantref*, represent not, as has been suggested, a pattern of small early bishoprics on an Irish model in south-west Wales, but rather the minsters or *clas* churches of a diocese, serving individual *cantrefi*, as in western Glamorgan. Most sculptured stones from the Dyfed 'bishop house' churches are late however, tenth or eleventh century, and it is doubtful if the pattern can be projected back to the sixth or seventh century. The other memorial stones from Glamorgan, however, come from quite different contexts. The *cantref* of Margam has a cluster of three, two alongside the main Roman coast road (along with a similar cluster of third-fourth century Roman milestones), the third from one of an alignment of four upland Bronze Age barrows. Another further east is associated not with a major church but with an obscure minor chapel, Capel Llanillterne.[17]

In Gwynedd, at the opposite end of Wales, most early memorial stones are associated with existing churches which in some cases, as at Llanerfyl or Tywyn, show other signs of having been important early ecclesiastical sites. Of the remainder, a few may have been associated with now vanished churches, and sometimes, as at Penmachno, there are 'satellite' stones a few miles from a major church which may represent a transitional phase before its churchyard became the normal place of burial for the people of its *parochia*. The Pentrefoelas stone for example (no. 183), a few miles from Penmachno, was associated with a long cist cemetery with no sign of an associated church. Whilst chance and the accidents of discovery must be borne in mind, a few conclusions can perhaps be drawn. A pattern of Christian churches seems to have existed by the sixth century (though of course churches could have been added to existing cemeteries). Some, for example Tywyn, may have been the chief church of their *cantref*, but more commonly, to judge by the pairs of churches with memorial stones in some *cantrefi*, they may have been associated with some smaller unit like the *commote*. Memorial stones in open country are for the most part to be found in marginal areas like the mountainous uplands of Merioneth.[18]

Those memorial stones not associated with Christian churchyards may be particularly useful in defining the relationship of such stones to contemporary secular society. Rural cemeteries of the pre-Roman or Roman Iron Age in Wales were mostly small and associated with an individual settlement, rather than being centrally organised burial places like later Christian churchyards. Groups of long cists and other burials associated with early memorial stones but with no associated church, at Arfryn in Anglesey, Pentrefoelas in Denbighshire and at Cae Maen Hir ('Standing stone field') on Penprys Farm, Llanor (Caernarvonshire), may have been similar. Elsewhere a group of memorial stones from the Upper Taf Valley above Merthyr Tydfil may have been associated with individual farms sited where tributary streams joined the river in optimum positions for exploiting the varied natural resources of the valley.[19]

As in northern Gaul we may be looking at a phase after initial contacts with Christianity, and with Christian literacy, but before the Church had established a network of rural churches, or had brought even people of rank and status within the compass of Christian burial. This interpretation is borne out by two other aspects of the Welsh memorial stones. A number are associated with Bronze Age barrows. This has sometimes been seen as a continuation, or even a continuity, of prehistoric traditions. Though no Iron Age or Roman burials are known from them, it has been assumed that the mounds remained 'sacred' or 'special' for the intervening two millennia, and that their use for burial was resumed in the Early Middle Ages. Alternatively, it has sometimes been suggested that some of the mounds may have been Christian *memoria*, contemporary with the inscribed stones.

Six memorial stones sited on Bronze age barrows are known from Wales, all from two upland areas in Clwyd and in Glamorgan. All save one are normal Bronze Age barrows. That at Abercar in Glamorgan stood among farm buildings, built into which were two early inscribed stones. When the mound was removed, long after the stones had been taken away, it produced a cremation with two Bronze Age pots. The line of barrows on Margam mountain associated with the Bodvoc stone and the ruined cairns at Gelligaer and Banwen Pyrddin with early memorial stones are typical of many other Bronze Age cairns in upland Glamorgan. The only exception is a significant one. Near Clocaenog in Denbighshire three farms called Maes Tyddin (Uchaf, Isaf and Canol — Upper, Lower and Middle) occupy a sheltered and well watered valley. From Maes Tyddin Uchaf at the head of the valley, a track climbs to the crest of the ridge of Bryn Y Beddau (Hill of the Graves) on which are two mounds. Beside these once stood two tall stones, 'Two stones at the head of a grave, four foot asunder' as Edward Lhwyd described them in 1693. One, the memorial stone of Similinus Tovisacus, is now in the National Museum of Wales. The other, uninscribed, still lies on the site. The mounds are not Bronze age barrows, but natural mounds mistaken for barrows by the people who put up the stones. There can have been no 'continuing tradition' of burial or of sacredness. Rather, they were mistaken

47   *An early medieval memorial stone (E.C.M.W. 197) on a Bronze Age barrow, Gelligaer Mountain (Glamorgan) from J.O. Westwood* Lapidarium Walliae *(1877)*

for ancient monuments marking the graves of those who had once owned and worked the land whose successors its present occupants claimed to be.[20]

This identification of ancient sites as the graves of fictive ancestors who reinforced the rights of possession of the present owners is found in other societies, particularly where there has been a cultural or social upheaval leading to the emergence of a new social élite. In Dark Age Greece, Mycenaean tholos tombs, already ancient monuments, were identified as the tombs of heroes like Agamemnon or the 'Seven Against Thebes', and became centres for religious cult and for burial. Similarly, Robert van der Noort has drawn attention to the use or re-use of barrows in areas of western Europe peripheral to its more romanised core in the period 550–750, a phenomenon which he associates with the re-assertion of traditional sources of power against the rising influence of the Christian church. In Wales, however, the status and rights of possession of the person commemorated and his family may have been more relevant than any perceived threat from the church whose influence was still weak in these upland areas.[21]

Something of the process of establishing churches to serve such upland areas, and something of its chronology, can be seen in the same upland areas of Glamorgan which have produced several of the memorial stones sited on Bronze Age barrows. In medieval times, this area contained a series of huge moorland parishes centred on the churches of Gelligaer, Merthyr Tydfil, Eglwysilan and Llantrisant. The fifth to seventh-century memorial stones in this area (not only the ones on barrows) stand in open country away from any church. In contrast, three of the four churches have early cross-slabs of possible seventh to ninth-century date. Merthyr has a simple cross slab with the name Artbeu, Eglwysilan a slab with the incised figure of a warrior, and Llantrisant a slab with three crosses, representing the crucifixion. Both the latter have interesting Merovingian and Irish parallels. It was presumably at this period that the pattern of rural churches, which had already existed for some time in the adjacent lowlands, was finally established in these upland areas with the resources and priests to serve them.

Anglo-Saxon England: late cemeteries and early minsters

In Britain we have no equivalent to the record of the bishops of Tours founding churches in the *vici* of Touraine, or the dispute over the *parochiae* of Citharista and Gargarius. In most areas of Anglo-Saxon settlement, the late Roman pattern was (so far as one can tell) obscured by the pagan incomers, and largely erased by the new Roman church order introduced by Augustine. Something of the pattern of the conversion period can, however, be recovered from two sources. One is a series of Anglo-Saxon cemeteries similar to the second east-west phase of the French twin cemeteries, the other the literary evidence for the pastoral organization of the early English Church.

The 'late phase' cemeteries of Anglo-Saxon England represent a post-conversion but pre-churchyard phase in the development of the English Church, after the Augustinian mission of 597. Their Christian nature was first recognised by E.T. Leeds in 1931 and their date (c.650–750) and significance have been made clear by Sonia Hawkes. They belong to an initial phase of Christianisation, before churches were widely available for burial, and their ending coincided with the establishment of an effective network of rural pastoral care. Like the French cemeteries, they are frequently 'paired' with an earlier pagan cemetery as at Winnall (Hampshire) or Chamberlain's Barn (Bedfordshire), though the distance apart is usually greater than in France. Usually orientated east-west, they contain grave goods, though these differ from those in earlier 'pagan' cemeteries and are usually confined to costume jewellery, belt fittings and similar possessions. Some graves contain rich items of personal jewellery with Christian crosses, as at Desborough (Northants) or Roundway Down (Wiltshire). The recognition of this transitional phase reinforces the view that models based on the Gallic evidence may be equally valid in Britain.[22]

The same conclusion can be drawn from some of the evidence relating to churches. Bede's names for churches follow the pattern of Merovingian Gaul, though with changes due to the radical growth of monasticism in the intervening period. A cathedral is an *ecclesia*, as in Gaul. The word *basilica*, however, seems to have lost much of its primitive meaning of an important early church where the body of a saint lay. This was either because almost any major church would now possess important relics, or because churches distinguished by the graves of early saints (as opposed to simply relics) would be few in the period of the conversions. *Oratoria*, as Cambridge and Rollaston point out, were probably far more common than Bede's relatively infrequent usage would suggest. In one case he refers specifically to an *oratorium villulae*, like the *oratoria villara* of Gallic sources. This relates to a landowner at Cunningham in Northumbria and an estate church founded by him on his own property. All this suggests that the pattern of churches in pre-Viking England was very like that in contemporary Gaul, but changes like that in the use of the term *basilica* show that this was an evolving process, not a static *status quo*.[23]

The role of monks and monastic foundations in the process of conversion and the provision of rural churches is uncertain. Though communities of monks under abbots had existed in Britain from an early date (Gildas for example speaks of them), it seems to have been Bede who first made the distinction in English between monastery and minster — the one a community of monks living under a written monastic rule or *Regula* (hence Regular clergy), the other a community of secular canons living in the world (*Saeculum*) and having the cure of souls. Hitherto, the single Latin word *monasterium* had served for both. English usage came to distinguish between monastery and minster, but the two words are etymologically identical.

Wales: Defining the boundaries. Dedications and mother churches

In Wales, the earlier phases of the existing pattern of parish churches was often associated in the past with the missionary activities of monastic saints like David, Teilo or Cadoc. It was thought that something of their activities could be reconstructed from the pattern of their monastic foundations like St Davids, Llandeilo Fawr and Llancarfan, and that of the churches dedicated to them — the various Llandewis, Llandeilos, Llangattocks, and the like. These had been founded either by the saints whose names they bore or by an immediate follower, much as the bishops of Tours had founded their rural churches in the *vici* of Touraine. This model was explored by the late Professor Emrys Bowen in a series of important and influential books, but it has its problems, quite apart from the fundamental one that the bulk of parish formation was a much later process than Bowen envisaged. Churches are dedicated to God under the invocation of a particular saint. Cases are certainly known of late Roman churches named after their founders, like the *Basilica Joviana* in Reims, but generally church dedications are likely to derive from relics brought from major churches, centuries — perhaps many centuries — after the death of the saint concerned. In the case of a monastic saint, this would be the monastery which he had founded and where his bones lay. This process would be fuelled by the devotion and local *pietas* of landowners, coupled with the extension of the property and estates of the monastic house. Though we have little idea when precisely men like Cadoc and David lived, the pattern of monastic expansion in western Europe would suggest that this was not before the mid-sixth century. An earlier, pre-monastic phase of church organization must have existed, as the history of the term *monasterium* or Gildas's comments on the married secular clergy show. In fact this has long been recognised. As long ago as 1911, the closing chapters of Sir John Edward Lloyd's magisterial *History of Wales* listed the ancient mother churches of Wales, *cantref* by *cantref*.[24]

The nearest Welsh equivalent to the English 'Minster' — a community of secular canons — is 'Clas church'. This means a portionary church whose revenues are shared by a community of canons. It may be convenient, though, to borrow the English term for the purposes of discussion without too much regard for modern political boundaries. In some cases it is possible to argue for a sub-Roman origin for such minsters, particularly in the English Midlands and Welsh Marches, where Anglo-Saxon settlement came late, if at all. Llanerfyl, as we have seen, may have been a rural church associated with a sub-Roman episcopal see based on Wroxeter. Whether it was a minster serving a rural area, equivalent to a Gallic *Ecclesia Diocesana*, or an estate church cannot be known, though the later cult of St Erfyl might indicate the former. In some cases, similar early foundations might be indicated by the way in which a church retained in medieval times a *parochia* with rights and revenues over much of a *cantref*, *commote* or hundred, but had been superseded in other respects at an early date by another nearby major church. In such cases there is an assumption that it already possessed such rights before the foundation of the latter and somehow managed to hang on to them.

Llanerfyl was eclipsed from an early date by nearby Meifod, a major church associated with the princes of Powys. Stephen Bassett has argued that St Helen's church within the walls of the Roman small town of Worcester may similarly have been a British minster before the establishment of Archbishop Theodore's cathedral for the kingdom of the Hwicce around 675–80. The sources are admittedly late, but since the two churches filled different functions there is no reason why the establishment of one should have entailed the extinction of the latter. Similar in some respects is the church of Bassaleg where the Roman road running west from Caerleon in Monmouthshire crosses the river Ebbw. Bassaleg is the only British example of the place name *Basilica*, denoting a major early church with important relics. Like Llanerfyl it was the church of an obscure female saint, Gwladys, whose *Eglwys Y Bedd* or grave chapel survived until the mid-nineteenth century. Two miles away is the church of St Gwynllyw, now Newport Cathedral, whose patron was the eponym of the *cantref* of Gwynlliog and which in the twelfth century was served by a community of canons under a dean. Despite St Gwynllyw's importance, however, it was Bassaleg which was mother church of the *cantref*, and retained rights over a series of churches in its uplands well into medieval times.[25]

Sometimes in western Britain, a high status fortified site with finds of imported Mediterranean and Gallic pottery and glass stands within a short distance of a major early church of the kind we have been discussing. In two cases, at Tintagel in Cornwall and at Llandough in Glamorgan (two miles from Dinas Powys), excavation in the cemetery area has produced sherds of the same types of import ware found at the fortified site. Ewan Campbell has suggested that the fortified site at Dunadd and the monastery of Iona may have had similar links of patronage and trade. Llandough stands on the site of a Roman villa and was a major monastic church by the mid-seventh century. Llanilltud Fawr (Llantwit Major) in the neighbouring *cantref* of Gorfynydd has the same combination of Roman villa with post Roman burials cut into it; a major early monastic foundation, in this case later a royal memorial church; and a royal *llys* or court, all set within a huge medieval parish occupying some of the finest cornlands of the Vale of Glamorgan and in a particularly favourable micro-climate. Once again, we may be seeing the survival of a Roman villa estate into the Early Middle Ages and the establishment, under royal or noble patronage, of an early minster or monastery to serve its territory.[26]

Such early minsters and royal monasteries were not the only kinds of church in Early Medieval Wales. Castell Dwyran in Carmarthenshire produced the royal memorial stone of Votepor, king of Dyfed, castigated by Gildas in *De Excidio*, yet it is a minute parish of 680 acres, and the church has no known dedication. The parish of Castell Dwyran contains a rectangular earthwork with substantial banks, not obviously Iron Age or Medieval but never tested by excavation. Similarly Capel Llanillterne, a minor chapelry in the parish of St Fagans (Glamorgan), has a seventh-century memorial stone, the only one in eastern lowland Glamorgan. Presumably what mattered about Castell Dwyran was not the church but the estate associated with it. It may be an estate church, an *oratoria villara*, albeit a royal one. A possible archaeological context is suggested by the contemporary

Anglo-Saxon site of Cowage Farm near Malmesbury in Wiltshire. This has rectangular timber buildings, including a large hall, and a probable timber church with an eastern apse. The core of its associated estate may be represented by the tiny later parish of Bremilham, first attested in the tenth century, which stands some 450m from its predecessor.[27]

Another aspect of rural pastoral care can be seen in ten early memorial stones from churches with the place name *Merthyr* or dedicated to St Michael, guardian of souls in death. *Merthyr* is from the Latin *Martyrium*, originally a place where a martyr was buried. The equivalent French place name is *Martre* or *Martres*, often associated with early churches with important cemeteries and most familiar in the name of the early Christian and medieval church at Montmartre in Paris. As the cult of the martyrs spread to include the graves of a variety of other men and women accounted holy or 'special', so *Merthyr* came to mean a place where the body of such a person lay and where those buried might find his or her protection on the Last Day. Often it was joined with a personal name, as at Merthyr Tydfil or Merthyr Enfael, giving the name of the man or woman whose tomb it held. Though an early memorial stone does not necessarily prove the existence of a contemporary church, the three from Welsh Merthyrs (four, if one counts the only slightly later Artbeu stone from Merthyr Tydfil) show that such sites were an early feature of Welsh church organisation, and some also have groups of later cross slabs and sculpture. Bede refers to a cemetery dedicated to St Michael the Archangel across the Tyne from Hexham in 687–705. Seven Latin memorial stones from six sites are from churches dedicated to St Michael, among them the now vanished church of Llanfihangel Croes Feini (St Michael of the crossed stones) at Newchurch near Carmarthen, with two memorial stones and several early cross slabs.[28]

Thus by the eighth century we can distinguish a number of overlapping categories of church in Wales — the territorial minster, often a portionary church served by a community of canons, the monastic church, royal or noble estate churches, and cemetery churches. These correspond with the types listed in tenth-century English law codes. A law of Edgar of 959–62 divides churches into three categories (since the law deals with the payment of tithes by lay folk, monastic churches are omitted). These are 'Old Minsters', churches with graveyards on thegn's land (ie estate churches), and minor chapels without cemeteries. Another law of Aethelraed II of 1041 divides churches into four groups, though by size rather than function. How far, though, can we distinguish such categories of church in practice?[29]

Eric Cambridge has suggested that, in County Durham, pre-Norman sculpture may be a feature of monastic churches in the strict sense of the term, and that secular minsters may be distinguished by a lack of sculpture since lay patrons may have felt the stricter living monks more worthy of their gifts than the secular canons. This opens out a new approach to the distribution of pre-Norman sculpture in Wales. Here, some sculptured crosses are specifically royal memorials on royal sites, but there is a marked tendency for sculptures to occur on a limited number of major churches which usually lack earlier memorial stones. In north Wales, where the impact of the Viking invasions was perhaps greatest, churches like Bangor (Caernarvonshire), Penmon (Ynys Mon) or Llanrhaiadr-Ym-Mochnant (Denbighshire) have important groups of pre-Norman sculptures but no earlier memorial stones or cross slabs, and there may have been a major reshuffle of ecclesiastical property or patronage. In south Wales, whilst the smaller sculptured cross slabs — more portable and perhaps less costly — have a wider distribution, standing crosses again tend to be confined to a narrower range of sites. These often have documentary evidence for monastic communities, as at Llandough or Llantwit Major with their documented lists of abbots, or Margam where the medieval Cistercian Abbey probably succeeded a pre-Norman monastery. None of these sites, or St Cadoc's monastery of Llancarfan, have produced early memorial stones (though, as always, it is risky arguing from negative evidence). The standing crosses often carry a personal name, either that of the donor or of the person in whose memory the cross was erected. This is usually a single name, Irbic, Ebissar or Conbelin, with no indication of status, but the crosses are best interpreted as costly votive gifts from lay magnates to major monastic houses.[30]

All this suggests that the later pre-Norman church in Wales was dominated by a series of major monastic churches which had pushed into the background, so far as patronage is concerned, an early pattern of territorial *clas* churches or minsters. They had not wholly replaced the latter, which often retained their property rights well into medieval times. In some cases early communities of canons may have been re-formed at some stage as monasteries, but at times, as at St Gwynllyw's minster at Newport or at Caerwent, twelfth-century saint's lives refer specifically to a community of canons under a *decanus* or dean. In the Anglo-Norman period, some small communities of secular canons in Wales and Ireland were re-formed as houses of Augustinian Regular Canons, following a rule said to have been written by St Augustine of Hippo for his cathedral clergy. In some cases, as at Chirbury on the Shropshire-Montgomery border, when this involved replacement of the existing clergy the re-formation had to wait, often for decades, until the holders of existing portionary rights died out or were found new livings.[31]

In the meantime, the pattern of parish formation was continuing. The church of Merthyr Mawr (more properly Merthyr Mymor) in Glamorgan has a sixth-century memorial stone and a collection of pre-Norman sculpture. It was probably the mother church of the eastern of the two commotes of Margam *cantref*. The process by which the Anglo-Norman parishes of Newcastle Bridgend, Newton and Kenfig were formed out of its *territorium* during the early twelfth century can, unusually, be followed in the documentary evidence. In upland areas the huge parishes created in the original period of church organization still survive, but in lowland areas like the Vale of Glamorgan a pattern of tiny parishes emerged as land-hungry Anglo-Norman settlers created small estates and parishes, nibbled out of corners of much larger earlier land units. At the opposite end of Wales, an inscription standing in the churchyard of Llanfihangel-y-Traethau is a reminder of how the pattern of parish formation continued for many centuries. Llanfihangel is in the *cantref* of Ardudwy, a few miles north of the church of Llandanwg which has two early memorial stones. Dedications and the shapes of parishes suggest that the existing pattern within the *cantref* is probably late, and that Llandanwg was the mother church of Ardudwy. The tall, slender pillar stone at Llanfihangel carries a vertical inscription; 'Here', it reads, 'is the tomb of Wleder, the mother of Odeleu, who first built this church in the time of King Owain'. This was Owain Gwynedd (1137–1170). Like the much earlier cemetery churches it was dedicated to the Archangel Michael, the guardian of the soul in death.[32]

8. Ancient Economics: Britain, Gaul and the Atlantic interface

But we have this treasure in earthen vessels

St Paul *Second Epistle to the Corinthians* 4.7

Until the late eighteenth century, when the new industrial and mercantile classes were able to challenge the age-old social dominance of the land-owning aristocracy, the western world had no word for economics in the modern sense. The Greek *Economica* ('Household rules') meant either domestic science or politics, changing, as Snodgrass has put it, 'from the world of Mrs Beeton to that of Machiavelli, without including that of Adam Smith'. Thus the many books published in recent years on the Roman and early medieval economies may be dealing to some extent with concepts which most contemporaries would have found unfamiliar. Similarly, despite the use of Roman coinage as a means of storing wealth, as shown by the innumerable coin hoards from all parts of the Roman world, the word 'capital' was only coined by Jeremy Bentham in the 1780s.[1]

Much recent work on the ancient economy has emphasised that exchange patterns in the late Empire were determined, not by normal commercial factors, but by state control and such factors as the free distribution of wine, grain and olive oil to the plebs of Rome from the time of Antoninus Pius onwards. Most agricultural production was controlled by the Imperial fisc, or by wealthy Roman senators with estates throughout the west Mediterranean. Under the Severi many senatorial estates were confiscated, so increasing the degree of Imperial control. Writing of the bulk export of olive oil from Tunisia, Keay, for example, has argued that by the fourth century, the west Mediterranean was one regional system with most land under Imperial or senatorial control, and that within this common market traders were usually agents of the Emperor, the Church, or the senatorial landowners. He shows how the export of oil in characteristic large cylindrical amphorae reflects the Imperial dole to the people of Rome until the time of the Vandal conquest of Africa in 439–442. Thereafter African amphorae become rare at Rome and Ostia, and the huge surplus cash crop was diverted northwards to southern Gaul and Spain. With the Byzantine conquest of Africa in 533–4, however, much of this surplus was diverted to the Byzantine army and administration and to the re-imposed annona, and the export of African oil and other goods northwards dries up.[2]

However, this may not have been the whole story. This international corporate trade did not exclude a great deal of economic activity at a lower level. Our literary sources for the ancient world reflect the values of a land-owning élite which may not have been universally shared outside their own circle. Gregory of Tours has two stories which bring out the ambiguity of contemporary attitudes. Both involve people engaged in what we would describe as capital accumulation in the form of *trientes*, small gold coins worth a third of an aureus. In one, a woman hides a pot of coins under the floor of her room. In the other, a man worked hard to acquire a single *triens*. With this he bought wine, which he then sold retail for silver coins (having well watered, it says Gregory), so accumulating a hundred gold solidi. Both were cautionary tales involving divine wrath for the individuals involved in such sordid and wicked activities, but despite Gregory's displeasure they show a society where coin use, commercial trade, and the storage of wealth were everyday events. Almost every detail of the stories can be confirmed from archaeological and literary sources, and elsewhere Gregory himself tells with approval of a priest buying wine for a church supper with a gold triens miraculously provided by his amiable patron saint. To Gregory, traders were often suspect outsiders, Jews, or eastern Christians of uncertain orthodoxy, who hoarded gold solidi and gave little in charity. Paul Veyne has made the point that in the ancient world trade was usually seen in terms of speculation rather than of sustained commercial strategy, and one cause of Gregory's hostility may have been the assumption that such gain was only possible by trafficking in foodstuffs essential to the poor, so raising their price and leading to hardship and starvation. Such activities were not unknown, even among the clergy. An early sixth-century church council in Tarragona forbade clerics to buy cheap and sell dear, and ruled that any cleric lending money to a peasant on the security of his fruit or wine harvest was, should the crop fail, to receive back only the sum loaned, without interest.[3]

Fairs, markets and Emporia: forms of early medieval exchange

Thus, a variety of forms of exchange existed at a variety of levels. In a traditional rural society a wide range of goods and services can be exchanged without formal economic structures, as reciprocal gifts to give support to certain groups such as the old, or the young just setting up house, or in return for communal labour at harvest. At the same time, however, the community will need access to an outside market to exchange its surplus produce or any specialist crops for essential goods. These include salt and iron that depend on raw materials of localised distribution, and manufactured goods like pottery and cloth that the village does not produce itself. It will also need seasonal fairs, geared to the annual round of the agricultural year, for the exchange of livestock, the hiring of labourers and servants, and the sale of specialist seasonal products like grain, wool, or cheese. Even today, such fairs will often be on religious festivals, though the religious and economic aspects may now be merely residual. At the next level up, medieval seigneurial estate documents record similar exchange. Early medieval charters refer to food rents in agricultural surplus — beer, bread, or livestock. One early Welsh charter records a census or food render of 'forty little pigs' (*douceint torth*) paid to an estate. The breeding pig is the villager's capital, raised and fattened on an annual cycle whilst its predecessor is eaten. The annual surplus of young porkers (the interest, as it were, on the capital) can be sold as a cash crop, or to pay taxes. Exchange at estate level is sometimes discussed in terms of broader economic patterns, but seen at its own level is remarkably constant. Pliny's negotiations over the sale of his grape harvest, or the renders in kind paid by Egyptian potters under the late Empire can readily be matched in medieval stewards accounts. Sixth-century estate owners in Gaul brewed beer for their reapers, like later landowners, though the aristocratic Gregory of Tours has to explain to his wine drinking readers what this was.[4]

Markets and fairs were the interface between this local small world and that outside. Like estate transactions and the imposition of monetary taxation, they were central to the initial stimulus of a rural monetary economy. They could also be used by a local élite, acting as representatives of a state, to demonstrate their power and prestige by religious festivals, or their coercive power, as with a formal legal Assize. The rural power structures of the Romano-Gallic countryside focussed in part on the rural cult centres. They declined in the late Empire because of changes in rural power structures, but the scale of their market squares and theatres suggest the crowds that flocked to them on religious festivals and the importance of their associated markets. Their successors in post Roman Gaul were the rural Christian shrines. Gregory of Tours has a story of a shoplifter at the shrine of the martyr Eugenius at Vieux (Tarn), in the countryside west of Albi. On his feast day, crowds from the surrounding region gathered at the shrine and much business was done in the atrium or courtyard before the shrine. The girl stole a piece of jewellery from a merchant's stall, but the martyr proved very effective in policing his own festival.[5]

At one level, the coastal trading emporium was simply a maritime extension of the rural trading fair which often specialised in locally produced goods with a widespread demand, such as wool, cloth, or dyestuffs. It was held on an agreed date, often a religious festival, and was held under the authority of someone who could keep law and order among the crowds who assembled, settle disputes, deal with petty crime, oversee the quality of goods offered and the genuineness of weights and coin, and in return collect a toll on behalf of the ruler. Urban emporia were usually outside the walls of the city, a natural extension of the quayside *vicus portensis* in Roman cities such as Nantes or Bordeaux. At Nantes, the *vicus portensis* had its own magistrates, like vici elsewhere, and we meet them on inscriptions from the quayside area, setting up dedications to Vulcan, patron of trade and manufacture, along with the Corporation of Loire boatmen, or donating a Tribunal or public platform for official ceremonies. At Bordeaux, the quayside area has produced a seventh-century hoard of gold solidi, including some from Visigothic Spain, indicating the continued importance of the maritime trading suburb. In London, the '*emporium* visited by many peoples, coming by land and by sea' of Bede's day lay west of the walled city, in the Strand and Aldwych, whilst in Paris the great fair of St Denis, founded in 634 and already frequented by Anglo-Saxon merchants in 710, lay around the great suburban church. This is often seen as reflecting the changed role of the city whose walled area was now the preserve of the King, his count or reeve, and of the bishop, with their palaces and churches, with economic life pushed outside the religious and administrative area. The economic role of the Gallo-Roman city may have been much less than is often assumed, however, and Nantes shows that the *vicus portensis* was already flourishing in Gallo-Roman times, even before the distinction between the walled city and its suburbs existed.[6]

Pottery: a fifth-century industry

The Merovingian pottery kilns at Haucourt (Nord) were discovered in 1972 by an archaeologist travelling on a bus along the Roman (and modern) road from Cambrai to Arras. He noticed areas of burnt material in ploughed fields east of the village of Vis-en-Artois, the probable location of the *Vicus Helenae* where Aetius defeated the Franks. We have seen how, in Gallo-Roman times, it was the vici rather than the towns which were the centres of primary industrial production. This was particularly true of the pottery industry. Many vici, like Famars (Nord), not far from Vis-en-Artois, had kilns which supplied the surrounding area with grey coarsewares. Others like Lezoux, Mayen, or the vici of the Argonne forest, developed large scale fineware industries which sometimes exported their products over much of the western Empire. The excavated kilns at Haucourt are largely seventh century, with the combination of carinated-rouletted bowls of ultimate Germanic inspiration, and plainware vessels of devolved Gallo-Roman form found through most of northern France. It confirms the evidence for the continuance of a vicus based pottery industry into post-Roman times. Possibly the potters were working under the control of a local magnate. Two late Roman legal edicts describe a man with potteries on his estate, who employed the potters seasonally on the land when the climate made potting in the open impossible, and another who has pottery workshops in which the products of his estate were sent for sale. Medieval parallels suggest that the potters may have been free tenants rather than belonging to the demesne of the estate, marketing their own wares locally (or in the vicus itself on market day), and paying a render, in cash or in kind. It is valuable, though, to be reminded that the potters would need not only land to dig clay and cut firing, but land to cultivate outside the potting season.[7]

The division between coarse wares for local use, like those of Famars or Haucourt, and fine wares with much wider distribution also continued. One distinctive fineware of north Gaul was the red-slipped pottery produced in the vici of the Argonne forest. This, like the English Oxfordshire ware, was one of the regional industries which under the late Empire replaced the vanished Samian ware. It produced a range of forms often derived from earlier samian types, one of the most distinctive being a bowl with rouletted decoration imitating the form Dragendorf 37 (the hemispherical bowls with elaborate pictorial decoration familiar to anyone who has visited a museum with Roman collections). Until the 1960s it was believed that the industry ended with the invasions of 406–7. It is now known that it continued to be produced, and to develop, through the fifth century and into Merovingian times. This is important for our understanding of the later history in the Rhine frontier defences, but also provides data about an important fifth-century industry. Didier Bayard has divided this later production into four phases, based on detailed study of the individual wheels used to produce the rouletted decoration. The first phase is basically fourth century. Interestingly it occurs on British sites, whereas all later phases are absent. The second phase (of the first half of the fifth century) is found on only two or three villas, and is best represented in military sites of the Rhine frontier, the Belgian limes, and the Armorican coastal defences. Not only does the main fourth-century production centre continue in use however, but a new one actually opens about 410. The third phase, of c.425–75, sees the appearance of a new range of decoration with Christian motifs, whilst a fourth and final phase carries production down to about 530. To anyone familiar with the latest phases of the British pottery industries, which rely on a limited range of old types and show little innovation or development, one of the most striking features of the Argonne industry is the way it not only survived, but continued to evolve. An accompanying range of distinctive hand made coarsewares including lid-seated jars, flanged mortarium-like bowls, and small handled jugs is known from excavation at sites such as Metz and Maastricht.

These sub-Roman forms recur in the wheel-made Roman derived coarsewares seen at Haucourt and in a variety of types and fabrics through much of post Roman Gaul.[8]

Much the same pattern emerges with the other main pottery production centre of northern Gaul in this period. The vicus of Mayen, west of Koblenz in the Rhineland, had important potteries in Roman times, and production of its hard-fired coarsewares continued uninterrupted into medieval times. The ware circulated mainly in the Rhineland, but it much influenced pottery production in north Gaul through a range of copies in sandy wares. Similar conclusions could be drawn from other industries of north Gaul, such as glassware, or the metalworking industry of the Meuse Valley which produced decorated belt and sword fittings and bronze vessels including 'Vestland' cauldrons with triangular ears or projections for the iron handles. These had a wide circulation in Scandinavia, Germany, and Anglo-Saxon England. Three even ended up in a lead mine at Halkyn Mountain in Flintshire. Most of the recent debate on Pirenne's *Mohammed and Charlemagne* has centred on the role of eastern imports in the Gallic economy, but he also put much stress on the scale of the economic activities of indigenous merchants and artisans within Gaul. Our understanding of the ways in which Gaul served as an intermediary between the Mediterranean and Insular worlds has to take this into account.[9]

More directly relevant to Britain and Ireland are the pottery industries of southern Gaul. Over most of Gaul, the predominant post Roman coarsewares comprise the series of fairly standard Roman-derived forms already referred to. These include a ubiquitous ovoid jar, often lid-seated (with the rim hollowed internally to take a lid); a pitcher which is basically the jar with a handle and a pinched spout added; a distinctive open bowl inspired by similar open glass bowls; a few lids to go with the jars, and, in the south, a few mortaria. In the north, these occur alongside the carinated-rouletted bowls of ultimate Germanic tradition in the Merovingian cemeteries. The carinated bowls are often technically highly proficient wheel thrown wares from production centres in the Rhineland and Belgic Gaul, with a black reduced surface which shows carefully controlled firing. The Roman derived wares, sometimes with distinctive inclusions, must have been produced at a great many local centres, and one hard-fired late sixth and seventh-century version from an unlocated centre in western Gaul (Insular 'E' ware) was exported to Britain and Ireland in some quantity, in part as containers for goods such as dyestuffs. 'E' ware, in common with some other south Gaulish wares in this tradition, sometimes has irregularly fired dark grey/light grey surfaces suggesting firing in clamp kilns rather than permanent structures.[10]

South of the Loire, the late slip-coated and decorated fineware tradition represented further north by Argonne ware was taken up by early Christian grey and orange stamp-decorated wares — *sigillées paléochrétiens grises et orangées*. These are ultimately in the tradition of decorated samian, but unsurprisingly the strongest influence, and the immediate source of much of their decoration, was African red-slip ware, imported into southern Gaul in quantity at this time. Madame Rigoir has identified three main groups, centred on the hinterlands of Marseille (the Provencal group); Narbonne (the Languedoc group) and Bordeaux (the Atlantic group), though smaller centres produced similar wares in Aveyron-Lozère, the Rhône valley and Poitou. They are the work of experienced professional potters of good quality, wheel-thrown, with an even slip coat, neat decoration, and were fired under controlled conditions to produce even orange or slate grey surfaces. The earliest was probably that in the Narbonne area in the mid-fourth century. The Provencal kilns seem to have begun in the early fifth century, whilst the Bordeaux atelier belongs to the later fifth and sixth century. Excavations in Bordeaux have produced the ware in quantity, suggesting that it must have been produced in the city itself or its immediate vicinity.[11]

This Atlantic group (known in Britain as Insular 'D' ware) has a number of distinctive features. Unlike Languedoc, where orange and grey wares are broadly equal in numbers, orange-fired wares are rare elsewhere, accounting for some 5% of the output at Bordeaux. The decoration is also distinctive. The radiating palm fronds, circles and rosettes derived from African red slip ware were supplemented by rouletted ornament and circular stamped medallions in the centre of the inside of a plate, with a stag surrounded by other motifs. Sometimes there is an inscription, one recording that it came from the workshop of Eosocus — *Ex Of(f)icina Eosoci*. The slate coloured slip coats may reflect a fashion for imitations of pewter or silver, and central internal decorated medallions are commonplace on late Roman silver dishes. The output of the Bordeaux group includes flat plates and dishes, decorated internally; hemispherical bowls, with external rouletted or cordoned decoration; pot lids and mortaria. The ware is also an indicator of maritime contacts along the Atlantic seaways, northwards to Nantes and Rouen and across the Channel to western Britain and Ireland.[12]

The amount of *sigillée paléochrétiene grise* from Britain and Ireland is small. The largest, and most characteristic group is that from Dinas Powys (Glamorgan), with some ten vessels. Totals from south-west England, the rest of south Wales and Scotland are probably all in single figures, and there is a single vessel from Ireland. On virtually all sites it is accompanied by much larger quantities of amphorae and fine wares from the east Mediterranean, and it is to the problems of these that we must now turn.[13]

The furthest shores: Syrian merchants and villagers

The recognition of post Roman pottery from Syria, Asia Minor and Greece on sites in western Britain and Ireland was one of great surprises of post-war early medieval archaeology. Some had been found in the late 1930s, but it was Radford's study of 1956 followed by that of Charles Thomas in 1959 that identified the main types. Tintagel (later Insular) 'A' wares are red-slipped fine ware bowls, mostly Phocean red slip ware from Phocea on the west coast of Asia Minor near Izmir (Smyrna), with smaller amounts of African red slip ware from the Carthage area. The 'B' wares comprise various types of amphorae.[14]

Insular 'Bi' are globular amphorae with a band of horizontal combing on the shoulder from the Aegean, perhaps the Argolis peninsula south of Corinth, or one of the Greek islands. 'Bii' amphorae have a longer oval body and a characteristic tegulated body ribbing (rather like the overlapping boards of a wooden fence). Fabric variations suggest more than one source, probably in the Antioch-Tarsus area of north Syria and south-west Turkey or in western Asia Minor or Cyprus. 'Biv' amphorae (*Caesarea* type 4) are smaller carrot shaped vessels in a micaceous fabric, possibly from around Sardis, inland from Smyrna. Phocea is nearby and the adjacent island of Chios was noted in antiquity for its wine. Unlike 'Bi' and 'Bii', however, these micaceous lagenae reached Britain in small numbers both in Roman and post Roman times. Large cylindrical north African amphorae ('Byzacena', 'Africana Grande' or Insular 'Bv') are now being recognised on late Roman sites in Britain and

Ireland. Insular 'Bvi' amphorae(*Caesarea* type 2), known from a few scattered examples, are of particular interest in that they are from the Gaza area in Palestine, and probably held the wine of Gaza whose quality (and price) were almost proverbial in late antiquity.[15]

The way in which overseas trade in post-Roman Gaul was dominated by Syrians, and to a lesser extent by Jews, has been familiar since the time of Pirenne. One Syrian merchant had a relic of St Sergius from Resafa on the upper Euphrates in a private chapel in his house at Bordeaux. Another *negotiator, genere Syrus*, named Eusebius, became bishop of Paris by bribery and replaced the previous bishop's household with his own countrymen, whilst the Greek merchants of Orleans joined with the Jews and the Gallo-Romans in the Adventus ceremony to welcome king Guntram to their city. However, this does not wholly explain the mechanism of the trade which brought amphorae of east Mediterranean oil and wine to Cornwall, Galloway or County Cork. Our best hope of doing this may be to follow the Syrian merchants back to their homeland.[16]

The great trading metropolis of north Syria was Antioch. For Gregory, the most celebrated inhabitant of the region was Simon Stylites, who in 423 began to live on a pillar at Telanissus in the countryside fifty miles east of Antioch. His fame brought offerings from the surrounding country folk and from much further afield, and after his death in 459 a huge cruciform pilgrimage complex was built around his pillar. Simon had not settled in the desert, but in a prosperous countryside whose villages soon came to acquire impressive churches based on the architecture of the pilgrimage church and monastery at Qalat Sem'an. Tchalenko's field survey of the interior of northern Syria, long famous for the ruins of its ancient churches, revealed large numbers of villages whose prosperity in the fifth and early sixth century was based on large scale production of olive oil, evidenced by the huge number of oil presses which they contain. Subsequent survey, accompanied by some excavation, has to some extent modified Tchalenko's view of a monoculture economy based on olive oil, but this is not very surprising — no villagers can subsist on a diet of olives and olive oil alone.[17]

This period of prosperity corresponds with the appearance of the 'Bii' amphorae, probably from the Antioch area, on sites in the west in the period 475–550. The village churches, like the numerous large villages themselves, attest the prosperity of the area in the period after the death of Simon Stylites. Qualat Sem'an dates from about 480. The area evidently produced at this time a large surplus cash crop of olive oil, a jar of which was worth radically more in Marseille or Bordeaux (to say nothing of in Cornwall or Cork) than it was in the east Mediterranean. The prosperity of the region may have been badly affected when it was sacked by the Persians in 541 and large numbers of people carried off into captivity. Although the main street of Antioch was rebuilt in good style after the sack, its great days were over. In 573 Antioch and Apamea were again sacked by the Persians and many of their inhabitants led off into slavery.[18]

Geographically, the Mediterranean is divided into two basins of unequal size, the lands around each of which correspond broadly to the Latin and Greek speaking areas of the Roman Empire. Access from the much larger eastern half to the west Mediterranean is by the straits between Sicily and Tunisia, a gap a hundred miles wide dominated by Carthage (and its Arab successor Tunis), and by the islands of Malta and Pantellaria. The wide range of pottery imports from the east Mediterranean at Carthage mirrors both the greatest prosperity of the oil producing north Syrian countryside and the chronology of the Insular imports. Types found in Britain were already present in the early fifth century, but the highest ratios of eastern imports at Carthage occur between the mid or later fifth century and the mid-sixth century. Thereafter, quantities decline. In the west Mediterranean, however, eastern imports are, unsurprisingly, heavily outnumbered by African products. Anyone familiar with late Roman pottery assemblages in the west Mediterranean will know the huge amounts of Tunisian wares — African red-slip, cylindrical amphorae and decorated lamps — that occur, and the modest amounts of eastern imports. This is only partly due to the fact that the African products enjoyed a much longer period of import, for it is equally true of shorter lived assemblages. To quote only one example, the coastal site at Benalua near Alicante had over a hundred vessels of Phocean red-slip ware — the largest assemblage in Spain — but nearly nine hundred of African red-slip ware.[19]

The African slip wares and amphorae are directly related to the trade in essential African foodstuffs, particularly olive oil and grain, on which the cities of the west Mediterranean had come to depend. The mechanisms by which food from estates in the surrounding countryside reached many Spanish cities and parts of Gaul may have broken down. The Goths in particular were now dependant on imported food. Constantius's blockade in 417–8 quickly led to their submission, and in return for agreeing to re-settlement in Gaul they received 600,000 measures (around 150,000 bushels) of wheat. Their repeated attempts to secure a Mediterranean port, whether Marseille, Arles or Narbonne, was an attempt to obtain access to these essential supplies on their own terms, and after the Vandal conquest of Africa in 429–39, an interruption in the grain supply led to famine, and to famine prices. These were exceptional times, however, and the quantities of north African pottery on west Mediterranean sites attest a normally flourishing trade. Such interruptions in supply, and the high prices which resulted would be a powerful stimulus to eastern merchants, in the decades after the fall of Carthage in 442, to try to break into a western market previously dominated by African products.[20]

Byzantine traders and the Spanish Levant

'In the Mediterranean', said the Genoese admiral Andrea Doria, 'there are three ports: Cartagena, June, and July'. It is not, as is sometimes assumed, a placid inland sea, but has strong currents, seasonal winds that can blow a fleet of sailing ships off course, and few good natural harbours. This helps to explain why places like Smyrna and Phocea, Marseille, Syracuse and Cartagena recur throughout its history. From Carthage, eastern trade goods, best represented in the archaeological record by the pottery containers in which some of the goods travelled, were shipped north to Marseille and Narbonne, or via the Balearic Islands to Catalonia, or due west, aided by a strong and direct ocean current, to New Carthage — Carthago Nova (Cartagena). In the sixth century, Marseille was still the great commercial port of Gaul, where papyrus, spices, eastern textiles, wine and oil were traded. There were many merchants and traders, mainly Syrians and Jews, and a flourishing gold coinage was supported by local small change in silver and bronze. In one characteristic episode in 573 some servants of an archdeacon stole seventy jars 'of the kind called *orcae* full of oil and other goods' from a merchant in the Vieux Port. Their master was fined 400 gold solidi by the Governor. However, it is clear that the Insular import wares arrived in Britain not through southern Gaul, but by way of the Straits of Gibraltar and the Atlantic seaways.[21]

The distribution of Phocean red-slip ware (Late Roman 'C') in the Mediterranean basin is instructive on the chronology of eastern imports. In the late fourth and early fifth centuries, it was confined east of a line from Benghazi to Albania. By the later fifth century, after the Vandal conquest of Africa, it had spread over the central and western Mediterranean, and thence to Britain and Ireland. Keay has suggested that the collapse of the western Empire coincided with an opening of the west Mediterranean to eastern imports. He explains this in terms of a relaxation of official control of trade, though one wonders how effective the fifth-century Empire was at enforcing such control. So far as the organization of the trade is concerned, Fulford has argued that the Insular import wares were not trans-shipped in France or Spain, but travelled direct from the east Mediterranean. 'Britain', he concludes, 'was a deliberate objective of certain ships setting out from eastern ports', from the Aegean, or Constantinople, and one objective is likely to have been British tin. The small amounts of north African amphorae and red-slip wares on early medieval insular sites contrast with the much greater bulk of eastern wares, reversing the pattern on west Mediterranean sites. We have already noted Benalua, where African red-slip outnumbers Phocean red slip by almost 9:1. In contrast, in 1981 Charles Thomas was able to list some 45 vessels of the latter from Insular sites, compared with 16 of African red-slip (10 being from Tintagel).[22]

The coastal areas of south-east Spain had long been supplied with Mediterranean fine wares by sea, supplementing, or at times excluding, inland wares. Italian Arretine and south Gaulish samian had been replaced, from the second century onwards, by African red-slip wares, excluding Spanish samian ware from coastal areas. The African wares are not wholly coastal, but reach inland sites within Levantine Spain in some quantity. Not only is Phocean red-slip ware much rarer than its African equivalent in Spain, but it has a significantly different distribution. It is almost entirely coastal, and shows a tendency to cluster on a limited number of sites or areas which may represent coastal emporia or trading centres. The African wares, however, are consumer goods. They include amphorae of oil, wine, or other foodstuffs, decorated oil lamps, usually with traces of burning around the nozzle, and fine wares to supplement local Roman and post-Roman coarsewares.

Benalua lies on a low hill bounded by the sea and by river gullies on the outskirts of Alicante, where the Emperor Majorian assembled his fleet for his ill-fated attempt at invading north Africa in 460. It evidently retained its importance as a harbour or coastal anchorage. The finewares are accompanied by amphorae, African lamps, and local coarsewares. In contrast to over a hundred vessels of Phocean red-slip ware from Benalua, Monastil near Elda, 30km inland, has only a single vessel. To the west, in Murcia, the ware is now known from Cartagena, and there is a good group from the Isla de Fraile off Aguilas, a coastal island with large surface collections of amphorae, mostly African, but including eastern types like Insular 'Bi'. There is another good group of Phocean red slip wares, again of form 3, like the insular examples, from the old excavations at Villaricos, a coastal site at the mouth of the Rio Almanzora, occupied from Carthaginian to Moorish times. Coastal Murcia had important Roman mines of argentiferous lead, and in the nineteenth century both Aguilas and the Cuevas de Almanzora were important centres of the silver and lead industry. Whatever the case with tin, Byzantine merchants would have had little reason to sail to the islands of Britain for lead and silver.[23]

From Murcia, there is a scatter of Phocean red-slip ware westwards as far as Malaga and the Straits of Gibraltar. Byzantine merchants are said to have sailed up the Guadiana in the late sixth century to Merida and there may have been a Greek Byzantine colony in the city. That the main eastern contacts were specifically with the Murcia-Cartagena area is, however, emphasised by the very thin scatter of PRS ware northwards from Alicante to Catalonia. This coast has plenty of other evidence for late and post Roman trade in the form of African and Baetican amphorae, Insular 'Bii' amphorae from northern Syria, and early Christian grey stamped ware from southern Gaul, some of which got as far south as Elche, Benalua and Alicante. Phocean red-slip ware is, however, rare in Catalonia, even on sites like Tarragona, Barcelona and Ampurias, which have seen much excavation. Fragments of five vessels of PRS ware from Port-Vendres (Pyrenees-Orientales), just over the border into France, were thought to be from the Port-Vendres 'A' wreck, as part of a mixed cargo. This would have been an important discovery, but it is now believed that they may have been debris from the harbour bottom, not part of the cargo.[24]

Beyond the Pillars of Hercules

A generation or two ago, contacts along the Atlantic seaways were sometimes seen as an historical-geographic continuum from prehistoric times onwards, with bands of 'Megalith builders' or 'Beaker folk' travelling north from Iberia to colonise Britain or Ireland. Such models drew support from modern cultural and religious affinities between Brittany and Wales, or Catholic Spain and Ireland, as well as from undoubted historical contacts of long standing. The fact that the archaeological models so invoked are now largely outmoded should not, however, be allowed to get in the way of a fresh exploration of the Atlantic sea routes of early historic times.

A good port at which to begin such an exploration would be Sanlucar de Barrameda at the mouth of the Guadalquivir, down river from Seville and well west of the Straits of Gibraltar. In the sixteenth century, Seville was the terminus of the treasure fleets of the Indies and of the Asian spice route, but Sanlucar was the destination of traders and sailors from England, Holland, Ireland and Brittany. 'Breton' became a generic term for northern traders, as the Calle de los Bretones near the Ducal Palace still testifies. 'In Sanlucar', said a local proverb, 'the Bretons find their Indies', and many entries in port books from Wales and south-west England record voyages there. These 'Bretons' came not only for wine, oil and spices, but for salt from the coastal salterns. The trade has archaeological trace elements in Iberian redware ('Merida' type ware), olive jars and Spanish costrels from Insular sites. We cannot project this trade backwards in time, but Sanlucar is instructive, not least as a warning against assuming that all trade north from the Straits of Gibraltar was necessarily carried in Mediterranean ships. To the north, a scatter of Phocean red slip ware is known from four sites along the Portuguese coast. At Conimbriga, the only site where such comparisons can as yet be made, the proportion to African red-slip is much higher than on Mediterranean sites, and closer to Insular figures. This reflects the fact that relatively little African ware was travelling outside the Mediterranean, and again shows that the mechanisms by which the two wares were distributed may have been quite different, and that comparisons of the quantities of the two on insular sites may be misleading.[25]

Beyond the coast of Portugal we move into historically difficult waters. Contacts between the world of Visigothic Spain and the Insular world of Britain and Ireland involve two separate controversies. On the level of intellectual contacts, Hillgarth has argued that the early distribution of manuscripts of writers like Isidore of Seville show direct contacts in the seventh century between Spain and Ireland. Roger Collins, though, has pointed to the absence of any references to Irishmen in Visigothic Spain, and suggested indirect contact through the monasteries of Columbanus in France rather than by 'itinerant booksellers afloat on the Bay of Biscay'. A parallel problem is that of the identity of the merchants who brought Mediterranean import wares to the Insular sites. Fulford and Thomas have argued for direct trade between the Byzantine world and Britain, but other alternatives are possible. Syrian or even Gallic sailors may have sailed from ports in Spain or western France, and we know that in the seventh century Irish and British sailors were to be found in ports at the mouth of the Loire. It may be difficult to decide whether Mediterranean goods arrived in the west as a result of direct eastern trade or were filtered through intermediaries in Mediterranean or Atlantic ports.[26]

The seventh-century Life of St John the Almsgiver, Patriach of Alexandria in 610–19, contains a remarkable story which has sometimes been cited as evidence for direct trade between Byzantium and western Britain. This biography has a complex textual history. The original version written by Sophronius bishop of Jerusalem in 633–7 is now lost, but a supplement — which contains the episode involving the ship captain said to have sailed to the Islands of Britain — was added by one Leontius, who describes himself as bishop of Neapolis. Some ten places of this name are known (it was the equivalent of the modern English Newport or Newcastle), but it was probably Neapolis in Cyprus. Later a conflated text combining the two earlier lives was produced. The story tells of an Alexandrian ship-captain down on his luck who is given the money for a new boat by the Patriach John. After two unsuccessful attempts he sails to the Islands of Britain with a loading of corn, with the aid of a magic mist and a ghostly helmsman. He returns with a cargo of lead which is miraculously turned to silver. Egyptian bishops are known from other sources to have owned and operated trading boats, but in its present form the story is clearly fiction. It begins with the familiar folk lore theme of 'third time lucky' (three brothers, three little pigs, etc) and then follows the framework of Vladimir Proop's morphology of the folk tale closely. It is rather like the pantomime history of Dick Whittington (a soundly historical character) and may be about as reliable a source for economic history. Nevertheless, it gives an insight into how an educated seventh-century Byzantine audience may have regarded Britain. Any contacts reflected in the pottery imports would have been a century in the past, and at one level the story could reflect a nostalgic look back from the disasters which befell the Byzantine Empire in the seventh century to the days when such things were possible. The Life was written to appeal to the mercantile community of Alexandria and says much about commerce and finance. Britain retained the reputation it held in the classical world as a rich source of metals. Tin was known in seventh-century Egypt as 'the British metal', though there is archaeological evidence that it was also being produced and traded in Brittany at this time.[27]

Visigoths, solidi and Syrians at Bordeaux

There is no doubt, however, about the eastern merchants of Bordeaux. Gregory of Tours' wealthy Syrian merchant of Bordeaux Eufronius, had, about 585, an oratory with a relic of the martyr St Sergius of Resapha (on the Euphrates east of Antioch) in his house. When a Merovingian usurper tried to take this from him for a battle charm, Eufronius offered a hundred gold solidi to buy him off. In 1803, a hoard of about eighty-five Frankish and Visigothic gold coins from the final decades of the seventh century was found near the Palais de l'Ombrière in the quayside area outside the Roman walls of Bordeaux. Most were from south-west Gaul, but there were seventeen from Spanish mints including Toledo, Merida and Seville. The Ilot-Saint-Christoly site within the Roman city has now produced intact sixth-century levels with rich artefactual and environmental evidence. This includes Phocean red-slip ware, an imitation gold triens of Justinian and *sigillée paléochrétienne grise* in such quantity as to reinforce strongly the view that it was a local product. It is a reasonable assumption that much of our insular import wares passed through the quays at Bordeaux, and even if Eufronius and his counterparts in the previous century did not themselves venture as far as Cornwall (and they may well have done so), they may well have had a profitable hand in its passage.[28]

Nantes: an Atlantic seaport

Sailing north from Bordeaux along the coasts of Charente and the Vendée, one comes after 300km to the mouth of the Loire. Nantes, the Roman *Condivicum*, was a port 30km from the open sea, at the navigational limit of the Loire for large sea going vessels and at its junction with the Erdre. The maritime port suburb, the *vicus portensis*, had its own magistrates in Roman times. It lay along the quays of the now vanished Erdre, west of the Roman walls. In the sixth century Nantes still maintained something of its old way of life. Fortunatus describes the cathedral of St Peter and St Paul built by bishops Eumenius and Felix between 548 and 568, marble columns and capitals from which were found in excavations early this century. Its builders seem to have been familiar with church building in north Italy and further afield. Felix is said to have improved the channel of the Loire for navigation, and it is possible that the tolls from maritime trade could have contributed towards the building of his cathedral.[29]

There have been no large scale modern excavations at Nantes to match Bordeaux, but older work at the Bishop's palace, the Place St Pierre and elsewhere, and salvage on nineteenth-century building sites produced much *sigillée paléochrétienne grise*. Most surviving sherds are decorated, and it would seem that only such sherds were kept. Any associated coarse wares or amphorae sherds were apparently also discarded. Some sherds have decoration from identical stamps to vessels from Bordeaux. There are also indications that Nantes was involved in trade along the Atlantic seaways with Visigothic Spain, one commodity involved being tin. At Abbaretz and Nozay north of Nantes, deep trenches have been dug into tin bearing schists. These workings have produced a radiocarbon date of 650 ± 100 AD, a Frankish triens, a Visigothic triens, and a sherd of unidentified amphora. A series of gold tremisses with the mint signature of Nantes also have a Victory carrying a wreath on the reverse in the very distinctive sixth-century style of Visigothic Spain. Nantes also had links in quite other directions. In 610 St Columbanus, under sentence of deportation for refusing to bless the illegitimate offspring of Theuderich II, arrived at Nantes and found a boat to Ireland with little difficulty. These links between the Loire estuary, the Seine, Ireland, Britain and Gascony recur in the Life of another seventh-century Frankish saint, whose career was much influenced by the Irish mission of Columbanus and by an English born Frankish queen.[30]

Noirmoutier and St Philibert

South of the Loire estuary is the broad sheltered Baie de Bourgneuf, with the Pornic peninsular to the north and the long narrow island of Noirmoutier to the south. Noirmoutier, an offshore island like Lindisfarne or Iona, was a ready-made *insula* for early monks. The name 'Black monastery' derives from the seventh-century Benedictine foundation of St Philibert, a Gascon of good family from *Vico Julii* (Aire) in Landes, where his father Philibald was bishop. In the household of Dagobert I (obit 630), that Parisian 'nursery of bishops', Philibert met St Ouen, a court official and founder of the monastery of Rebais, where Philibert became a monk and later abbot. In 654 Philibert founded the monastery of Jumièges in the Seine valley near Rouen (where Ouen was now bishop), on land given by Clovis II and his English-born wife Baldhild, herself founder of the aristocratic nunnery of Chelles outside Paris which attracted many Anglo-Saxon women. These royal and courtly foundations may seem to have brought us away from the Baie de Bourneuf with its coastal salt pans and oyster beds, but in 674 Philibert denounced the powerful Mayor of the Palace Ebroin, who had expelled the Irish monks of Luxeuil, and was exiled from Neustria. He withdrew south of the Loire and founded Heri Monasterium or Noirmoutier.

With a career which encompassed Gascony, the Loire estuary, the Irish mission of Columbanus, Rouen, Paris, and the Seine Valley, Philibert is a saint of the Atlantic interface. His eighth or ninth-century Life contains much about ships and the people who sail in them. Three stories near its end (c.40–42) involve visits to Noirmoutier by Irish ships, *Scothorum naves*, and by British or Breton sailors and ships — *Brittones nautici* and *naves Britannicae*. The life was written at Jumièges. It describes at first hand the wooded scenery of the Seine Valley, the architecture of Jumièges, and the foundations of the nearby nunneries of Pavilly and Montivilliers. The stories of shipping would appeal to the sailors and traders of the Seine river traffic, many of whom, at least today, are Bretons. Their offerings to St Philibert, who could still storms and tempests, would have brought a useful income to his monastery on the heights above the river. Only the final section of the life, dealing with the decade before his death in 684, is set in Noirmoutier.[31]

The theme of this section is Philibert's care for his monks under divine providence. He cures monks of fever and of accidental injury with holy oil and the sign of the cross (c.35–6). There follow the 'providence' miracles, with their details of the seventh-century Atlantic coasts. Once Sidonius, his cellarer (probably Sidonius the Irishman, patron of St-Saens near Dieppe, birthplace of the composer), came to him because he had no oil for the lamps save a little he kept in reserve for guests. Philibert told him to use this. That evening, as it was getting dark, a ship arrived from Bordeaux with forty *modii* of olive oil, sent to

Philibert by friends or kinsmen in Gascony (c.37). The olive tree does not grow in south-west France, and the oil must have been brought to Bordeaux from Spain or from Provence or Languedoc in the course of normal commercial trade. One would dearly like to know what the containers were made of (the quantity involved is about 365 litres). They had presumably been sent to Philibert as a personal present or pious gift. When the monks were once more short of oil, a school of porpoises were stranded on the island (c.38). When Mediterranean imports were not available, local resources could serve instead. The consignment of oil from Bordeaux would have been exactly contemporary with the hoard of Merovingian and Visigothic gold *trientes* from there. This was put together about 675–80 in the years when Philibert was abbot of Noirmoutier, and the coins from Spain and the Garonne valley show the routes by which the oil might have reached Bordeaux.

The British ships and sailors could have been Bretons though, if so, it is hard to know why their origin was noted, for Noirmoutier is virtually in Brittany. There is no doubt, however, about the Irish ships, matched by that which earlier in the century Columbanus had found at Nantes, having unloaded its cargo, and awaiting the return trip. Philibert thanked God for the providence that brought his monks all their needs from maritime parts. Soon after, an Irish ship arrived with footwear (*calciamenta*) and clothing. Giraldus Cambrensis noted five hundred years later that the Irish, in return for wine from Poitou, traded leather and hides. The Irish at Noirmoutier were also calling at one of the major salt producing areas of medieval Europe. The museum there has photographs of nineteenth-century salt ships, and a large collection of Sunderland lustre ware brought back on the salt boats via Jersey for wedding presents. Like Philibert's olive oil, this is a reminder that gifts can be as potent a source of goods exchange as commerce.[32]

Today, much of Noirmoutier is taken up with French holiday villas, fenced and private, not ideal terrain for archaeological fieldwork. Among the small collection of local archaeological material in the museum is a flanged roof tile with a seventh or eighth-century graffito, cut before firing, reading *S(an)c(t)a Ec(c) elesia* ('The Holy Church'). The suggestion of a ceramic industry on the island at that date is interesting. The decorated moulded bricks with late classical and early Christian motifs from churches in Nantes, Angers and the Vendée point in the same direction. Such architectural decoration would have been little use in the timber churches of the Irish and British, but it is scarcely surprising that pottery was, in the seventh century, reaching Insular sites from some unlocated pottery-making centre in western Francia.[33]

Late Roman trade in the Atlantic seaways

By the fourth century, the bulk commerce that had earlier brought Gaulish samian ware, Italian wines and Spanish olive oil to Britain was a thing of the distant past. A few amphorae from north Africa or jars of the celebrated wine of Gaza still arrived at British ports, but these were rare luxuries. North African amphorae are common as far north as Bordeaux, and one from the Roman port of Dournenez in Finistere, which has also produced the burial of a woman in a lead coffin with hairpins of Yorkshire jet, helps to close the gap with the British and Irish finds. Surviving barrels of impressive size re-used as well linings suggest that much wine now travelled in cask, and this may have been

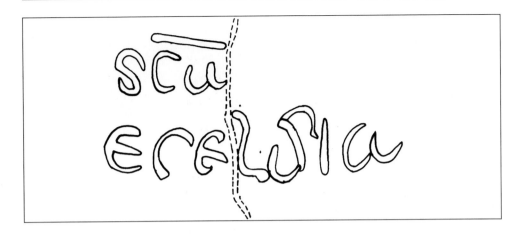

48   *'Sancta Ec(c)elesia' (Holy Church). Graffito cut before firing on a flanged pottery roof tile. Noirmoutier (Vendée), seventh-eighth century (drawing — the author)*

accompanied by a distinctive orange fineware from Poitou with dark red decoration made with a sponge — the *céramique a l'éponge*. These may have been no more than archaeological trace elements, but we can only guess what other goods travelled with them. The Atlantic coasts of Gaul have a tradition of salt making going back into prehistoric times. It was well established in south Brittany by the ninth century, and the medieval salt ports of Gascony and the Charente supplied much of Atlantic Europe. Late Roman pottery from Oxfordshire, the New Forest and Surrey reached the Channel coasts from Holland to the Loire, evidence of British coastal trade, and the concentration in south Brittany corresponds well with the distribution of Roman salt pans.[34]

North African amphorae of the 'Africana Grande' class from Tintagel, from Dalkey Island near Dublin, and from the coastal promontory fort of Loughshinny, a few miles north of Dalkey, may form a link between this late Roman trade and the post Roman imports of Mediterranean and Gallic pottery and glass. All three sites are ideally placed for maritime trading emporia, sited as they are on coastal islands or near islands. The medieval word *insula* differed in meaning from our own 'island'. An island in our sense had to be qualified as an *insula maris* 'an island in the sea', for an insula was a piece of land largely surrounded by rivers or by water, as with the Ile de France around Paris, between the Seine, the Oise and the Marne. The basic meaning is something enclosed, like a Roman insula or city block. Thus a coastal site flanked by water courses, as at Benalua, or a promontory (a sixteenth-century coinage for an 'almost island') or headland like Tintagel would have been, in medieval times, simply an island.[35]

If the finds of late Roman amphorae near Dublin imply that traders from Gaul were already venturing into the Irish sea in the fourth century, there is a hint of them in north Wales also. About 1760, lead miners were sinking a shaft at Long Rake on the eastern part of Halkyn Mountain in Flintshire when they discovered a hoard of eight late Roman bronze vessels 'several yards below the surface'. Possibly they had broken into old workings. Three were 'Irchester' bowls, a British type known from other hoards of the

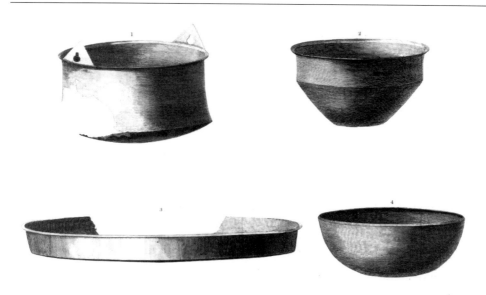

49   *Late Roman bronze bowl hoard from Halkyn Mountain (Flintshire), probably early fifth century. From* Archaeologia *Vol. XIV (1809)*

later fourth century and probably the ancestor of post-Roman hanging bowls. The broad, flat pan, and the carinated bowl can be matched in fourth-century contexts elsewhere, and none would be out of place in a late Romano-British context. The remaining three vessels ,however, were more surprising things to find in a lead mine in north Wales. They were cauldrons with broad convex bases, a gently incurving body above a sharp carination, and a pair of triangular perforated lugs which would originally have carried an iron cauldron handle. The keyhole shape of the perforations is due to wear. 'Westland' cauldrons were one of several types produced in the Meuse Valley in Belgium in the fourth and fifth centuries. They are known from rich graves in Denmark and Norway, and from Belgium and the Rhineland. Two very like the Halkyn Mountain cauldrons, from Bensheim south of Mainz, still have their iron handles. There is another from an early fifth-century grave at Vieuxville in Belgium. Three others ended up in fifth-sixth century Anglo-Saxon graves in eastern England and the Thames Valley, that from Long Wittenham in Berkshire with a stoup with relief decorated bronze panels with Christian scenes from the same area of production in the Somme-Meuse-Upper Rhine area of north-east France. These Westland cauldrons are unparalleled in the other hoards of late Roman bronze vessels from Britain, and traders, whether British or foreign, in search of Flintshire lead (mined since early Roman times) are the most probable explanation for them.[36]

Into the dark, into the light

Within little over half a century of this late Roman trade in the Atlantic seaways, east Mediterranean pottery and Frankish pottery and glass appear on sites in western Britain and Ireland, most of which show a consistent range of features and are usually interpreted as the seats of local rulers. They are fortified promontory forts or ring forts, set near but not on the coast, close to rivers and navigable waters. Dinas Powys, close to the Vale of Glamorgan and its metal rich hinterland, lies halfway between two natural harbours at Cardiff and Barry. Hen Gastell is on the estuary of the River Neath in west Glamorgan, again with easy access to a metal producing hinterland. Cadbury-Congresbury is near the estuary of the River Yeo and the Avon-Mendip area. The triple-banked ringfort of Garranes in County Cork lies inland from Kinsale Harbour. Such sites would have controlled a variety of natural resources, which may have reached the fortified sites as renders from the surrounding population. Their distribution is far wider than the few sites with late Roman African amphorae.[37]

Tintagel, on the north coast of Cornwall, has produced a radically greater amount of imported pottery, including coarse wares which may have been brought in by the traders themselves for their private use and fragments of glass which may be of Spanish origin. Tintagel would thus seem to be a true emporium rather than simply one part of a trade network, and here at least the probable objects of trade were the small, dark lumps of Cassiterite or tinstone (Stannic Dioxide) which wash out from veins in the Hercynian granites of Brittany and Cornwall. Tin can be traded as tinstone concentrate, in jars or bags, or as ingots of smelted metal. Both types are known from Mediterranean shipwrecks ranging in date from Phoenician times to the third century AD. They occur in mixed cargoes with lead and copper ingots, iron bars and a range of other trade goods, including south Spanish amphorae. The number of tin ingots in any one wreck is not large save in one exceptional case, and the shapes and weights of individual ingots vary considerably, even in the same wreck. They thus seem to have been collected by merchants from a variety of sources, rather than being the product of large scale merchant traffic. The immediate source was probably southern Spain, as the amphorae and a Greek stamp on a southern French wreck of c.100 BC referring to Aistor, an estuary near Huelva, show. They must have been traded along the Atlantic seaways from Brittany, Cornwall, or some area with similar tin bearing granites.[38]

The involvement of Ireland in such a trade is in contrast to the situation in Roman times. Though many Roman coins have been recorded from Ireland, almost all are chance finds without an archaeological context, and a high proportion must be recent losses. They include Alexandrian issues and other types which did not circulate in the west in ancient times. A trickle of Roman coins has probably been reaching Ireland from ancient times until the present day from a variety of sources, and this makes it difficult to use such finds as evidence. A few coins hoards, usually of silver denarii, and a few Roman brooches and similar trinkets are known, however, and sometimes correspond with periods of Roman military activity in southern Scotland, as under Agricola or Severus, when refugees might be expected. The most striking absence, however, is the total lack of Roman coarse pottery. The contrast with other areas beyond the Imperial frontiers, such as Scandinavia or Free Germany, is striking. If Ireland had relatively few natural products to attract Roman traders, it may well be that Irish society at that stage had little need of the prestige goods which those traders had to offer.[39]

This situation changed radically in the late fourth century, when late Roman gold and silver coins and pieces of silver plate cut up into convenient sized units (hacksilver) appear in Ireland, evidence of a sudden influx of wealth. Early in 1854, a small farmer digging peat

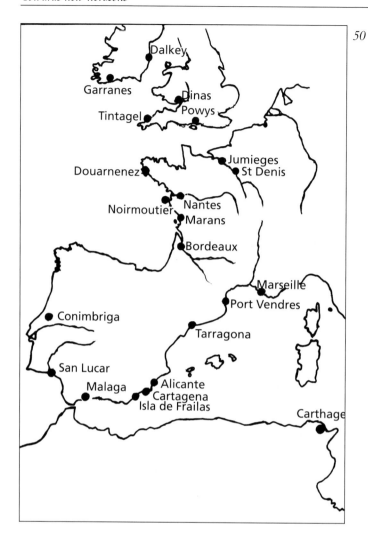

50 The west Mediterranean and the Atlantic interface, showing some of the sites mentioned in the text

in the townland of Ballinrees, west of Coleraine in County Derry, found a collection of coins and scrap silver, including 1500 silver siliquae, the latest being of Constantine (407–11). There were also pieces of cut-up silver plate and spoons, and of the silver stamped ingots given to late Roman soldiers and officials as donatives. There were fragments of silver gilt fittings from a military belt of exceptional quality, from the same workshop and perhaps the same hand as the silver-gilt fittings from the Vermand warrior grave. One coin, originally seen as a Trier issue of about 419–23, has now been recognised as a British imitation no later than the rest of the hoard. With parallels in hoards from London and Essex, it shows that some at least of the bullion was from British sources, rather than from, for example, Gaul. A start had been made in melting the silver down, for there were also six finger shaped bar-ingots of Insular type.[40]

We cannot say how all this bullion, and that from the similar hoard from Balline in County Limerick, came into Irish hands, or into those of its final owner. It may have been loot from raiding, payment or subsidy from sub-Roman authority in Britain in the years after the end of Roman rule, or a by-product of dealing in slaves abducted from Britain (like St Patrick). However it was acquired, it had clearly been obtained by armed force, directly or indirectly, rather than by normal trade. This means that the influx of wealth came into the hands of a warrior class whose status and economic position would be radically increased by it. The silver had been cut into smaller pieces, perhaps as units of value to facilitate some form of exchange. This may have been done by some British authority paying wages or protection money to a band of Irish warriors. Equally, it might have been done in Ireland to facilitate trade in some commodity such as slaves. In either case, the new wealth, the enrichment of a warrior elite, and the creation of a means of high value exchange, must have acted as a powerful catalyst to bring about change in Irish society. The establishment of a coastal emporium at Dalkey and Loughshinny, the beginnings of literacy in the Ogam script and later in Latin, and the changes in society that facilitated the beginnings of Irish Christianity may well be connected with this catalyst.[41]

It is less clear whether the appearance of Mediterranean import wares in the third quarter of the century was a continuation of the late Roman Atlantic trade or something new. A phase of early fifth-century blackout, when the latest types of Roman artefact had ceased to evolve and the earliest identifiable post Roman types had yet to emerge, is widespread in western Europe at this time. In north Gaul, the phase when grave goods shrank to an undiagnostic few led to debate on discontinuity in the cemetery evidence. Similar problems arise in relation to the continuity of fifth-century Roman towns such as Canterbury. In Ireland there is, of course, no earlier Roman occupation to complicate matters. In western Britain, however, the late antique trappings by which, by the later fifth century, an élite segment of society was using Latin memorial inscriptions, imported oil or wine, and Roman style tableware and glass to maintain something of a Romanized life style, seem to represent fresh beginnings rather than a stem grown from Romano-British roots. Dinas Powys is situated in the most heavily romanized and well-populated part of south Wales, with some evidence for the survival of villa estates into post Roman times. Despite this, the Roman pottery and coins from the site seem to be entirely residual, and there is no continuity with earlier Roman occupation in the area, despite continued occupation and burial nearby at the Llandough villa. Similarly, the Latin memorial stones seem to be a fresh development of the fifth century, and do not depend on Romano-British tombstones. Thus, at the time when Ireland was beginning to discover the uses of literacy, and starting the relationship with Christian Europe that was to bear such spectacular fruit in the seventh century and in Carolingian times, the situation in western Britain is less clear. The import wares, the fifth-century memorial formulae, and even a sixth-century consular date, show that we should not exaggerate any isolation, but in the seventh century it was to be Ireland, not the residual British petty kingdoms, that was to influence so radically their neighbours in England and in Francia.[42]

9. The End of Antiquity? Seventh century change in Insular and Atlantic Europe

All Continuity of history means, is, after all, perpetual change.

William Morris

The decline of the old south: the legacy of Henri Pirenne

Anyone who has tried to write a book will not be surprised that two of the major historical works of this century were written in the enforced leisure of prisoner of war camps. Henri Pirenne's *Medieval Cities* originated in a series of lectures to his fellow internees when that Belgian and European patriot was imprisoned for his resistance to the German occupation of Belgium in the First World War. Fernand Braudel's book *The Mediterranean and the Mediterranean World in the Age of Phillip II* was largely written when its author was a prisoner of war after the collapse of France in 1940. Pirenne had died in 1935, leaving a remarkable legacy in the form of the manuscript of his *Mohammed and Charlemagne*, which he had finished a few days before his death. The 'Pirenne thesis' has been debated by historians ever since, and the debate shows little sign of being concluded. His view that the economic unity of the Mediterranean world continued until destroyed by the Arab invasions of the seventh century is now supported by much archaeological evidence still below the ground when Pirenne wrote. Whether we are looking at cause and effect, however, or whether the vitality of the Mediterranean world had already been ended before the Arab invasions — by urban decline, Persian invasions, plague, and the long wars in Italy and elsewhere following Justinian's re-conquest of the shores of the west Mediterranean — is another matter. Similarly, whilst Pirenne paid much attention to the relationship of Charlemagne and the Papacy, he took less notice of developments in areas like Spain, Ireland and Anglo-Saxon England which were already underway before the Arab conquest of the eastern and southern shores of the Mediterranean.[1]

Much of this new evidence derives from the trade with the west represented by east Mediterranean amphorae and fine wares. This depended upon the continued existence of active ports like Antioch or Smyrna, with hinterlands producing large agricultural surpluses of goods such as oil and wine. There has been much debate about the conditions of the cities of the eastern Empire in the sixth and seventh centuries. Cities like Antioch and Constantinople flourished in the earlier sixth century, but the sack of Antioch by the Persians in 541 may have marked the turn of the tide. The Justinianic revival was brief, as it was in the Balkans, where Justinian's work of urban renewal was largely lost to the Slavs within twenty years of his death in 565. The Persian invasions were accompanied by mass deportations of townspeople, and the flight of others, particularly clergy, to the west. Gregory of Tours heard of the second Persian sack of Antioch in 572 from a refugee Syrian bishop who turned up at Tours. Clive Foss and John Haldon have argued that the later wave of Persian invasions of 611 onwards were a 'mortal blow from which the classical civilization of Asia Minor never recovered' and that they were 'the first stage in the process which marked the end of Antiquity in Asia Minor'. The catalogue of burning and destruction in cities such as Ancyra, Sardis, Ephesus or Aphrodisias, often dated by sealed coins or the hiding of coin hoards, is impressive. Anyone familiar with the similar evidence for the third-century invasions of Gaul will know, however, that problems of coin use and a tendency to attribute archaeological evidence to some destruction recorded in historical sources mean that such evidence needs careful scrutiny, and Foss concludes his second article with a note of caution as to cause and effect. Nevertheless, it does seem that many cities were devastated and largely depopulated well before the Arabs made their appearance in Asia Minor.[2]

By the mid-sixth century, eastern trade with the west was already in decline. The prolonged wars following Justinian's invasions of Italy (535 on) and Spain (552) coincide with the end of the main period of eastern exports. From about 550, Phocean red slip ware, probably traded through Smyrna, was confined to the east Mediterranean where it continued to circulate until about the time of the Persian invasions of 611–14 when it was replaced by Cypriot and Egyptian wares. This was presumably due to eastern factors rather than to western ones. At the death of Justinian, the Byzantines still held the shores of the Mediterranean save for eastern Spain and Provence, but their control of its western and central shores did not last. In 568, the Lombards invaded Italy and Byzantine rule was soon confined to Sicily and a few enclaves in the south, and around cities such as Ravenna, Rome and Naples. Baetica, save for a few fortified cities such as Cartagena, fell to a gradual and systematic Visigothic re-conquest, and Berber revolts made much of north Africa a liability. The loss of these peripheral western regions might, if anything, have strengthened the hold of the overstretched Byzantines on their core east Mediterranean territories, but worse was to follow. In the early years of the Emperor Maurice (582–602) the Balkans and Greece were invaded by the Slavs, and direct Byzantine control was soon limited to cities and coastal areas, though Byzantine armies continued to campaign in the Balkans for the rest of century. In some respects the scattered fortified cities and coastal tracts under Byzantine control recall the later maritime Venetian Empire. Though we should not confuse political control with trade, by the early seventh century the ruined cities and impoverished countryside of the east Mediterranean, with their heavy defence and tax burdens, would hardly have a sufficient production surplus for a viable export trade with the west.

There were still wealthy Syrian merchants in Gaul in the late sixth century, and in the early years of the seventh century papyrus continued to arrive at Marseille from Egypt, along with oil, spices and other goods, accompanied by east Mediterranean pottery. Between about 580 and 613 (when Provence was finally annexed by the Frankish kings), Marseille and other cities of Provence struck a distinctive 'pseudo-Imperial' or 'quasi-Imperial' gold coinage in the names of successive Byzantine Emperors, at a time when the rest of Gaul had gone over to a 'national' coinage bearing only the names of the mint and moneyer. After that date the coinage continued, but in the names of Frankish kings. It is doubtful if they were intended for external trade, however, and a letter of Pope Gregory the Great shows that 'Gallic solidi' were not accepted in Italy. Similarly in southern Spain, African red slip wares continued to arrive from Byzantine Carthage until the early years of the seventh century, despite the diversion of much African produce to the Byzantine army and administration. Thus the disappearance of Phocean red slip ware from the west about the time of Justinian's attempted re-conquest was the harbinger of a period of decline in eastern trade contacts, though it did not become critical until at least half a century later.[3]

In 636, four years after the death of Muhammed, the Arabs destroyed the Byzantine army at the Battle of the Yarmuk. In the following six years Syria, Palestine and Egypt fell to them, Alexandria being taken in 642. The eastern Roman Empire, as it had remained since the time of Augustus, no longer existed. By this time the eastern trade with the west was largely a thing of the past, nor did the Arabs, always a trading people, halt what was left of it. Not long after *Mohammed and Charlemagne* appeared, Robert Lopez showed that one of Pirenne's famous ' four disappearances' had little to do with Islam. Marseille was almost synonymous with the import of papyrus into Gaul. About 575, bishop Felix of Nantes wrote a maliciously unpleasant letter to Gregory of Tours. 'What a pity', wrote Gregory in reply 'that it was not Marseille which elected you its bishop. Instead of bringing cargoes of oil and other wares, its ships could have carried only papyrus, which would have given you much more scope for writing malicious letters'. The papyrus plant (*Cyperus papyrus*) is native to Egypt. Pirenne himself showed that its use by the Merovingian chancery extended well into the seventh century, and Lopez demonstrated that the Arab conquest of Egypt in 639–42 did not mark the end of its export. However, a diplomatic quarrel with the Emperor Justinian II led to a trade embargo by the Caliph Abd al Malik (685–705), and the placing of a Muslim religious formula on the opening authentication of each sheet. Presumably Pope John VII was unaware that one of his Papal Bulls opened with the statement (in Arabic) that there was no God but Allah. This embargo coincided with the end of its use by the Merovingian chancery, but it continued in use at Rome and Ravenna until the eleventh century. The disuse of this expensive imported material, so unsuited to a damp climate, may have owed more to the run down state of Marseille and the ruin of its merchants than to any short lived Arab trade embargo. Thus the end of the east Mediterranean trade with the west had little to do with the Arab invasions. It was already in serious decline by the later years of Justinian, though Syrian merchants were active in Gaul until at least 575–80. The disasters to the eastern Empire in the early seventh century may have marked its virtual end, but one of its most distinctive trade goods survived the Arab conquest unscathed.[4]

The end of Marseille as a trading city can now be charted archaeologically. The imports of papyrus, spices, oil and wine and cloth were used by Pirenne to demonstrate the continuance of a late antique economy in Merovingian Gaul. More recently, excavations at the Bourse site have reinforced this with a sequence of African and east Mediterranean pottery, supplemented by a scatter of coarse wares from across the Mediterranean, perhaps brought in by merchants and sailors for domestic use. By the mid-seventh century, this ends. Pottery imports dry up and only resume in the tenth century when Italian *vetrina pesante* coarsewares appear. Similarly, a cartulary of the Abbey of St Victor at Marseille shows many of the (admittedly never very fertile) estates of the Abbey empty and deserted by the end of the seventh century, and the remainder with no more than a few sheep.[5]

This long term decline of southern Gaul, with its self conscious late antique culture, can be followed in other spheres. The Parisian Abbot Domnolus, offered the see of Avignon by Lothar I about 559, regarded it as no better than a sentence of exile. His plea to the king to save him from tedious dinner table conversations with members of old senatorial families and counts who only wanted to talk philosophy had more than a touch of ironic humour about it, but the south was already a political backwater. There were still 'senatorial' families there, however, in the early seventh century. Desiderius, bishop of Cahors in 630–50, was from an aristocratic Gallo-Roman family from Albi on the eastern margin of Aquitaine. His brothers included Syagrius, named from the great aristocratic dynasty of Lyon; Rusticus, who bore the name of a notable fifth-century bishop of Narbonne, and a sister, Avita, from the family of the Emperor Avitus. The claimed family connections add up to a virtual Who's Who of fifth-century Gaul, but Desiderius and his brothers sought their fortune, not in their native cities, but in the Merovingian court in Paris under Chlotar II and Dagobert I. Rusticus and Desiderius were successive bishops of Cahors, near Albi, whilst Syagrius became count of Albi and patrician of Provence. We shall need to look at the relationships of periphery and centre in seventh-century Francia in more detail later. For the moment we need only note that, however useful their local connections made them to the Merovingian kings, they made their careers not as local magnates but as royal appointees. Another aristocratic seventh-century bishop, a namesake (and possibly kinsman) of Desiderius, left his huge collection of family silver to the churches of Auxerre. The cathedral alone was bequeathed 140kg of plate, and another church 40kg. This great treasure survived until the sixteenth century. This is eloquent both of the surviving inherited wealth of seventh-century 'senatorial' bishops, and of the fact that they were often the last of their line.[6]

Something of what Domnolus was complaining of can even be seen in the tombstones. By the later sixth century, the simple memorial inscriptions of the fifth century had developed into florid, long-winded epitaphs which were both archaic and stereotyped. In place of the simple 'Here lies' or 'Here rests in peace', they open with a formula on the lines of 'In this tomb rests in peace, of blessed memory . . .', and usually end with what was by then a wholly irrelevant post-consular dating. Justinian had abolished the consulship in 541 by subsuming it with his own titles, and commanded that legal documents should carry a regnal dating and the year of the Indiction (a fifteen year tax cycle). In the absence of a consul who gave his name to the year, the monumental masons of southern Gaul had a genuine problem. The Indiction was of little use for dating purposes, since, for example, the tenth indiction meant only the tenth year of a fifteen year cycle, without specifying which particular tax cycle you had in mind. Regnal datings presented problems, not least the shifting and regional nature of much Merovingian kingship. Dating by the years of the Incarnation, from the birth of Christ, were not yet in use. However pedantic and archaic they might appear, post-consular datings ('Forty-five years after the consulship of Justinus, *vir clarissimus* and consul') were for the moment the only realistic alternative. By the time of the Frankish annexation of Provence around 613, when the names of the Byzantine Emperors on the 'quasi-Imperial' gold coinage were replaced by those of Frankish kings, regnal datings had become the norm. The final inscriptions with post consular datings at Lyon are of 601 and 622, but in the Choulans cemetery there the latest inscriptions, of the decade 650–60, all have regnal or indictional dates.[7]

By the mid-sixth century, the Visigoths and Franks had been settled within the Roman Empire for five generations, longer than the time that separates us from the Indian mutiny or the American Civil War. There was no longer an emperor in the west, even a distant Italian one. The name of the Greek Emperor still appeared on the gold coinage, more to guarantee it for international trade than for reasons of politics. There were still 'senatorial' families, but their strategy of retaining local power by becoming bishop of their city (now something in the gift of the king) meant that fewer aristocrats were raising families. Above all, the legal fiction by which Germanic rulers were simply allies of Rome or rulers of their own people, rather than kings of a territorial state, was becoming more and more threadbare. There were counterbalancing forces, however. Many barbarian peoples were still pagan, like the Anglo-Saxons, or had heretical views on the Trinity, like the Goths and Vandals. Elements of the aristocracy, Gallo-Roman or 'barbarian', may have seen the differences that divided them from the other as features which defined their own status and identity. This, though, was eroding rapidly, as the two parallel nobilities alike sought advancement at the courts of their kings. Overall, as the century proceeded, the transition from barbarian successor state to territorial kingdom gathered pace.

Toledo and the making of a kingdom

In Spain, the kingdom of the Visigoths still had many attributes of a barbarian successor state in the late sixth century, despite a strong Byzantine influence. The coinage bore the name of the Roman Emperor, not that of the Visigothic king, even when the two were at war. Romans and Goths had their own law codes, and marriage between the two communities was forbidden. Catholic Romans and Arian Goths had their own churches and church hierarchies, and many Gothic nobles seem to have regarded their Arianism as a defining characteristic, surrender of which would weaken their own national identity. As throughout Spanish history, regionalism and local independence were strong, and individual cities could and did maintain self-rule against the royal power for years, sometimes decades.[8]

The Visigothic king Leovigild (570–86) was one of the chief architects of a Romano-Gothic territorial state. He ended the semi-autonomous rule of cities like Cordoba, and of a mysterious *senatus Cantabriae*, an enclave controlled by sub-Roman magnates in the Cantabrian mountains. More importantly, he provided the Visigothic state with a literally central capital at Toledo, previously a city of no outstanding importance. His reasons for choosing Toledo were almost identical to those of Phillip II when he abandoned Toledo as the Spanish capital and moved it to Madrid just short of a thousand years later. Toledo was geographically in the centre of Spain, and lacked most of the pre-existing power structures, ecclesiastical or civil, of other cities, which might have made the effective exercise of Leovigild's authority more difficult. After about 580 the coinage bore the king's name, not that of the Roman Emperor, and the apartheid that forbade marriage between Goths and Gallo-Romans ended.[9]

Not all of Leovigild's reforms took root. His revised laws are now lost, but Romans and Goths seem to have retained their separate codes until the mid-seventh century. His attempts at formulating a revised form of Arianism acceptable to both Romans and Goths failed, but under his son Reccared I in 589, religious unity was attained on the basis of a Catholic conversion of the Goths. This was largely the work of bishop Leander of Seville, brother of Isidore of Seville and an ally and friend of Pope Gregory the Great, who eight years later sent St Augustine to Canterbury to begin the conversion of another group of peripheral barbarian successor states. The significance of these two missions goes far beyond the religious sphere. They created an alliance of the Roman church with territorial rulers in Spain and England that prefigured in some ways the relationship of the Papacy with the Carolingian rulers. The Papacy could not look to distant Toledo or Canterbury for protection against Lombards, Greeks or Arabs in Italy, as it could with the Franks, but its relationship with the two cities, and the rulers who controlled them, was to become a major theme of European history.[10]

Periphery and centre: the Frankish kingdoms

These attempts to forge a centralised kingdom out of a barbarian successor state and from areas with strong regional identities and an often almost autonomous aristocracy, can be matched in Francia where the central monarchy was much weaker. If the sixth-century Frankish realm was treated as the private family property of its king, to be divided among his heirs, this strategy made sense at one level. It was better to have a possible candidate for the throne, and his followers, as a regional king controlling that area and its magnates, rather than plotting at court. Such a king could check regional autonomy and prevent his region passing out of royal control, as Aquitania was to do in the next century. In his final few years (558–61), Chlotar I united the four kingdoms of Metz, Orleans, Paris and Soissons, but they were divided again on his death, giving rise to the fratricidal wars and blood feuds chronicled by Gregory of Tours. It was not until the time of Chlotar's grandson Chlotar II in 613 that there was again a single king of the Franks, who now ruled also in Provence.

The intervening period had, however, seen one important development. The various fifth-century copies of the Imperial coinage that had circulated in Gaul were followed about 500 by the first Merovingian coins, gold solidi and tremisses (third solidi) with the names and titles of the Emperor on the obverse and various types of winged Victory on the reverse. They begin in the reign of Anastasius I (491–518) and are very similar to those struck by other barbarian peoples such as the Ostrogoths, Burgundians and Visigoths, from which they can only be distinguished on grounds of distribution and style. There is nothing about them specifically royal. The only exception are those struck by king Theodebert I of Metz (534–48) in his own name. He had acquired much gold in subsidies and booty through Frankish intervention in Italy, and though his breach of the Imperial prerogative caused grave scandal in Byzantium they were a political statement rather than a sustained attempt at a regal coinage. Theodebert's source of bullion is significant, for some of these 'pseudo-Imperial' coins show Ostrogothic influence and the profitable Frankish interventions in Italy may account for their new gold coinage. From about 570, a decade before Leovigild introduced a specifically royal coinage in Spain, these copies of

Imperial coinage were replaced by a 'National' series, but in contrast to Visigothic Spain these show no sign of being regal. They rarely carry a royal name, but have a profile bust and the name of the mint on the obverse, with various forms of cross or other emblem and the name of the moneyer on the reverse. Direct royal supervision must have been slight, for the coins were struck not at a few mints centres but at 800 cities, towns and villages in all regions of France. This local mintage did not mean, however, that the coinage was wholly unregulated. Most significant mints had a distinctive and recognisable style, often with a mint signature such as M.A. (Marseille) or A.C. (Autun) or some distinctive device like the chalice on the plentiful coins of the *vicus* of Banassac (Lozère). These, with the name of the moneyer, must have protected the coinage against debasement and fraud and given merchants and others confidence in the currency, as Gregory of Tours' anecdotes about coin use involving gold tremisses show. Indeed, the phased dilution of the gold with increasing amounts of silver must have been carefully controlled from the centre if it was not to result simply in uncontrolled debasement.[11]

The reigns of Chlotar II (584–629) and his son Dagobert I (629–39) mark the high point of the Merovingian monarchy. Chlotar had brought to an end the regional kingships of Gregory of Tours' day, and Dagobert worked towards a centralised Frankish state based on Paris. The concept of a single, undivided kingship was still not really established. Chlotar associated Dagobert with himself in a period of joint rule (623–9) and established his other son Charibert (d.632) as ruler of Aquitaine. Again, the need to control semi-autonomous peripheral regions, in this case threatened by the Basques, outweighed the claims of a fully monarchical system. However, it was Dagobert who rebuilt the fifth-century martyrial church of St Denis outside Paris, close to the great royal estate at Clichy, and established it as the burial place of the kings of France. In the thirteenth century the gilt effigies of Dagobert and of Charles the Bald were on the north side of Suger's choir at St Denis, those of the Capetian kings of France on the south. His founding of the fair of St Denis in 634 was closely associated with his rebuilding of the basilica, consecrated in 636. No doubt the tolls from the fair helped to pay for the work, and it quickly became an international emporium for a wide variety of goods from France, the Rhineland and Anglo-Saxon England. Such an emporium would not stand in isolation, and a charter of St Denis, ninth century in its present form but possibly with some seventh-century text behind it, brackets the fair of St Denis with those of Rouen and Quentovic and with merchants who come from beyond the sea to buy wines, honey and *garantia* (madder). In view of the Pirenne thesis, it is worth noting that the reign of Dagobert coincided with the Arab conquests of Syria and Egypt. The Prophet Muhammed died in 632. In the year when the new basilica of St Denis was dedicated, the Arabs destroyed the Byzantine army at the Battle of the Yarmuk. Jerusalem fell to the Arabs in 638, Egypt in 639–42. The foundation of the emporium of St Denis preceded all but the first of these events, and it is hard to see any logical connection with them.[12]

A new wind from the west

In Ireland, the influx of wealth from fourth-century Britain, in the shape of silver and of slaves, must have radically enhanced the status of the aristocratic warrior class. The first major churches of the mission led by St Patrick were sited in relation to royal seats. Armagh was within two miles of Emain Macha, the ancient capital of Ulster. Auxilius's church at Killashee was near Dun Ailline, Secundinus's foundation of Dunshaughlin close to both Tara and Lagore. By the sixth century, in Ireland as elsewhere in western Europe, monastic foundations were rapidly increasing in number. The amount of sixth-century imported east Mediterranean pottery in Ireland is small, but amphora sherds from monasteries at Reask in County Kerry, Inishcaltra in Co. Clare and Derrynaflan in Co. Tipperary, may represent princely gifts of oil for the lamps and wine for the Mass rather than any form of monastic trade. This is now matched in Wales by similar pottery from the monastery at Llandough in Glamorgan, close by Dinas Powys.[13]

By the end of the century, it was Ireland that was influencing Gaul. About 585, an opinionated forty-five year old Irishman landed in western Gaul, perhaps at Nantes, with twelve companions. Columbanus had been given leave by his abbot, St Comgall of Bangor (Co. Down), to travel to Gaul (not by his bishop, which would have been the norm elsewhere). He built a monastery in a deserted fort at *Castrum Anagrates* (Annegray) in the wooded Vosges mountains of northern Burgundy, later moving to the deserted Roman spa town of Luxeuil-les-Bains nearby. His stay in Gaul was fairly short, for in 610 he offended the formidable Queen Brunhild by refusing to bless her illegitimate grandchildren. He and his monks were to be deported to Ireland. Arriving at Nantes they found an Irish ship, which had discharged its cargo and was waiting to sail, with little difficulty. However, they evaded their captors and fled. Eventually, in 612 they left Gaul and crossed the Alps to Lombardy. Columbanus died there in 615 at Bobbio, which he had founded the previous year.[14]

Columbanus and his fellow Irish emigrants acted as a powerful catalyst on the Merovingian Church. Apart from their influence on its spirituality, in such matters as private penance, through their influence on the Frankish kings and aristocracy they changed the nature of much of Gallic monasticism. In the sixth century most monasteries had been urban, part of the complex of basilicas and funerary churches that surrounded the civitas city and its bishop. Monasteries, at least those of men, had, it is true, ventured outside the walls, since it was usual for monks and their servants to work the land on their extra mural properties. Neither was Columbanus's emphasis on rural monasteries entirely new, since it had been prefigured to some extent by the monks of the Jura mountains at the beginning of the century. Nevertheless, the new wave of Hiberno-Frankish monasteries founded by Frankish nobles and kings were often rural, endowed with large estates, and organized on manorial lines. Many were in areas of eastern and northern France where earlier monastic foundations had been few, and there was still scope for evangelising the *pagenses* of wooded and remote regions. In many ways (save in that of missionary activity) the colonization of the Frankish countryside by this new wave of Hiberno-Frankish monasteries recalls that of the Cistercians five hundred years later. At the same time, the resources of such major monastic houses lent themselves to building up traditions of scholarship and literary activity, and to the creation of a new monastic architectural tradition.[15]

Monks as landowners

The sixth century, and particularly its second half, was the major period of monastic expansion in the cities of Gaul. Two estimates would place the number of monasteries in Gaul in 500 at forty and at about seventy-five. By 600, the same two would put the total number of monastic houses at about two hundred and forty and at three hundred. By AD 700 there may have been as many as 600, the great majority of the new foundations being filiations of Columbanus and of Luxeuil. These figures can be illustrated at a more local level by Christian Sapin's survey of monastic foundations in Burgundy before 750. In the fifth century the city of Autun had two monasteries, St Pierre l'Estrier, originally a Gallo-Roman funerary chapel in the suburban cemetery, and St Étienne. St Symphorien followed about 500, in an earlier basilica over the tomb of a martyr. The second half of the sixth century saw three new foundations — St Andoche, St Mary and St John — St Martin, the last a royal foundation by Queen Brunhaut and bishop Syagrius just before 600. Only one new urban monastery followed in the seventh century. The neighbouring city of Chalons shows a similar pattern, with one possible fifth-century foundation, and at least three of the sixth century. Not all cities followed quite the same pattern, for this depended on chance local circumstances and available patronage, and some latecomers may have made up their numbers with new seventh-century foundations. At Cahors, for example, there is said to have been no monastery until after Desiderius became bishop in 630. However, the overall pattern is clear enough.[16]

As Sapin has emphasised, the pattern of rural foundations was quite different. Burgundian rural monasteries were rare before the late seventh century. The diocese of Auxerre had three late sixth-century rural foundations, but that of Autun had no certain rural monastery before 700. The evident crudity of these figures reflects the sparsity and difficulties of our sources, but it is at least clear that in Burgundy between about 550 and 650 there was a decisive shift from monasteries in the city to monasteries in the country. Available urban resources were now fully subscribed, making new foundations difficult. The main reason, however, was the Irish mission of St Columbanus. This drew on a tradition of rural monasteries in Ireland, both in his own foundations and those of his followers, and his influence, direct and indirect, on the Frankish kings and aristocrats led to them giving large rural estates for the foundation of new monasteries.

By the end of the Merovingian period, the Church in Gaul may have held a third of all land under cultivation. With the acquisition of large-scale rural property it acquired the duty, like any other landowner, of the provision of spiritual care for the tenants of its ecclesiastical estates. One seventh-century example brings out something of what this might mean. The Abbey of St Evre at Toul (Meurthe-et-Moselle) had been founded in the early sixth century and was a favoured burial place of the bishops of the city from its founder, St Evre, onwards. In 1974 work on the site of the demolished abbey uncovered some late Merovingian sarcophagi. Two, with personal belongings and jewellery, were identified from inscribed finger rings as the graves of bishop Endulus of Toul (c.600–22) and of a rich woman, Pretoria, who gave a large estate to the church in his time. This estate, north of the city across the Moselle, comprised six villages and the tithes of a seventh. One of these, Villey-Saint-Étienne, was the site of a Merovingian cemetery of seventy graves, in use from the late fourth century until the seventh. The cemetery was on a hilltop, close to a late Roman occupation site, and some 1400m away from the present church and village. Here again we see the familiar pattern of burial shifting from an open country site next to the settlement to the Christian graveyard of a newly founded church, perhaps after Pretoria's gift of the estate, whose date corresponds broadly with that of the end of the cemetery. Later, it would seem, the settlement itself gravitated to the site of the church. We do not know if the estate was a single poly-focal unit, but we see once again why ecclesiastical organization often mirrored the secular. There may have been other reasons why Pretoria granted the church only the tithes of the seventh village, St Maximin (which, from its name, already had a church). It may have been an estate centre for rents and lands not in her direct demesne ownership, and which she therefore needed to retain. Such munificent gifts of land to the Church posed problems for the monarchy, for such land was exempt from many royal taxes and reduced the lands from which the king and the Mayor of the Palace could reward or recruit their military followers. Reaction, in the form of the alienation of Church lands to form estates for such followers, was perhaps inevitable.[17]

Insular change in the seventh century

In 651, Aidan bishop of Northumbria died at an unnamed *villa regalis*, the centre of a royal estate, whose tenants would owe food rents and services to the king, and look to the estate centre for elements of administration and justice. As Bede explains:

> Having a church and lodging there, Aidan would often stay at the place, travelling around the surrounding countryside to preach. This was his practice at all the royal estates, for he had no personal possessions there save for his church and a few fields around it.

The church was reliant on the kings and aristocracy for the resources with which to preach, baptise, and build churches. Bede is writing of the early days of the Northumbrian church before Aidan's few fields of glebe had grown into the great monastic and episcopal estates of his own day, able to support monasteries and to command the services of stonemasons, sculptors, scribes and painters.[18]

These new large monastic estates created a fresh situation. Not only were the old diocesan minsters eclipsed, but the monastic churches were now responsible for the spiritual welfare of the people living on their lands. Eric Cambridge has argued that in County Durham the pattern of early Saxon stone churches and sculpture can be linked to monasteries in the strict sense of the term. Where early minsters can be identified, they lack buildings in stone, or early sculpture. Even later pre-Norman sculpture is rare on such sites. Monks and bishops were expected to provide churches and clergy for areas like Hexhamshire, or the great poly-focal estate of the Archbishops of York around Otley in Wharfedale. Ian Wood has looked at Otley and the sculptured crosses in the church there. The estate may originally have been given to St Wilfred in the seventh century. Wood re-interprets the figure on the eighth-century 'Angel cross', previously seen as a cowled

51   *Chi-rho monograms (1–3), Monogram crosses (4–6) and crosses (7–10) from early Christian memorial stones, Vienne, mostly mid-late fifth century*

monk, as a Mass priest vested in a stole, with evangelists, angels and a vine scroll of eucharistic significance ('I am the True Vine'). The theme is evangelism through preaching and the Mass. Otley, perhaps served by canons rather than monks, was the centre of pastoral care for the people of Wharfedale. Sculpture from other centres, including Ilkley, suggests churches on other elements of the estate, much as Cambridge has shown the poly-focal nature of some early Northumbrian monasteries.[19]

Similar eucharistic and evangelical symbolism can be found on early sculpture in Wales and Ireland. Two figures of Christ represented as a vested priest in the Orante position of the Mass are known on eighth or ninth-century crosses from upland Glamorgan. Cefn Hirfynydd and Mynydd Gellionen are both remote parts of the huge parish of Llangyfelach, and may represent secondary centres for pastoral work within this upland area. Llangyfelach was the mother church of the *commote* of north Gower, and later one of the major estates of the see of St Davids. A similar iconography is seen on the seventh-century Bantry pillar in western Ireland, best known perhaps from its representation of a curragh or skin boat. The other face has a cross, an orante figure and a sculpture of St Paul and St Anthony in the desert, another eucharistic motif. The process of rural pastoral care was continuing.[20]

Archaeologically Ireland and western Britain share two distinctive features which, though they begin in the sixth century, seem to be characteristic of the seventh. These are a new wave of pottery imports from western France, and the early uninscribed stone cross-slabs. The latter also go back to Gallic prototypes. The fifth to seventh-century memorial stones of Gaul have a range of early Christian motifs above the inscription, including eucharistic symbols (chalices, vine scrolls and feeding birds), chi-rho monograms, monogram crosses (which show the chi-rho symbol in an upright cross form, rather than as an X), or simple crosses, sometimes encircled like the wreathed crosses or chi-rhos found on fourth-century wall paintings and sculpture. Both monogram crosses and ringed crosses occur on sixth-century British memorial stones, as at Treflys (Caernarvonshire) or Castell Dwyran (Carmarthen), sometimes above the text in the continental manner, and a number of unaccompanied chi-rhos, without text, are also known, particularly in Ireland. In some cases, however, the cross was added later to an earlier Latin or Ogam inscribed stone, and it can often be difficult to tell whether a cross is contemporary with the inscription or was added later. The cross was certainly an addition in the case of a group of inscribed stones from the Brecon area where the stone was inverted, perhaps to emphasise its change of role, and a cross cut on the former butt. Such cases emphasise the separateness of the early Latin or Ogam inscribed memorial stones and the uninscribed cross slabs that succeeded them.

The latter are individually almost undateable. Few carry inscriptions, and confusingly similar types of simple cross continued to be cut well into the full Middle Ages, sometimes on datable medieval buildings. The numerous Irish examples still lack a full corpus, though recent regional surveys have gone a long way towards making good this lack. These uncertainties make general statements difficult. However, a cross-slab from Reask in County Kerry has a pair of doves flanking the cross, borrowed from the Gallic series (or from even further afield), presumably via some portable medium such as metalwork. A series of seventh-century cross-inscribed grave markers from the Paris

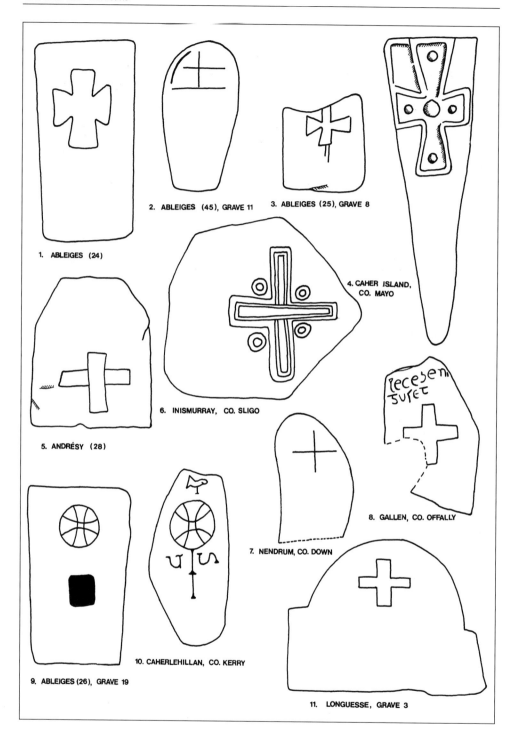

1. ABLEIGES (24)

2. ABLEIGES (45), GRAVE 11

3. ABLEIGES (25), GRAVE 8

4. CAHER ISLAND, CO. MAYO

5. ANDRÉSY (28)

6. INISMURRAY, CO. SLIGO

7. NENDRUM, CO. DOWN

8. GALLEN, CO. OFFALLY

9. ABLEIGES (26), GRAVE 19

10. CAHERLEHILLAN, CO. KERRY

11. LONGUESSE, GRAVE 3

52   *Cross slabs from late seventh-century graves in the French Vexin (after Sirat), and from sites in Ireland*

region, some found in situ over late Merovingian graves, have a range of cross forms very similar to those on the earliest Insular cross slabs. Early monastic literature has many stories showing the power of the sign of the cross. Crosses were cut on food bowls and on tool handles. The sign of the cross was made over food before eating, and one unfortunate nun who omitted to do so swallowed a devil who happened by chance to be sitting on her lettuce leaf. It had the power to kill dragons or other vermin, replenish jars of honey, detect poison in a glass vessel or heal the sick. The sixth-century Saint Sampson of Dol is said to have cut a cross on a prehistoric standing stone in Cornwall, and this was still to be seen in the following century.[21]

The replacement of Latin epitaphs by uninscribed cross slabs may thus be associated with the growth of a more specifically monastic Insular church in the late sixth and seventh century. Anne Hamlin has equated Ogam inscriptions, the Irish counterpart of the Latin memorial stones, with a pre-monastic episcopally organized phase of the Irish church, the stones being often associated with ecclesiastical sites of early importance, but of obscurity in the later monastic orientated literature. Similarly in eastern Scotland, the Group II sculptured crosses banish the earlier Pictish symbols to the margins or back of stones, showing, as Stephen Driscoll has put it, 'the point at which the importance of the Church is outstripping that of the ancestors'. The Latin inscriptions of Wales and western Britain are the memorials of an élite who recorded their names and ancestry on their tombstones, as Roman Emperors did on milestones. The early cross slabs served various purposes, as their inscriptions show, but as memorials they commemorate anonymous Christians, save where they ask for a prayer for the dead. Literacy may now have been more exclusively a clerical preserve.[22]

Even if there was no direct link between the rise of a monastically organized church and the greatly increased Gallic trade with western Britain and Ireland in the seventh century, our sources suggest that monks and traders were no strangers to each other, whether we are looking at St Columbanus at Nantes or St Philibert and the Irish sailors at Noirmoutier. Links between western Francia and Ireland through Nantes are also shown by two Merovingian gold trientes from Leinster, both from mints in Maine, on the river network inland from the Loire estuary, that from Portlaoghise (Co. Leix) being from Le Mans, another at Trim (Co. Meath) from Beaufoy (Sarthe). It may be an oversimplification to say that the range of hard fired jars, open bowls and pitchers from somewhere in western France known to archaeologists as ' Insular 'E' ware' replaced the earlier Aegean imports. The two seem to have different patterns of distribution. 'E' ware is absent from Tintagel, despite its huge collection of Mediterranean imports. Perhaps some political event ended the trade emporium there during the sixth century. This may also be reflected in the almost total absence of 'E' ware from south-west England, for the twenty or so sites here with Mediterranean imports may have relied on redistribution from Tintagel. 'E' ware did reach the Isles of Scilly in some quantity, however, so that the changes in Dumnonia are likely to reflect internal events rather than external causes.[23]

In contrast, the quantities of imports in Scotland and Ireland increase dramatically. The twenty or so vessels of Mediterranean wares from Ireland increase threefold, and the very sparse imports in Scotland to a total of over forty vessels (not counting the recent finds from Whithorn). Of about 150 vessels so far published from Britain and Ireland, almost

100 are ovoid jars, usually with an internal groove to the rim for a lid, a characteristic sub Roman type in Gaul. There are around thirty smaller carinated beakers and smaller numbers of open bowls, jugs and spouted pitchers, plus a few pottery lids to go with the jars. It is doubtful if such pottery would have been imported as kitchen wares, and the jars and beakers would have made excellent containers for high value goods. Residual deposits inside a number of 'E' ware jars contain traces of madder (*Rubia tinctorum*), a dye plant not native to these islands, which produces a high quality purple-red dye. A charter of St Denis refers to it, with wine and honey, as one of the main items of commerce sought by overseas merchants at the emporium there.[24]

The end of Antiquity

By the final decades of the century, the generation of aristocratic Frankish churchmen and churchwomen who had known the courts of Dagobert I and Clovis II was disappearing from the scene. Balthild, Clovis's English born queen, died in 677 at her nunnery of Chelles outside Paris where she had spent the last decade of her life as abbess. Philibert died in 684 at Noirmoutier, as did Bishop Audoenus (Ouen) of Rouen, his partner in the foundation of Jumièges. All three were soon made saints. Monastic foundations still continued, but the great seventh-century houses of Picardy and the Paris basin — Jouarre, St Riquier, Jumièges, St Wandrille, Rebais, or Balthild's foundations of Corbie and Chelles — were accomplished fact, and most new foundations were now more modest. There were still Irish *peregrini* like Philibert's former cellarer Sidonius the Irishman who founded the little monastery of St Saens near the later Dieppe, or Romanus, to whom bishop Ansoald of Poitiers gave the church of Mazerolles outside Poitiers around 675, but by the early 690s the Northumbrian monk Willibrord and his companions had begun their mission to the Frisians which developed into the English mission to Germany of the following century.[25]

The common factor to many things that were happening in Francia at this time was the rising power of the Mayors of the Palace. After the death of Dagobert I in 639, Erchinoald became Mayor in Neustria and regent for Dagobert's infant son Clovis II. On Erchinold's death in 658, Balthild and the Neustrian aristocracy chose as *maior domus* an aristocrat from the Soissons region, Ebroin. It may have been Ebroin who, in about 670, was responsible for one of the decisive changes between the world of Antiquity and that of the Middle Ages. Late Roman coinage was based on the gold solidus and its third, the triens or tremissis. It was in gold that taxes were collected and the Roman army and civil service paid. The Frankish tremissis of the seventh century was the direct descendant of this gold coinage, though its gold content had been increasingly diluted with silver, either from shortage of bullion or through inflation. This (which should not be confused with debasement of the coinage) again suggests that although the locally minted Merovingian coins were not regal in the sense that the Visigothic coinage was (it did not normally carry the name and image of the king), it was nevertheless centrally controlled. About 670 someone, probably Ebroin, replaced this 'pale gold' coinage with silver deniers which were the immediate ancestors of the multitude of silver deniers and silver pennies of the medieval European currency. The English coinage rapidly followed suit. About 675 the pale gold English 'shillings' were replaced by new silver coins, the two primary series emanating from Kent and Essex, perhaps from the trading centres of Canterbury and London, where trading links with Francia would be strongest. By the early 690s, the laws of King Ine of Wessex were already calling the new coins 'Pennies', though the replacement of the small thick flans of the 'sceattas' by the broad silver penny had to wait for King Offa. The new silver coinage was not, however, universal. Most of Aquitaine was outside its sphere, and in Spain the Visigoths retained their rather idiosyncratic gold tremisses until their kingdom was destroyed by the Arabs in 711. The source of the silver for the Frankish deniers is another problem. The prolific silver mines at Melle, the Roman *Metellum*, in Poitou are not known to have been re-opened before the Carolingian period, though there could have been an earlier phase of unsigned coins without a mint name. Grierson has suggested that the massive hoards of family silver given to the Church by Gallo-Roman bishops may have also contributed to the bullion supply. It is at least certain that the similar switch to silver coinage by the Arab world was not a factor, for this did not occur until thirty years later.[26]

Pirenne, writing when European countries were going off the gold standard in the aftermath of the First World War, saw gold coinage as one of the 'four disappearances' that marked the end of the Mediterranean economy in Gaul. Later scholars, more concerned with the rise of medieval Europe, have seen the shift to silver in a more positive light, marking an increase in trade and commerce in northern and central France, Frisia and England. It was certainly an event that cast a long shadow — in England down to the replacement of silver by cupro-nickel in 1947. The views are not incompatible. Gold coinage was perhaps more suitable for long distance trade and the silver deniers could mark a decline in this, as Pirenne argued, and its replacement by a network of small local markets. This is not borne out, however, by the growth of new trading emporia like Hamwic, the predecessor of Southampton, or Lundenwic, the port of London, a mile west of the walled Roman city. Lundenwic, in the area of the present Covent Garden and Aldwich, developed from the mid-seventh century, perhaps under the aegis of King Wulfhere of Mercia. First mentioned in a charter of 672–4, it was striking its own silver sceatta coinage by about 675. Hamwic came into being around 700 with a street grid and enclosing ditch. Imported pottery from the Rhineland and northern France shows its overseas contacts, and before long it was also minting its own distinctive sceattas. Its foundation must fall within the long reign of King Ine of Wessex (689–726), who may have played a part in its foundation like that of Dagobert at St Denis.[27]

By this time much of the structure of medieval Europe was in place. There had been a decisive shift away from the Mediterranean to northern waters, where emporia were developing from periodic trading fairs into true trading towns, using a plentiful silver currency for local and international trade and administered by royal officials on behalf of territorial kings. The Church, now with a strong monastic element, had great wealth and large estates together with the beginnings of a monumental church architecture, though its relations with the secular power, which had its own priorities, remained an unsolved problem. Seventh-century Gaul was not noted for its learning or literacy, but when these revived in Carolingian times what had been the late antique was now in many fields (though not that of architecture) merely the antiquarian.

Appendix

The Notitia Galliarum: The Cities and Provinces of Late Roman Gaul

Lugdunensis Prima
Metropolis | Lugdunum | (Lyon)
2. Civitas Aeduorum | Augustodunum | (Autun)
3. Civitas Lingonum | Andematunnum | (Langres)
4. Castrum Cabillonense | Cabillonum | (Chalons-sur-Sâone)

Lugdunensis Secunda
Metropolis | Rotomagus | (Rouen)
2. Civitas Baiocassium | Augustodunum | (Bayeux)
3. Civitas Abrincatum | Ingena | (Avranches)
4. Civitas Ebroicorum | Mediolanum | (Evreux)
5. Civitas Saiorum | | ? Séez
6. Civitas Lexoviorum | Noviomagus | (Lisieux)
7. Civitas Constantia | Constantia | (Coutances)

Lugdunensis Tertia
Metropolis- | Civitas Turinorum | Caesarodunum (Tours)
2. Civitas Cenomannorum | Vindinum | (Le Mans)
3. Civitas Redonum | Condate | (Rennes)
4. Civitas Andecavorum | Juliomagus | (Angers)
5. Civitas Namnetum | Condivincum | (Nantes)
6. Civitas Coriosolitum | Fanum Martis | (Corseul)
7. Civitas Venetum | Darioritum | (Vannes)
8. Civitas Osismorum | Vorgium | (Carhaix)
9. Civitas Diablintum | Noviodunum | (Jublains)

Lugdunensis Senonia
Metropolis- | Civitas Senonum | Agedincum (Sens)
2. Civitas Carnotum | Autricum | (Chartres)
3. Civitas Autisiodorum | Autessiodurum | (Auxerre)
4. Civitas Tricassium | Augustobona | (Troyes)
5. Civitas Aurelianorum | Cenabum | (Orleans)
6. Civitas Parisiorum | Lutetia | (Paris)
7. Civitas Melduorum | Iatinum | (Meaux)

Belgica Prima
Metropolis- | Civitas Treverorum | Augusta (Trier)
2. Civitas Mediomatricum | Divodurum | (Metz)
3. Civitas Leucorum | Tullum | (Toul)
4. Civitas Verodunensium | Virodunum | (Verdun)

Belgica Secunda
Metropolis- | Civitas Remorum | Durocortorum (Reims)
2. Civitas Suessionum | Augusta | (Soissons)
3. Civitas Catalaunorum | Durocatalaunum | (Châlons-sur-Marne)
4. Civitas Veromandorum | Augusta | (Vermand)
5. Civitas Atrabatum | Nemetacum | (Arras)
6. Civitas Camaracensium | Camaracum | (Cambrai)
7. Civitas Turnacensium | Turnacum | (Tournai)
8. Civitas Silvanectum | Augustomagus | (Senlis)
9. Civitas Bellovacorum | Caesaromagus | (Beauvais)

10. Civitas Ambianensium	Samorobriva	(Amiens)
11. Civitas Morinum	Tarvenna	(Therouanne)
12. Civitas Bononiensium	Bononia	(Boulogne)

Germanica Prima

Metropolis-	Civitas Moguntiacensium	Moguntiacum (Mainz)
2. Civitas Argentoratensium	Argentorate	(Strasbourg)
3. Civitas Nemetum	Noviomagus	(Speyer)
4. Civitas Vangionum	Borbetomagus	(Worms)

Germanica Secunda

| Metropolis- | Civitas Agrippiensium | (Cologne) |
| 2. Civitas Tungorum | Atuatuca | (Tongres) |

Maxima Sequanorum

Metropolis-	Civitas Vesontiensium	Vesontio (Besançon)
2. Civitas Equestrium	Noviodunum	(Nyon)
3. Civitas Helvetiorum	Aventicum	(Avenches)
4. Civitas Basiliensium	Basilia	(Basle)
5. Castrum Vindonissense	Vindonissa	(Windisch)
6. Castrum Ebrodunense	Ebrodunum	(Yverdon)
7. Castrum Argentariense	Argentia	(Horburg)
8. Portus Bucini		(Port Sur Sâone)

Alpes Poeninae et Graiae

| Metropolis- | Civitas Ceutorum | Tarantasia (Moûtiers) |
| 2. Civitas Vallensium | Octodurus | (Martigny) |

The Seven Provinces

Viennensis

Metropolis	Vienna	(Vienne)
2. Civitas Genavenensium	Genava	(Geneva)
3. Civitas Gratianopolitana	Gratianopolis	(Grenoble)
4. Civitas Albensium	Alba	(Alba, formerly Aps)
5. Civitas Deensium	Dea Augusta	(Die)
6. Civitas Valentinorum	Valentia	(Valence)
7. Civitas Tricastinorum	Augusta	(St Paul Trois Chateaux)
8. Civitas Vasensium	Vasio	(Vaison)
9. Civitas Arausicorum	Arausio	(Orange)
10. Civitas Cabellicorum	Cabellio	(Cavaillon)
11. Civitas Avennicorum	Avennio	(Avignon)
12. Civitas Arelatensium	Arelate	(Arles)
13. Civitas Massiliensium	Massilia	(Marseille)

Aquitanica Prima

Metropolis-	Civitas Biturigum Avaricum	(Bourges)
2. Civitas Arvernorum	Augustonemetum	(Clermont Ferrand)
3. Civitas Rutenorum	Segodunum	(Rodez)
4. Civitas Albigensium	Albiga	(Albi)
5. Civitas Cadurcorum	Divona	(Cahors)
6. Civitas Lemovicum	Augustoritum	(Limoges)
7. Civitas Gabalum	Anderitum	(Javols)
8. Civitas Vellavorum	Ruessio	(S. Paulien)

Aquitanica Secunda

Metropolis- — Civitas Burdigalensium — Burdigala (Bordeaux)
2. Civitas Aginnensium — Aginnum — (Agen)
3. Civitas Ecolisnensium — Ecolisina — (Angoulême)
4. Civitas Santonum — Mediolanum — (Saintes)
5. Civitas Pictavorum — Limonum — (Poitiers)
6. Civitas Petrocoriorum — Vesunna — (Périgueux)

Novempopulana

Metropolis- — Civitas Elusatium — Elusa (Eauze)
2. Civitas Ausciorum — Elimberrum — (Auch)
3. Civitas Aquensium — Aquae — (Dax)
4. Civitas Lactoratium — Lactora — (Lectoure)
5. Civitas Convenarum — Lugdunum — (St Bertrand de Comminges)
6. Civitas Consorannorum — — — (St Lizier)
7. Civitas Boatium — — — (La Teste de Buch)
8. Civitas Benarensium — Beneharnum — (Lescar)
9. Civitas Aturensium — Aturum — (Aire)
10. Civitas Vasatica — Cossio — (Bazas)
11. Civitas Turba — Turba — (Tarbes)
12. Civitas Elloronensium — Iloro — (Oloron)

Narbonensis Prima

Metropolis- — Narbo — (Narbonne)
2. Civitas Tolosatium — Tolosa — (Toulouse)
3. Civitas Beterrensium — Baeterrae — (Béziers)
4. Civitas Nemausensium — Nemausus — (Nimes)
5. Civitas Lutevensium — Luteva — (Lodève)
6. Castrum Ucetiense — Ucetia — (Uzès)

Narbonensis Secunda

Metropolis- — Civitas Aquensium — Aquae Sextiae (Aix-en-Provence)
1. Civitas Aptensium — Apta Julia — (Apt)
2. Civitas Regensium — Reii Apollinares — (Riez)
3. Civitas Foroiuliensium — Forum Julii — (Frejus)
4. Civitas Vappincensium — Vappincum — (Gap)
5. Civitas Segesteriorum — Segustero — (Sisteron)
6. Civitas Antipolitana — Antipolis — (Antibes)

Alpes Maritimae

Metropolis- — Civitas Ebrodunensium — Ebrodunum (Embrun)
2 Civitas Diniensium — Dinia — (Digne)
3. Civitas Rigomagensium — Rigomagus — (Barcelonnette)
4. Civitas Saliniensium — Salinae — (Castellane)
5. Civitas Sanitiensium — Sanitium — (Senez)
6. Civitas Glanatina — Glannativa — (Gladeves)
7. Civitas Cemenelensium — Cemenelum — (Cimiez)
8. Civitas Vintiensium — Vintium — (Vence)

References

1: Mid-life crisis: Gaul and the west in the third century

1. *Severus* — Cassius Dio LXXVI, 5.2. *Julian* — Ammianus Marcellinus XX, 4
2. *Disc*— Cagnat *Rev. Archéologique* 26 (1895), 23. *Lessened mobility of the legions from Marcus Aurelius onwards* — Luttwak (1976), 24–6 'provincial security had been sacrificed for the security of the Empire as a whole, and the provincials can be excused for their faliure to accept the logic of the system'. *Caerleon* — R.I.B. 327–8 and 334. *Similar evidence from Chester* — R.I.B. 449 and 488
3. *Amiens* — Bayard and Massey (1983), 214–20. *Boulogne* — Seillier and Demolon (1984), 24–6. *Langres* — T.C.C.G. IV (1986), 48–52
4. J. Sumption *The Hundred Years War: Trial by Battle* (London 1991), 11. Wightman (1985), 98 estimated the population of all save the very largest towns in Gallia Belgica at 2,000–5,000. Thus between 5,000 and 14,000 acres of grain would be needed for each town, without other foodstuffs
5. *Pillars of Tutela* — Etienne (1962), 187–91, *Archéologia* 47 (June 1972), 10–11. *Inscriptions* — Bordeaux— C.I.L. XIII, 583 and 584 and Courteault (1921). *Vieux* — C.I.L. XIII, 362 and Pfaulm (1948). *Sens* — C.I.L. XIII, 2949. *Beauvais* — Leman (1982)
6. Poulter (1995), 12 and n.38; Herodian V, 2
7. *Vienne* — J.L. Prisset *et al.* 'Evolution urbain à Saint-Romain en Gal', *Gallia* 51 (1994), 1–133. F. Baratte *et al* 'Le Trésor de la Place Camille — Jouffray à Vienne: un dépot d'argenterie et son contexte archéologique' (50th supplement to *Gallia* 1990)
8. *Amiens* — Bayard and Massey (1983), 214–20
9. Whittaker (1990), 113. Cleere in D. Miles *The Romano-British Countryside* (B.A.R. 103, 1982), 23. 'The tendency to equate industry with towns . . . is fallacious and misleading . . . The current picture of Roman industry suggests that major primary industries were almost exclusively located outside urban centres'. Provost (1993), 35–6
10. Agache (1970, 1978). Drinkwater (1983), 29. *Historia Augusta, Gallieni Duo* VI (Atrebatic cloaks as almost synonymous with Gaul). Do *Probus* IV, 5 'Pallia Gallica'. Diocletian's Price edict (ed S. Lauffer) 19. 32, 54; 259. Van Ossel (1992). Maps 4–16. Wightman (1978)
11. Gechter and Kunow (1986, 1988). Potter (1979), 116 and 38–46. Hodges and Whitehouse (1983), 33–40. Potter (1987), 195–7
12. *Larch and fir* — Boon (1975), 56. *Wine barrels in north-east Italy in the third century* — Herodian VIII, 4
13. See n.7 above. J. Mertens in Maloney and Hobley (1983), 42–57
14. *Concordia* — I.L.S. 9479. *Aquilea* — C.I.L. V, 808. See Eadie (1980). *Leg XX.* — C.I.L. XIII, 6780 (AD 255). *Coins* — R.I.C. Vol 5, part 1. *Gallienus* Victoria Germanica (AD 256); Victoria Augg It(er) Germ (AD 257). Germanicus Maximus Ter. (AD 257). Restitutor Galliarum AD 256–9. *Architects and engineers* — *Historia Augusta, Triginta Tyranni* 23, 3,6. *Cologne* — Hellenkemper in Maloney and Hobley (1983), 20–28. *Italy* — C.I.L. V, 3329, Richmond and Holford (1935). N. Christie 'Urban defences in later Roman Italy' in Herring, Whitehouse and Wilkins *Papers of the Fourth Conference of Italian Archaeology* Vol 2 (1991), 185–99
15. Arnheim (1972), 34, 37 casts doubt on the alleged edict of Gallienus cited by Aurelius Victor. He argues that the change from senatorial to non-senatorial governors in senatorial provinces was gradual, and the edict simply a 'neat and handy device' by Aurelius Victor to explain a more protracted development
16. Aurelius Victor *De Caesaribus* XXX, 3. Eutropius IX, 8. Orosius *Adversos Paganos* VII, 22,7.; 24, 2
17. *Historia Augusta, Probus* 3. *Rome* — Richmond (1930). M.Todd (1978) and 'The Aurelianic wall of Roman and its analogies' in Maloney and Hobley (1983), 58–68. *Dacia* — L. Okamura 'Roman withdrawls from three transfluvial frontiers' in Mathisen and Sivan (1996), 11–19. *Aurelian* — *Historia Augusta, Aurelian* 38, 2–4. Aurelius Victor *De Caesaribus* XXXV, 6. *Restitutor Galliarum* — C.I.L. XII, 2673, 5553. *Situation on the frontier* — Eadie (1980)
18. *Haccourt* — de Boe *Archaeologia Belgica* 132 (1971), 15–32; 174 (1975); 182 (1982). *Archéologia* 93 (1976), 22–37. *Vodelée* — A. Rober *Archaeologia Belgica* new series, 3 (1987), 133–64. *Echternach* — J. Metzler (1981); *Archáéologia* 168 (July 1982), 38–50. *Fuller survey* — P. Van Ossel (1992). *Settlement patterns* — Van Ossel (1987), Gechter and

Kunow (1978, 1986)

19. J. Sumption *The Hundred Years War* (1990), 28–9. Geronimo de Uztariz *Théorie et Pratique du Commerce et de la Marine* (1753), 171, quoted Braudel (1973), Vol 1, 458. *Hoards* — Fabre and Mainjonet in *Tresora Monétaires et Plaques-Boucles de la Gaule Romaine* ed Gricourt *et al* (12th supplement to *Gallia* 1958), 121–271

20. *Historia Augusta, Probus* 13, 5. Julian *Convivium* 314.b. Frere *Britannia* (1987), 329 suggests that Probus may have created the Saxon shore system in Britain

21. *Jublains* — C. Roach Smith *Collectanea Antiqua* III (London, 1854), 103–8. *Gallia* 38 (1980), 381–4. Rebuffet (1985) Naveau (1986)

22. *Peasant unrest in Gaul* — Eutropius IX, 20.3; Orosius VII, 29.2. *Britannicus Maximus* — C.I.L. XIV, 126

2: Soldiers and civilians in the Gallic late Empire

1. For examples see J.P.C. Kent *Roman Coins* (1978), plates 606, 612

2. *Panegyrici* VIII, 5,2; VII, 6,2. Herodian VI, 4

3. Rivet (1976), J. Harries (1978)

4. Johnson (1983). R.M. Butler 'The construction of urban defences' in Maloney and Hobley (1983), 125–9. *Dax* — C. Roach Smith *Collectanea Antiqua* 5 (1861), 226–40. *Will of Bishop Bertram* — *Actus Pontificum Cenomannis* p.99. Biarne T.C.C.G. V (*Lugdunensis Tertia*) 50

5. A. Invernizzi 'Kifrin and the Euphrates Limes' Freeman and Kennedy (1986), 357–81. *Rome* — Todd (1978) and 'The Aurelianic wall of Rome and its analogies' in Mahoney and Hobley (1983), 58–67. *Ain Sinu* – D. and J. Oates 'Ain Sinu, a Roman frontier post in northern Iraq' *Iraq* 21 (1959), 207–42. D. Oates *Studies in the History of Northern Iraq* (1968), 80–92. *Groups of walls* — Johnson (1973) and 1983 figs 42, p.115 and 79, p.172

6. *Grenoble* — C.I.L. XII, 2229. *Xanten* — G. Precht 'The town walls and defensive systems of Xanten' Mahoney and Hobley (1983), 34–6. *Beauvais* — Johnson (1973), Leman (1982), 213 and n.45 and *Gallia* 7 (1949), 95. *Tours*— J. Wood (1983), 45. *Orleans* — *Rev Archéol du Loiret* 19–20 (1994), quoted N. Gauthier in Gauthier and Galinié (1997), 52, n.9

7. *Bourges* — *Gallia* 42 (1984), 275–7. *Rouen* — Halbout (1989). *Poitiers* —Le Masne de Chermont (1987), 168–9

8. L.Saulnier — Pernuit. *La Facade des Thermes de Sens* 7th supplement to *Rév Archéol de l' Est* (Dijon 1987)

9. Le Masne de Chermont (1987), 162–9

10. *Evreux* — *Gallia* 40 (1982), 293–5. *Amiens* — Bayard and Massey (1983), 237–24, 253–4. *Bavai* — E. Will 'Les enceintes du Bas-Empire a Bavay' *Revue du Nord* 44 (1962), 39–40. H. Bievelet 'L'exploration archéologique de Bavai' *Revue du Nord* 46 (1964), 193–204. J. Mertens in Maloney and Hobley (1983), 51–3. *Famars* — Bersu and Unverzagt (1961). Mertens, loc cit, 53

11. Sulpicius Severus *Dialogues: Gallus* 4. L. Pietri T.C.C.G. V (*Lugdunensis Tertia*) citing Ph. Lauer, *Recueil des Actes de Charles III, Le Simple* (Paris 1940), nos. 46 and 101

12. H.A. Thompson (1959)

13. Ausonius *Mosella* 456–7. Goffart (1974). Ammianus Macellinus XIV, 2.3, XIV,10, XVII, 8, XV, 2–3. C. Young 'The late Roman water mill at Ickham and the Saxon Shore' in A. Detsicas *Collectanea Historica : Essays in Memory of Stuart Rigold* (Maidstone 1981), 32–40

14. R. Lane-Fox *Pagans and Christians* (1986), 13. Rebuffet (1985). *Alchester* — Esmonde Cleary (1989), 50. *Oretum* — C. I.L. II, supplement 6340. *Praeses* — Keay (1988), 183–4. 'A city . . .' quoted Antonio Dominguez Ortiz *The Golden Age of Spain, 1516–1659* (1971), 130–1. The same distinction between 'Civitas' — (Roman) city and 'Villa' — (non-Roman) town appears on the English coinage of Edward I and his successors

15. *Notitia Dignitatum* Occ. XLII

16. Luttwak (1986), 127–145. *Bordeaux* — I.L.C.V. 554, C.I.L. XII, 11, 032. *Arras* — A. Jacques 'Le presence militaire a Arras au Bas-Empire' in Vallet and Kazanski (1993), 195–207. *Tours* — Galinié (1997), 69. – *Poitiers* — Zeiss (1941), Abb. 36,1

17. Pilloy and Jumel (1886); Pilloy (1886–92) Vol 2 (1891), 38–51; Eck (1891). Böhme (1974), 69–75, 330–34. *Christian objects* — Eck plates III, XIV — glass dish with Christian motifs and the motto VIVAS IN DEO and a casket with relief decorated panels with Biblical scenes

18. Eck (1891) 22–3 and 121–37. Pilloy (1895), 38–52. Böhme 331–2 and Taf. 137

19. Elton (1996), 115. *Late Roman weapon grave in timber chamber at Rouen* — *Gallia* 44 (1986), 371–2. *Later examples* — C. Hills *Medieval Archaeol* 21 (1977), 67–76. *St Quentin* — Eck (1891), 286–308. *Vermand* — *Marteville* Agache (1978), 402–4, plates 224–6 and exhibition catalogue *Gallien in der Spätantike: Von Kaiser Constantin zur Frankenkönig Chideric* (Römisch-Germanisches Zentralmuseum, Mainz, 1980), 166–73 and nos. 257–70

20. *Passio of St Marcellus of Tingitana* — Musurillo (1972), 250–1. Sulpicius Severus *Dialogues, Postumianus 2* c. 11, *Vita Martini* 3. Constantius of Lyon *Vita Germani* 4. *Stilicho* — Delbrueck (1929), pl.63. Van der Meer and Mohrmann (1966), pl. 200. *Missorium of Theodosius* — Toynbee and Painter (1986), pl.X no 6. Van der Meer and Mohrmann pls. 78, 80

21. *Decorated baldrics* — B. Sternquist 'Runde Beschlagplatten mit Befestigungöse' *Saalburg Jahrbuch* 13 (1954), 59–68 (Abb.4, p.65). *Saint-Croix* — Gricourt *et al.* (1958), 275–341 and pl. I and V. *Historia Augusta, Claudius Gothicus* 4, 5 a 'sword belt of silver, gilded' as a rich gift. Gregory of Tours *Gl. Mart* 60 — a richly ornamented gold belt with its fittings, as a gift to a church at Nantes. *Spoilt castings* — Bishop and Coulston (1993), 187, fig 134. *Typology* — Böhme (1974), 357–62 and maps 11–12

22. J. Lafaurie in Gricourt *et al* (1958), 275–341. Discussion — Knight (1984) 360, n65 and (with the slightly different 'lost lead' process) P. Craddock in S. Youngs *The Work of Angels* (1989) 170–1 and 194–5. *Saucer brooches* — T. Dickinson (1982)

23. Bayard and Massey (1983), 237–41, 253. *Notitia Dignitatum* Occ. IX, 32–9. The state armaments factories are mapped by Wightman (1985, 254–7, fig 42). Simon James (1988), 262 discusses the 'often astounding level of specialistation' and (271–2) the factory-like production line, their urban siting and the role of the city councils in assembling raw materials and other supplies. *Miséry* — Böhme (1974), Taf. 128

24. *Made within the Empire* — eg the Cortrat and Oudenberg types of Tutulus brooch, from the Seine Valley and Normandy, and between the Rhine and Seine. Böhme (1974) Karte 6 and Fundliste 6. *Laeti* — *Panegyrici* VII, 6.2, VIII, 5, 21. *Historia Augusta Probus* 13.5. *Kentish laeti* — Attenborough (1922), 237–9. *Julian* — Ammianus Marcellinus XX, 3.18

25. *Praefectus Nerviorum* — *Notitia Dignitatum* Occ. XLII, 41. *Famars* — Bersu and Unverzagt (1961), 187. *Menapii and Nervii* — Wightman (1985), 205. Paulinus of Nola *Letters* 12. 18 (C.S.E.L. 29. 1, 347–65). It was characteristic of monk-bishops like Martin of Tours that they did not confine their activities within their own diocese

26. *Vron* — Seillier (1976, 1978, 1986). Seillier and Demolon (1983), 28–31 (Grave 209 A). 75 and colour plate opp. p.80 (Grave 200 A). Belt set — Seillier (1986), 15

27. *Cortrat* — France-Lanord (1963). *Frenouville* — Perin (1974)

28. Wightman (1988), 246–50. Distribution maps — Johnson (1983) figs 87–8 and Wightman (1985), 254–5, fig 42. J. Mertens 'Le Luxembourg meridional au Bas Empire' *Archaeologia Belgica* 76 (1964). *Echternach* — Metzler (1981). Brulet (1990) divides the Gallia Belgica series into three groups — third century, late fourth century and exclusively later. *Massif Central* — *Gallia* 24 (1966), 484, 27 (1969), 416. Sidonius *Letters* 1, 4; VI, 4

29. Nenquin (1953), Brulet (1978)

30. J. Mertens and H. Remy 'Un refuge du Bas-Empire a Éprave' *Archaeologia Belgica* 144 (1973). R. Brulet 'La Roche a Lomme a Dourbes: Fortification du Bas-Empire et refuge Medieval' *Archaeologia Belgica* 160 (1974), fig 4, B.2

3: **How the West was Lost: Valentinian I to Valentinian III**

1. Ammianus Marcellinus XXVII, 1–3. *British evidence* — J. Casey 'Imperial campaigns and fourth-century defences in Britain'. Maloney and Hobley (1983), 121–4

2. Matthews (1975), 50–87. *Jovinus* — C.I.L. XIII, 3256. P.L.R.E. Jovinus 6. Sivan (1993)

3. Mathisen (1989), 12–19

4. *Letter of St Ambrose* — P.L. 16, 1036, c, quoted Macmullen *Corruption and the Decline of Rome* (1988), 230. *Sulpicius Alexander* — Gregory of Tours H.F. II, 9. Books 1–2 covered the rule of Gratian, 3–4 Magnus Maximus, later books Arbogast and Eugenius

5. Claudian *Panegyric on the Fourth Consulship of Honorius* 439–458. *Consulship of Stilicho* I , 188–245. *Gothic Wars* 416–8

6. Orosius VII, 40. C.E. Stevens (1957). Parallel accounts by Photius (Blockley 170–1), Sozomon (9.11–12.3) and Zosimus (6, 1–5) all derive from Olympiodorus of Thebes. 'They thought', says Sozomon, 'that with such a name Constantine would conquer the whole empire.'

7. Mathisen (1988), 27–37. Ammianus Marcellinus XV, 5. *Defender of Gaul* — Prosper of Aquitaine *Chronicle* 1247, sub anno 412. *Pope Zosimus* — Jaffé (1885) 329 and 340

8. Orosius VII, 40. Sozomon 9. 12–15 (Blockley 175–8). Renatus Frigedarius (Gregory of Tours H.F. II, 9). Matthews (1975), 313–14

9. Sidonius *Letters* III, 12, V.9. Mathisen 33–5. *Dardanus* — P.L.R.E. II, 3, 965. Benoit *Rivista di Archeologia Cristiana* 27 (1951), 69–89. *Carte Archéologique de la Gaule Romaine* VI (1937), pl. 1. *Retirement* — Sidonius *Letters* IV, 9 and 24

10. Matthews (1975), 330–49. Mathisen (1984), 159–70

11. The Council of the Seven Provinces (south of the Loire and upper Rhône), established shortly before the invasions of 406–7, lapsed during the subsequent disorder. Mathisen (1989), 19 n. 78 and 43

12. Kent (1979). White (1988). *Fifth century imports* — Evison (1985) Böhme (1986)

13. *Furfooz* — Nenquin (1953), 20 and pl. VIII, D.11. *Vieuxville* — Alenus-Lecerf (1985, 1986). See also Werner (1958)

14. Böhme (1974), 368–70

15. *Indented bowls* — Harden (1956), 136. Morin-Jean (1913) type 76. Another from Fel was with a silver siliqua struck c.445. *Moulded bowls* — Werner and Dasnoy in Breuer and Roosens (1957), 307–11, 360–75. *Darenth bowl* — Webster *et al* (1980)

16. Lemant (1985), Böhme (1974), 316–17, Taf. 123–4

17. Lafaurie (1964–80). C.E. King (1992)

18. Hübener (1968), Bayard (1993)

19. *Magnentius* — Zonares XIII,6. British father — Zosimus II, 54.1. See Bastien (1964), 7

20. Gregory of Tours H.F. 2, 8 (from Renatus Frigeridus). Prosper of Aquitaine *Chronicle* 1288, 1290, 1292 (AD 425 and 428). *Chron. Gall* p.658. Merobaudes *Panegyric* 1 pp.32–4. Hydatius *Chronicle* 92, 94. *Goths at Marseille* — Photius 80 (Blockley 185–6). Mathisen (1989), 73–5

21. Thompson (1982), 3–36. G. Alfoldy *Noricum* (1974), 208–20

22. C.I.L. VI, 1724. *Chron Gall* pp.660, 662. Prosper of Aquitaine *Chronicle* 1322, sub anno 435. Hydatius *Chronicle* 108. Sidonius *Panegyric on Avitus* 234–5, 244–99. Merobaudes *Panegyric 1*, 9–16, 55. Mathisen (1989), 102–8

23. Sidonius *Letters* VI, 4. Van Dam (1985), 25–6. Drinkwater (1992). *Peasant revolt* — Thompson (1952)

24. Merobaudes *Panegyric II* , 10–15 (Clover 13–15). *Querolus* (*Alularia*) ed. Havet (Paris 1880), 217. Drinkwater (1992, 210) suggests that the passage may not directly refer to Bacaudae, but reflect a more general Massiliot or Provencal view of north Gaul. *Panegyrici Latini* 2.4.3

25. R. Mc Kitterick *The Frankish Kingdoms under the Carolingians* (1983), 232

26. R. Hutton *The Royalist War Effort 1642–1646* (1982), 159–73. D. Underdown 'The chalk and the cheese: contrasts among the English Clubmen' *Past and Present* 85 (1979), 25–48. Sidonius *Letters* II, I. The actions of Seronatus were 'filling the woods with dangerous fugitives from the estates'

27. Sidonius *Panegyric on Majorian* 211–56. *Location of Vicus Helenae* — Boudelles 'Le problem linguistique dans l'affaire du Vicus Helena' *Revue du Nord* 66 (1984), 351–9. Another possible location is Hélesmes (Nord). Procopius *History of the Wars* V, xii, 8–9

28. *Xanten* — Ruger 'Die spatromische Grossfestung in der Colonia Ulpia Traiana' *Bonner Jahrbuch* 179 (1979), 499–524. Bayard (1993), 227–9. *Alzey* — Oldenstein 'Le fortification d'Alzey et la défence de la frontière romaine le long du Rhine au Ive'. Vallet and Kazanski (1993), 125–33. *Duisberg* — G. Krause *Stadtarchäologie In Duisburg 1980–90* (Duisburg 1992). I am very grateful to Dr Krause for valuable discussion of the Duisburg sequence, and for the generous gift of a copy of his work

29. Merobaudes *Second Panegyric on Aetius* 13–15, 41–59. Gildas *De Excidio* I, 20. (for a different view see M.E. Jones 'The appeal to Aetius in Gildas' *Nottingham Medieval Stud 32* (1988), 141–55). Thompson (1982), 140

30. Loriot and Delaporte (1980), no.32. Galliou and Jones *The Bretons* (1991), 125–7 and pl. 21

31. Lafaurie (1964–78), C.E. King (1992)

32. *Varying views on Aetius* — Stein *Histoire du Bas Empire* I (Paris 1959), 337. Oost (1964), Twyman (1970), Moss (1973). *End of Empire* — Marcellinus Comes *Chronicle*, Bede H.E. I, 21

33. *Soissons and fall of Syagrius* — Gregory of Tours H.F. II, 27. Gregory's summary of events (II, 8), from a lost *Annals of Angers* is important, but capable of more than one explanation. D Frye 'Aegidius, Childeric, Odovacer and Paul' *Nottingham Medieval Stud 36* (1982), 1–4. E James 'Childeric, Syagrius et la disparition du Royaume de Soissons' *Rev. Archéol de Picardie* 3–4 (1988), 9–12

34. Constantius of Lyon *Vita Germani* 10

35. Pliny *Letters* VII, 27, to Licinius Sura. I owe this parallel to my daughter, Delia Knight

36. Fullest discussion — Thompson 1984. *Dux* — S. Johnson 'Channel commands in the Notitia' Goodburn and Bartholemew (1976), 81–102

37. *Hagiography and its audience* — B. de Gaiffier (1947), emphasising the role of public readings. *St Alban* — Levison (1941). H. Williams (1912), 108

38. Prosper of Aquitaine *Chronicle* sub anno 429

39. Wood (1984), 9. *Seven offices* — Griffe (1966), II, 313–22

40. *Rhual* — Grid ref. SJ 223647. *Rhetoric* — Hodgkin *A History of the Anglo-Saxons* (1952), I, 61. A. Cameron *Claudian :Poetry and Propaganda at the Court of Honorius* (Oxford, 1970), 96–7. Sidonius *Panegyric on Avitus* II, 88–92. Claudian *Panegyric on the Fourth Consulship of Honorius*

4: The Christian City

1. Rouché (1964)

2. Sidonius *Letters* 1, 6

3. Kurth (1919), Stroheker (1948) Gilliard (1979) Brennan (1985)

4. *Thorigny marble* — C.I.L. XIII, 3162. Pflaum (1948). *Caerwent stone* — R.I.B. 311. Constantius of Lyon *Vita Germani* 19

5. *Counts* — James (1982), 58–9. An older but valuable source, with a list of known counts is Kurth 'De la nationalité des comtes Francs en VI e siècle' *Études Franques* I (1919), 169–181

6. *Vita Germani* 28. Sulpicius Severus *Dialogues-Gallus* 4. *Postumianus 2* 4–6

7. Klingshirn (1985). Patrick *Epistola* 14. Sulpicius Severus *Dialogues-Gallus* 14. *Severinus of Noricum* — Thompson (1982), 122. *Eugenia* — I.C.G. 544, C.I.L. XII, 480

8. Sidonius *Letters* V, 1, VI, 2–10. Gregory of Tours H.F. II, 24. Jews, merchants and clergy were useful letter carriers, and could carry more confidential verbal messages. Some of Sidonius's more bland epistles could have been cover for such. Not all were reliable — letters lost in the post — Sidonius *Letters* IV,2. Harries (1994), 207–10

9. Maillé (1959), 160–66. *Current Archaeology* 120 (June 1990), 406–8

10. Gregory of Tours H.F. X, 31. Kraeling *Excavations at Dura Europos: Final Report 8, part 2: The Christian Building* (New Haven 1967). J Ramon Melida 'Una casa Romana Cristiana' *Junta Superior de Excavaciones: Memoria 12* (Madrid 1917)

11. Le Blant I.C.G. 617–19. C.I.L. XII, 5356. Marrou (1970). The sums involved may be 600 + 600 (reading the second numeral as ID(em) or 600 + 1500. Jill Harries (1994, 34) suggests that they represent 600 for the workforce, 1500 for materials. *Consentius* — Sidonius *Letters* VIII, 4, *Carmina* 23. The villa estate, the *ager Octavianus*, survived as the medieval Cistercian grange of *Octabian*, with the church of St Etienne, belonging to the Abbey of Fontfroide. The area, in the communes of Ornaisons and Boutenac, would repay detailed fieldwork. Griffé (1965), 292–3, n79

12. *Concilia Galliae* I, 76–93, II, 65. *First Council of Orleans* 511, c.25. No one shall keep Easter, Christmas or Pentecost on their estate (*villa*) unless sick. *Council of Clermont* 535, c.15. If a priest . . . lives on an estate (*villa*) . . . he must celebrate Christmas, Easter and Pentecost with the bishop in the city. So must all adult citizens. *Fourth Council of Orleans 541* c.3. It is not permitted for distinguished laymen to celebrate Easter outside the episcopal city. *Crowds* — Sidonius *Letters* V, 17

13. Guild, Guyon and Rivet (1980, 1983). Kauffman (1983). J. Guyon T.C.C.G. II *Narbonensis Secunda et Alpes Maritimae* (1986), 7–28. M Gauthier *Gallia* 44 (1986), 379–83

14. *Valence* — A. Blanc (1957, 1971). *N.D. le Ronde* — E. James (1977), 272–5

15. *Geneva* — C. Bonnet (1987, 1989)

16. *St Stephen* — Griffé (1947–65) III, 34–5. *Relics at Clermont* — Gregory of Tours H.F. X, 31, *Gl. Mart* 8–33

17. *Bishop's houses* — Gregory of Tours H.F. II, 23 (Clermont); IX, 2 (Verdun). The *domus ecclesiae* at Tours was still partly plank built in 575 — H.F. V.4. *Camera of episcopa* — *Second Council of Tours* 567, c.12. For an episcopa and her maids who broke this rule see H.F. IV, 36. *Episcopae* — Brennan (1985). *Dogs* — *Second Council of Macon* 585, c.13. *Bishop Audoveus* — H.F. X, 14. *Bishop Bertram* — *Actus Pontificum Cenomannis* pp.99, 115–16 . *Poitiers* — Masne de Charmant (1987)

18. *Pipe burial* — G.C. Boon *Isca: The Roman Legionary Fortress at Caerleon* (1972), 107–8 and n.37, pp.138–9, citing others from Britain and Rhine. *Gervasius and Protasius* — H. Delehaye *Les Origines du Culte du Martyrs* (Brussels, 2nd ed 1933), 75–8. *Martin the equal of the martyrs* — Sulpicius Severus *Letters* 2

19. Augustine *Sermon 273*. Migne P.L. 38 (1865). *Martin* — Sulpicius Severus *Vita Martini* 11. *Dijon and Troyes* — Gregory of Tours *Gl. Mart* 50, 63

20. *Symphorian of Autun* — *Passio S. Symphoriani* (*Acta Sanctorum* August IV, 496–7) possibly from the time of bishop Euphronius (452–75) Gregory of Tours *Gl. Mart* 51. *Patroclus of Troyes* — *Acta Sanctorum* January II, 343–5. *Gl. Mart* 63. Van der Straeten 'La passion de S Patrocle de Troyes' *Analecta Bollandiana* 78 (1960), 145–53 — related to those of Symphorian of Autun and Alban of Verulamium and probably mid-sixth century. *Saturninus of Toulouse* — The early passio (Ruinart *Acta Sincera* (ed of 1859), 177–80) used by Gregory of Tours H.F. I, 30, may be the earliest Gallic martyr text, written soon after the death of bishop Exuperius, who finished the basilica begun by his predecessor, and translated the martyr to it. de Gaiffier *Analecta Bollandiana* 66 (1948), 53–8. There was a similar sequence at Clermont, where bishop Illidius was buried c.383–5 in a wooden coffin in a suburban crypt. A basilica was built over his tomb in the next century, and bishop Avitus (572–94) later translated the remains to a new church

21. Sapin (1982). *Pectorius* – Cabrol — Leclerq D.A.C.L. article 'Autun' cols. 3193–4 *Inscription of 378* — Le Blant I.C.G. 7, C.I.L.XIII, 2798. *Hic Iacet* — I.C.G. 600, C.I.L.XIII, 2799

22. Sidonius *Letters* V, 17. *Poundbury* — Farwell and Mollison (1993). *Dijon* — Gregory of Tours *Gl Conf.* 41–2. Pietri T.C.C.G. IV *Lugdunensis Prima* 43–4. *Autun* — *Gl. Conf* 72–6. Sapin (1982)

23. *Vienne* — Jannet-Vallat *et al* (1986), 42–59. Reynaud (1977). *Xanten* — Bader 'Ausgrabungen unter dem Xantener Dom' *Germania* 18 (1934), 112–17. Borger 'Die Ausgrabungen im Bereich des Xantener Domes' in W. Kramer *Neue Ausgrabungen in Deutschland* (1958), 368ff. Bridger *Archaologie in Deutschland* 1990 8–11. *St Viktor* — Gregory of Tours *Gl.Mart* 62

24. *Adventus ceremony* — Mac Cormack (1972), Gussone (1978). *Sermon* — Victricius of Rouen *De Laude Sanctorum* Migne P.L. 20, cols 443–458. *Trier ivory* — frequently reproduced — eg Van der Meer and Mohrmann (1966), pl.509

25. *Tarbes* — Gregory of Tours *Gl. Mart* 73. *Thiers* — *Gl Mart* 66. See also Gregory's account of the martyrs Nazaire and Celsus 'of Embrun' — in fact of Milan *Gl.Mart* 46

26. The most comprehensive survey is the series *Topographie Chrétienne des Cites de la Gaule des Origines au Milieu du Ve. Siecle* (Paris 1986 on). The following accounts inevitably draw heavily on this. *Marseille* — Loseby (1992 a)

27. Good account of Roman Vienne in Rivet (1988), 305–15. *Possible late circuit* — Jannet-Vallat (1986), 9–22. *Palace fire* — Gregory of Tours H.F. II, 34. *Coffins* — Esperandieu *Inscriptions latines de Gaule Narbonnaise* (1929), no.263. *Temple* — Jannet-Vallat fig 8

28. Reynaud (1978), Jannet-Vallat 61–4. The passio of St Ferreolus (*Acta Sanctorum* September V, 764–7) may date from soon after his discovery by bishop Mamertius c.476. The body was moved to a new intra-mural basilica in the eighth century after Arab attacks. *Bishop list* — Duchesne (1894–5) 'Vienne'. Griffé (1966) I, 93–4. *Julian* — Ammianus Marcellinus XXI, 2,5. *Cathedral* — Hubert (1952), 52, Beck 1950), 383–4

29. Gregory of Tours *Gl Mart* 46, H.F. X, 31. *Foedula* — Le Blant I.C.G. 412, C.I.L. XII, 2115. *Cemetery* — Cabrol Leclerq D.A.C.L. 15, cols. 3070—9, Le Blant I.C.G. II, p. 46. *Inscriptions* — Four with *Hic Iacet* (c.420–50), nine beginning *Hic Requiescit in Pace* (c.450–80). None of the dated sequence of Vienne stones, which begins in 481, is from St Gervaise. I.C.G. 401–441, C.I.L.XII, 2104–2149 (with others)

30. *Oldest inscription* — I.C.G. 410. C.I.L. XII, 2110. *St Pierre* — Allmer *Bull._Soc.Antiq. de France* Nov 1860, 26–7. *Plan* — Jannet-Vallat fig 7, p.15 and pl IV (arcolositum tomb). *Earliest tomb* — I.C.G. 448, C.I.L. XII, 2057

31. Jannet-Vallet 28–30. *Inscriptions* — St Martin — I.C.G. 458 EE, C.I.L. XII, 2059. N.D. de Outre Gére — Esperandieu op. cit. in n.25, no 296. St Severe — I.C.G. 437, C.I.L. XII, 2063. The life of St Severus (*Analecta Bollandiana* V (1886), 416–24) is Carolingian, but based on good local sources. Queen Brunhild (d.613) is a figure of the fairly distant past, but the life was used by Ado of Vienne c.850. It gives two variant dates for the foundation of St Severe, centreing on 435–50. Beck (1950), 380–3. *St Andre le Bas* — Beck (1950) 386, Reynaud (1975), Jannet-Vallet 31–4

32. Caesar *De Bello Gallico* VII, 1–3. *Bishop list* — Duchesne (1894–5) 'Bourges'

33. Gregory of Tours H.F. I, 31. *Gl.Conf* 79. The early life of bishop Sulpicius, written 647–67 refers to the baptistery and bishop's palace. M.G.H. *Scr.Rer.Merov* IV, 364–8. Prevot T.C.C.G. VI *Aquitania Prima* 17. *Vita S.*

Eustandiolae — cited Prevot, 22. *Spolia* — Prevot, p.21

34. *Genesius of Tarbes* — Gregory of Tours *Gl.Mart* 73. *Fides and Caprasius of Agen* — H.F. VI, 2 — church of the martyr Capraisius. There is no reference to Fides, whose first passio has no reference to Capraisius (*Acta Sanctorum* October III, 288–9). Presumably there were two martyr shrines at Agen. *Palladius of Saintes* — *Gl.Mart* 55 and Peter Llewellyn *Rome in the Dark Ages* (1971), 175, quoting Gregory the Great *Registrum* VI, 48. *Eutropius of Saintes* — *Gl. Mart* 55. Fortunatus *Carmen de Basilica S. Eutropis* (M.G.H. *Auct Ant* IV, I, p.5). The passio of St Eutropius is a late composition — de Gaiffier *Analecta Bollandiana* 69 (1951), 57–66

35. *Cemetery* — de Maillé (1959), 9–59. Etienne (1962), 80–86. *Inscription* — I.L.C.V. 554, C.I.L. XII, 11,032. *Severinus* — Gregory of Tours *Gl. Conf* 44, citing a local life, Fortunatus *Vita Severini* (Levison, M.G.H. *Scr. Rer. Merov.* 7 (1920), 29–124). *Origins of cult* — de Maillé 160–66, James, (1977), 177. *Miracles* — Gregory of Tours H.F. VII, 31, *Gl Mart* 33

36. Gregory of Tours H.F. IV, 26, V, 48–9. For an unflattering account of Bertram's mother and sister, who had founded a nunnery in Tours see H.F. IX, 33

37. *Dijon* — Gregory of Tours H.F. III, 19.*Demolition of walls* — Blanchet (1907), 20–24. *Relics* — Picard T.C.C.G. IV *Lugdunensis Prima* 11–14. They were already regarded as local martyrs in the time of Gregory of Langres (505–40). *Ceolfrith* — Bede *Historia Abbatum* 21

38. R.M. Butler (1958). Biarne T.C.C.G. V *Lugdunensis Tertia* 52. *Gervasius and Protasius* — Gregory of Tours *Gl.Mart* 46. *Actus Pontificum Cenomannis* (see n.15 above) *Gesta Juliani* pp.30–31, *Gesta Innocenti* p.54. *Will of Bishop Bertam* p.103

39. *Abbey of St Vincent* — Gregory of Tours H.F. VI, 9. Latouche (1961), 107

40. *Chapel of St Michael* — *Will of Bishop Bertram* p.103 *Chapel of St Albinus* — *Actus Pontificum Cenomannis* 192

41. N.H. Baynes 'The supernatural defenders of Constantinople' *Byzantine Studies and Other Essays* (1955), 248–60. *Nantes* — Gregory of Tours *Gl.Mart.* 59. *Intaglio* — Gruter (1615), 115. Le Blant N.R. 20

5: The Buildings of Jerusalem: Churches and Inscriptions in Post Roman Gaul

1. *Christian basilicas* — Krautheimer (1965), 19–22 and in *Dumbarton Oaks Papers 21* (1967), 117–40. J.B. Ward Perkins 'Constantine and the origins of the Christian basilica' *Papers British School at Rome* 22 (1954), 29–90. *Trier* — Reusch 'Die Aula Palatina in Trier' *Germania* 33 (1955), 180–210 and Ward-Perkins (1981), 442–4. *Metz* — Wightman 1985, 23

2. *S. Aquilino* — Krautheimer (1965), figs 20, 22. He suggests (41–2, n.47) that it may also have been an Imperial mausoleum in origin. Like the Honorian mausoleum at St Peter's, it is attached to the south transept. Van der Meer and Mohrmann (1966) plates 189–90

3. *Trier cathedral* — Kempf *Germania* 29 (1951), 47–58 and in Kramer *Neue Ausgrabungen in Deutschland* (Berlin 1958), 368ff. Krautheimer (1965), 60–62 and fig 9. Wightman (1970), fig 8, p.112. *Geneva* — Bonnet (1987, 1989). *Vienne* — Hubert (1952), 52. *Rouen* — Le-Maho *Gallia Informations* 1989, 2, 25 ;1991, 57–8. The latter comprises an aisled nave with a large masonry rotunda near the east end. Initially interpreted as a baptistery, the rotunda is now seen as a shrine for the relics brought to Rouen by St Victricius in 395–6

4. *St Gereon* — Deckers 'St Gereon in Köln-Ausgrabungen 1978–9' *Jahrbuch für Antike und Christentum* 25 (1982), 102–31. Krautheimer (1965) 62 and fig 24. *Reims* — P.L.R.E. I, *Jovinus* 6, 462–3 and Flodoard *Historia Remensis Ecclesiae* 6 (=C.I.L. XIII, 3256. *Lion hunt sarcophagus* — Wightman (1985), 293–4 and Pietri *Revue du Nord* 52 (1970), 443–53. *Golden saints* — Gregory of Tours *Gl. Mart* 6

5. Dieulafoy 'Basilique Constantinienne de Lugdunum Convenarum' *Comtes-rendus de l'Académe des Inscriptions et Belles-Lettres* 1914, 59–90. *Gallia* 44 (1986), 36–8

6. Hubert (1952), fig 8, p.47. Sapin (1986), 143–6

7. Reynaud 1973, 1984, 1986, 66 and 104–5

8. The church at Briord (Ain) has stones with consular dates of 497–501 and regnal dates of 557–633, but the cemetery is continuous since Roman times and to make matters more complicated, the church is believed to have been destroyed before the final period of the cemetery. *St Martin* — Sulpicius Severus *Vita Martini* 3 'where he destroyed a (pagan) shrine, he straightway built there either a church (*ecclesia*) or a monastery'

9. *Lyon* — Reynaud (1973, 1975, 1976,89–111). *Vienne* — Reynaud (1974–5) Jannet-Vallat (1986), 42–59. *Parallels* — Ephesus, basilica of St Mary c.400 (Krautheimer 1965, fig 27) Meriamlik, basilica of St Tecla c.480

(Krautheimer fig 29) Salona — (Krautheimer fig 56). *St Ferreol* — Reynaud (1978). Jannet-Vallat 61–4

10. *Justus* — Griffé (1965), III, 253–5. *Churches* — Reynaud (1973, 1986, 54–76)

11. Sulpicius Severus *Dialogues* — *Postumianus II* 1. The word used is *'secretarium'* Gregory of Tours *Gl Conf* 20, *Gl Mart*. 33

12. P. Wuilleumier, A. Audin and A. Leroi-Gourhan *L'Eglise et la Nécropole Saint-Laurent dans le Quartier de Choulans: étude archéologique et étude anthropologique* (Lyon, 1949). *Excavations of 1976–8* — Reynaud 'Fouilles recentes de l'ancienne église Saint-Laurent a Lyon' *Comtes-rendus de l' Academe des Inscriptions et Belles-Lettres* July–October 1976, 460–487 and Reynaud (1986), 77–87

13. Pirenne (1937), Loseby (1992a). *Primacy* — Mathisen (1989), 22–5 and 52–60

14. Krautheimer (1965), 70. *Carignan* — Van Ossel (1992), 319

15. Barral I Altet and Drocourt (1974). I have not seen the original account of the 1850s discoveries — F. Roustan *La Major et le Premier Baptistere de Marseille* (Marseille 1905). *Riez* — G. Bailhache *Congrés Archéol de France* XCV (1933), 75–8. Cimiez (Alpes-Maritimes) is similar, bur re-uses a room of the Roman West Baths — P.A. Fevrier *Gallia* 22 (1964), 600–07

16. *Aix* — Guyon T.C.C.G. II *Narbonensis Secunda* 1986, 7–28. Fig 29 shows baptismal annexes revealed in excavation, including a large aisled building to the west. Guild, Guyon and Rivet (1980, 1983). *Mosaic pavement from baptistery* — *Gallia* 16 (1958), 416–7. *Valence* — see below, n.17. *Porec* — Krautheimer (1965), fig 78, p.97. *Provencal baptisteries generally* — A. Katchatrian *Les Baptisteres Paléochretiens* (Paris 1962) and Guyon (1989). *Easter in town* — See Chapter 4, n.10 above. *Spain* — Keay (1988)

17. *Valence* — H. Epailly 'Découverte d'un ancien baptistere a Valence' *Congrés Archéol de France* 33 (1866), 191–204. A.Blanc (1957, 1971). *Life of St Apollinaris* — Krusch M.G.H. *Scr.Rer.Merov.* III, 197–203. *Italian parallels* — Krautheimer (1965), 131–2 and fig 54 (SS Felice e Fortunato, Vicenza). *Grenoble* — *Gallia Informations* 1996, 102–5

18. R.P. Camille de la Croix *Etude Sommaire du Baptistere Saint Jean de Poitiers* (Poitiers 1904) and F. Eygun (1964). For the history of the study of the monument see James (1977), 275–9

19. *Relics* — Gregory of Tours *Gl.Mart* 23–4

20. M.Cahour 'Découverte du baptistere primitif de la cathedrale de Nantes' *Bull. Soc. Archéol de Nantes* 5 (1876), 273–85. G. Durville 'Les fouilles de l'eveche de Nantes en 1910–11'. *Rev Archéol* 1912, 222–64. Do. *Les Fouilles de l'Éveche de Nantes 1910–1913* (supplement to *Bull. Soc. Archéol de Nantes* 1913). Do. 'L'ancienne église de Saint Jean le Baptist a Nantes' *Bull Soc Archéol de Nantes* 56 (1914), 57–140

21. P.D.C. Brown 'The church at Richborough'. *Britannia* 2 (1971), 225–31. *Chedworth* — R. Goodburn *The Roman Villa, Chedworth* (National Trust, 1972), 24 and pl.11. For the archaeology of baptism in Roman Britain see C. Thomas (1981), 202–27. *Civaux* — Eygun *Gallia* 19 (1961), 402–11, 21 (1963), 453–6. *Lerins* — the chapel of St Sauveur is octagonal, with semi-circular niches in each internal wall. Its purpose is disputed. Taylor 'The monastery at Lerins' *J. Brit Archaeol. Assoc.* 133 (1980), 27–8. *Port-Bail* — de Bouard *Cahiers Archéologiques* 9 (1957), 1–22. *Easter baptisms in rural baptistery near Bordeaux* — Gregory of Tours *Gl.Conf* 47. *Primuliacum* — Paulinus of Nola *Letters* XXII

22. *Chronicle of Nantes* (ed R. Merlet, Paris 1896), quoted Pietri T.C.C.G. V *Lugdunensis Tertia*, 90

23. Fortunatus *Carmina* III, 7, IV, 1 (Bishop Eumerius) and III, 6 (dedication, AD 559–73). St Martin d'Autun, built by bishop Syagrius and Queen Brunehaut in 589–600 had triple apses at the east end, closing nave and aisles (Fig 23). Hubert (1962), 47–51 and fig 18, Sapin (1986), 143–6. *Transepts* — Viellard-Troiekouroff (1976), 180

24. *Capitals* — Fossard (1947)

25. L.H. Cottineau *Répetoire topo-bibliographique des Abbayes et Prieurés* (Macon 1935–7), col 1800. For a sixth-seventh-century cemetery at Mazerolles see *Gallia Informations* 1989, 2, 287. *Nantes fragments* — Costa (1964), nos. 180–97. Pietri T.C.C.G. V. 88–9

26. Costa (1964), nos 4–20, 205–11. *St Jouin* — Eygun *Gallia* 28 (1969), 275–8 and plan. The earliest phase comprises a rectangular nave, and polygonal apse with a *confessio* or square crypt. Cocquet thought that this was fourth century, but it is probably ninth, when the bones of St Martin de Vertou were brought here. *Sarcophagus* — Provost (1993), 324

27. Costa (1964), nos 21–177. *Church* — Pietri T.C.C.G. V, 92–3

28. *Arches turned in 'opus mixtum'* — eg Saint-Romain-en-Gal, Vienne (Isére); St Philibert de Grandlieu (Loire Atlantique) or the crypt of St Laurent at Grenoble

29. Gregory of Tours *Gl.Conf* 51. *Jarrow* — Cramp (1969). *Nivelles* (founded c.650) — James (1981), 43

30. Gregory of Tours *Gl. Mart* 58 (Yzeures), H.F. VI, 10 (Tours). At both Monkwearmouth and Jumieges, some monastic buildings were glazed by the seventh century. *Ruricus of Limoges* — *Letters* Krusch M.G.H. *Auct. Ant* 8 (1887). *Benedict Biscop* — Bede *Historia Abbatum* V

31. *Wall paintings* — Gregory of Tours H.F. II, 7, VII, 22, X.3. The seventh-century church at Nivelles (Belgium) had red painted wall plaster. *Stucco* — *Chronicle of Nantes* 9 see n.22 above. *Grenoble* — Colardelle (1992), 46. Chatel in M.S.F. II, pl.XV

32. Ward-Perkins (1938), Briesenick (1962), James (1977), 29–67 and 301–42 (all with catalogues). Christe and Duval (1993) contains the papers from an important conference on Aquitanian sarcophagi. *'Seventh century Renaissance'* — J. Hubert *L'Art Preroman* (Paris 1938), 143–6 and D. Fossard 'La chronologie des sarcophages d'Aquitaine' *Actes du V.eme Congres International d' Archéologie Chretienne, Aix en Provence 1954* (Paris and Vatican 1957), 321–33, with Ward Perkins's rejoinder (1960)

33. *Marseille* — Benoit (1954), Ward Perkins (1938). James (1993) suggests a lengthy period of production (very reasonably since over 200 are known, and new ones continue to appear) spanning the fifth and sixth centuries. *Caskets* — Sivan (1986) *Other sources* — James (1977), 39–49. *Mosaics* — C. Balmelle 'Le répétoire végétal des mosaistes du Sud-Ouest de la Gaule et des sculptures de sarcophages dits d'Aquitaine' (Christe and Duval 1993, 101–10)

34. Briesenik (1962), James (1977), 39–49. *Pau quarries* — Cabanot in Christe and Duval (1993), 5–24. *Stencils* — R.N.Bailey *Viking Age Sculpture in Northern England* (1980), 238–54. *St Bertrand* — Michael Jones — lecture to Society of Antiquaries, 1998

35. *Relationship of sarcophagi and capitals* — Hubert and Fossard saw the capitals in seventh-century buildings like Jouarre as evidence of a 'seventh century renaissance' embracing both capitals and sarcophagi. Ward-Perkins and Cabanot on the other hand did not see a close relationship. Over six hundred capitals are known, implying a long period of manufacture, and there is no reason why this could not extend into the seventh century. Most recent discussion — Cabanot 'sarcophages et chapiteaux de marbre en Gaule' Christe and Duval (1993), 111–124. *Quarries* — Parizoult *Gallia* 19 (1961), 429–30. Vinon-Faviere — 'les sarcophages antiques du Cher' *Rev. Archéol du Centre* 6 (1955), 40–54 and *Gallia* 30 (1972) 320–1. Arcy-sur-Cure — Poulain *Rev Archéol Est et Centre Est* 5 (1954), 29–45. Maine-Zeiss (1941). *Place name evidence* — James (1977) 90–91. Suggestions on the organization of the industry — Lebel 'Comment s'achetait un sarcophage a l'epoque merovingienne?' *Rev.Archéol Est et Centre Est* 2 (1951), 166–71

36. *Autun* — Cabrol-Leclerq D.A.C.L. Vol 1 (1913), cols. 3193–4. *Bordeaux* — C.I.L. XIII, 633, Etienne (1962), 266–8 and pl.XXI. *Marseille* — I.C.G. 548A. C.I.L. XII, 489. The stone may be third century and Christian, but Le Blant's reading depends upon reading the word 'Ignis' from its final letter, as opposed to (say) 'Maris'. It could equally commemorate shipwreck victims like the *optio* from Chester whose body had not been recovered (R.I.B. 544)

37. *Selentiosus* — I.C.G. 62, C.I.L. XIII, 235. *St Bertrand* — N.R. 297, C.I.L.XIII, 229. *Autun* — I.C.G. 7, C.I.L. XIII, 2798. *Angouleme* — N.R. 276–277, C.I.L. XIII, 7–8. Finds at the same time included two grey ware pots, one inscribed LEA VIVAS (N.R. 278). *Civaux* — I.C.G. 576, C.I.L. XIII, 6. *Rom* — C.I.L. XIII, 76. *St Cyr* — N.R. 256, C.I.L. XIII, 82 (Ecomusée de Vendée, Fontenay le Comte). *St Croix du Mont* — C.I.L.XIII, 92

38. *Camiac* — Coupry *Gallia* 25 (1967), 341–2. *Bordeaux* — C.I.L. XIII, 11,032. *Gaillardon* — I.C.G. 575, C.I.L. XIII, 1185. *Protet* — (Haute-Garonne) — N.R. 297A. *Insular connections* — Nash-Williams (1950), 55. *Western French origin* — Knight (1992)

39. I.L.T.G. 921

6: The World Turned Upside Down: The Christianisation of the Gallic Countryside

1. Grenier (1931–60), vols II–IV. Picard (1970). Provost (1993), 145–55. *Vendoeuvre* — I.L.S. 9361

2. Provost (1993), 154–5. *Drevant* — M.G. Mallard *Bull. Archéol du Comité* 1906, 43–71, 1914, 95–212. *Mem.Soc Antiq du Centre* 1906, 3–54. New excavations and plan — C. Cribellier 'Un quartier d'habitat de l'agglomération antique de Drevant (Cher)' *Rev Archéol du Centre de la France* 35 (1996), 113–52. *Aubigny* — *Gallia* 39 (1981), 343–5; 41 (1983), 302–4. *Ribemont-sur Ancre* —Cadoux (1978, 1982), Bayard and Cadoux

(1982), Agache (1978), 404–10. *Genainville* — Mitard (1982). *Coins* — *Gallia* 36 (1978), 307–9. At Sanxay by contrast, the coins are post-conquest

3. The temple at Sanxay is also Antonine on architectural evidence — Pillard (1982), 124. *Lillebonne* — *Gallia* 44 (1986), 366–8

4. Mangard (1982). *Berthouville* — Babelon (1916), C.I.L. XIII, 382. *Paterninus* — C.I.L. XIII, 2949

5. Whittaker (1990), 114–117. For the possible survival of *vicus* as a place name in post Roman Britain see M. Gelling (1967). *Gargarius* — C.I.L. XII, 594. *Yzeures* — C.I.L. XIII, 3075. *Carte Archéologique de la Gaule Romaine* XIII (Indre-et-Loire) 5–6

6. Of 342 Roman and 12 Gaulish coins from Sanxay, 27 survive in the Musée d'Echevinage at Poitiers. Eygun (*Gallia* 2 (1944), 20) published a list of emperors represented, from Vespasian to Tetricus. A coin of Justinian now in the collection could be intrusive. *Ribemont* — Cadoux (1978). The bath building may have been destroyed, and its site levelled, in the early third century (Agache 1978, 410). *Bouchards* — Y Marion *et al.* 'Le sanctuaire gallo-romain de Bouchards (Charente)' *Aquitania* 10 (1992), 45–94 (p.84). *Drevant* — Cribellier op. cit. in n.2, 47. *Collapse of pagan religion* — Frend (1974)

7. *Avallon* — Grenier IV, 709–10, *Sanxay* — Pillard (1982), 30, C.I.L. XIII, 1172–1174. *Berthouville* — Babelon (1916), Grenier (1958), 956–8

8. D. Cannadine 'the transformation of civic ritual in modern Britain — the Colchester oyster feast' *Past and Present* 94 (1982), 107–30

9. *Regional surveys* — Etienne (1962), 302–8 and map 20 (Gironde); Jacob, Laredde and Loriot (1983, Yonne); Loriot and Delaporte (1980, Seine Maritime); Jigan (1986, Manche). *Rural shrines* — *eg* Jacob, Laredde and Loriot no 96, Grenier (1958), 709–10, De Vesly (1908)

10. ed J. Fontaine. Translation — Hoare (1954), 1–144. The account of Martin and the alpine brigands (*Vita Martini* c.5) uses martyr iconography — compare Hertling and Kirschbaum *The Roman Catacombs and their Martyrs* (1980) pl.12, from the basilica of SS. Nereus and Achilleus. On the 'audience' for hagiography, particularly public reading in chapter and cloister, see de Gaiffier (1947). *Bricius* — *Dialogues-Gallus* 15

11. J. Fontaine (1963. *Legionary martyrs* — Musurillo (1972), 250–9 (*Acta Marcelli*), 244–9 (*Acta Maximiliani*). The cult of St Maurice of Agaune and the Theban legion owed much to Theodore of Octodunum, an eastern immigrant bishop. It was already well established by 450. Frend *Martyrdom and Persecution: the early church* (1965), 486

12. There is a large literature on St Martin. The principal works are Ch. Babut *St Martin de Tours* (Paris 1920), published posthumously after the writer's death in the First World War; H. Delehaye 'St Martin et Sulpice Severe' *Analecta Bollandiana* 38 (1920), 5–136; J. Fontaine (1963, 1967–9); Prinz (1965) and, most recently, Stancliffe (1983)

13. Grenier III, 727–9, C.I.L.XIII, 307. Lane-Fox *Pagans and Christians* (1986), 66–7 cites coins of Magnesia on the Maeander in Asia Minor showing a god being processed on a stretcher-like device, with four bearers, like some later Christian reliquaries. *Pine tree* — Sulpicius Severus *Dialogues-Gallus* 8. *Temples* — *Vita Martini* 14

14. Matthews (1967, 1975, 40–45). Theodoret *Historia Ecclesiastica* 5.2. Sozomon *Historia Ecclesiastica* 7.5.3. Macmullen (1984, 98) cites a law of 398 – 'If there are temples in rural areas, they shall be destroyed without disturbance or commotion'

15. *Codex Justinianus* 11.66. 4. (AD 382–4). *Codex Theodosianus* 6.3.1. (AD 393); 6.10.4. (AD 396); 6.10.19 (AD 407)

16. *Richborough* — Bushe-Fox (1932), 34–6, P.D.C. Brown (1971), 225–31. *Amboise* – *Gallia* 43 (1985), 299

17. E. James (1977), 174–6 and 421. *Gallia* 19 (1961), 402–3; 21 (1963), 453–461. *Inscription* — I.C.G. 576, C.I.L. XIII, 1161

18. Mauss (1950), 16. *Miracles* — *Vita Martini* 11–12

19. Flint (1991)

20. For an important collection see R.S.O. Tomlin 'The curse tablets' in B. Cunliffe *The Temple of Sulis Minerva at Bath. Vol 2. The Finds from the Sacred Spring* (Oxford 1988), 59–277. *Béthune* — Muchembled (1992), 200. The practice persists — of two friends of the writer, one, a woman from Jaen in southern Spain, habitually conjured part of the Devil's person into a handkerchief, using two small coins, and forced him to divulge where he had 'hidden' the missing object. The other, an Anglican priest, prayed to St Anthony

21. Alban Dold (1948). For the manuscript see E.A. Lowe C.L.A. 953. The secondary texts comprise extracts from the Fathers, and a glossary in eighth-century miniscule. *Medieval survivals of pagan oracle books* — Lane Fox

(1986), 210–11 and 677. *Sortes* — Gregory of Tours H.F. IV, 6, V, 14. *Council of Agde* (506), c.42. *Council of Orleans* (511), c.30. *Council of Auxerre* (578–85), c.4

22. Aline Rousselle (1982). George Boon (1983) suggests itinerant doctors. For a resident doctor in a north French *vicus* (Hermes, Oise) see I.L.T.G. 358. *Oculists* — Thevenot (1950). *Gold eye plaque from Wroxeter* — *Antiq. J.* 51 (1971), 329–31. *Medical spatulae* — eg Vieil-Evreux and Berthouville (Eure) — Grenier III, 956–8. *Surgical instruments* — Areines (Loir-et-Cher), which has also produced bronze eye-plaques. (Grenier IV, 739–40)

23. *Concilia Galliae* II, 264–272. It was signed by the bishop, 34 priests and 7 abbots. E.C. Cawte *Ritual Animal Disguise* (1978). Arbesmann (1979)

24. Gregory of Tours *V.Pat* VI, 2. *Gl. Conf* 2 (Javols, Aveyron)

25. Flint (1991), 211–12. Gregory of Tours H.F. IV, 6. V.4. *Ambivalent Christian attitudes to the 'Sortes'* — Flint 273–86

26. *Digest* L.15, 4, quoted Percival 1985, 12. *Writing tablet* — R.S.O. Tomlin *Ant.J.* 68 (1988), 306 and 'A five acre wood in Roman Kent' *Interpreting Roman London: Papers in Memory of Hugh Chapman* ed. J Bird *et al* (1996), 209–15. *Rennes* — C.I.L. XIII, 3148–3152. Galliou (1976), 68

27. eg *Council of Tarragona* (516), c.8. Many *Ecclesiae Diocesanae* in bad condition, bishops to visit yearly. Gregory of Tours *Gl. Conf* 104

28. Letters of Pope Zosimus, 22 March and 22 September 417 (P.L. 20, cols 642, 661) Griffe (1965), III, 269–70. For the background see Frye (1991) and Mathisen (1989), 51–7. *Inscription* — C.I.L. XII, 594. Rivet (1988), 196. *Early Gallic parishes* — de la Tour (1900)

29. Gregory of Tours H.F. X, 31. Sulpicius Severus *Dialogues* II, 8

30. *Yzeures* — Gregory of Tours H.F. VI, 2. X.31 and *Gl.Mart* 58. *Roman sculptures* — C.I.L. XIII, 3075. *Carte Archéologique de la Gaule Romaine* XIII, (Indre-et-Loire) 1960, 15–16 and 121–4. *Merovingian graves* — *Gallia* 43 (1985), 323. *Loches* — Gregory of Tours H.F. X, 31. *Gallia* 32 (1974), 316. *Chinon* — Gregory of Tours *Gl.Conf* 22 (Aegidius). *Carte Archéologique de la Gaule Romaine* XIII (Indre-et-Loire) 35–36, 121–4. *Cemetery* — *Gallia* 43 (1985), 302–3. *Archéol Medievale* 15 (1985), 235 and 21 (1991), 441–2

31. Council of Clermont (535) c.15. *Oratoria villara* — First Council of Orleans 511 c.25, Council of Epaon (517), c.25, Council of Clermont (5350, c.14. Fourth Council of Orleans (541), cc.3, 33. Griffé III, 291–8

32. Ausonius *Ephemeris* ('the daily round') II–III. Sidonius *Letters* V, 4 to Consentius on his villa at Octaviana (Ornaisons, near Narbonne). On its location and survival as a medieval monastic property see Griffé III, 292–3 and n.79. *Primuliacum* — Paulinus of Nola *Letters* 31 (AD 403), 32 (AD 404). P.L. 61, cols. 325–30. Griffé III, 274–6, 326–8. Sulpicius Severus *Dialogues* III, I

33. M. Larrieu *Gallia* 24 (1966), 431–2; 26 (1968), 431. 28 (1970), 45–7. *Mosaics* — Balmelle (1987)

34. Serra-Rafols (1943). *Inscriptions* — C.I.L. XIII, 912, N.R. 256

35. Gregory of Tours *Gl.Conf.* 18, *Gl. Mart* 30. Addleshaw (1954, 1970)

7: The Prehistory of the Parish

1. *Frenouville* — Pilet (1980). *St Martin de Fontenay* — Pilet (1994). Wightman (1978)

2. *Vron* — Seillier (1978, 1986). *Saxons* — C. Lorren *Studien zur Sachsen Forschung* 2 (Hildershein 1980), 123–259. Seillier and Demolon (1983), 43–46

3. *Maule* — J. Sirat (1978). I owe the point about settlement and cemetery patterns in the Vixit to M. Sirat. *Krefeld Gellep* — Pirling (1966–79). *Rhenen* — Ypey 1978. *Bulles* — R. Legoux *Rev. Archéol de Picardie* 1988, 3–4. (Actes des Ve. Journées Internationales d'Archéologie Merovingiennes de Soissons 1986), 81–84. *Goudelancourt-les Pierrepont* A. Nice. ibid 127–37

4. Pilet (1980), Vol 1, 1–3, 154–7

5. Sulpicius Severus *Vita Martini* 13

6. Nice, op. cit. in n.3, figs 6 B and 12 p.137. *Nouvion* — *Gallia* 39 (1981), 287

7. Seillier and Demolon (1983), 57

8. Pilet, (1980), 1–3, 154–7. *Tithes* — Addleshaw 1954, 1970. Levison (1946), 106–7) cites references in early Irish sources, and by St Boniface, and suggests that Pippin's legislation may have been intended to compensate the church for its losses through alienation of church property. *Meaux* — quoted Latouche (1961), 66

9. Migne P.L. 30 (1846), cols 152–67, Griffé II, 313–32. The issue was still alive in the early sixth century. In 529 a church council had to affirm that in rural churches (*parrociis*), priests might preach *Council of Vaison c. 2*

10. *Gildas a deacon* — O. Chadwick (1984). Gildas *De Excidio* 67, 69. *Capel Anelog* — E.C.M.W. 77–78, now in Aberdaron church. *Sacerdos* — E.C.M.W. 83 and 33, C.I.I.C. 56. *De Excidio* 66 and 26.2. Similar use by Sidonius — Hanson (1970), 2. Wyn Evans has suggested that in later Welsh contexts *sacerdos* could mean 'archpriest', head of a community of secular canons; 'Aspects of the early church in Carmarthenshire', *Sir Gar: Studies in Carmarthenshire History* ed H. James (Carmarthen 1991), 248

11. Brennan (1984)

12. Gildas *De Excidio* 66.3. Compare Council of Angers (453), 4. Council of Orleans (511), 29. Council of Clermont (535), 16. Council of Lerida (524), 15. Fifth Council of Orleans (549), 3

13. Gildas *De Excidio* 26. A.L. Kroeber *Anthropology* (New York 1948), 334–57. R.W.V. Elliot *Runes: An Introduction* (Manchester 1959), plates VI–VIII. D. McManus *A Guide to Ogam* (Maynooth 1991)

14. *Milestone* — R.I.B. 2254, E.C.M.W. 258. *Llanerfyl* — E.C.M.W. 294. *Formulae* — E.C.M.W. 7 and 54

15. R.P. Wright and K. Jackson 'A late inscription from Wroxeter' *Ant. J.* 48 (1968), 269–300

16. *Excavated stone* — R. White 'Excavations at Arfryn, Bodedern' *Trans. Anglesey Antiq. Soc* 1971–2, 19–51 (interim report)

17. For individual Welsh stones see Nash-Williams E.C.M.W. *passim. Seven bishop houses of Dyfed* — Charles Edwards (1971)

18. *Penmachno etc.* — Knight (1995)

19. *Iron Age burials in Wales* — K. Murphy 'Plas Gogerddan, Dyfed, a multi-period burial and ritual site' *Archaeol. J.* 149, (1992), 1–38 (pp.30–35). *Long cist cemeteries* – Pentrefoelas — E.C.M.W. 83, *Gentleman's Magazine* 1820, 443. Cae Maen Hir field — E.C.M.W. 96–97, *Archaeologia Cambrensis* 1847, 20. Two stones found re-used nearby (E.C.M.W. 94–95) may be strays from the same cemetery. *Taff Valley* — J.K.Knight *Merthyr Historian* 2 (1970), 105–10

20. *Abercar* — E.C.M.W. 40–41, Knight (1984), 338. *Bodvoc* — E.C.M.W. 229, A. and C. Fox (1934). *Gelligaer* — E.C.M.W. 197. *Banwen Pyrddin* — E.C.M.W. 268. *Settings* — A. Fox (1939). *Bryn Y Beddau* — Camden *Britannia* ed Gough (1789), 111. E. Lhwyd — letter — *Archaeologia Cambrensis* 1848, 310. The stone is E.C.M.W. 76

21. A.M. Snodgrass *The Dark Age of Greece: an archaeological survey from the eleventh to the eighth centuries* (Edinburgh 1971), 192–5. R. Van der Noort 'The context of early medieval barrows in western Europe' *Antiquity* 67 (1993), 66–73

22. S.C. Hawkes in Meaney and Hawkes (1970), 45–55, with full references

23. Cambridge and Rollaston (1995), 89–90. Bede H.E. V,2

24. E. Bowen *Antiquity* 18 (1944), 16–28 and 19 (1945), 175–86. Do *The Settlements of the Celtic Saints in Wales* (Cardiff, 1954)

25. Bassett (1989)

26. *Llantwit Major villa* — V.E. Nash Williams 'The Roman villa at Llantwit Major' *Archaeologia Cambrensis* 1953, 89–163. A.H.A. Hogg 'The Llantwit Major villa: a reconsideration' *Britannia* 5 (1974), 225–50. *Later history* — Knight (1984), 375–6. *Royal llys* – M. Richards 'Gwrinydd, Gorynydd and Llyswyrny' *Bull. Board Celtic Stud.* 18 (1960), 383–8. *Llandough* — Knight (1984), 377–9 and N. Holbrook (forthcoming). *Dunadd-Iona* — Campbell (1987)

27. J. Hinchcliffe 'An early medieval settlement at Cowage Farm, Foxley, near Malmesbury' *Archaeol J.* 143, (1986), 240–59

28. This is not the modern basilica of Sacre Coeur, but the more interesting St Pierre de Montmartre, thankfully ignored by tourists, and one of the churches in the Paris area with Merovingian capitals of St Béat marble. A rival etymology would make Montmartre the Hill of Mercury, from a pagan shrine said to have once existed there. Such legends however are common with major French churches. *Chapel of St Michael* — Bede H.E. V, 2. *Merthyr* — C. Thomas (1971), 89, T. Roberts (1992), 42. *Memorial stones from Merthyrs* — Merthyr Mawr (Glamorgan) E.C.M.W. 238, Merthyr Enfael, Carms (E.C.M.W. 70), Mathry (Pembs) E.C.M.W. 346, Merthyr Tydfil, Glamorgan (E.C.M.W. 248)

29. Addleshaw (1970).

30. E. Cambridge (1984). For individual Welsh sites see Nash Williams E.C.M.W. *passim*

31. *Saints lives* — Wade Evans (1944), *Vita Gundleii* and *Vita Tatheii. Chirbury* — M. Chibnall *Victoria County History, Shropshire* Vol 2, 59–62

32. *Merthyr Mawr* — F. Cowley in *Glamorgan County History* Vol III, ed T.B. Pugh, 116–17. *Llanvihangel Y Traethau* — E.C.M.W. 281

8: Ancient Economics: Britain, Gaul and the Atlantic Interface

1. A. Snodgrass *Archaic Greece: The Age of Experiment* (London 1980), 124. M.I. Finley *The Ancient Economy* (1973, revised ed 1985), was a seminal work on this topic. See also Whittaker (1993)

2. Keay (1984), 416–28

3. Gregory of Tours *Gl. Mart* 105, *Gl.Conf* 110. Veyne (1990), 67. Council of Tarragona 516, cc 2 and 3

4. W. Davies (1982), 129–31, 165–6. *Forty little pigs* — Gospels of St Chad, *Chad* 3 (ninth century) — *Liber Landavensis* ed J. Gwenogvryn Evans and John Rees (1893), xiv. Pliny's Letter (V.2) finds a parallel in nineteenth-century Ireland. Somerville and Ross 'The man that came to buy apples' (*Further Experiences of an Irish R.M.*). *Egyptian potters* — H Cockle 'Pottery manufacture in Roman Egypt: a new papyrus' *J. Roman Stud* 71 (1981), 87–97. *Beer* — Gregory of Tours *Gl. Conf* 1

5. Gregory of Tours *Gl. Mart* 57

6. *Nantes* — C.I.L. XIII, 3105 and 3106. *Bordeaux* — P. Le Gentilhomme (1936). James (1977), 225–9. *London* — Bede H.E. II, 3

7. P. Leman 'Fours du haut moyen age a Haccourt: étude preliminaire' Fleury and Perin (1978), 199–209. *Digest* XXX, 7.25 and V.3.6 preface and 1, quoted Veyne (1990), 67 n.81

8. *Argonne* — Chenet 1941, Hubener 1968, Bayard 1990, 1993. *Coarsewares* — Bayard (1990), fig 3 p.278 (Metz), Dijkman *Gallia* 49 (1992), 129–172 (Maastricht). At Arras these first appear c.375 — M. Tuffreau-Libre and A. Jacques 'Le céramique gallo-romaine du Bas-Empire à Arras' *Gallia* 49 (1992), 271–319 (fig 9)

9. M. Redknap *Mayener Ware: The Roman and Medieval Pottery Industry at Mayen, Kreis-Mayen-Koblenz* (forthcoming). I am very grateful to Dr Redknap for allowing me access to this important study before publication. *Bronzework* — H.J. Eggars *Der romische Import im freien Germanien* (Hamburg 1951), types 11–14. *Halkyn Mountain* — *Archaeologia* 14 (1809), 275, pl. XLIX. Pirenne (1939), 75–107

10. *E Ware forms* — C. Thomas (1990), fig 1, p.7. *Dyestuffs* — E. Campbell (1996), 92–3

11. *Stamped wares* — Rigoir (1968). *Atlantic group* — Rigoir and Meffre (1973) *Chronology and relationship with African red slip* — Hayes (1972), 402–4. *Bordeaux* — D. Barraud 'Le site de 'La France': origins et évolution de Bordeaux Antique' *Aquitania* 6 (1988), 3–60 (pp.39–40)

12. Rigoir (1968), fig.4, p.82. *Eosocus* — Rigoir and Meffre 254–6. *Nantes* — Costa (1958), *Rouen* — Rigoir (1968), 242 and fig 5, p.184

13. Alcock (1963), fig 28 p.36

14. Radford in Hoden (1956 ed), 59–70; C. Thomas (1959)

15. Peacock and Williams (1986), 82–4 (Class 43=Bi), 85–7 (Class 44=Bii). C. Thomas (1981), 4–5. The wines of Chios were known, if only by repute, in sixth-century Spain. J. Herrin (1987), 222. *African amphorae* — D. Williams and C. Carreras 'North African amphorae in Roman Britain: a reappraisal' *Britannia* 26 (1995), 23–52. *Wine of Gaza* — Peacock and Williams 98–9 (Class 49). C Thomas (1981), 16. Anecdotal material — Gregory of Tours H.F. VII, 29, *Gl.Conf* 60

16. Pirenne (1939), 79–82. Gregory of Tours H.F. VII, 3 (Bordeaux), X, 26 (Paris), V, 1 (Orleans)

17. Tchalenko (1953–8) discussion — Kennedy and Liebeschuetz (1988)

18. G. Downey *A History of Antioch in Syria* (1961) thought the city already in decline by 541, but more recent work has questioned this. Kennedy and Liebeschuetz op. cit. *Sack of Antioch* — Gregory of Tours heard of the event from a refugee Syrian bishop, who turned up at Tours. H.F. IV, 40, X, 23. By an odd slip, Gregory says in one place that Antioch was in Egypt

19. Fulford and Peacock (1984), 118. Fulford (1989), 3. *Benalua* — Reynolds (1987). The Marseille Bourse site has 86 illustrated vessels of African red-slip ware, and 20 sherds of Late Roman C (Phocean red slip). Bonifay and Pelletier (1983)

20. *Gothic famine* — Olympiodorus of Thebes 29–30 (Blockley 92–5)

21. Quoted Braudel (1973), I, 257. *Ocean current* — Jauregi (1949). *Marseille* — Gregory of Tours H.F. IV, 43

22. Hayes (1972), maps 4–5, pp. 459–60. Keay (1984), 428–31. Fulford (1989), 4. Thomas (1981), 6–9

23. *Benalua* — Reynolds (1987 and 1993, 14–17). *Monastil* — A. Poveda (1988). *Isla de Fraile* — A. Gonzalez Blanco (1985), 264–5 and fig, p.279. *Villaricos* — L. Siret *Villaricos Y Herrerias, Antiguedades Romanos, Visigoticas Y Arabes: Memoria Descriptiva Y Historica* (Madrid 1908). Mayet and Picon (1986), 130 no.9 and plates I–III. See also Nieto Prieto (1984)

24. *Merida* — Collins (1980), 202–4. *Grey stamped ware* — Reynolds (1993). *Port Vendres* — Mayet and Picon (1986), 30 no. 6 and pl. IV, 3–6 and 8. *P.R.S. ware, Marseille* — n.19 above

25. *Conimbriga* — M. Delgado, F. Mayet and A. Alarcao *Fouilles de Conimbriga IV: Les sigillées* (Paris 1975), 285–291 and pl.LXXVI–VII — 85 fragments, virtually all of Hayes form 3. *Troia (Setubal)* — M.G. Pereira Mala 'Ceramica fina oriental de Troia de Setubal': 'Late Roman C ware' *III Congresso Nacional de Arqueologia (Porto 1973)* Porto 1974, 333–41

26. Hillgarth (1962, 1964, 1965). Collins, review of Hillgarth (1985) in *J. Ecclesiastical Hist* 37 (1986), 145–6

27. E. Dawes and N.H. Baynes *Three Byzantine Saints* (Oxford 1948). Vladimir Proop *The Morphology of the Folk Tale* (1926, trans. L Scott 1970). The story follows the standard pattern — preliminary misfortune, consent to counteraction, hero given magic device, transference to distant place, victory, liquidation of misfortune. R.D. Penhallurick *Tin in Antiquity* (1986), 237

28. Gregory of Tours H.F. VII, 30. *Coin hoard* — see n.6 above. *Excavations* — *Gallia* 33 (1975), 461–65. *Archaéologia* 158 (Sept.1981), 36–39

29. C.I.L. XIII, 3105–6. Fortunatus *Carmina* 6–7. *Bishop Felix* — Mc Dermott (1975)

30. *Pottery* — Costa (1958). *Tin mining* — Provost (1993), 250, *Carte Archéologique de la Gaule* 44 (Loire Maritime) 140–1. *Coins* — Grierson and Blackburn (1986), no. 459, pl.22. Compare nos. 171–85, 192–208 (pl. 10–11) in the names of Anastasius I (491–518), Justinian (527–65) and Justin II (565–78). *Columbanus* — Jonas *Vita Columbani* I, 22–3

31. *Vita Filiberti*. On Sidonius the Irishman see p.602, n.1

32. Giraldus Cambrensis *Topographia Hiberniae* I, chapter 6. ed J. O'Meara *Proc. Roy. Irish Acad* C (1948–50), 113–78

33. *Tile* — in castle museum, Noirmoutier. I am very grateful to Marcel Baudoin for drawing my attention to it, and to Carlo Tedeschi for comments on its epigraphy. *Moulded tiles* — Costa (1964)

34. *African amphorae* — see n.15 above. P. Galliou (1983), 76–8. *Céramique á l'éponge* — Raimbuilt (1973), Galliou, Fulford and Clement (1980). *Salt* – Galliou (1983), 182, and fig. 53

35. Thomas (1981), 15, and information from Ewan Campbell. *Islands* — Marc Bloch *The Ile de France: the country around Paris* (trans. J.E. Anderson, 1966), 8–10

36. *Archaeologia* 14 (1809), 275, and pl. XLIX

37. *Dinas Powys* — Alcock (1963). *Cadbury-Congresbury* — Rahtz (1992). *Garranes* — O'Kelly (1962). *Full list of sites* — E. Alcock (1988)

38. *Tintagel* —Thomas (1993). *Tin from shipwrecks* — Parker (1992) — wrecks nos. 77, 83, 540, 541 (all BC); 153, 218, 585, 875, 980 (first century AD); 918 (third century AD)

39. Bateson (1973, 1976) estimates that perhaps 20% of Roman coins from Ireland are genuine ancient losses. Casey draws similar conclusions re. Scotland — in R. Miket and C. Burgess *Between and Beyond the Walls: Essays on the Prehistory and History of North Britain in Honour of George Jobey* (Edinburgh 1984), 295–304

40. R.H.M. Dolley 'Roman coins from Ireland and the date of St Patrick' *Proc. Roy. Irish Acad* 76 C (1976), 18–90. *Ballinrees* — Mattingley and Pearce (1937). *Belt set* — compare Böhme (1974), Taf 37, Mattingley and Pearce pl. IV. *Imitation* — A. Burnett 'Clipped siliquae and the end of Roman Britain' *Britannia* 15 (1984), 63–8

41. McManus (1991). Swift (1997)

42. *Gaulish cemeteries* — James (1979). *Canterbury* — D.A. Brooks (1986, 1988)

9: The End of Antiquity? Seventh Century Change in Insular and Atlantic Europe

1. Hodges and Whitehouse (1983). R. Van Dam 'The Pirenne thesis and fifth-century Gaul' in Drinkwater and Elton (1992), 32–3

2. Bintliff (1991). *Antioch* — G. Downey *A History of Antioch in Syria* (1961). Kennedy and Liebeschutz (1988). *Balkans* — Poulter (1995) and Averil Cameron (1993), 59–63. *Refugee bishop* — Gregory of Tours H.F X, 24. *Seventh century* — C. Foss (1975, 1977), Haldon (1990), 92–124. Quotations from Foss 1975, 721 and 747 and 1977, 486

3. *Phocean red slip* — Hayes (1972), 423–4. *Spain* — P. Reynolds 'African red-slip ware and African imports in Valencia'. T. Blagg, R. Jones and S. Keay *Papers in Iberian Archaeology* (B.A.R. Int. ser. 193, 1984), 474–84. *Coins* — S.E. Rigold 'An Imperial coinage in southern Gaul in the sixth and seventh centuries?' *Numismatic Chronicle*

6th series, 14 (1954), 93–133. Grierson and Blackburn (1986), 13. Loseby (1992a), 175–8

4. R. Lopez 'Mohammed and Charlemagne, a revision' *Speculum* 18 (1943), 14–38. *Letter* — Gregory of Tours H.F. V, 5

5. Bonifay and Pelltier (1983), Bonifay, Paroli and Picon 'Ceramiche a vetrina pesante scoperta a Rome et a Marsaglia' *Archaeologia Medievale* 13 (1986), 85–6. *Cartulary* — Latouche (1961), 282

6. *Domnolus* — Gregory of Tours H.F. VI, 9. *Desiderius* — P.L.R.E. III A, *Desiderius* 5, p.398 and *Syagrius* 3, p.1209. Geary (1988), 60–2. Earlier generations of the family already had links with the Merovingian kings. Duke Desiderius, from Albi, was Childeric's military commander, killed at Carcassone in 587 (Gregory of Tours H.F. V, 45, P.L.R.E. III A. *Desiderius* 2, p.396–8. In the previous year, a namesake had become bishop of Albi by simony (H.F. V, 22). *Family plate* — Grierson and Blackburn 96–7

7. *Latest post-consular datings* — I.C.G. 17 and N.R. 16 (C.I.L. XIII, 2381). *Choulans* — I.L.T.G. 291–5. The latest inscriptions from Vienne are of 661, with a regnal dating (N.R. 107) and of 625+ (Wuilleumier *Rev. Études Anciennes* 1946, 98

8. R. Collins (1980), *Ebro valley* — Van Dam (1985), 50–3

9. *Cantabrian senate* — Braulio *Vita Aemiliani* 24, quoted Collins (1980), 190. An inscription from Vildé (Soria Prov.) records the building of a church by a husband and wife, both claiming the title *vir illustris* (Vives I.C.E. 505). I am grateful to Charles Thomas for drawing my attention to this in a quite different context. *Visigothic coinage* — G.C. Miles *The Coinage of the Visigoths of Spain: Leovigild to Achila II* (New York 1952) and Grierson and Blackburn 39–54

10. P.D. King 'King Chindasvind and the first territorial law code of the Visigothic kingdom' E. James (1980), 131–57

11. Grierson and Blackburn 111–17. *Theodobert* — Procopius *Bell Goth* 33, 5–6. *Ostrogothic influence* — Grierson and Blackburn, 463–4. Gregory of Tours *Gl.Mart* 105, *Gl. Conf.* 5, 110

12. *Charter* — M.G.H. *Diplomatum Imperii* I, ed Pertz, 140, quoted E. Campbell (1996), 93

13. K. Hughes (1966), 76. C Thomas (1981a) gives a list of imports recorded to that year

14. Jonas *Vita Columbani* Clarke and Brennan (1981)

15. *Vitae Patrum Jurensium* ed F. Martine *Sources Chrétiennes* 142, (Paris 1968)

16. J. Besse *Les Moines del'Ancienne France* (Paris 1906). L. Cottineau *Répetoire Topographique-Bibliographique des Abbayes et Prieures* (Macon 1939). C. Sapin (1986), 23–5. *Cahors* — *Vita Desiderii* Krusch M.G.H. *Scr. Rer. Merov.* 4, part 2, 586–8

17. *Rev Archéol d'Est* 35 (1984), 301–17. *Villey-St Étienne* — E. Salin *Le Haut Moyen Age en Lorraine d'apres le mobilier funéraire (1939)* 79–254

18. Bede H.E. III, 17

19. E. Cambridge (1984), I. Wood (1987a)

20. E.C.M.W. 256 and 268 — both stones now in Swansea Museum

21. *Catalogue of Irish cross slabs* — H.S. Crawford *J. Roy.Soc.Antiq. Ireland* vols 42–44 (1921–4). *Reask* — T. Fanning 'Excavation of an early Christian cemetery and settlement at Reask, Co. Kerry' *Proc.Roy.Irish Acad* 81 C (1981), fig 3, H. *Nun and lettuce leaf* — Gregory the Great *Dialogues* 1, 4. (P.L. 77, 69), quoted P. Brown *Religion and Society in the Age of Saint Augustine* (1972), 35. *St Sampson* — *Vita Sampsonis* c.35, 48, 55–6. *Vexin crosses* — Knight (1996), fig 2, p.118

22. A. Hamlin (1982), 285. S.T. Driscoll in Driscoll and Nieke (1988), 84

23. *Portlaoghise* — found 1842–3. British Museum, ex Graves collection. *Trim* — once in collection of Dean Butler of Clonmacnois. S.E. Rigold in R.L.S. Bruce-Mitford *The Sutton Hoo Ship Burial* I, (1975), 669–70. *E Ware* — Thomas (1990), Campbell (1996), 90–4

24. Figures from Thomas (1981) with additions. These do not include the new material from Whithorn. *Madder* — Campbell (1996), 92–3

25. *English missions to Germany* — Levison (1946)

26. Grierson and Blackburn (1986), 38–49, 84–9

27. R. Hodges *The Hamwih Pottery: local and imported wares from Middle Saxon Southampton and their European context* (C.B.A. Research Report 37, 1981). P. Andrews *The Coins and Pottery from Hamwic* (Southampton 1988)

Bibliography

1. Collections of Inscriptions

A.E.   *L'Année Épigraphique*

C.I.I.C.   *Corpus Inscriptionum Insularum Celticarum*, R.A.S. Macalister, (Dublin 1945, 1949)

C.I.L.   *Corpus Inscriptionum Latinarum* T. Mommsen, Berlin 1863 ff (16 vols)

E.C.M.W.   *The Early Christian Monuments of Wales* V.E. Nash Williams, (Cardiff 1950)

F.I.M.   Die Frühchristlichen Inscriften des Mittelrheingebietes W. Boppert (Mainz 1971)

F.I.T.   *Katalog der Früchristlichen Inscriften in Trier* E. Gose (Trier 1958)

I.C.E.   *Inscriptiones Cristianas de la Espana Romana y Visigoda* J. Vives (Barcelona 1942)

I.C.G.   *Inscriptions Chrétiennes de la Gaule Antérieures au VIII Siècle* E. Le Blant Vol 1 *Provinces Gallicanes*, Vol 2 *Les Sept Provinces* (Paris, 1856, 1865)

I.L.C.V.   *Inscriptiones Latinae Christianae Veteres* E. Diehl (Berlin, 1925–31)

I.L.T.G.   *Inscriptions Latines des Trois Gaules* P. Wuilleumier (Paris 1963 — 17th supplement to *Gallia*)

N.R.   *Nouveau Recueil des Inscriptions Chrétiennes de la Gaule Antérieures au VIII e. Siècle* E. Le Blant (Paris 1892)

R.I.B.   *The Roman Inscriptions of Britain I. Inscriptions on Stone* R.G. Collingwood and R.P. Wright (Oxford, 1965)

R.I.C.G. XV.   *Recueil des Inscriptions Chrétiennes de la Gaule antérieures à la Renaissance Carolingienne t. XV. Viennoise du Nord* F. Descombes (Paris 1980)

2. Primary documentary sources

Actus Pontificum Cenomannis   *Actus Pontificum Cennomannis in Urbe Degentium* Busson-Ledru (Le Mans 1901). Also in Cabrol-Leclerq D.A.C.L. X (1932), cols. 1499–1502

Acta Sanctorum   J. Bollandus et al. Antwerp, Brussels and Tongerloo, 1643 ff

Adamnan   *Vita Columbii: Adomnan's Life of Columba* A.O. and M.O. Anderson (London and Edinburgh 1961)

Ammianus Marcellinus   J.C. Rolfe (Loeb, 3 vols)

Augustine   *Sermons* J. Migne P.L. 38 (1865)

Ausonius   *Poems* H.G. Evelyn White (Loeb, 2 vols)

Bede *Historia Ecclesiastica*   *Historia Ecclesiastica Gentis Anglorum* B. Colgrave and R.A.B. Mynors (Oxford Medieval Texts, 1969)

Cassius Dio   *History* E. Cary and H.B. Foster (Loeb, 9 vols)

Claudian   *Poems* M. Platnauer (Loeb, 2 vols)

Constantius of Lyon   *Vita Germani* W. Levison M.G.H. *Scriptores Rerum Merovingicrum* 7 (Berlin 1920), 247–83 R. Borius *Sources Chrétiennes* 112 (Paris 1965) F.R. Hoare *The Western Fathers* (London, 1954), 283–320

Eddius Stephanus   *The Life of Bishop Wilfred by Eddius Stephanus* B. Colgrave (Cambridge 1927) J.F. Webb *Lives of the Saints* (Penguin Classics), 131–206

Gildas   Mommsen M.G.H. *Auctores Antiquissimi* 3, part 1 (*Chronica Minora* 3), 25–85 *Gildas: The Ruin of Britain* H. Winterbottom (Chichester 1978)

Gregory of Tours:

Historia Francorum	W. Arndt and B. Krusch M.G.H. *Scriptores Rerum Merovingicrum* I (Hanover, 1885), 1–140
	The History of the Franks by Gregory of Tours O.M. Dalton (Oxford, 2 vols 1927)
	Gregory of Tours: The History of the Franks L. Thorpe (Penguin Classics, 1974)
In Gloria Confessorum	Krusch M.G.H. loc. cit. 744–820
	R. Van Dam *Gregory of Tours: Glory of the Confessors* (Liverpool, 1988, Translated texts for Historians 4)
In Gloria Martyrum Beatorum	Krusch M.G.H. loc. cit. 484–561 R. Van Dam *Gregory of Tours: Glory of the Martyrs* (Liverpool, 1988, Translated texts for Historians 3)
De Passione et Virtutibus S Juliani Martyris	ed Krusch, M.G.H. loc. cit. 562–85
Vitae Patrum	Krusch M.G.H. loc. cit. 661–744 E. James *Gregory of Tours: Lives of the Fathers* (Liverpool, 1985, Translated Texts for Historians 1)
De Virtutibus Beati Martini Episcopi	Krusch M.G.H. loc. cit. 584–661
Herodian	*History* C.R. Whittaker, (Loeb, 2 vols)
Historia Augusta	*Scriptores Historiae Augustae* D. Magie (Loeb, 3 vols)
Hydatius	*Chronicle* T. Mommsen M.G.H. *Auctores Antiquissimi* II (*Chronica Minora* 2) 225–39
John the Almsgiver	Life. E. Dawes and N.H. Baynes *Three Byzantine Saints* (Oxford 1948) — combines the surviving part of the Life by Leontius, bishop of Neapolis (Migne *Patrologia Graeca* 93) with the opening chapters of a later conflate version edited by Delehaye
Jonas	*Vita Columbani* W. Levison M.G.H *Scriptores Rerum Merovingicrum* 4, part 1
Marcellinus Comes	Mommsen M.G.H. *Auctores Antiquissimi* II (*Chronica Minora* 2) 37–108
Merobaudes	F.M. Clover *Flavius Merobaudes: A Translation and Historical Commentary* (Trans. American Philosophical Society, new series 61, part I, 1971)
Notitia Dignitatum	O Seeck (Berlin 1896)
Notitia Galliarum	T. Mommsen M.G.H. *Auctores Antiquissimi 9* (*Chronica Minora* 1) 552–612
Panegyrici Latini	E. Galletier (Bude, Paris 3 vols 1949–55)
	R.A.B. Mynors Oxford Classical Texts 1964
Patrick	*Libri Epistolarum Sanctii Patricii* L Bieler (Dublin 1952)
	St Patrick: His Writings and Muirchu's Life A.B.E. Hood (Chichester 1978)
Paulinus of Pella	*Eucharisticos* H.G. Evelyn White in Ausonius *Poems* Vol 2 (Loeb)
Procopius of Caesarea	*History of the Wars* H.B. Dewing (Loeb, 7 vols)
Prosper of Aquitaine	*Chronicle* T. Mommsen M.G.H. *Auctores Antiquissimi 9* (*Chronica Minora* 1), 464–85
Prudentius	*Peristephanon* H.J. Thomson in *Poems* (Loeb, 2 vols)
Sidonius Apollinaris	*Poems and Letters* W.B. Anderson (Loeb, 2 vols)
Sulpicius Severus	*Vita Martini* J. Fontaine *Sulpice Severe: Vie de Saint Martin* Sources Chrétiennes 133–35 (Paris, 3 vols)
	F.R. Hoare *The Western Fathers* (London, 1954), 1–144
Victricius of Rouen	*De Laude Sanctorum* Migne *Patrologia Latina* 20, 443–58
Vitae Patrum Jurensium	F. Martine *Sources Chrétiennes* 142 (Paris 1968)
Vita Filiberti	W. Levison M.G.H. *Scriptores Rerum Merovingicrum* 5, part 5, 568–610
Vita Sampsoni	*La Vie de S. Samson* R Fawtier (Paris, 1912)
	The Life of St Sampson of Dol trans T. Taylor (London, 1925)
Zosimus	*Historia Nova* L. Mendelsohn (Leipzig 1887)

Abbreviations

B.A.R.	*British Archaeological Reports* (Oxford)
C.B.A.	Council for British Archaeology
M.G.H.	*Monumenta Germaniae Historica* (Berlin)
M.S.F.	*Recueil Général des Monuments Sculptés en France* (Paris)
P.L.	*Patrologia Latina* (Paris)
P.L.R.E.	*The Prosopography of the Later Roman Empire* Vol 1, AD 260–395. A.H.M. Jones, J.R. Martindale and J. Morris (Cambridge 1972) Vol. 2, AD 395–527 and Vol. 3, AD 527–640 J.R. Martindale (Cambridge, 1980, 1983)
R.I.C.	*Roman Imperial Coinage* H. Mattingley, E.A. Sydenham *et al* (London)
T.C.C.G.	*Topographie Chétienne des Cities de la Gaule des Origines au milieu du VIII e siècle* N. Gauthier and J-Ch. Picard (Paris)

3. Books and articles

Actes du Colloque	1978	*Actes du Colloque International d' Archéologie, Rouen 3–5 Juillet, 1975: Centenaire de l'Abbe Cochet*
Addleshaw, G.W.O.	1954	'The beginnings of the Parochial system' *St Anthony's Hall Publications 3, Borthwick Institute of Historical Research, York*
	1970	*The Beginnings of the Parochial System from Charlemagne to Urban II* (2nd ed, York)
Agache, R.	1970	*Détection Aérienne de Vestiges Protohistoriques, Gallo-Romaines et Médiévaux dans la Somme et ses Abords* (Musée de Picardie, Amiens)
	1978	*La Somme Pre-Romaine et Romaine* (Amiens)
Alcock, E.	1988	'Enclosed places AD 500–800' Driscoll and Nieke 40–6
Alcock, L.	1963	*Dinas Powys, an Iron Age, Dark Age and early Medieval settlement in Glamorgan* (Cardiff)
	1987	*Economy, Society and Warfare among the Britons and Saxons* (Cardiff)
	1988	*The activities of Potentates in Celtic Britain, AD 500–800: A Positivist approach* Driscoll and Nieke 22–40
	1995	*Cadbury Castle, Somerset. The Early Medieval Archaeology* (Cardiff)
Alenus-Lecerf, J.	1985	'Le cimetière de Vieuxville, bilan des fouilles 1980–84' *Archaeologia Belgica* new series 1.1. 129–39
	1986	'Le cimetière de Vieuxville: 6.e. campagne de fouilles' *Archaeologia Belgica* new series 2, 75–80
Antiguedad y Christianismo		*Antigueded y Christianismo: Monografias Historicas Sobre La Antigueded Tardia* (University of Murcia, series editor Antonio Gonzalez Blanco)
Arbessman, R.	1979	'The *cervuli* and *anniculae* in Caesarius of Arles' *Traditio* 35, 89–121
Arnhcim, M.T.W.	1972	*The Senatorial Aristocracy in the Later Roman Empire* (Oxford)
Atsmar, H.	1976	'Die Christlichen Inschriften Galliens als Quelle fur Kloster und Klosterbewohner bis zum ende des 6 Jahrhunderts' *Francia* 4, 1–57
Attenborough, F	1922	*The Laws of the Earliest English Kings* (Cambridge)
Audin, A. and Burnand, Y.	1959	'Alla ricerca della trace di Cristianesimo sulle tombe di Lione Prima della pace della Chiesa' *Rivista di' Archaeologia Cristiana* 35, 51–70
	1959a	'Chronologie des epitaphs romaines de Lyon' *Rev. des Études*

	Anciennes 61, 320–52
	1961 'Chronologie des epitaphs romaines de Vienne' *Rev.des Études Anciennes* 63, 291–311
Babelon, E.	1916 *Le Trésor d'Argenterie de Berthouville, pres Bernay, Eure* (Paris)
Balmelle, C.	1980 *Receuil Generale des Mosaiques de la Gaule IV: Aquitaine 1: Partie Meriodionale* (Paris, 10th supplement to *Gallia*)
Barley, M.W. and Hanson, R.P.C.	1968 ed *Christianity in Britain, 300–700* (Leicester)
Barnish, S.J.B.	1988 'Transformation and survival in the western senatorial aristocracy AD 400–700' *Papers Brit. School at Rome* 56, 120–55
	1989 'The transformation of classical cities and the Pirenne debate' *J. Roman Archaeol 2, 385–400*
Barral y Altet, X and Deocourt, D.	1974 'Le Baptistere Paléochrétien de Marseille' *Archéologia* 73 (August 1974), 6–19
Bassett, S.	1989 ed *The Origins of Anglo-Saxon Kingdoms* (Leicester)
	1989 'Churches in Worcester before and after the conversion of the Anglo-Saxons' *Antiq. J.* 69, 225–56
Bastien, P.	1964 *The Monnayage de Magnence, 350–3* (Wetteren)
Bateson, J.D.	1973 'Roman material from Ireland, a reconsideration' *Proc. Roy. Irish Acad.* 73, C, 21–98
	1976 'Further finds of Roman material from Ireland' *Proc Roy. Irish Acad* 76, C, 171–80
Bayard, D.	1990 'L'ensemble du Grand Amphithéâtre de Metz et la sigillée d'Argonne au Ve. Siècle' *Gallia* 47 (1990), 271–319
	1993 'Le fin de la domination romaine dans le nord de la Gaule: l'apport de la sigillée d'Argonne' Vallet and Kazanski (1993), 223–33
Bayard, D. and Cadoux, J.L.	1982 'Les thermes du sanctuaire Gallo-romain de Ribemont-sur-Ancre (Somme)' *Gallia* 40, 83–105
Bayard, D. and Massy, J.L.	1983 *Amiens Romain* (*Rev. Archéol de Picardie*)
Beck, H.G.	1950 *The Pastoral Care of Souls in South-East France During the Sixth Century* (Rome — Analecta Gregoriana II)
Benoit, F.	1954 *Sarcophages Paléochretiens d'Arles et de Marseille* (5th supplement to *Gallia*)
	1977 Cimiez, La Ville Antique: Fouilles de Cemenelum I (Paris)
Bernier, G.	1982 *Les Chrétientes Bretonnes Continentales Depuis les Origines Jusqu'au IX éme Siécle* (Rennes)
Bersu, G. and Unverzagt, W.	1961 'Le castellum de Fanum Martis (Famars, Nord)' *Gallia* 19, 159–90
Bishop, M.C. and Coulston, J.	1993 *Roman Military Equipment*
Blagg, T.F.C.	1983 'The re-use of monumental masonry in late Roman defensive Walls' Maloney and Hobley (1983 ed)
Blagg, T.F.C., Jones, R.F.J. and Keay, S.J.	*Papers in Iberian Archaeology* (B.A.R. Int. series, 193)
Blair, J.	1988 ed *Minsters and Parish Churches: The Local Church in Transition* (Oxford)
Blair, J. and Sharpe, R.	1992 ed *Pastoral Care Before the Parish* (Leicester)
Blanc, A.	1957 'Le Baptistere de Valence (Drôme)' *Gallia* 15, 87–116
	1971 'Autour de Saint-Jean — l'Evangeliste de Valence' *Rivista di Studi Liguri* 37, 77–82
Blanchet, A.	1907 *Les Enceintes Romaines de la Gaule* (Paris)
Blanco, A.G.	1985 *Del Conventus Carthaginensis a la Chora de Tudmir: Perspectives de la Historia de Murcia entre los Siglos III–VIII* (*Antiguedad y Cristianismo* 2)
Böhme, H.W.	1974 *Germanische Grabfunde des 4 bis 5 Jahrhunderts Zwischen Unterer Elbe und Loire* (Munich, 2 vols)

	1986 'Das ende der Römerherrschaft in Britannien und die Angelsachsische Besiedlung Englands im 5 Jahrhundert' *Jahrbuch Röm-Germanischen Zentralmus. Mainz* 33, 469–574
Bonnet, C.	1987 'The archaeological site of the cathedral of St Peter, Geneva' *World Archaeology* 18.3, 330–40
	1989 'Baptisteres et Groupes Episcopaux d'Aoste et de Geneva: Evolution architectural et amenegements liturgiques' *Actes du X I e Congrés International d' Archéologie Chrétienne* II, 1407–26
Boon, G.C.	1975 'Segontium fifty years on I' *Archaeol. Cambrensis* 124, 52–67
	1983 'Potters, oculists and eye troubles' *Britannia* 14, 1–12
Boussard, J.	1954 'Essai sur le peuplement de Touraine du 1 e. au VIII e. siècle' *Le Moyen Age* 60, 273–6
Brandt, R. and Slofstra, J. (eds)	1983 *Roman and Native in the Low Countries: Spheres of Interaction* (B.A.R. Int. series, 184)
Braudel, F.	1983 *The Mediterranean and the Mediterranean World in the Age of Philip II* (2 vols)
Brennan, B.	1985 '*Episcopae*: Bishops wives viewed in sixth-century Gaul' *Church History* 54, 311–23
	1985a 'Senators and social mobility in sixth-century Gaul' *J. Medieval Hist* 11, 145–61
Briesenick, B.	1962 'Typologie und chronologie der südwest-Gallische sarkophage' *Jahrbuch Römische-Germanischen Zentralmus. Im Mainz* 9, 76–182
Brooke, C.N.L.	1982 'Rural ecclesiastical institutions in England: a search for their Origins' *Settimane di Studio del Centro Italiano di Studi sull Alto Medioevo* (Spoleto), 28, 2, 685–711
Brooks, D.A.	1986 'A review of the evidence for continuity in British towns in the fifth and sixth centuries' *Oxford J. Archaeol* 5, 77–102
	1988 'The case for continuity in fifth-century Canterbury re-examined' *Oxford J. Archaeol* 7, 99–114
Brown, P.D.C.	1971 'The church at Richborough' *Britannia* 2, 225–31
Bruer, J. and Roosens, H.	1957 'Le cimetière de Haillot' *Archaeologia Belgica* 34
Brulet, R.	1990 'La chronologie des fortifications du Bas-Empire dans l' hinterland de la Gaule septentrionale' *Der Römische Limes in Osterreich, Aktendes 14 Internationalen Limeskongressus 1986 in Carnuntum* (Vienna, 1990), 301–9
Bullinger, H.	1960 *Spatantike Gürtelbeschlage: Typen, Herstellung, Trageweise und Datierung* (Dissertationes Archaeologicae Gandenses XII, 2 vols, Bruges)
Bullough, D.A.	1966 'Urban change in early medieval Italy: the example of Pavia' *Papers Brit. School at Rome* 34, 82–130
Burlock, J.D.	1956 'Early Christian memorial formulae' *Archaeol. Cambrensis* 105, 49–53
Burnett, A.	1984 'Clipped siliquae and the end of Roman Britain *Britannia*' 15, 163–8
Bushe-Fox, J.P.	1932 *Third Report on the Excavation of the Roman Fort at Richborough, Kent*
Butler, R.M.	1958 'The Roman walls of Le Mans' *J. Roman Stud.* 48, 33–9
	1961 'Late Roman town walls in Gaul' *Archaeol. J.* 116, 25–50
Cabanot, J.	1993 'Sarcophages et chapiteaux de marbre en Gaule' *Antiquite Tardive* I, 111–124
Cabrol, F. and Leclerq, H.	1913–53 *Dictionnaire d'Archéologie Chrétienne et du Liturgie* (Paris, 15 vols)

Cadoux, J.L.	1978	'Un sanctuaire Gallo-romaine isolé: Ribemont-sur-Ancre' *Latomus* 37, 325–60
Cahour, M.	1876	'Découverte du baptistere primitif de la Cathedrale de Nantes' *Bull. Soc. Archéol de Nantes* 15, 273–85
Cambridge, E.	1984	'The early Church in County Durham: A Re-assessment' *J. Brit Archaeol Assoc.* 137, 65–85
Cambridge, E. and Rollaston, D.	1995	'The pastoral organization of the Anglo-Saxon Church: A review of the minster hypothesis' *Early Medieval Europe* 4.1, 87–104
Cameron, Averil	1993	*The Mediterranean World in Late Antiquity*
Cameron, A. and Schauer, D.	1982	'The last Consul: Basilius and his diptych' *J. Roman Stud* 72, 126–45
Campbell, E.	1987	'A cross-marked quern from Dunadd and other evidence for relations between Dunadd and Iona' *Proc. Soc. Antiq. Scotland* 117, 105–17
	1996	'The archaeological evidence for external contacts: Imports, trade and economy in Celtic Britain AD 400–800' K.R. Dark (1996 ed), 83–96
Carney, J.	1971	'Three Old-Irish accentual poems' *Eriu* 22, 23–80
Casey, P.J.	1979	ed *The End of Roman Britain* (B.A.R. Brit. Series 71)
Charles-Edwards, T.M.	1971	'The seven Bishop Houses of Dyfed' *Bull. Board Celtic Stud* 24, 247–62
	1979	'The distinction between land and moveable wealth in Anglo-Saxon England' P.H. Sawyer (ed) *English Medieval Settlement* 97–104
Chenet, G.	1941	*La céramique Gallo-Romain d'Argonne du IVe Siècle et la terre sigillée décorée à la Molette* (Macon 1941)
Christe, Y. and Duval, N.	1993	ed *Les Sarcophages d' Aquitaine* (Antiquite Tardive 1), 9–170
Clarke, H.B. and Brennan, M. (ed.)	1981	*Columbanus and Merovingian Monasticism* B.A.R. Int. series 113
Collins, R.	1980	'Mérida and Toledo 550–85' E. James (1980), 189–219
	1983	*Early Medieval Spain: Unity in Diversity 400–1000*
Conges, A. and G. and Kauffman, A.	1980	'Aix-en-Provence' in *Archéologie Urbaine Actes du Colloque International, Tours 1980* (Paris)
Conway, J.M.	1914–15	'The Abbey of St Denis and its ancient treasures' *Archaeologia* 66, 103–58
Costa, D.	1958	'Céramique paléochrétienne découverte à Nantes' *Bull. Soc. Archéol et Hist. de Nantes* 97, 65–76
	1959	'La decor architectonique a l'époque Mérovingienne dans le pays Nantais' *Bull. Soc.Archéol et Hist de Nantes* 98, 173–93
	1964	*Nantes, Musée Th. Dobree, Art Mérovingienne* (Inventaire des Collections Publiques Françaises 10, Paris)
Courteault, P.	1921	'An inscription recently found at Bordeaux' *J. Roman Stud* 11, 101–7
Cramp, R.	1969	'Excavations on the Saxon monastic sites of Wearmouth and Jarrow, Co. Durham: an interim report' *Medieval Archaeol* 13, 21–66
Crawford, H.S.	1912–14	'A descriptive list of early cross slabs and pillars' *J. Roy. Soc. Antiq. Ireland* 43–4
Cunliffe, B.W.	1968	*Fifth Report on the Excavations of the Roman Fort at Richborough, Kent*
Dark, K.R.	1994	*Civitas to Kingdom: British Political Continuity, 300–800* (Leicester)
	1996	ed *External Contacts and the Economy of Late Roman and Post Roman Britain* (Woodbridge)

Davies, W.   1978a   Land and power in early medieval Wales *Past and Present* 81, 3–23

    1982   *Wales in the Early Middle Ages* (Leicester)

Deanesly, M.   1941   'Early English and Gallic minsters' *Trans. Roy. Hist. Soc.* 4th series 23, 25–69

Delbruck, R.   1929   *Die Consulardiptychen* (Berlin, 2 vols)

Delehaye, H.   1920   'Saint Martin et Sulpice Severe' *Analecta Bollandiana* 38, 5–136

    1921   *Les Passions des Martyrs et les Genres Litteraires* (Brussels)

de la Croix, C.   1883   *Mémoire Archéologique sur les découvertes d' Herbord ,dites de Sanxay* (Niort)

de la Tour, I.   1900   *Les origines Religieuses de la France: Les Paroisses Rurales du IV é au XI é Siècle* (Paris)

Delgado, M., Mayet, F. and Moutinho de Alarrcao, A.   1985   *Fouilles de Conimbriga IV Les Sigillées* (Paris)

Demolon, P.   1979   'L'Implementation du Christianisme dans le bassin superieur de l'Escaut' *Francia* 7, 533–

De Palol, P.   1967   *Arqueologia Cristiana de la Espana Romana* (Madrid)

De Vesly,   1908   *Les Fana ou Petits Temples Gallo-Romaines de la Région Normande* (Rouen)

Dickinson,T.M.   1982 'Ornamental variation in pairs of cast saucer brooches: a case study from the Upper Thames Region' L. Webster (ed) *Aspects of Production and Style in Dark Age Metalwork: Selected papers given to the British Museum Seminar on Jewellery AD 500–600*, 21–50

Doherty, C.   1984   'The Basilica in early Ireland' *Peritia* 3, 303–15

Dold, A.   1948   *Die Orakelspruche im St Gallener Palimpsestcodex 908* (Sitzungesbericht der Osterreichischen Akademie der Wissenschaften Phil-hist klasse 2254, Vienna)

Drinkwater, J.F.   1987   *The Gallic Empire: Separatism and Continuity in the Northwestern Provinces of the Roman Empire* (Stuttgart)

    1992   'The Bacaudae of Britain and Gaul' Drinkwater and Elton (1992 ed), 208–17

Drinkwater, J.F. and Elton, H.   1992   ed *Fifth Century Gaul. A Crisis of Identity?* (Cambridge)

Driscoll, S.T.   1988   'The relationship between history and archaeology in artefacts, documents and power' Driscoll and Nieke (1988 ed) 162–87

Driscoll, S.T. and Nieke, R.   1988   ed *Power and Politics in early Medieval Britain and Ireland* (Edinburgh)

Duchesne, L.   1894–5   *Fastes Episcopaux de l'Ancienne Gaule* (Paris)

Eadie, J.W.   1980   'Barbarian invasions and frontier politics in the reign of Gallienus' *Roman Frontier Studies 1979* ed W.S. Hanson and L.J.F Keppie (B.A.R. Int. series 71), vol 3, 1043–50

Eck, T.   1891   *Les deux Cimetières Gallo-Romains de Vermand et de St Quentin* (Paris and St Quentin)

Edmondson, J.C.   1989   'Mining in the later Roman Empire and beyond: continuity or disruption?' *J. Roman Stud* 79, 84–102

Edwards, N. and Lane, A.ed   1992   *The Early Church in Wales and the West* (Cardiff)

Elton, H.   1992   'The defence of Gaul' Drinkwater and Elton (1992 ed), 167–76

    1996   *Warfare in Roman Europe, AD 350–425* (Oxford)

Esmonde Cleary, A.S.   1989   *The Ending of Roman Britain*

Etienne, R.   1962   *Histoire de Bordeaux I: Bordeaux Antique* (Bordeaux)

Evison, V.I.   1965   *The Fifth-Century Invasions south of the Thames*

	1981 'Distribution maps and England in the first two phases' Evison (ed) *Angles, Saxons and Jutes: Essays Presented to J.N.L. Myres* (Oxford)
Eygun, F.	1964 Le Baptistere Saint-Jean de Poitiers *Gallia* 22, 137–71
Fabre, G. and Mainjonet, M.	1965 'La trouvaille Monetaire de Fontaines-Salees' *Gallia* 23, 151–233
Farwell, D.E. and Molleson, T.	1993 *Excavations at Poundbury 1966–80, Vol 2: The Cemeteries* (Dorchester, Dorset)
Finley, M.I.	1973 *The Ancient Economy*
Fletcher, E. and Meates, G.W.	1969 'The ruined church of Stone by Faversham' *Antiq J.* 49, 273–94
	1977 do. Second report. *Antiq J.* 57, 67–72
Fleury, M. and Périn, P.,	1978 ed *Problemes de Chronologie Relative et Absolue Concernant les Cimetières Mérovingiens d'entre Loire et Rhine* (Paris)
Flint, V. I.	1991 *The Rise of Magic In Early Medieval Europe* (Oxford)
Fontaine, J.	1963 Sulpice-Severe, 'a-t-il travesti Saint Martin de Tours en Martyr Militaire' *Analecta Bollandiana* 81, 31–58
Forster, R. and Ranum, O.	1982 *Ritual, Religion and the Sacred: Selections from the Annales, Economies, Societes, Civilisations*
Foss, C.	1975 'The Persians in Asia Minor and the End of Antiquity' *English Hist. Rev* 90, 721–47
	1977 'Archaeology and the Twenty Cities of Byzantine Asia' *American J. of Archaeol* 81, 469–86
Fossard, D.	1947 'Les chapiteaux de marbre du VII e siècle en Gaule, style et Évolution' *Cahiers Archéologiques* 2, 69–85
	1957 'La chronologie des sarcophages d'Aquitaine' *Actes du Vê Congrès Int. d'Archéol Chrétienne 1954* (Vatican-Paris) 321–33
Fouracre, P.	1979 'The work of Audoenus of Rouen and Eligius of Noyon in extending episcopal influence from the town to the country in seventh-century Neustria' *Stud. In Church Hist.* 16, 77–91
Fox, A.	1939 'The siting of some inscribed stones of the Dark Ages in Glamorgan and Breconshire' *Archaeol. Cambrensis* 94, 30–41
Fox, A. and C.	1934 'Forts and farms on Margam mountain, Glamorgan' *Antiquity* 8, 395–413
France-Lanord, A.	1963 'Un cimetière des Letes a Cotrat (Loiret)' *Rev. Archéol* 1963, 15–35
Freeman, P. and Kennedy, D.	1986 *The Defence of the Roman and Byzantine East* (B.A.R. Int. series 297)
Frere, S.S.	1976 'The Silchester church: the excavation by Sir Ian Richmond' *Archaeologia* 105, 277-302
Frye, D.	1991 'Bishops and pawns in early fifth-century Gaul' *J. Ecclesiastical Hist* 42, 349–61
Fulford, M.	1977 'Pottery and Britain's foreign trade in the late Roman period' D.P.S. Peacock (ed) *Pottery and Early Commerce* 35–84
	1978 'The interpretation of Britain's late Roman trade: the scope of medieval historical and archaeological analogy' Taylor and Cleere (1978 ed), 59–69
	1979 'Pottery production and trade at the end of Roman Britain: the case against continuity' Casey (1979 ed), 120–32
	1989 'Byzantium and Britain; a Mediterranean perspective on post-Roman Mediterranean imports in western Britain and Ireland' *Medieval Archaeol* 33, 1–6

De Gaiffier, B. 1947 'L'hagiographie et son public au XI e siècle' *Miscellanea Historica in Honorum Leonis van der Essen* (Brussels and Paris), I, 135–66

Galinie, H. 1978–82 Fouilles Archéologique à Tours (rapports préliminaires) *Bull. Soc. Archéol Touraine* 38 (1978) — 40 (1982)

1997 'Tours de Grégoire, Tours des archives du Sol' Gauthier and Galinié, 65–80

Galliou, P. 1976 'Celtic permanence or Roman change? Roman Brittany revisited' *Oxford J. Archaeol* 5, 67–76

1983 *L'Armorique Romaine* (Braspars)

Galliou, P., Fulford, M. and Clement, C. 1980 'La diffusion de la céramique a l'éponge dans le nord-ouest de l'Empire Romain' *Gallia* 38, 265–78

Gauthier, N. 1980 *Histoire et Numismatique en Haute Normandie* (Cahier des Annales de Normandie 12 A, Caen)

Gauthier, N. and Galinié H. 1997 *Grégoire de Tours et l'espace Gaulois (Actes du Congres International, Tours 1994)* 13th Supp. to Rev. Archéol du Centre de la France

Geary, P.J. 1988 *Before France and Germany: The creation and transformation of the Merovingian World* (Oxford)

Gechter, M. and Kunow, G. 1986 'Zur landlichen Besiedlung des Rheinlandes in Romischer Zeit' *Bonner Jahrbucher* 186, 377–96

1988 'Zur landlichen Besiedlunges Rheinlandes vom I. Jahrhundert v. bis ins V. Jahrhundert n. Chr. Geb' R.F.J. Jones *et al* (1988 ed), 109–28

Gelling, M. 1967 'English placenames derived from the compound *wicham*' *Medieval Archaeol* 11, 87–104

Gillard, F. 1979 'The senators of sixth-century Gaul' *Speculum* 54, 685–97

Goffart, W. 1974 *Caput and Colonate: Towards a History of Late Roman Taxation* (Toronto)

1980 *Barbarians and Romans AD 418–585: The techniques of Accomodation* (Princeton)

1982 'Old and new in Merovingian taxation' *Past and Present* 96, 3–21

Goodburn, R. 1972 *The Roman Villa, Chedworth* (National Trust)

Goodburn, R. and Bartholemew, P. 1976 ed *Aspects of the Notitia Dignitatum* (B.A.R. Supp. Series 15)

Green, C.J.S. 1987 *Excavations at Poundbury, 1966–80. Vol 1 the Settlements* (Dorchester, Dorset) For Vol 2 see Farwell and Molleson, 1993

Greenslade, S.L. 1965 'The unit of pastoral care in the early Church' *Stud. In Church Hist* 2, 102–8

Grenier, A. 1931–60 *Manuel d'Archéologie Gallo-Romaine* (Paris)

Gricourt, J., Fabre, G., Mainjonet, M. and Lafaurie, J. 1958 ed *Trésors Monetaires et Plaques-Boucles de la Gaule Romaine: Bavai, Montbuoy, Checy* (12th supplement to *Gallia*)

Grierson, P. and Blackburn, M. 1986 *Medieval European Coinage, with a catalogue of the coins in the Fitzwilliam Museum Vol 1. The Early Middle Ages (fifth to tenth century)* (Cambridge)

Griffe, É. 1947–66 *La Gaule Chrétienne à l'Époque Romaine* (Paris-Toulouse, 3 vols)

1. Des Origines Chrétiennes à la fin du IV e Siècle (1947, revised ed 1964)

2. L'Eglise des Gaules au V e. Siècle part 1 (1957, revised ed 1966)

3. L'Eglise des Gaules au Ve Siècle part 2 (1957, revised ed 1965)

Groenman-van-Waateringe, W 1983 'The disasterous effects of the Roman Occupation' Brandt and Slofstra (1983 ed), 147–58

Gruter, J. 1615 *Inscriptionum Romanorum Corpus* (Heidelberg)

Guild, R., Guyon, J. and Rivet, L. 1980 'Recherches archéologiques dans le clôitre Saint-Sauver d'Aix-en-Provence' *Rev. Archéol de Narbonnaise* 13, 115–64

1983 'Les origines du baptistere de la cathedrale Saint-Sauveur; étude de topographie Aixoise' *Rev. Archéol du Narbonnaise* 16, 171–232

Gussone, M. 1978 Ceremonial d'Adventus et translation des reliques en Victrice de Rouen 'de Laude Sanctorum' *Actes du Colloque* 3, 287–300

Halbout, P. 1989 'Une Halle aux poissons à Rouen aux II e -III e siécles?' *Gallia* 46, 163–72

Haldon, J.F. 1990 *Byzantium in the Seventh Century* (Cambridge)

Hamlin, A. 1972 'A chi-rho carved stone at Drumaqueran, Co. Antrim' *Ulster J. Archaeol* 35, 22–8

1982 'Early Irish stone carving: Content and context' S. Pearce *The Early Church in western Britain and Ireland* (B.A.R. Brit. Ser. 102), 283–96

Hanson, R.P.C. 1970 'The church in fifth-century Gaul: evidence from Sidonius' *J. Ecclesiastical Hist* 21, 1–10

Harden, D.B. 1956 'Glass vessels in Britain and Ireland, AD 400–1000' Harden (1956 ed), 136–67

1956 ed *Dark Age Britain: Studies Presented to E.T. Leeds*

Harries, J. 1978 'Church and state in the Notitia Galliarum' *J. Roman Stud* 68, 26–43

1994 *Sidonius Apollinaris and the Fall of Rome* (Oxford)

Hayes, J.W. 1973 *Late Roman Pottery*

1980 *Supplement to Late Roman Pottery*

Heather, P 1991 *Goths and Romans 332–489* (Oxford)

Herrin, J. 1987 *The Formation of Christendom*

Hillgarth, J.N. 1961 'The east, Visigothic Spain and the Irish' *Studia Patristica* 4, 442–56

1962 'Visigothic Spain and Early Christian Ireland' *Proc. Roy. Irish Acad* C. 62. 167–94

1984 'Ireland and Spain in the seventh century' *Peritia* 3, 1–16

1985 *Visigothic Spain, Byzantium and the Irish* (Varorium)

Hitchner, R.B. 1992 'Meridional Gaul, trade and the Mediterranean economy in late antiquity' Drinkwater and Elton (1992 ed), 122–31

Hodges, R. 1982 *Dark Age Economics: The Origin of Towns and Trade AD 600–1000*

Hodges, R. and Whitehouse D., 1983 *Mohammed, Charlemagne and the Origins of Europe*

Hubener, W. 1968 'Eine studie zur spatromische Radchensigillata (Argonnesigillata)' *Bonner Jahrbucher* 168 (1968), 240–98

Hubert, J. 1952 *L'Architecture Religieuse du Haut Moyen Age en France*

Hughes, K. 1966 *The Church in Early Irish Society*

Jacob, J.P., Leredde, H. and Loriot, X. 1983 'Trésors monétaires Gallo-romains du département de l'Yonne' *Rev. Archéol Est et Centre Est* 34, 301–

Jaffe, E. 1885 *Regestra Pontificum Romanorum I*

James E. 1977 *The Merovingian Archaeology of South-West Gaul* (B.A.R. Supp. Series 25, 2 vols)

1979 'Cemeteries and the problem of Frankish settlement in Gaul' P.H. Sawyer (ed) *Names, Words and Graves* (Leeds), 55–89

1980 ed *Visigothic Spain: New Approaches* (Oxford)

1981 'Archaeology and the Merovingian monastery' Clarke and Brennan (1981 ed), 33–55

	1982	*The Origins of France: from Clovis to the Capetians*
	1983	'Ireland and western Gaul in the Merovingian period' Whitlock (1983 ed), 362–86
	1988	*The Franks* (Oxford)
	1993	'The historical and archaeological context of the south-west Gallic sarcophagi' Christe and Duval, 23–7
James, S.	1988	'The Fabricae: state arms factories of the late Roman Empire' J.C. Coulston (ed) *Military Equipment and the Identity of Roman Soldiers* (B.A.R. Int. series 394), 257–331
Jannet-Vallat, M., Lauxerois, R. and Reynaud, J.F.	1986	*Vienne aux Premiers Temps Chrétiens* (Paris)
Jauregi, J.	1949	*I.o Congreso Arqueologico del Sudest Espanol, Almeria 1947* (Cartagena, 1949)
Jigan, C.	1986	'Inventaire provisoire des trésors de monnaies découvértes dans le département de la Manche' *Annales de Normandie*3, 188–203
Johnson, S.	1973	'A group of late Roman city walls in Gallia Belgica' *Britannia* 4, 210–23
	1976	*The Roman Forts of the Saxon Shore*
	1983	*Late Roman Fortifications*
Jones, A.H.M.	1964	*The Later Roman Empire, 284–602: A Social, Economic and Administrative History* (Oxford, 3 vols)
Jones, R.F.J, Bloemers, J.H.F., Dyson, S.L. and Biddle, M. (ed)		*First Millenium Papers: Western Europe in the First Millenium AD* (B.A.R. Int. series 401)
Kaufffman, A.	1983	'Cardo et place dallées à Aix-en-Provence' *Rev. Archéol de Narbonnaise* 16, 233–46
Keay, S.J.	1984	*Late Roman Amphorae in the West Mediterranean* (B.A.R. Int. series 196)
	1984a	'Decline or continuity? The coastal economy of the Conventus Tarraconensis from the fourth century until the late sixth century' Blagg *et al* (1984 ed), 552–70
	1988	*Roman Spain*
Kennedy, H. and Liebeschuetz, J.	1988	'Antioch and the villages of northern Syria in the fifth and sixth centuries AD' *Nottingham Medieval Stud.* 32, 65–90
Kent, J.P.C.	1979	'The end of Roman Britain: the literary and numismatic evidence reviewed' Casey (1979 ed), 15–27
Kent, J.P.C. and Painter, K.S.	1977	*Wealth of the Roman World: Gold and Silver AD 300–700*
King, A. and Henig, M. 1981 ed		*The Roman West in the Third Century: Contributions from Archaeology and History* (B.A.R. Int. series 109)
King, C.E.	1992	'Roman, local and barbarian coinages in fifth-century Gaul' Drinkwater and Elton (1992), 184–95
Klingshirn, W.	1985	'Charity and power: Caesarius of Arles and the ransoming of captives in sub-Roman Gaul' *J. Roman Stud* 75, 183–203
Knight, J.K	1984	'Early Medieval Glamorgan' *Glamorgan County History Vol 2. Prehistory and Early History* ed H.N. Savory Cardiff, 315–409
	1992	'The early Christian latin inscriptions of Britain and Gaul: chronology and context' Edwards and Lane (ed), 45–50
	1995	'Penmachno revisited: the Consular inscription and its context' *Cambridge Medieval Celtic Stud.* 29, 1–10
	1996	'Seasoned with salt: Insular-Gallic contacts in the early memorial stones and cross-slabs' K.R. Dark (1996),109–120
Krautheimer, R.	1965	*Early Christian and Byzantine Architecture*
	1982	*Three Christian Capitals: Topography and Politics: Rome,*

	Constantinople, Milan
Kurth, G.	1919 'Les sénateurs en Gaul au VI e. siècle' *Etudes Franques* Vol 2 (Paris-Brussels), 97–115
Lafaurie, J.	1964 'Monnaie en argent trouvée à Fleury-sur-Orne' *Annales de Normandie* 14, 173–96
	1971 'Etude Numismatique' in J. Decaeans Hérouvillette *Archéologie Médiévale* 1, 173–82
	1978 'Monnaies d'argent Franques trouvées à Envermu (Seine-Maritime)' *Actes du Colloque* Fasc 3, 421–8
	1980 'Trouvailles de monnaies Franques ey Mérovingiennes en Seine-Maritime' Gautier (1980 ed), 93–107
Lapidge, M.	1984 'Gildas's education and the Latin culture of sub-Roman Britain' Lapidge and Dumville (1984 ed), 27–50
Lapidge, M. and Dumville, D.	1984 ed *Gildas: New Approaches* (Woodbridge)
Latouche, R.	1956 *Les Origines d'Economie Occidentale* (Paris) trans E.M. Wilkinson *The Birth of Western Economy: Economic Aspects of the Dark Ages* (1961)
Le Gentilhomme	1936 'Trouvaille de monnaies d'or des Mérovingiens et des Wisigoths faite a Bordeaux en 1803' *Rev Numismatique* 39, 87–133
Leman, P.	1982 'Un quartier Romaine de Beauvais (Oise)' *Gallia* 40, 195–217
Lemant, J-P.	1985 *Le Cimetière et la fortification du Bas-Empire de Vireux-Molhain, Dép. Ardennes* (Mainz)
Levison, W.	1941 'St Alban and St Albans' *Antiquity* 16, 337–59
	1946 *England and the Continent in the Eighth Century* (Oxford)
Loriot, X. and Delaporte, J.	1980 'Les trésors de monnaies romaines découverts dans le département de Seine Maritime' Gauthier (1980 ed), 27–59
Loseby, S.T.	1992 'Bishops and cathedrals: order and diversity in the fifth century urban landscape of south Gaul' Drinkwater and Elton (1992), 167–176
	1992a 'Marseille, a Late Antique success story?' *J. Roman Stud.* 82, 165–183
Loyen, A.	1972 'L'oeuvre de Flavius Merobaudes et l'histoire de l'occident de 430 à 450' *Revue des Études Anciennes* 74, 155–74
Luttwak, E.N	1976 *The Grand Strategy of the Roman Empire from the First Century AD to the Third* (Baltimore and London)
Lynn, C.	1984 'Some fragments of exotic porphyry found in Ireland' *J. Irish Archaeol* 2, 19–32
MacCormack, S.	1972 'Change and continuity in late antiquity: the ceremony of Adventus' *Historia* 21, 721–52
McManus, D.	1991 *A Guide to Ogam* (Maynooth)
Maillé, Marquise de	1959 *Recherches sur les Origines Chrétiennes de Bordeaux* (Paris)
	1971 *Les cryptes de Jouarre* (Paris)
Maloney, J. and Hobley, B.	1983 ed *Roman Urban Defences in the West*
Mangard, M.	1982 'L'inscription dédicatoire du Théâtre du Bois l'Abbé a Eu (Seine-Maritime)' *Gallia* 40, 35–51
Marrou, H.I.	1970 'Le dossier epigraphique de l'évêque Rusticus de Narbonne' *Rivista di Archeologia Cristiana* 46, 331–49
Martin, J.B.	1904 'Inscriptions Chrétiennes decouverts à Lyon' *Bull Archéol du Comité* 41, XLI–XLIV
Masne de Chermont, N. le	1987 'Les fouilles de l'ancien Évêchede de Poitiers (Vienne)' *Aquitania* 5, 149–75

Mathisen, R.W.

1979 'Resistance and reconciliation: Majorian and the Gallic aristocracy after the fall of Aetius' *Francia* 7, 597–627

1984 'Emigrants, exiles and survivors: aristocratic options in Visigothic Aquitaine' *Phoenix* 38, 159–70

1989 *Ecclesiastical Factionalism and Religious Controversy in Fifth Century Gaul* (Washington, DC)

Mathisen, R.W. and Sivan, H. S.

1996 ed *Shifting Frontiers in Late Antiquity* (Aldershot and Brookfield, Vermont)

Matthews, J.F.

1967 'A pious supporter of Theodosius I: Maternus Cynegius and his family' *J. Theological Stud.* new series 18, 438–46

1975 *Western Aristocracies and Imperial Court AD 364–425* (Oxford)

Mattingley, H. and Pearce, J.W.E.

1937 'The Coleraine hoard' *Antiquity* 11, 39–45

Mauss, M.

1925 *Essai Sur Le Don* (Paris). Trans. I. Cunnison *The Gift: Form and Function of Exchange in Archaic Societies* (1954)

Mayet, F., and Picot, M.

1986 'Une sigillée Phoceene tardive (Late Roman C) et sa diffusion en Occident' *Figlina* 7, 129–42

McDermott, W.C.

1975 'Felix of Nantes: A Merovingian Bishop' *Traditio* 31, 1–24

Meaney, A.L. and Hawkes, S.C.

1970 *Two Anglo-Saxon Cemeteries at Winnall* (Soc. Med. Archaeol Monograph 4)

Metzler, J.

1981 *Ausgrabungen in Echternach* (Luxembourg)

Millar, F.

1969 'Herennius Dexippus: The Greek world and the third century invasions' *J. Roman Stud* 59, 12–29

Morin-Jean

1913 *La Verrerie en Gaule sous l'Empire Romain*

Moss, J.R.

1973 'The effects of the policy of Aetius on the history of western Europe' *Historia* 22, 711–31

Muchembled, R.

1982 'Witchcraft, popular culture and Christianity' Forster and Ranum (1982 ed), 213–26

Musurillo, H.

1972 *The Acts of the Christian Martyrs* (Oxford)

Nash-Williams, V.E.

1950 *The Early Christian Monuments of Wales* (Cardiff)

Naveau, J.

1986 'Le plan antique de Jublains (Mayenne)' *Rev Archéol de l'Ouest* 3 (1986), 107–17

Nenquin, J.

1953 *La Nécropole de Furfooz* (Dissertationes Archaeologices Gandenses 1, Bruges)

Nieto Prieto, F.J.

1984 'Algunos datos sobre las importaciones de ceramica Late Roman C en la Peninsula Iberica' Blagg *et al* 1984 ed, 540–8

O'Kelly, M.J.

1962 'Two ring-forts at Garryduff, Co. Cork' *Proc. Roy. Irish Acad* 63 C. 17–124

Oost, S.I.

1964 *Aetius and Maiorian Classical Philology* 59, 27–8

O'Riordain, S.P.

1942 'The excavation of a large earthern ring fort at Garranes, Co.Cork' *Proc.Roy. Irish Acad.* 47 C. 77–150

Ortiz, R.M.

1988 'El transito a la Dominacion Bizantina en Cartagena; Las producciones ceramicas de la Plaza de las Tres Reyes' *Arte y Pobliamento en el S.E. Peninsular durante los ultimos siglos de Civilizacion Romana* (Antiguedad y Christianismo V), 31–164

Page, W.

1915 'Some remarks on the churches of the Domesday survey' *Archaeologia* new series 16, 61–102

Painter, K.S.

1972 'A late Roman silver ingot from Kent' *Antiq J.* 52, 84–92

1977 *The Water Newton Early Christian Silver*

Parker, A.J.

1992 *Ancient Shipwrecks of the Mediterranean and the Roman Provinces* (B.A.R. Int. ser. 580)

Peacock, D.P.S. and Williams, D.F.

1986 *Amphorae and the Roman Economy: An Introductory Guide*

Percival, J.

1969 'Seigneurial aspects of Roman estate management' *Eng. Hist.*

	Review 84, 449–73
	1976 *The Roman Villa: An Historical Introduction*
Périn, P.	1980 *La datation des tombes Mérovingiennes: Historique, Methodes, Applications* (Geneva)
	1987 'Des nécropoles Romaines tardives aux nécropoles du Haut Moyen Age: Remarques sur la topographie funéraraire en Gaule Mérovingienne et à sa périphérie' *Cahiers Archéologiques* 35 (1987), 9–30
Pfaulm, H.G.	1948 *Le Marbre de Thorigny* (Paris)
Picard, G.	1969 'Les théâtres ruraux sacrés en Gaul' *Archéologia* May-June 1969, 69–77
	1970 'Les théâtres ruraux en Gaul' *Rev. Archéol.* 185–92
	1970a 'Les *Conciliabula* de la Gaule' *Bull. Soc. Nat. Antiq. de France* 66–9
Pilet, C.	1980 *La Nécropole de Frenouville* (B.A.R. Int. series 86, 3 vols)
	1994 *La Nécropole de Saint-Martin-Fontenay (Calvados)* 54th supplement to *Gallia*
Pillard, G.	1982 *Les Ruines d'Herbord, Commune de Sanxay* (Niort)
Pilloy, J.	1895 *Études sur d'Anciens Sépultures dans l'Aisne* (St Quentin, 2 vols)
Pilloy, J. and Jumel, M.	1896 'Le tomb du chef militaire de Vermand' *Mem. Soc. Acad. De St Quentin* 353–67
Pirenne, H.	1937 *Mahomet and Charlemagne*
Pirling, R.	1966–79 *Das Romisch Frankische Graberfeld von Krefeld-Gellep* (6 vols)
Piton, D. and Schuler, R. 1993	'La nécropole de Nouvion-en-Ponthieu, Somme. IV e.–VII e Siécle' *Cahiers Archéol de Picardie* 9, 217–84
Potter, T.W.	1979 *The Changing Landscape of South Etruria*
	1987 *Roman Italy*
Poulter, A.	1995 *Nicopolis ad Istrum: A Roman, Late Roman and Early Byzantine City* (Soc. for Promotion of Roman Studies Monograph 8)
Poveda, M.A.	1988 *El Poblado Ibero-Romano de El Monastil* (Alicante)
Prinz, F.	1965 *Frühes Monachtum Im Frankenreich* (Munchen-Wien)
Provost, M.	1993 *Le Val de Loire dans l' Antiquité* 52nd Supplement to *Gallia*
Rahtz, P.A.	1992 *Cadbury-Congresbury 1968–73: A Late / Post Roman Hilltop Settlement in Somerset* Tempus Reparatum Brit. Ser. 223
Raimbuilt, M.	1973 'La céramique gallo-romaine dite a l'éponge dans l'Ouest de la Gaule' *Gallia* 31, 348–50
Rebuffet, R.	1985 'Jublains: un complexe fortifié dans l'Ouest de la Gaule' *Rev. Archéol* 1985, 2, 237–56
Reynaud, J.F.	1973 'Les fouilles de l'église Saint-Just et du groupe épiscopal de Lyon' *Acad. Des Inscriptions et Belles Lettres: Comtes rendus 1973* 346–64
	1974 'La nécropole de St Just' *Rev. Archéol d'Est et du Centre Est* 25, 111–23
	1975 'Le group épiscopal de Lyon: découvertes recentes' *Acad des Inscriptions et Belles Lettres: Comtes rendus Nov-Dec 1975*
	1975a 'Vienne la Sainte au Moyen Age' *Archaéologia* 88, Nov 1975, 44–54
	1977 'Les églises Saint-Pierre et Saint-Georges de Vienne. Documents du XIX e. siècle et études archéologiques récentes' *Bull. Archéol du Comité des Travaux Historiques* new series 10–11, fasc A. 1974–5, 7–32
	1978 Saint-Ferreol, une des plus anciennes eglises Viennoises *Archeologia* 122 (Sept. 1978), 44–51

	1980 'Le baptistère Saint-Etienne du groupe épiscopal de Lyon' *Actes du X e Congrès Int d' Archéol Chrétienne, 1980* (Thessalonica 1984), 2, 463–75
	1986 *Lyon aux Premiers Temps Chrétiens* (Paris)
Reynolds, P.	1987 *El Yacimento Tardoromano de Lucentum (Benalua-Alicante) Las Ceramicas Finas* Catalogo de Fondos del Museu Arqueologico II, Alicante
	1993 *Settlement and Pottery in the Vinalopó Valley (Alicante, Spain) AD 400–700* (B.A.R. Int ser. 588)
Richmond, I.A.	1930 *The City Walls of Imperial Rome*
	1943 'Roman legionaries at Corbridge, their supply base, temples and religious cult' *Archaeologia Aeliana* 4th series, 21, 127–224
Richmond, I.A. and Holford, W.G.	1935 'Roman Verona: The archaeology of its town Plan' *Papers Brit School at Rome* 13, 69–76
Rigoir, J.	1968 'Les sigillées paléochretiennes grises et orangées' *Gallia* 26, 177–244
	1971 'Les derivées des sigillées paléochrétiennes en Espagne' *Rivista di Studi Liguri* 37
Rigoir, J and Meffre, J.F.	1973 'Les derivées paléochrétiennes du groupe Atlantique' *Gallia* 31, 207–64
Rivet, A.L.F	1976 'The Notitia Galliarum: some questions'. Goodburn and Bartholemew (1976), 119–42
	1988 *Gallia Narbonensis: Southern France in Roman Times*
Roberts, T.	1992 'Welsh ecclesiastical place names and archaeology' Edwards and Lane (ed) 40–2
Rouché, M.	1964 'Le changement de nom des chefs-lieux de cite en Gaule au Bas Empire' *Mém et Travaux Soc.Nat. Antiq.de France* 84, 47–64
	1979 *L'Aquitaine des Wisigoths aux Arabes: Naissance d'une Region* (Paris)
Rouselle, A.	1982 'From sanctuary to miracle worker: healing in fourth-century Gaul' Forster and Ranum (ed)
Sapin, C.	1982 'L'ancienne église de Saint-Pierre l'Estrier à Autun' *Archéologie Medievale* 12, 50–105
	1986 *La Bourgogne Préromane: Construction, décor et fonction des édifices religieux* (Paris)
Seillier, C.	1976 Vron (Somme), une nécropole de l'époque des invasions *Archaéologia* 90 (Jan 1976), 37–43
	1978 'Quelques tombes du Ve siècle et du debut du VI e siècle de la nécropole de Vron' Fleury and Perin (1978 ed), 71–85
	1986 Développement topographique et caracteres generaux de la nécropole de Vron (Somme) *Archéologie Medievale* 16, 7–23
Seillier, C. and Demolon, P.	1984 ed *Le Nord de la France de Theodose à Charles Martel* (exhibition catalogue, Lille)
Serra-Rafols, J.C.	1943 'Villa de Fortunatus' *Ampurias* 5, 1–35
Sirat, J.	1966 'Les steles Mérovingiennes du Vexin Français' *Bull Archól Vexin Français* 2, 73–83
	1970 'Les steles Mérovingiennes du Vexin Français — inventaire complementaire' *Bull Archól Vexin Français* 6, 95–103
	1978 'La nécropole de Maule (France, Yvelines) — Essai de chronologie' Fleury and Perin (1978 ed), 105–7
Sivan, H.S.	1986 'Funerary monuments and funerary rites in late antique Aquitaine' *Oxford J. Archaeol* 5, 339–53

	1992 'Town and country in late antique Gaul: the example of Bordeaux' Drinkwater and Elton (1992 ed), 132–43
	1993 *Ausonius of Bordeaux: the Genesis of a Gallic Aristocracy*
Stancliffe, C.E.	1979 'From town to country: Christianisation of the Touraine 370–600' *Studies in Church History* 16, 43–59
	1983 *St Martin and his Biographer: History and Miracle in Sulpicius Severus* (Oxford)
Stevens, C.E.	1933 *Sidonius Apollinaris and his Age* (Oxford)
	1957 Marcus, Gratian, Constantine *Athenaeum* 35, 316–47
	1976 'The Notitia Dignitatum in England' Goodburn and Bartholemew (1976 ed), 211–24
Stroheker, K.F.	1948 *Der Senatorische Adel in Spatantiken Gallien* (Tubingen)
Swift, C.	1997 *Ogam Stones and the Earliest Irish Christians* (Maynooth)
Tchalenko, G.	1953–8 *Villages antiques de la Syrie du Nord: le Massif de Bélas à l'époque Romaine* (3 vols)
Thevenot, E.	1950 'Medecine et religion aux temps gallo-romains: le traitement des affections de la vue' *Latomus* 9, 415–26
Thomas, A.C.	1959 'Imported pottery in Dark Age western Britain' *Medieval Archaeol* 3, 89–111
	1981 *Christianity in Roman Britain to AD 500*
	1981a *A Provisional List of Imported Pottery in Post-Roman Western Britain and Ireland* (Redruth, Inst. of Cornish Stud.)
	1990 '*Gallici Nautae de Galliarum Provinciis* — a sixth-seventh century trade with Gaul reconsidered' *Medieval Archaeol* 34, 1–26
	1993 *Tintagel: Arthur and Archaeology*
	1994 *And Shall These Mute Stones Speak? Post-Roman Inscriptions in western Britain* (Cardiff)
Thompson, E.A.	1952 'Peasant revolts in late Roman Gaul and Spain' *Past and Present* 2, 11–23, reprinted M.I. Finley (ed) *Studies in Ancient Society* (1974), 304–20
	1982 *Romans and Barbarians: The Decline of the Western Empire*
	1984 *St Germanus of Auxerre and the End of Roman Britain*
Thompson, H.A.	1959 'Athenian Twilight, AD 267–700' *J. Roman Stud* 49, 61–72
Todd, M.	1978 *The Walls of Rome*
Tomlin, R.S.O.	1988 *Tabellae Sulis: Roman Inscribed Tablets of Tin and Lead from the sacred spring at Bath* (Oxford)
Toynbee, J. and Painter, K.	1986 'Silver picture plates of late antiquity: AD 300–700' *Archaeologia* 108, 15–66
Trout, D.	1996 'Town, countryside and Christianisation at Paulinus's Nola' Mathisen and Sivan (1996 ed), 175–86
Twyman, B.	1970 'Aetius and the aristocracy' *Historia* 19, 480–503
Vaiselle, F.	1954 'Les trésors monétaires gallo-romain du département de la Somme' *Revue du Nord* 36, 447–69
Vallet, F. and Kazanski, M.	1993 ed *L'Armée Romaine et les Barbares du IIIe au VII e Siècle* (Mem. Assoc. Français d'Archéol Merov. 5)
Van Dam, R.	1985 *Leadership and Community in Late Antique Gaul* (Berkeley)
	1986 '*Sheep in wolves clothing*, the letters of Consentius to St Augustine' *J. Ecclesiastical Hist* 37, 515–35
Van der Meer, F. and Mohrmann, C.	1978 *Atlas of the Early Christian World*
Van Ossel, P.	1987 'Les établissements ruraux au Bas-Empire dans le nord de la Gaule' *Archaeologia Belgica* 111, 185–96
	1992 *Établissements ruraux de l'Antiquité tardive dans le Nord de la*

	Gaule 51st supplement to *Gallia*
Viellard-Troiekouroff, M.	1976 *Les Monuments Réligieux de la Gaule d' apres les Oeuvres de Gregoire de Tours* (Paris)
Wade-Evans, A.W.	1944 *Vitae Sanctorum Britanniae et Genealogiae* (Cardiff)
Ward Perkins, J.P.	1938 'The sculpture of Visigothic France' *Archaeologia* 87, 79–128
	1960 'A carved marble fragment from Riom (Puy-de-Dôme), and the chronology of the Aquitanian sarcophagi' *Antiq J.* 40, 25–34
	1981 *Roman Imperial Architecture*
Webster, L. and Brown, M.	1997 *The Transformation of the Roman World, AD 400–900* (British Museum, exhibition catalogue)
Webster, L., Harden, D. and Hassall, M.	1980 'The Darenth Park bowl' *Ant J.* 60, 338–40
Werner, J.	1958 'Kriegergraber aus der ersten halfte des 5 Jahrhunderts' *Bonner Jahrbucher* 158, 372–413
Wheeler, R.E.M.	1954 *Rome Beyond the Imperial Frontiers*
White, R.H.	1988 *Roman and Celtic Objects from Anglo-Saxon graves* (B.A.R. Brit. Series 191)
Whitlock, D. *et al*	1982 *Ireland and Early Medieval Europe: Studies in Memory of Kathleen Hughes* (Cambridge)
Whittaker, C.R.	1993 *Land, City and Trade in the Roman Empire*
Wickham, C.J.	1981 *Early Medieval Italy: central power and local society, 400–1000*
Wightman, E.M.	1970 *Roman Trier and the Treveri*
	1978 'North-eastern Gaul in late Antiquity: the evidence of settlement patterns in an age of transition' *Berichten Rijksdienst Oudheidkundig Bodenmonderzoek* 28, 241–50
	1979 'Peasants and potentates: An investigation of social structure and land tenure in Roman Gaul' *American J. Anc. Hist*
	1985 *Gallia Belgica*
Wood, I.N.	1979 'Early Merovingian devotion in town and country' *Stud. in Church Hist* 16, 61–76
	1982 'The Vita Columbani and Merovingian hagiography' *Peritia* 1, 63–80
	1983 'The ecclesiastical politics of Merovingian Clermont' Wormald *et al*, 1983 ed, 34–57
	1984 'The end of Roman Britain: Continental evidence and parallels' Lapidge and Dumville (1984 ed), 1–25
	1987 'The fall of the western Empire and the end of Roman Britain' *Britannia* 18, 251–62
	1987a 'Anglo-Saxon Otley: an archepiscopal estate and its crosses in a Northumbrian context' *Northern Historian* 23, 20–38
Wood, J.	1982 *Le Castrum de Tours, étude architecturale du rempart du Bas Empire* (Recherches sur Tours 2)
Young, B.K.	1977 'Paganisme, Christianisation et rites funeraires' *Archéol Medievale* 7, 5–81
	1988 'Sacred topography and early Christian churches in late Antique Gaul' Jones *et al* (1988 ed), 219–40
Ypey, J.	1978 'La chronologie du cimetière Franc de Rhenen' Fleury and Perin 1978 ed, 51–7
Zeiss, H.	1941 'Die Germanischen Grabfunde des fruhen Mittelalters zwischen mittlerer Seine und Loirmundung' *31 Bericht Romische-Germanischen Kommission* part 1, 5–173 (Berlin)

216

Index